T0185109

Lecture Notes in Computer Science 12596

Diana Maimut · Andrei-George Oprina ·
Damien Sauveron (Eds.)

Innovative Security Solutions for Information Technology and Communications

13th International Conference, SecITC 2020
Bucharest, Romania, November 19–20, 2020
Revised Selected Papers

 Springer

Editors
Diana Maimut 🆔
Advanced Technologies Institute
Bucharest, Romania

Andrei-George Oprina
Advanced Technologies Institute
Bucharest, Romania

Damien Sauveron 🆔
Faculté des Sciences et Techniques
University of Limoges
Limoges, France

ISSN 0302-9743   ISSN 1611-3349   (electronic)
Lecture Notes in Computer Science
ISBN 978-3-030-69254-4   ISBN 978-3-030-69255-1   (eBook)
https://doi.org/10.1007/978-3-030-69255-1

LNCS Sublibrary: SL4 – Security and Cryptology

This Springer imprint is published by the registered company Springer Nature Switzerland AG
The registered company address is: Gewerbestrasse 11, 6330 Cham, Switzerland

Preface

This volume contains the papers presented during the 13th International Conference on Information Technology and Communications Security (SECITC 2020) held on November 19–20, 2020 online via ZOOM.

There were 41 submissions. Each submission was reviewed by at least 2, and on average 3 program committee members. The committee decided to accept 17 papers. The program also included 3 invited talks.

The SECITC conference started 13 years ago, when, in a small room at the Bucharest University of Economic Studies, was held the first edition of the event. At that time, the auditorium held approximately 15 students and professors.

Since then, the conference has grown significantly: the quality of the TPC and of the submitted papers has been improved from year to year, and, of course, we had valuable keynote speakers. Our conference is now indexed in several databases and probably a notable thing to mention is that SECITC is listed within the IACR cryptologic events calendar. Also, Springer agreed to publish the post proceedings (since 2015). The conference covers topics from cryptographic algorithms to digital forensics and cyber security and if this conference were to be initiated today, probably a better name for it would be "CyberSecurity Conference", but for now SECITC is already a brand and is not yet the time for rebranding.

The conference was organized by the master programs for information security within the Military Technical Academy and the Bucharest University of Economic Studies, as well as the Institute for Advanced Technologies (two of this year's co-chairs are representatives of the Institute). At the same time, partners of the conference included the master program Coding Theory and Information Storage within the Faculty of Applied Sciences, Politehnica University of Bucharest and the Center for Research and Training in Innovative Techniques of Applied Mathematics in Engineering from the same university.

A special word of gratitude to the invited keynote speakers, Constantin Catalin Dragan, Rémi Géraud-Stewart and Gerhard Hancke, who have certainly improved the quality of our conference SECITC 2020.

Last but not least, we would like to thank all the TPC members for reviewing the papers, the organizers and the technical committee for their efforts, and the sponsors for their support.

November 2020

Diana Maimut
Andrei-George Oprina
Damien Sauveron

Organization

Program Committee

Raja Naeem Akram	ISG Smart Card and IoT Security Centre, Royal Holloway, University of London, UK
Ludovic Apvrille	Télécom Paris, France
Claudio Ardagna	Università degli Studi di Milano - Dipartimento di Informatica, Italy
Lasse Berntzen	University of South-Eastern Norway, Norway
Ion Bica	Military Technical Academy, Romania
Catalin Boja	Bucharest University of Economic Studies, Romania
Guillaume Bouffard	National Cybersecurity Agency of France (ANSSI), France
Samia Bouzefrane	CEDRIC Lab, Conservatoire National des Arts et Métiers, France
Paolo D'Arco	University of Salerno, Italy
Roberto De Prisco	Dip. Informatica ed Appl., Università di Salerno, Italy
Eric Diehl	Sony Pictures Entertainment, USA
Pooya Farshim	University of York, France
Dieter Gollmann	Hamburg University of Technology, Germany
Johann Groszschaedl	University of Luxembourg, Luxembourg
Rémi Géraud-Stewart	École normale supérieure, France
Gerhard Hancke	City University of Hong Kong, China
Julio Hernandez Castro	University of Kent, UK
Shoichi Hirose	University of Fukui, Japan
Nesrine Kaaniche	The University of Sheffield, UK
Mehmet Sabir Kiraz	De Montfort University, UK
Chhagan Lal	University of Padova, Norway
Jean-François Lalande	CentraleSupélec, France
Maryline Laurent	Institut Mines-Télécom, France
Giovanni Livraga	University of Milan, Italy
Diana Maimut	Advanced Technologies Institute, École normale supérieure, University of Bucharest, Bucharest, Romania
Sjouke Mauw	University of Luxembourg, Luxembourg
Kazuhiko Minematsu	NEC Corporation, Japan
Stig Mjølsnes	Norwegian University of Science and Technology, Norway
David Naccache	ENS, France
Vincent Nicomette	University of Toulouse, France
Svetla Nikova	KU Leuven, Dept. ESAT/COSIC and iMinds, Belgium

Ruxandra F. Olimid	Norwegian University of Science and Technology and University of Bucharest, Norway
Victor Valeriu Patriciu	Military Technical Academy, Romania
Cezar Pleşca	Military Technical Academy, Romania
Andrei-George Oprina	Advanced Technologies Institute, Bucharest, Romania
Marius Popa	Bucharest University of Economic Studies, Faculty of Cybernetics, Statistics and Economic Informatics, Romania
Joachim Posegga	Univ. of Passau, Germany
Reza Reyhanitabar	TE Connectivity Germany GmbH, Germany
Peter Rønne	SnT, University of Luxembourg, Luxembourg
Damien Sauveron	University of Limoges, Limoges, France
Emil Simion	University Politehnica of Bucharest, Romania
Daniel Smith-Tone	NIST, USA
Agusti Solanas	Rovira i Virgili University, Spain
Riccardo Spolaor	University of Oxford, UK
Pantelimon Stanica	Naval Postgraduate School, USA
Rainer Steinwandt	Florida Atlantic University, USA
Ferucio Laurentiu Tiplea	Alexandru Ioan Cuza University, Romania
Mihai Togan	Military Technical Academy, Romania
Cristian Toma	Bucharest University of Economic Studies, Romania
Denis Trček	University of Ljubljana, Slovenia
Valérie Viet Triem Tong	CentraleSupélec, France
Qianhong Wu	Beihang University, China
Sule Yildirim-Yayilgan	Norwegian University of Science and Technology, Norway
Alin Zamfiroiu	Bucharest University of Economic Studies, Romania
Stefano Zanero	Politecnico di Milano, Italy
Lei Zhang	East China Normal University, China

Additional Reviewers

Atashpendar, Arash	Mohammadi, Farnaz
Berro, Sahar	Nugier, Cyrius
Claudepierre, Ludovic	Panait, Andreea-Elena
Deo, Amit	Perez Kempner, Octavio
Dhooghe, Siemen	Sedaghat, Mahdi
Diehl, Eric	Shen, Kunyu
Fang, Qihao	Soroush, Najmeh
Han, Shangbin	Tronel, Frédéric
Hristea, Cristian	van Wier, Jeroen
Klement, Felix	Velciu, Alexandru
Madhusudan, Akash	Zhong, Liangyu

Contents

Elementary Attestation
of Cryptographically Useful
Composite Moduli

Rémi Géraud-Stewart[1,2(✉)] and David Naccache[2]

[1] QPSI, Qualcomm Technologies Incorporated, San Diego, USA
`rgerauds@qti.qualcomm.com`
[2] ÉNS (DI), Information Security Group, CNRS, PSL Research University,
75005 Paris, France
`david.naccache@ens.fr`

Abstract. This paper describes a non-interactive process allowing a prover to convince a verifier that a modulus n is the product of two primes (p, q) of about the same size. A further heuristic argument conjectures that $p - 1$ and $q - 1$ have sufficiently large prime factors for cryptographic applications.

The new protocol relies upon elementary number-theoretic properties and can be implemented efficiently using very few operations. This contrasts with state-of-the-art zero-knowledge protocols for RSA modulus proper generation assessment.

The heuristic argument at the end of our construction calls for further cryptanalysis by the community and is, as such, an interesting research question in its own right.

1 Introduction

Several cryptographic protocols rely on the assumption that an integer $n = pq$ is hard to factor. This includes for instance RSA [RSA78], Rabin [Rab79], Paillier [Pai99] or Fiat–Shamir [FS86]. A user generating their own keys can ensure that n is indeed such a product; however this becomes a concern when n is provided by a third-party. This scenario appears e.g. with Fiat–Shamir identification, or in the context of certificate authentication: carelessly using an externally-provided n may compromise security if n is incorrectly generated. Naturally, one cannot ask for the factor(s) p, q to check n.

The state of the art in the matter are the zero-knowledge procotols of Auerbach–Poettering [AP18] and Camenisch–Michels [CM99], which ascertain that a given n is the product of safe primes of prescribed size. While correct and very useful, these protocols are difficult to implement and analyze, and have high computational costs. This motivates the search for simpler and more efficient solutions.

This paper introduces an alternative protocol that nearly achieves the same functionality with fewer operations and communication. The new protocol is also simpler to understand and therefore to implement.

© Springer Nature Switzerland AG 2021
D. Maimut et al. (Eds.): SecITC 2020, LNCS 12596, pp. 1–12, 2021.
https://doi.org/10.1007/978-3-030-69255-1_1

2   Preliminaries and Building Blocks

This paper uses the following notations: $a|b$ denotes the concatenation of the bitstrings a and b. If c is an integer, $\|c\| = \lceil \log_2 c \rceil$ denotes the size of c, i.e. the minimal number of bits needed to write c. We denote by 0^ℓ the ℓ-bit all-zero string. For $A \in \mathbb{N}$ we denote by $[A]$ the set $\{0, 1, \ldots, A-1\}$. If X is a finite set, then $x \xleftarrow{\$} X$ indicates sampling uniformly at random from X.

2.1   Camenisch–Michels Proofs

While this paper does not rely on [CM99] we feel that it is important to recall Camenisch and Michels' protocol (hereafter, CM) given that it is currently considered as the state-of-the-art tool for achieving the functionality that we try to approach by our construction.

CM provides provable guarantees that an RSA modulus is well-formed. At its heart is a pseudo-primality proof, combined with zero-knowledge proofs of knowledge of a discrete logarithm, of a conjunction, and for belonging to a range. We recall here the protocol for the sake of completeness, using the following syntax [CS97]:

$$\mathrm{PK}\{(w) : P(x, w)\}$$

refers to a *proof of knowledge* that property P holds, i.e., that the prover (henceforth $\mathcal{P}$) knows a witness w that makes $P(x, w)$ true.

Let $n = pq$ be the number of interest, $\varepsilon > 1$ be a security parameter, ℓ such that $2^\ell > n$, G a cyclic group of prime order $Q > 2^{5+2\varepsilon\ell}$, and $g, h \in G$. There are two main phases to the protocol [CM99, Sec 5.1]:

1. $\mathcal{P}$ computes

$$c_p \leftarrow g^p h^{r_p} \qquad\qquad c_p' \leftarrow g^{\frac{p-1}{2}} h^{r_p'}$$
$$c_q \leftarrow g^q h^{r_q} \qquad\qquad c_q' \leftarrow g^{\frac{q-1}{2}} h^{r_q'}$$

   where r_p, r_p', r_q, r_q' are random integers. The values (c_p, c_p', c_q, c_q') are sent to the verifier (henceforth $\mathcal{V}$).

2. Run the protocol

$$\begin{aligned}
\mathrm{PK}\{(x_1, &\ldots, x_{11}) : \\
&c_p' = g^{x_1} h^{x_2} \wedge c_q' = g^{x_3} h^{x_4} \wedge c_p = g^{x_5} h^{x_6} \wedge c_q = g^{x_7} h^{x_8} \\
&\wedge\, c_p g^{-1} c_p'^{-2} = h^{x_9} \wedge c_q g^{-1} c_q'^{-2} = h^{x_{10}} \wedge g^n c_p^{-1} c_q^{-1} = h^{x_{11}} \\
&\wedge\, x_1 \in [-2^{\ell'}, 2^{\ell'}] \wedge x_4 \in [-2^{\ell'}, 2^{\ell'}] \\
&\wedge\, x_1 \in \texttt{pprimes(t)} \wedge x_3 \in \texttt{pprimes(t)} \\
&\wedge\, x_5 \in \texttt{pprimes(t)} \wedge x_7 \in \texttt{pprimes(t)} \\
\}&
\end{aligned}$$

The pprimes(t) sub-algorithm denotes t rounds of the Lehmann primality test for a committed number [CM99, Sec 4.2] and $\ell' = \varepsilon\ell + 2$. The above protocol is a statistical zero-knowledge proof that $n = pq$ is an RSA modulus where p, q are safe primes.

Remark 1. As noted by [CM99], under some conditions running the protocol of Gennaro et al. [GMR98] after the first phase we can remove the two last pseudo-primality tests and reduce the number of rounds to $t = 1$. However this assumes that n was not adversarially constructed and we cannot rely on this hypothesis here.

Remark 2. As discussed in [CM99], the protocol can be extended to ensure additional properties of p and q, e.g. that $(p + 1)/2$ is prime, or that p and q satisfy some lower bound.

The protocol's cost is dominated by the four pseudo-primality tests, which use $O(t \log n)$ exponentiations and exchange $O(t \log n)$ group elements.

2.2 Goldberg–Reyzin–Sagga–Baldimtsi Modulus Tests

Our first building block is a very elegant protocol published by Goldberg, Reyzin, Sagga and Baldimtsi (GRSB) [GRSB19]. This protocols allows to verify that n has exactly two prime factors.

A first GRSB protocol checks that a pair (n, e) defines a permutation over $\mathbb{Z}/n\mathbb{Z}$. For typical parameter settings, this proof consists of nine integers, with proof generation and verification requiring both about nine modular exponentiations.

A further protocol in [GRSB19] allows $\mathcal{V}$ to check that n is the product of two distinct primes [GRSB19, Sec. 3.4] in a zero-knowledge fashion. We recall the protocol here:

1. $\mathcal{P}$ and $\mathcal{V}$ agree on a security level κ, integer $m := \lceil 32 \cdot \kappa \cdot \ln 2 \rceil$, and n.
2. $\mathcal{V}$ checks that n is a positive odd integer and that n isn't a prime power, otherwise the protocol stops with a failure.
3. $\mathcal{V}$ chooses m values ρ_i whose Jacobi symbol $(\rho_i | n) = 1$, and sends them to $\mathcal{P}$ as challenge.
4. $\mathcal{P}$ checks for each ρ_i whether it is a quadratic residue modulo n: if it is, $\mathcal{P}$ returns a square root σ_i of ρ_i to $\mathcal{V}$; otherwise $\mathcal{P}$ returns $\sigma_i = 0$.
5. $\mathcal{V}$ checks that there are at least $3m/8$ non-zero σ_i and that they all satisfy $\sigma_i^2 = \rho_i \bmod n$.

As is, this protocol assumes that $\mathcal{V}$ is honest. The honest verifier assumption is removed through a classical derivation of the ρ_is by hashing. Both protocols are very efficient for $\mathcal{P}$ and $\mathcal{V}$.

2.3   Girault–Poupard–Stern Signatures

The GPS signature scheme was first proposed by Girault in 1991 [Gir91] without a security proof; a first analysis was given in 1998 [PS98, PS99] by Poupard and Stern. This was further refined by all three authors in 2006 [GPS06]. GPS has been standardized as ISO/IEC 9798-5 in 2004.

Algorithms. GPS consists of four algorithms (Setup, Keygen, Sign, Verify) that we now describe.

- GPS.Setup(λ) $\rightarrow$ pp: the public parameters consist of integers A, B and a hash function $h : \{0,1\}^* \rightarrow [B]$. They are chosen so that a security level λ is achieved.

- GPS.Keygen(pp) $\rightarrow$ (sk, pk): The signer chooses two safe primes $P = 2p + 1$, $Q = 2q + 1$, computes $n \leftarrow PQ$, and finds an element $g \in \mathbb{Z}/n\mathbb{Z}$ whose order is divisible by pq.[1] The order of g (and therefore of the subgroup generated by G) needs not be explicitly known.
  The signer's secret key is sk $:= n - \varphi(n)$, while the public key is given by pk $:= (n, g)$.

- GPS.Sign(pp, sk, m) $\rightarrow \sigma$:
  1. $r \xleftarrow{\$} [A]$
  2. $x \leftarrow g^r \bmod n$
  3. $c \leftarrow h(m, x)$
  4. $y \leftarrow r + c \cdot$ sk
  5. If $y \geq A$, restart from step 1 with a new value of r.
  The signature is $\sigma \leftarrow (x, c, y)$.

- GPS.Verify(pp, pk, m, σ) $\rightarrow$ {valid, invalid}: $\mathcal{V}$ checks the ranges:

$$x > 0 \quad \text{and} \quad x \in [n] \quad \text{and} \quad c \in [B] \quad \text{and} \quad y \in [A]$$

If either of these checks fails the signature is invalid. Otherwise, $\mathcal{V}$ computes:
  1. $\widetilde{c} \leftarrow h(m, x)$
  2. $\widetilde{x} \leftarrow g^{y - n\widetilde{c}} \bmod n$
  3. If $c = \widetilde{c}$ and $\widetilde{x} = x$ then σ is valid otherwise σ is invalid.

Security of GPS Signatures. Under the discrete logarithm with short exponent assumption (DL-SEA, see below), and if sk $\cdot B/A$ and $1/B$ are negligible, GPS signatures are existentially unforgeable under adaptive chosen message attacks in the random oracle model [GPS06, Theorem 7].

DL-SEA is an *ad-hoc* strengthening of the usual discrete logarithm assumption, which formalizes the notion that it should be hard to recover a discrete logarithm, knowing that it is smaller than some known bound:

---

[1] This is the case if and only if $\gcd(g - 1, n) = \gcd(g + 1, n) = 1$, which happens with high probability.

Definition 1 (DL-SEA, [GPS06]). *For every polynomial Q and every PPT Turing machine $\mathcal{A}$ running on a random tape ω_M, for sufficiently large λ,*

$$\Pr_{\omega_p, \omega_M} [\mathcal{A}(n, g, \mathsf{sk}, g^x) = x \mid (n, g, \mathsf{sk}) \leftarrow \mathsf{Setup}(\omega_p, \lambda) \land x \in [\mathsf{sk}]\}] < \frac{1}{Q(\lambda)}$$

where Setup *is a randomized algorithm generating public parameters n, g from a security parameter λ using the random tape ω_p, and $\mathsf{sk} = n - \varphi(n)$.*

In summary, the choice of parameters for GPS to be secure are:

- An integer n which is hard to factor;
- Integers $B < A < n$ such that $2^\lambda B/A$ is negligible;
- A hash function h for which the random oracle model is appropriate.

For instance, at the 128 bit security level, $B \sim 2^{128}$, $A \sim 2^{80+128+128}$ and $n \sim 2^{3072}$, with SHA-3 as h.

2.4 RSA Moduli with a Prescribed Pattern

To preserve compatibility with the notations of [Joy08] we will temporarily rename the modulus N in this section. We will then revert back to the notation n introduced previously. An RSA modulus generator is a PPT algorithm that outputs p, q such that $N = pq$ is an RSA modulus. There exist several algorithms that output N with additional properties; one such family of algorithms gives *prescribed patterns*: a bitstring (the "pattern") is given as input to the generation algorithm, and will be found in N. We denote $n = \|N\|$.

Different methods are known to achieve this, depending on the pattern length being considered [Len98, LdW05a, Joy08, LdW05b]. To the best of our knowledge, no polynomial-time algorithm capable of imposing a pattern of more than $2n/3$ bits while respecting the constraint $\|q\| \cong \|p\|$ has been described. The leading motivations for such algorithms originates from the desire to compress RSA keys, so that they can be stored on less bits and the from the intention to speed-up modular reduction using "computation-friendly" moduli.

Let $n > n_0$ be integers, $\kappa \lesssim 2n/3$, a predetermined portion N_H of length κ. The following algorithm [Joy08] outputs a pair (p, q) such that $N = pq = N_H \| N_L$ along with N_L, with p of size $n - n_0$ and q of size n_0.

1. Sample p_0 uniformly of length $n - n_0$, and let

$$q_0 = \left\lfloor N_H \frac{2^{n-\kappa}}{p_0} \right\rfloor.$$

2. Define recursively the triples (d_i, u_i, v_i) as:

$$(d_0, u_0, v_0) = (p_0, 0, 1)$$
$$(d_{-1}, u_{-1}, v_{-1}) = (q_0, 1, 0)$$
$$(d_i, u_i, v_i) = \left(d_{i-2} \bmod d_{i-1}, u_{i-2} - \left\lfloor \frac{d_{i-2}}{d_{i-1}} \right\rfloor u_{i-1}, v_{i-2} - \left\lfloor \frac{d_{i-2}}{d_{i-1}} \right\rfloor v_{i-1}\right)$$

3. Define recursively the triples (x_i, y_i, z_i) as:

$$(x_0, y_0, z_0) = \left(0, 0, \left(N_H 2^{n-\kappa} \bmod p_0\right) + 2^{n-\kappa-1}\right)$$

$$(x_i, y_i, z_i) = \left(x_{i-1} + \left\lfloor \frac{z_{i-1}}{d_i} \right\rfloor u_i, y_{i-1} + \left\lfloor \frac{z_{i-1}}{d_i} \right\rfloor v_i, z_{i-1} \bmod d_i\right)$$

such that $|z_i - x_i y_i| < 2^{n-\kappa-1}$. (This value decreases and then increases, so once the condition is reached we can break out of the loop.)
4. Sieve the pairs (x_i, y_i) until both

$$p = p_0 + x_i$$
$$q = q_0 + y_i$$

are prime. If no such pair is prime, start over from Step 1.
5. Output $N_L \leftarrow N \bmod 2^{n-\kappa}$ and p, q.

Note that the generation process can be repeated until (p, q) satisfies any desired property (e.g., being safe primes).

3   Assembling the Puzzle to Get an Attestation

We decompose our construction into four steps.

Section 3.1 $\xrightarrow{\text{provable}}$ n is the product of exactly two primes p, q

Section 3.2 $\xrightarrow{\text{provable}}$ p, q are of about the same size

Section 3.3 $\xrightarrow{\text{heuristic}}$ p, q cannot be controlled

Section 3.4 $\xrightarrow{\text{trivial}}$ even if the adversary controls p, q they face a slow down

Fig. 1. The general outline of the construction proposed in this paper.

3.1   Checking that n Has Exactly Two Prime Factors

Our first building block is the GRSB protocol that we run, unmodified, between $\mathcal{P}$ and $\mathcal{V}$.

Note that GRSB does not suffice, in itself, to guarantee n is cryptographically useful. For instance, $n = 3p$ with $p > 3$ will pass this phase but is clearly a bad RSA modulus.

3.2   Checking for Factor Sizes

The second building block checks that the two factors of n have the appropriate size. We achieve this by requesting that $\mathcal{P}$ provides a valid GPS signature of some agreed-upon message (e.g. n) to $\mathcal{V}$.

The key observation here is that GPS signatures have a size that depends on the factors of n. More precisely, if $\sigma = (x, c, y)$ is the GPS signature and we are working modulo n, the size of y essentially reveals the size of n's factors (up to a relatively small constant).

The following lemma makes this statement more precise and more general.

Lemma 1. *Let p, q be two positive integers. Let $u = \|pq\|$, $v = \|p + q\|$, and $w = \|p - q\|$. Let $\Delta > 0$, if $v \geq \log_2(2^{2\Delta-1} + 2^u)$, then $w \leq \Delta$.*

Proof. Without loss of generality, assume $p \leq q$ and let $\delta = q - p$. Then

$$w = \|\delta\| = \frac{1}{2}\|\delta^2\| = \frac{1}{2}\|(p+q)^2 - 4pq\|$$
$$\leq \frac{1}{2}\|2^{v+1} - 2^{u+1}\| = \frac{1}{2}\left[1 + \log_2|2^v - 2^u|\right]$$
$$\leq \frac{1}{2}\left[1 + 2\Delta - 1\right] = \Delta.$$

$\square$

A valid GPS signature comprises $y = r + c \cdot \mathsf{sk}$ which is of size $\max(\|A\|, \|B\| + \|\mathsf{sk}\|)$. With A, B being a public parameters and sk being $p + q - 1$ we see that Lemma 1 can be used to set a threshold so that with typical GPS parameters, pq is large enough and at most a discrepancy between p and q of about 200 bits is possible.

This is unfortunately not enough: even if we know that $n = pq$ with p and q of similar size, partial Pohlig–Hellman factorization [vOW96] can exploit the smoothness of $p - 1$ or $q - 1$ to factor n. Thus we need an additional building block fill that gap.

3.3   Checking that n Is a Cryptographically Useful Modulus

What follows is only *conjectured* to be secure. The intuition is to restrict $\mathcal{P}$ to use only certain moduli, obtained through a verifiable procedure that (hopefully!) makes it hard to obtain smooth $p - 1$ and/or $q - 1$ or otherwise purposely weaken n. Indeed, from a practical standpoint [vOW96] fails whenever $(p-1)/2$ and $(q-1)/2$ have each a large factor: $(p-1)/2$ and $(q-1)/2$ being primes is ideal but not strictly necessary to resist this attack. This does not imply that methods other than [vOW96] would fail to factor n but we know of no such strategies and encourage the community to further scrutinize our proposal.

For preserving compatibility with Joye's notations we switch again to the notation N for the modulus.

We now want to ensure that the factors of N (which we know to be exactly two primes of comparable sizes), are not easy to factor. A complete but inefficient solution consists in plugging-in the CM sub-protocol for safe-primality testing [CM99]. Doing so has a sizable cost, so we take an alternative, cheaper route.

To illustrate the difficulty, consider the following procedure which generates a couple (p, q) of primes whose product features a prescribed bit pattern N_H:

1. Form a string $N' := N_H | \rho$ where ρ is a random bitstring.
2. Generate a prime p and compute $q \leftarrow \lfloor x/p \rfloor$
3. Increment q until the result is prime.

At the end of this procedure, p and q are prime and their product $N = pq$ features N_H in its MSBs. Informally, because q is constrained we expect q to be hard to control, and therefore it would be hard to ensure that $q-1$ is abnormally smooth using this procedure. A malicious generator could however manipulate p freely, so this approach is unsatisfactory. The above algorithm stops to work as N_H grows beyond $n/2$ bits while keeping the sizes of p and q balanced.

Joye's protocol described in Sect. 2.4 [Joy08, 4.1, 4.2] enables us to fix $\frac{2}{3}$ of N's bits to a prescribed pattern, with p and q being generated *simultaneously*. We *conjecture* that this causes $p - 1$ and $q - 1$ to "essentially" behave like large random numbers, which are likely to have a large prime factor as expected by the asymptotic distribution of factors in random integers[2]. This assumption is made explicit below.

Note that from $\mathcal{V}$'s viewpoint, checking that N features the prescribed pattern is cost-less and that only the LSBs of N need to be transmitted to $\mathcal{V}$. For the above to work it is crucial to enforce that N_H is beyond the control of $\mathcal{P}$. For instance set N_H as equal to the digits of $\pi = 3.14159\ldots$ or $e = 2.71828\ldots$.

One interesting question is whether RSA moduli indistinguishable from those generated by Joye's algorithm can be purposely crafted to be more vulnerable than moduli formed by multiplying two random equal-size primes. The case is clearly different with moduli generated by other bit prescription methods because, unlike Joye's algorithm, alternative methods pick p at random first and only then generate q as a function of p and N_H and. As we have already explained, in such a scenario p can be chosen to be weak (e.g. $p-1$ can be purposely selected to be smooth). Therefore the conjecture upon which the heuristic part of our construction relies is:

Conjecture: *Given a challenge N_H of size $\frac{2n}{3}$, it is hard to generate a vulnerable N featuring the MSB pattern N_H such that N has exactly two prime factors of roughly equal size.*

The above calls for a precise definition of the term "vulnerable". Evidently, a dishonest $\mathcal{P}$ could publish his random tape or run the proof with some public test values for p, q. To capture simply the requirement we construe the term "vulnerable" as follows:

---

[2] In particular, the Golomb–Dickman constant $\lambda \approx 0.624$ asymptotically governs the relative size of the largest prime factor of an integer [KP76, Dic30, Gol64].

A modulus of size n is vulnerable if its factoring is asymptotically easier than the factorization of a modulus generated by picking two random $\frac{n}{2}$-bit primes.

3.4 Optional Security Measures

In this section we describe three optional security measures. All are heuristic and incur additional computational cost for $\mathcal{P}$ and/or $\mathcal{V}$.

The rationale behind these measures is that if a cryptanalysis whose work factor is ω_1 is found, the proposed countermeasures will multiply ω_1 by a constant factor ω_2 that may put $\omega_1 \times \omega_2$ out of practical reach.

1. The first countermeasure consists in using an n larger than required. This reinforces the argument of Sect. 3.3, as larger smooth numbers are scarcer. We recommend to use moduli whose size is larger by 62% than normal for any desired security level. This is meant to account for the fact that the largest prime factor of a random ℓ-bit number is expected to be roughly 0.62ℓ-bits long [KP76].

2. The second countermeasure will put a burden on generation but leave verification unchanged: we require from n an additional *short* redundancy, e.g. $\text{SHA}(n) \bmod 2^{24} = 0$. It is reasonable to assume that there is no efficient algorithm allowing to achieve this property along with a prescribed pattern. Thus, to obtain n the generation procedure should be run on average 2^{24} times. This places no extra burden on $\mathcal{V}$ and because moduli are usually generated once for all in a device's lifetime, slowing the modulus generation process down on one occasion may pay back in case of an attack.

3. The third countermeasure is applicable when $\mathcal{V}$ witnesses the generation of n. It consists in performing a cut-&-choose protocol to ascertain the freshness and the conformity of the generated moduli:

   - $\mathcal{P}$ and $\mathcal{V}$ generate a common secret key u using e.g. Diffie-Hellman.
   - $\mathcal{P}$ picks t random w_is and computes $v_i = \text{hash}(w_i, u)$ for $0 \le i \le t-1$.
   - $\mathcal{P}$ uses v_i as a random tape to generate the modulus n_i
   - $\mathcal{V}$ picks a random index j and sends it to $\mathcal{P}$
   - $\mathcal{P}$ reveals to $\mathcal{V}$:

   $$w_0, w_1, \ldots, w_{j-1}, w_{j+1}, \ldots, w_{t-1}$$

   - $\mathcal{V}$ re-generates the corresponding $t-1$ moduli

   $$n_0, n_1, \ldots, n_{j-1}, n_{j+1}, \ldots, n_{t-1}$$

   and checks that all the above $t-1$ moduli were properly generated.
   - $\mathcal{V}$ tests using the first two phases of the protocol proposed in this paper that n_j has two large factors of equal size and if so, he signs n_j to certify it.

We see that this protocol reduces the cheating odds to $\frac{1}{t}$ where by "cheating" we mean generating factors so that n_j is easy to factor. It has the advantage of ascertaining, in addition, the freshness of n_j. Indeed, even if $\mathcal{P}$ would use a fixed random tape then the randomness injected by the $\mathcal{V}$ into the protocol would ascertain that no entities other than $\mathcal{P}$ and $\mathcal{V}$ would be able to factor n_j.

4   Efficiency

The global computational cost of our protocol is dominated by Sect. 3.3, as other phases essentially have the cost of a few full-sized modular multiplications. While the complexity of Joye's algorithm does not follow a simple expression, we can consider that around $1/\eta^2$ primality tests are performed, where η is the probability that an integer of size n is prime—by the prime number theorem η is of the order of $1/\ln(2^n) = 1/n \ln 2$. Thus the overall algorithmic complexity is essentially $\widetilde{O}(k \log N^3)$, where N is the modulus and k is the number of primality testing rounds.

If the optional measures of Sect. 3.4 are implemented, the impact on total complexity is a slowdown by a factor of about $4.25 \simeq (1+\lambda)^3$ for the GPS phase that dominates the slowdown in the other phases.

Note that if n is used to sign a message m, the protocol can made even more efficient. Instead of just signing n during the GPS phase, use GPS to sign $n|m$. This achieves both the goal of attesting the sizes of p, q and signing m. In such a case, the attestation of n comes at the minimal price of phases 3.1 and 3.3 only.

5   Conclusion

In this paper we introduced a cheap non-interactive process for proving that $n = pq$ is a product of two equal-size primes. The process is completed with a heuristic trick conjectured to be sufficient to ascertain that n is cryptographically useful.

This raises a number of interesting research questions. For instance, speeding-up or simplifying [CM99] by hybridizing it with the techniques. The same seems also applicable to [GMR98] although we haven't investigated this avenue.

More importantly, we invite the community to find attacks on the heuristic phase of our protocol. A successful attack consists in exhibiting a modulus n having exactly two equal-size prime factors and featuring $\frac{2}{3}\|n\|$ prescribed LSBs[3]. This n must be easier to factor than an $n = pq$ where p, q are randomly generated primes.

Acknowledgements. The authors are grateful to Arjen Lenstra for his pertinent remarks on an earlier version of this article.

References

[AP18] Auerbach, B., Poettering, B.: Hashing solutions instead of generating problems: on the interactive certification of RSA moduli. In: Abdalla, M., Dahab, R. (eds.) PKC 2018. LNCS, vol. 10770, pp. 403–430. Springer, Cham (2018). https://doi.org/10.1007/978-3-319-76581-5_14

---

[3] e.g. the binary digits of $\pi = 3.14159265\ldots$.

[CM99] Camenisch, J., Michels, M.: Proving in zero-knowledge that a number is the product of two safe primes. In: Stern, J. (ed.) EUROCRYPT 1999. LNCS, vol. 1592, pp. 107–122. Springer, Heidelberg (1999). https://doi.org/10.1007/3-540-48910-X_8

[CS97] Camenisch, J., Stadler, M.: Efficient group signature schemes for large groups. In: Kaliski, B.S. (ed.) CRYPTO 1997. LNCS, vol. 1294, pp. 410–424. Springer, Heidelberg (1997). https://doi.org/10.1007/BFb0052252

[Dic30] Dickman, K.: On the frequency of numbers containing prime factors of a certain relative magnitude. ArMAF **22**(10), A-10 (1930)

[FS86] Fiat, A., Shamir, A.: How to prove yourself: practical solutions to identification and signature problems. In: Odlyzko, A.M. (ed.) CRYPTO 1986. LNCS, vol. 263, pp. 186–194. Springer, Heidelberg (1987). https://doi.org/10.1007/3-540-47721-7_12

[Gir91] Girault, M.: Self-certified public keys. In: Davies, D.W. (ed.) EUROCRYPT 1991. LNCS, vol. 547, pp. 490–497. Springer, Heidelberg (1991). https://doi.org/10.1007/3-540-46416-6_42

[GMR98] Gennaro, R., Micciancio, D., Rabin, T.: An efficient non-interactive statistical zero-knowledge proof system for quasi-safe prime products. In: Gong, L., Reiter, M.K. (eds.) CCS 1998, Proceedings of the 5th ACM Conference on Computer and Communications Security, San Francisco, CA, USA, 3–5 November 1998, pp. 67–72. ACM (1998)

[Gol64] Golomb, S.W.: Random permutations. Bull. Am. Math. Soc **70**, 747 (1964)

[GPS06] Girault, M., Poupard, G., Stern, J.: On the fly authentication and signature schemes based on groups of unknown order. J. Cryptol. **19**(4), 463–487 (2006)

[GRSB19] Goldberg, S., Reyzin, L., Sagga, O., Baldimtsi, F.: Efficient noninteractive certification of RSA moduli and beyond. In: Galbraith, S.D., Moriai, S. (eds.) ASIACRYPT 2019. LNCS, vol. 11923, pp. 700–727. Springer, Cham (2019). https://doi.org/10.1007/978-3-030-34618-8_24

[Joy08] Joye, M.: RSA moduli with a predetermined portion: techniques and applications. In: Chen, L., Mu, Y., Susilo, W. (eds.) ISPEC 2008. LNCS, vol. 4991, pp. 116–130. Springer, Heidelberg (2008). https://doi.org/10.1007/978-3-540-79104-1_9

[KP76] Knuth, D.E., Pardo, L.T.: Analysis of a simple factorization algorithm. Theor. Comput. Sci. **3**(3), 321–348 (1976)

[LdW05a] Lenstra, A., de Weger, B.: On the possibility of constructing meaningful hash collisions for public keys. In: Boyd, C., González Nieto, J.M. (eds.) ACISP 2005. LNCS, vol. 3574, pp. 267–279. Springer, Heidelberg (2005). https://doi.org/10.1007/11506157_23

[LdW05b] Lenstra, A.K., de Weger, B.M.M.: Twin RSA. In: Dawson, E., Vaudenay, S. (eds.) Mycrypt 2005. LNCS, vol. 3715, pp. 222–228. Springer, Heidelberg (2005). https://doi.org/10.1007/11554868_16

[Len98] Lenstra, A.K.: Generating RSA moduli with a predetermined portion. In: Ohta, K., Pei, D. (eds.) ASIACRYPT 1998. LNCS, vol. 1514, pp. 1–10. Springer, Heidelberg (1998). https://doi.org/10.1007/3-540-49649-1_1

[Pai99] Paillier, P.: Public-key cryptosystems based on composite degree residuosity classes. In: Stern, J. (ed.) EUROCRYPT 1999. LNCS, vol. 1592, pp. 223–238. Springer, Heidelberg (1999). https://doi.org/10.1007/3-540-48910-X_16

[PS98]   Poupard, G., Stern, J.: Security analysis of a practical "on the fly" authentication and signature generation. In: Nyberg, K. (ed.) EUROCRYPT 1998. LNCS, vol. 1403, pp. 422–436. Springer, Heidelberg (1998). https://doi.org/10.1007/BFb0054143

[PS99]   Poupard, G., Stern, J.: On the fly signatures based on factoring. In: Motiwalla, J., Tsudik, G. (eds.) CCS 1999, Proceedings of the 6th ACM Conference on Computer and Communications Security, Singapore, 1–4 November 1999, pp. 37–45. ACM (1999)

[Rab79] Rabin, M.O.: Digitalized signatures and public key functions as intractable as intractable as factorization. MIT Laboratory of Computer Sciences, vol. 21 (1979)

[RSA78] Rivest, R.L., Shamir, A., Adleman, L.M.: A method for obtaining digital signatures and public-key cryptosystems. Commun. ACM **21**(2), 120–126 (1978)

[vOW96] van Oorschot, P.C., Wiener, M.J.: On diffie-hellman key agreement with short exponents. In: Maurer, U. (ed.) EUROCRYPT 1996. LNCS, vol. 1070, pp. 332–343. Springer, Heidelberg (1996). https://doi.org/10.1007/3-540-68339-9_29

Off-the-Shelf Security Testing Platform for Contactless Systems

Yuanzhen Liu[1], Gerhard Petrus Hancke[1(✉)], and Umair Mujtaba Qureshi[1,2]

[1] Department of Computer Science, City University of Hong Kong, Kowloon,
Hong Kong, SAR of China
{yuanzhliu3-c,gp.hancke,umqureshi2-c}@my.cityu.edu.hk

[2] Department of Telecommunication Engineering, Mehran University of Engineering
and Technology, Jamshoro, Sindh, Pakistan

Abstract. RFID is widely used in many security sensitive areas.
Researchers proposed many theoretical attacks and security implementation models on RFID devices. To test these theories and models is
challenging and difficult task. In this paper, we use three common-off-
the-shelf security testing platforms i.e. PN532, TI RF430CL330H and
Chameleon Mini, to test the most widely used standards ISO14443A,
ISO14443B and ISO18092. We present a detailed workflow of each platform. Furthermore, we highlight the advantages and disadvantages of
each platform in regards fast implementation, delays and support for
different types of RFIDs.

Keywords: Radio Frequency Identification · Near Field
Communication · Smart card

1 Introduction

Radio-frequency identification (RFID) is a technique that allows the system to
perform contactless data exchange [1]. Near Field Communication is a technique
based on high frequency (13.56 MHz) RFID, which is widely used in contactless
smart cards [2–4]. These contactless cards are widely used in many security sensitive scenes, e.g. payment [5,6] or access control [7,8]. Smart cards have drawn a lot
researchers to test security layers of the smart card by designing attacks to breach
the security and infer valuable information. Also to design add-on security layers
to make the smart cards more secure [9,10]. There are two main research stream
of attacking RFID i.e. skimming and relay attack [11]. One of the most frequently
used smart cards, Mifare Classic which is based on ISO14443A standard, had been
hacked by the researchers, using the weakness of the pseudo-random number generator to recover the keystream and read the information stored in the card [12].
Researcher also successfully hacked cards in ISO15692 standard [13]. Another possible attack method on NFC cards is the relay attack. Researchers had successfully
applied relay attack on NFC communication [14–17]. As alternative, researchers
also worked on defending NFC cards from attacks. Distance Bounding protocol is

© Springer Nature Switzerland AG 2021
D. Maimut et al. (Eds.): SecITC 2020, LNCS 12596, pp. 13–23, 2021.
https://doi.org/10.1007/978-3-030-69255-1_2

an effective method to prevent relay attacks, using the timing of data exchange to estimate the distance between two devices [18–20]. Work on security of short range communication is also of wider interest to mobile and IoT areas [21–23].

This paper aims at testing off-the-shelf security testing platform for RFID systems, emulating the communication between reader and tags in different standards. Three standards were considered, ISO14443A, ISO14443B and ISO18092. We tested three platforms, PN532, TI RF430CL330H and Chameleon Mini. Section 2 describes the basic modulation and bit coding of each standard and general information of the devices that we used. Section 3 shows the details of these standards. Section 4 shows the implementation of standards on different platforms. Section 5 draws a conclusion and discusses the pros and cons of each platform. This work follows on from prior work related to relay-resistant channels [24], focusing on underlying work of implmenting common contactless RFID channels using mostly COTS hardware.

2 Background

In this paper, we focus on three standards, ISO14443A, ISO14443B and ISO18092. These standards share some similarities. The communication radio is 13.56 MHz. When initializing and doing anti-collision, the bit rates of these channels are 106 kbits/s. The modulation and bit-coding when reader transmitting data to card are different. ISO14443A, ISO18092 at the bit rate 106 kbit/s in both passive and active mode use ASK 100% modulation and Modified Miller code. The ISO14443B, ISO18092 at 212 kbit/s in active and passive mode use ASK 10% modulation. However, ISO14443B uses NRZ code while ISO18092 uses Manchester code. Table 1 shows the communication specification when transmitting data from reader to card.

Table 1. Modulation and bit coding of transmission from reader to card [1]

Standard	Modulation	Bit coding
ISO14443A	ASK 100%	Modified Miller
ISO14443B	ASK 10%	NRZ Code
ISO18092 Passive Mode at 106 kbit/s	ASK 100%	Modified Miller
ISO18092 Active Mode at 106k bit/s	ASK 100%	Modified Miller
ISO18092 Passive Mode at 212 kbit/s	ASK 10%	Manchester Code
ISO18092 Active Mode at 212 kbit/s	ASK 10%	Manchester Code

The modulation and bit coding of data transmission from card to reader are different. ISO14443A, ISO14443B and ISO18092 in its passive mode at 106 kbit/s and 212 kbit/s, uses load modulation with sub carrier at 847 kHz. The subcarriers of ISO14443A and ISO18092 in passive mode at 106 kbit/s and 212 kbit/s are ASK modulated, while that of ISO14443B is BPSK. ISO18092 in active mode at 106 kbit/s use ASK 100% while ISO18092 active mode at 212 kbit/s use ASK 10%. ISO14443A, ISO18092 passive mode at both bit rate and active mode at 212 kbit/s use Manchester Coding. ISO14443B uses NRZ code and Modified Miller code for ISO18092 in active mode at 106 kbit/s. Table 2 shows the communication specification when transmitting data from card to reader.

We used TI RF430CL330H on TI MSP430G2, Chameleon Mini and PN532 breakout board to implement these standards. TI RF430CL330H is a transponder that works at 13.56 MHz and supports ISO14443B standard. It can both emulate card and reader. We attached RF430BP booster pack with RF430CL330H built-in from DLP design on the MSP430G2 launchpad to make it work. We need to write the code to the memory of MSP430G2 to control RF430CL330H. PN532 supports reader and card emulation with ISO14443A and ISO18092, however, it can only emulate ISO14443B reader. Different from TI RF430CL330H, we run the codes using LibNFC library in the host machine, computer or Raspberry Pi, to control PN532 through serial port. ChameleonMini has a ISO14443A card emulator, which can work wirelessly, using the battery on the board.

Table 2. Modulation and bit coding of transmission from card to reader [1]

Standard	Modulation	Bit coding
ISO14443A	Load modulation with sub carrier at 847 kHz%	Manchester Code
ISO14443B	Load modulation with sub carrier at 847 kHz%	NRZ Code
ISO18092 Passive Mode at 106 kbit/s	Load modulation with sub carrier at 847 kHz%	Manchester Code
ISO18092 Active Mode at 106 kbit/s	ASK 100%	Modified Miller
ISO18092 Passive Mode at 212 kbit/s	Load modulation with sub carrier at 847 kHz%	Manchester Code
ISO18092 Active Mode at 212 kbit/s	ASK 10%	Manchester Code

3   Communication Standards

We tested three standards in this paper, ISO14443A, ISO14443B, ISO18092. We emulated the full data exchange processes of ISO14443A and ISO18092. The hardware we used does not support ISO14443B, thus we only built an emulated reader for ISO14443B standard.

3.1 ISO14443A

ISO14443A is a widely used standard. The communication process of ISO14443A is, first initializing the reader and anti-collision. After that, the bit rate should be decided. In this paper, we tested this standard using 106 kbit/s. Many devices support the ISO14443A. We tried to build the ISO14443A card emulator using PN532. When we put the card close enough to the reader, the card will be charged. If the reader can provide enough power, the card will be turned on and the processor inside it will start to work. After the card activated, it is in IDLE state. The reader sends a REQA (Request-A) command to the card. The card should send back a ATQA (Answer to Request) command as a response. After that, the card will be in READY state. Then the reader will send a SELECT command with NVB (number of valid bits) parameter to the card and start the anti-collision algorithm. If the reader detected card's ID in the received ATQA command, the reader will embed this ID in the SELLECT command. After the card received the SELECT command with its ID, it will send back an SAK (SELECT-Acknowledge) command containing protocol information to the reader. Then the card will be in ACTIVE state. If the protocol is valid, the reader will send a RATS command (request for answer to select) to the card. The card will answer back an ATS (answer to select) command. After the reader received the ATS command, it will send a PPS (protocol parameter selection) command to decide the baud rate of communication. Figure 1 shows the initialization processes of ISO14443A. Then the card will keep waiting until the reader send data to it. The data frame has 5 components. PCB (protocol control byte) is at the start of the frame, the transmission behavior in the protocol is determined by this byte. After the PCB there is the CID (card identifier) is at the second place, it is used to distinguish different cards. The NAD (node address) is at the third place, it is used to check the compatibility between ISO14443-5 and ISO7816-3. The data payload is following the CID. At the end of a frame there is a CRC to check if error happened in the transmission. Besides, ISO14443A uses odd parity to check the data integrity. We first used two PN532 to emulate the reader and card. Instead send command to PN532 directly, we used an open

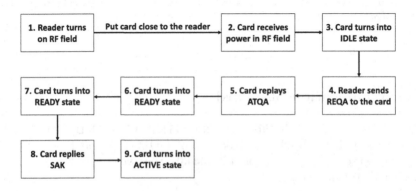

Fig. 1. ISO14443A initialization processes

source library, LibNFC to control PN532. With the help of Libnfc, we can complete the processes from initialization to READY state by writing a single line of function. We can even write the register of PN532 to control all the processes. We also tried Chameleon Mini and TI MSP430G2.

3.2   ISO14443B

When a type B card comes in the RF (radio frequency) field of a reader, it will be in IDLE mode and wait for the REQB (Request-B) command from the reader. After the card receives REQB, it will extract the parameter AFI (Application Family Identifier) search it in the applications stored in the card storage. If the AFI is found, the card will analyze another parameter M in REQB to confirm that there is more than one available slot. If yes, the card will generate a random slot number in ATQB (Answer to Request B) as a response to the reader. In the ATQB command, there are important parameters information and a 4-byte serial number. Different from type A cards, the serial number is not fixed. After the reader received ATQB from card, it will send an application command with 4-byte ATTRIB prefix to process card selection. Figure 2 shows the initialization of ISO14443B card. We build an ISO14443B reader by using PN532 and Libnfc. However, compared to ISO14443A, ISO14443B is less popular. Thus we have not found a card emulator to act as ISO14443B card. What we can do is using an emulated reader and a real card.

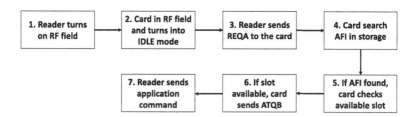

Fig. 2. ISO14443b initialization processes

3.3   ISO18092

ISO18092 standard contains two modes, passive and active. In active mode, during the data transmission, both the reader and the card will create an RF field to send data. In passive mode, only the reader creates the RF field to communicate with card, then the card modulates reader's RF field to answer the reader. These active or passive mode will remain the same in a single transaction. The data frame of ISO18092 has 5 components: Preamble, SYNC, Length, Payload and CRC. At the start of the frame, there are 48 bits of Manchester coded zeros or more, which is called the Preamble. The SYNC value B24D is next to the end of preamble. After the SYNC, there is one Length byte, which stored the length of payload plus one. Payload is the data to be sent. A two bytes CRC-CCITT checksum value of Length and Payload is appended at the end of the data frame.

At the beginning of the communication, the reader keeps trying to find an external RF field. If the reader receives response and it is in passive mode, the reader will process initialization and single device detection (SDD). Next, reader will decide the bit rate of data transmission. The reader uses time slot to detect and communicate with individual cards. The maximum time slot number is 16. The Time Slot Number (TSN) is defined in the polling request frame (ATR_REQ). When a card is in the RF field, it will select a random number R between 0 and TSN. The card will be waiting until the Time Slot becomes R. After that it will send the response of polling frame (ATR_RES) and wait for the reader's data. The polling frame's Length is 06h, 5 bytes payload and one-byte length. First byte of payload is 00h, the second and third bytes in Felica is the fixed system code 8008h. The fourth byte is 00h, also not changeable. The fifth byte is TSN. The Length of polling response frame is 12h. The first payload byte is fixed 01h, the next content of payload is NFCID2, a value that is used to distinguish different devices. The 8-byte Pad is appended at the end of NFCID2, but it is ignored when transferring data. If the reader finds changeable parameter in the ATR_REQ command, it may send a PSL_REQ command to modify parameters. After received by the card, the card should send command to answer PSL_REQ. The parameter selection can be ignored if there are no editable parameters.

4   Implementation

We have done experiments on NFC channels using ISO14443A, ISO14443B and ISO18092 standards, respectively using different platforms.

4.1   PN532

We used PN532 breakout board from Adafruit to implement ISO14443A and ISO18092 standard. We connected the PN532 board to the host machine by the UART to USB convertor. We need to run the program on the host, send the data to PN532 through serial port to control it. We used two PN532 to implement standards, one acted as card and the other acted as reader. The implementation process is, first we run our reader and card emulation program on the host machine. The host machine will send command to serial port which are connected by UART to USB convertor. The PN532 reader will receive command from UART and send data by RF interface. Then PN532 card will receive data from RF interface and send data to host by UART to USB convertor. The card emulation program will receive data from serial port and reply through serial port. The PN532 card will receive data and perform the response by RF interface. Figure 3 shows the workflow of exchanging data using PN532.

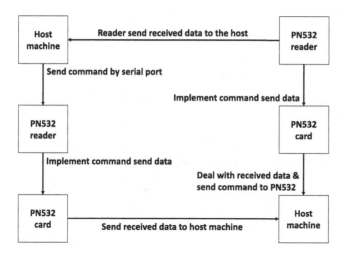

Fig. 3. Data exchange using PN532

To simplify the program development, we used Libnfc library such that we can perform a set of complicated data transmissions by only implementing a line of function, e.g. we initiate PN532 as reader using nfc_initiator_init function, implement nfc_initiator_select_passive_target function, the host machine will control PN532 to send REQA command to the card and handle the ATQA from card, then send SELECT command and deal with SAK from card. After implemented this function, we can start data exchange with the card. When we implement the functions in Libnfc in the program, Libnfc will receive the parameters, generate related data and send them through serial port. The PN532 will receive the data through the UART to USB convertor and implement the command. After that, the PN532 will receive data and send the raw result back to the host. The raw result will be analyzed by Libnfc and return a set of data as the result of the function. Figure 4 shows the workflow of Libnfc.

4.2   TI RF430CL330H

We used TI RF430CL330H transponder to build testing platforms for ISO14443B standard. The hardware we used is RF430BP booster pack with a RF430CL330H on it. We attached the booster pack on a MSP430G2 launchpad. The connection between these two board is I2C. After that, we connect the launchpad to computer by a USB cable. The control method of this device is different from PN532. We need to compile the program on PC using Code Composer Studio from TI, then write the compiled code to the MSP430G2 launchpad. The MSP430G2 launchpad run the program and write the register of the booster pack to control the RF430BP RF interface. When using PN532, we deal with the response data on the host machine, however, in RF430BP, we actually run the host program on MSP430G2. Sending data to host machine is optional. Figure 5 shows the workflow of TI RF430CL330H.

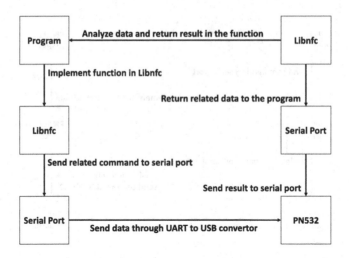

Fig. 4. Workflow of Libnfc

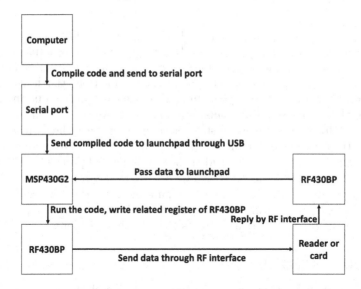

Fig. 5. Workflow of TI RF430CL330H

4.3 Chameleon Mini

Chameleon Mini is a hardware that we used for ISO14443A. The major difference between Chameleon Mini and the devices mentioned above is, it does not need a host. The firmware source code of Chameleon Mini is available on its website. We can modify the source code to customize it. After we compile the source code and write the data to the device, the device can start working with the power supply of USB port or its own battery. Send debug message to computer is an optional choice. Figure 6 shows the workflow of Chameleon Mini.

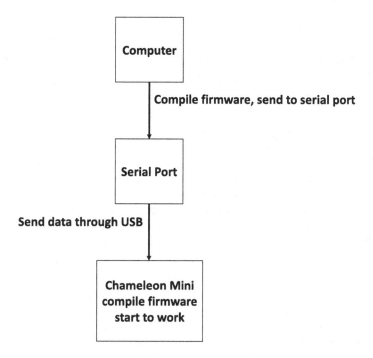

Fig. 6. Workflow of Chameleon Mini

5   Conclusion

In this paper we implemented off-the-shelf card and reader emulators in different standards and tested the possibility of using different configurations on each channel. Based on our analysis, it is suggested for ISO14443A, PN532 provides fast implementation and also provides support for ISO18092. Whereas ChameleonMini provides low delay for ISO14443A. TI RF430CL330H support ISO14443B card and reader emulation while PN532 only support ISO14443B readers. PN532 can be used to emulate reader and card in ISO14443A and ISO18092 standards. The advantage of PN532 is we can use Libnfc library to simplify the code and reduce development time. We can also use Libnfc to modify the register of PN532 directly. The example program shows how to access the register and we can add our own code to the example and compile them to write our data to the register of PN532. This means we can use this platform to test our own security implementation with flexibility. The drawback of PN532 is the delay. We need to control PN532 through a USB cable that will cost in order of milliseconds and may cause failure in some time sensitive applications. TI RF430CL330H can be used for ISO14443B standard. The advantage of TI RF430CL330H is, the launchpad MSP430G2 can directly write the register of the RF transponder to control the RF interface, which means the system delay is low. The disadvantage of TI RF430CL330H is, the firmware source code of MSP430G2 is complicated and not easy to modify, which may significantly increase the development time. Chameleon Mini is for ISO14443A, it can work wirelessly, using the built-in battery slot without cable. The weak point of Chameleon Mini is, though its hardware supports many modulation and codec, its official firmware only support ISO14443A. If we want to use Chameleon Mini to emulate other standards, we need to write the firmware by ourself.

Acknowledgements. This work was funded by an Industrial Technology Fund grant by the Industrial Technology Commission (ITS/047/16). Any opinions, findings, conclusions or recommendations expressed in this material/event (or by members of the project team) do not reflect the views of the Government of the Hong Kong Special Administrative Region, the Innovation and Technology Commission or the Panel of Assessors for the Innovation and Technology Support Programme of the Innovation and Technology Fund. This work was partly supported by the Research Grants Council of Hong Kong under Project CityU 21204716.

References

1. Finkenzeller, K.: RFID Handbook: Fundamentals and Applications in Contactless Smart Cards, Radio Frequency Identification and Near-Field Communication. Wiley, Chichester (2010)
2. Identification Cards-Contactless Integrated Circuit. ISO/IEC 15693–2 cards-vicinity cards-part 2: Physical characteristics, Int. Std. Technical report, ISO/IEC/JTC1 Information Technology (2006)
3. International Organization for Standardization/International Electrotechnical Commission, et al.: ISO/IEC 14443 identification cards-contactless integrated circuit cards-proximity cards. ISO/IEC, 14443, 2001
4. International Organization for Standardization/International Electrotechnical Commission, et al.: ISO/IEC 18092 information technology-telecommunications and information exchange between systems-near field communication-interface and protocol (NFCIP-1). ISO/IEC, 18092 (2004)
5. Pourghomi, P., Ghinea, G., et al.: A proposed NFC payment application. arXiv preprint arXiv:1312.2828 (2013)
6. Lee, D,: Wearable device and method for processing NFC payment using the wearable device, April 24 2018. US Patent 9,953,312
7. Dmitrienko, A., Sadeghi, A.-R., Tamrakar, S., Wachsmann, C.: SmartTokens: delegable access control with NFC-enabled smartphones. In: Katzenbeisser, S., Weippl, E., Camp, L.J., Volkamer, M., Reiter, M., Zhang, X. (eds.) Trust 2012. LNCS, vol. 7344, pp. 219–238. Springer, Heidelberg (2012). https://doi.org/10.1007/978-3-642-30921-2_13
8. Saparkhojayev, N., Dauitbayeva, A., Nurtayev, A., Baimenshina, G.: NFC-enabled access control and management system. In: 2014 International Conference on Web and Open Access to Learning (ICWOAL), pp. 1–4. IEEE (2014)
9. Qiao, H., Zhang, J., Mitrokotsa, A., Hancke, G.: Tangible security: survey of methods supporting secure ad-hoc connects of edge devices with physical context. Comput. Secur. **78**, 281–300 (2018)
10. Qureshi, U.M., Hancke, G.P., Gebremichael, T., Jennehag, U., Forsström, S., Gidlund, M.: Survey of proximity based authentication mechanisms for the industrial internet of things. In: IECON 2018–44th Annual Conference of the IEEE Industrial Electronics Society, pp. 5246–5251. IEEE (2018)

11. Madlmayr, G., Langer, J., Kantner, C., Scharinger, J.: NFC devices: security and privacy. In: 2008 Third International Conference on Availability, Reliability and Security, pp. 642–647. IEEE (2008)
12. de Koning Gans, G., Hoepman, J.-H., Garcia, F.D.: A practical attack on the MIFARE classic. In: Grimaud, G., Standaert, F.-X. (eds.) CARDIS 2008. LNCS, vol. 5189, pp. 267–282. Springer, Heidelberg (2008). https://doi.org/10.1007/978-3-540-85893-5_20
13. Hancke, G.P.: Practical eavesdropping and skimming attacks on high-frequency RFID tokens. J. Comput. Secur. **19**(2), 259–288 (2011)
14. Francis, L., Hancke, G., Mayes, K., Markantonakis. Practical , K.: FC peer-to-peer relay attack using mobile phones. In: International Workshop on Radio Frequency Identification: Security and Privacy Issues, pp. 35–49. Springer (2010)
15. Kfir, Z., Wool, A.: Picking virtual pockets using relay attacks on contactless smartcard. In: First International Conference on Security and Privacy for Emerging Areas in Communications Networks (SECURECOMM 2005), pp. 47–58. IEEE (2005)
16. Hancke, G.P., Mayes, K.E., Markantonakis, K.: Confidence in smart token proximity: relay attacks revisited. Comput. Secur. **28**(7), 615–627 (2009)
17. Thevenon, P.-H., Savry, O.: Implementation of a countermeasure to relay attacks for contactless HF systems. In: Radio Frequency Identification from System to Applications, Intech (2013)
18. Avoine, G., et al.: Security of distance-bounding: a survey. ACM Comput. Surv. (CSUR) **51**(5), 1–33 (2018)
19. Hancke, G.P., Kuhn, M.G.: An RFID distance bounding protocol. In: First International Conference on Security and Privacy for Emerging Areas in Communications Networks (SECURECOMM 2005), pp. 67–73. IEEE (2005)
20. Drimer, S., Murdoch, S.J., et al.: Keep your enemies close: distance bounding against smartcard relay attacks. In: USENIX Security Symposium, vol. 312 (2007)
21. Hu, Q., Liu, Y., Yang, A., Hancke, G.: Preventing overshadowing attacks in self-jamming audio channels. IEEE Trans. Depend. Secur. Comput. **18**(1), 45–57 (2018)
22. Zhou, L., Yeh, K.-H., Hancke, G., Liu, Z., Chunhua, S.: Security and privacy for the industrial internet of things: an overview of approaches to safeguarding endpoints. IEEE Sig. Process. Mag. **35**(5), 76–87 (2018)
23. Cheng, B., Zhang, J., Hancke, G.P., Karnouskos, S., Colombo, A.W.: Industrial cyberphysical systems: realizing cloud-based big data infrastructures. IEEE Ind. Electr. Mag. **12**(1), 25–35 (2018)
24. Liu, Y., Zhang, J., Zheng, W., Hancke, G.P.: Approaches for best-effort relay-resistant channels on standard contactless channels. In: 2019 IEEE 17th International Conference on Industrial Informatics (INDIN), vol. 1, pp. 1719–1724 (2019)

A New Generalisation
of the Goldwasser-Micali Cryptosystem
Based on the Gap 2^k-Residuosity
Assumption

Diana Maimuţ[1(✉)] [iD] and George Teşeleanu[1,2] [iD]

[1] Advanced Technologies Institute, 10 Dinu Vintilă, Bucharest, Romania
{diana.maimut,tgeorge}@dcti.ro
[2] Simion Stoilow Institute of Mathematics of the Romanian Academy,
21 Calea Grivitei, Bucharest, Romania

Abstract. We present a novel public key encryption scheme that enables users to exchange many bits messages by means of *at least* two large prime numbers in a Goldwasser-Micali manner. Our cryptosystem is in fact a generalization of the Joye-Libert scheme (being itself an abstraction of the first probabilistic encryption scheme). We prove the security of the proposed cryptosystem in the standard model (based on the gap 2^k-residuosity assumption) and report complexity related facts. We also describe an application of our scheme to biometric authentication and discuss the security of our suggested protocol. Last but not least, we indicate several promising research directions.

1 Introduction

The authors of [11] introduced a public key encryption (PKE) scheme[1] representing a rather natural extension of the Goldwasser-Micali (GM) [9,10] cryptosystem, the first probabilistic encryption scheme. The Goldwasser-Micali cryptosystem achieves ciphertext indistinguishability under the *Quadratic Residuosity* (QR) assumption. Despite being simple and stylish, this scheme is quite uneconomical in terms of bandwidth[2]. Various attempts of generalizing the Goldwasser-Micali scheme were proposed in the literature in order to address the previously mentioned issue. The Joye-Libert (JL) scheme can be considered a follow-up of the cryptosystems proposed in [13] and [7] and efficiently supports the encryption of larger messages.

Inspired by the Joye-Libert scheme, we propose a new public key cryptosystem, analyze its security and provide the reader with an implementation and performance discussion. We construct our scheme based on 2^k-th power residue symbols. Our generalization of the Joye-Libert cryptosystem makes use of two

---

[1] Reconsidered in [5].

[2] $k \cdot \log_2 n$ bits are needed to encrypt a k-bit message, where n is an RSA modulus as described in [9,10].

© Springer Nature Switzerland AG 2021
D. Maimut et al. (Eds.): SecITC 2020, LNCS 12596, pp. 24–40, 2021.
https://doi.org/10.1007/978-3-030-69255-1_3

important parameters when it comes to the encryption and decryption functions: the number of bits of a message and the number of distinct primes of a public modulus n. Thus, our proposal not only supports the encryption of larger messages (as in the Joye-Libert variant), but also operates on *a variable number of large primes* (instead of two in the Joye-Libert case). Both these parameters can be chosen depending on the desired security application.

Our scheme can be viewed as a flexible solution characterized by the ability of making adequate trade-offs between encryption speed and ciphertext expansion in a given context.

In biometric authentication protocols, when a user identifies himself using his biometric characteristics (captured by a sensor), the collected data will vary. Thus, traditional cryptographic approaches (such as storing a hash value) are not suitable in this case, since they are not error tolerant. As a result, biometric-based protocols must be constructed in a special way and, moreover, the system must protect the sensitivity and privacy of a user's biometric characteristics. Such a protocol is proposed in [6]. Its core is the Goldwasser-Micali encryption scheme. Thus, a natural extension of the protocol in [6] can be obtained using our generalization of the Joye-Libert scheme. Thus, we describe such a biometric authentication protocol and discuss its security.

Structure of the Paper. In Sect. 2 we introduce notations, definitions, security assumptions and schemes used throughout the paper. Inspired by the Joye-Libert PKE scheme and aiming at obtaining a relevant generalization, in Sect. 3 we propose a new scheme based on 2^k residues, prove it secure in the standard model and analyze its performance compared to other related cryptosystems. An application of our scheme to biometric authentication and its security analysis are presented in Sect. 4. We conclude in Sect. 5 and in Appendix A we present some optimized decryption algorithms for our proposed scheme.

2   Preliminaries

Notations. Throughout the paper, λ denotes a security parameter. We use the notation $x \overset{\$}{\leftarrow} X$ when selecting a random element x from a sample space X. We denote by $x \leftarrow y$ the assignment of the value y to the variable x. The probability that event E happens is denoted by $Pr[E]$. The Jacobi symbol of an integer a modulo an integer n is represented by $\left(\dfrac{a}{n}\right)$. J_n and $\bar{J}_n$ denote the sets of integers modulo n with Jacobi symbol 1, respectively -1. Throughout the paper, we let QR_n be the set of quadratic residues modulo n. We consider as $\mathcal{Z}_p = \{-(p-1)/2, \ldots, -1, 0, 1, \ldots, (p-1)/2\}$ the alternative representation modulo an integer p. The set of integers $\{0, \ldots, a-1\}$ is further denoted by $[0, a)$. Multidimensional vectors $v = (v_0, \ldots, v_{s-1})$ are represented as $v = \{v_i\}_{i \in [0,s)}$.

2.1 2^k-th Power Residue

In this paper, we consider the 2^k-th power residue symbol as presented in [15]. The classical Legendre symbol is obtained when $k = 1$.

Definition 1. *Let p be an odd prime such that $2^k | p - 1$. Then the symbol*

$$\left(\frac{a}{p}\right)_{2^k} = a^{\frac{p-1}{2^k}} \bmod p$$

is called the 2^k-th power residue symbol modulo p, where $a^{\frac{p-1}{2^k}} \in \mathcal{Z}_p$.

Properties. The 2^k-th power residue symbol satisfies the following properties

1. If $a \equiv b \bmod p$, then $\left(\dfrac{a}{p}\right)_{2^k} = \left(\dfrac{b}{p}\right)_{2^k}$

2. $\left(\dfrac{a^{2^k}}{p}\right)_{2^k} = 1$

3. $\left(\dfrac{ab}{p}\right)_{2^k} = \left(\dfrac{a}{p}\right)_{2^k} \left(\dfrac{b}{p}\right)_{2^k} \bmod p$

4. $\left(\dfrac{1}{p}\right)_{2^k} = 1$ and $\left(\dfrac{-1}{p}\right)_{2^k} = (-1)^{(p-1)/2^k}$

2.2 Computational Complexity

In our performance analysis we use the complexities of the mathematical operations listed in Table 1. These complexities are in accordance with the algorithms presented in [8]. We do not use the explicit complexity of multiplication, but instead we refer to it as $M(\cdot)$ for clarity.

Table 1. Computational complexity for μ-bit numbers and k-bit exponents

Operation	Complexity
Multiplication	$M(\mu) = \mathcal{O}(\mu \log(\mu) \log(\log(\mu)))$
Exponentiation	$\mathcal{O}(kM(\mu))$
Jacobi symbol	$\mathcal{O}(\log(\mu)M(\mu))$

2.3 Security Assumptions

Definition 2 (Quadratic Residuosity - QR, Squared Jacobi Symbol - SJS and Gap 2^k-Residuosity - GR). *Choose two large prime numbers $p, q \geq 2^\lambda$ and compute $n = pq$. Let A be a probabilistic polynomial-time (PPT) algorithm that returns 1 on input (x, n) or (x^2, n) or (x, k, n) if $x \in QR_n$ or J_n or $J_n \backslash QR_n$. We define the advantages*

$$ADV_A^{\text{QR}}(\lambda) = \left| Pr[A(x, n) = 1 | x \xleftarrow{\$} QR_n] - Pr[A(x, n) = 1 | x \xleftarrow{\$} J_n \backslash QR_n] \right|,$$

$$ADV_A^{\text{SJS}}(\lambda) = \left| Pr[A(x^2, n) = 1 | x \xleftarrow{\$} J_n] - Pr[A(x^2, n) = 1 | x \xleftarrow{\$} \bar{J}_n] \right|,$$

$$ADV_{A,k}^{\text{GR}}(\lambda) = \left| Pr[A(x, k, n) = 1 | x \xleftarrow{\$} J_n \backslash QR_n] - Pr[A(x^{2^k}, k, n) = 1 | x \xleftarrow{\$} \mathbb{Z}_n^*] \right|.$$

The Quadratic Residuosity assumption states that for any PPT algorithm A the advantage $ADV_A^{\mathrm{QR}}(\lambda)$ is negligible.

If $p, q \equiv 1 \bmod 4$, then the Squared Jacobi Symbol assumption states that for any PPT algorithm A the advantage $ADV_A^{\mathrm{SJS}}(\lambda)$ is negligible.

Let $p, q \equiv 1 \bmod 2^k$. The Gap 2^k-Residuosity assumption states that for any PPT algorithm A the advantage $ADV_A^{\mathrm{GR}}(\lambda)$ is negligible.

Remark 1. In [5], the authors investigate the relation between the assumptions presented in Definition 2. They prove that for any PPT adversary A against the GR assumption, we have two efficient PPT algorithms B_1 and B_2 such that

$$ADV_{A,k}^{\mathrm{GR}}(\lambda) \leq \frac{3}{2}\left(\left(k - \frac{1}{3}\right) \cdot ADV_{B_1}^{\mathrm{QR}}(\lambda) + (k - 1) \cdot ADV_{B_2}^{\mathrm{SJS}}(\lambda) \right).$$

2.4 Public Key Encryption

A *public key encryption* (PKE) scheme usually consists of three PPT algorithms: *Setup*, *Encrypt* and *Decrypt*. The *Setup* algorithm takes as input a security parameter and outputs the public key as well as the matching secret key. *Encrypt* takes as input the public key and a message and outputs the corresponding ciphertext. The *Decrypt* algorithm takes as input the secret key and a ciphertext and outputs either a valid message or an invalidity symbol (if the decryption failed).

Definition 3 (Indistinguishability under Chosen Plaintext Attacks - IND-CPA). *The security model against chosen plaintext attacks for a PKE scheme is captured in the following game:*

Setup(λ): The challenger C generates the public key, sends it to adversary A and keeps the matching secret key to himself.

Query: Adversary A sends to C two equal length messages m_0, m_1. The challenger flips a coin $b \in \{0, 1\}$ and encrypts m_b. The resulting ciphertext c is sent to the adversary.

Guess: In this phase, the adversary outputs a guess $b' \in \{0, 1\}$. He wins the game, if $b' = b$.

The advantage of an adversary A attacking a PKE scheme is defined as

$$ADV_A^{\mathrm{IND\text{-}CPA}}(\lambda) = |Pr[b = b'] - 1/2|$$

where the probability is computed over the random bits used by C and A. A PKE scheme is IND-CPA secure, if for any PPT adversary A the advantage $ADV_A^{\mathrm{IND\text{-}CPA}}(\lambda)$ is negligible.

The Joye-Libert PKE Scheme. The Joye-Libert scheme was introduced in [11] and reconsidered in [5]. The scheme is proven secure in the standard model under the GR assumption. We shortly describe the algorithms of the Joye-Libert cryptosystem.

Setup(λ): Set an integer $k \geq 1$. Randomly generate two distinct large prime numbers p, q such that $p, q \geq 2^\lambda$ and $p, q \equiv 1 \bmod 2^k$. Output the public key $pk = (n, y, k)$, where $n = pq$ and $y \in J_n \setminus QR_n$. The corresponding secret key is $sk = (p, q)$.

Encrypt(pk, m): To encrypt a message $m \in [0, 2^k)$, we choose $x \xleftarrow{\$} \mathbb{Z}_n^*$ and compute $c \equiv y^m x^{2^k} \bmod n$. Output the ciphertext c.

Decrypt(sk, c): Compute $z \equiv \left(\dfrac{c}{p}\right)_{2^k}$ and find m such that the relation $\left[\left(\dfrac{y}{p}\right)_{2^k}\right]^m \equiv z \bmod p$ holds. Efficient methods to recover m can be found in [12].

2.5   A Security Model for Biometric Authentication

We further consider the security model for biometric authentication described in [3] in accordance with the terminology established in [6]. We stress that the authors of [6] preferred a rather informal way of presenting their security model while the approach of [3] is formal.

Participants and Roles. The data flow between the different roles assumed in the authentication protocol of [3] is depicted in Fig. 1.

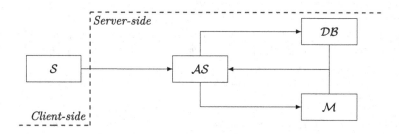

Fig. 1. Data flow and roles

The *server-side* functionality consists of three components to ensure that no single entity can associate a user's identity with the biometric data being collected during authentication. The roles assumed in the authentication protocol are:

– The *Sensor* ($\mathcal{S}$) represents the *client-side* component. As in [6], we assume that the sensor is capable of capturing the user's biometric data, extracting

it into a binary string[3], and performing cryptographic operations such as
PKE. We also assume a *liveness link* between the sensor and the server-side
components, to provide confidence that the biometric data received on the
server-side is from a present living person.

- The *Authentication Server* ($\mathcal{AS}$) is responsible for communicating with the
  user who wants to authenticate and organizing the entire *server-side* procedure. In a successful authentication the AS obviously learns the user's identity, meaning that it should learn nothing about the biometric data being
  submitted.
- The *Database* ($\mathcal{DB}$) securely stores the users' profile and its job is to execute
  the pre-decision part of classification. Since the $\mathcal{DB}$ is aware of privileged
  biometric data, it should learn nothing about the user's identity, or even be
  able to correlate or trace authentication runs from a given (unknown) user.
- The *Matcher* ($\mathcal{M}$) completes the authentication process by taking the output
  produced by the $\mathcal{DB}$ server and computing the final decision step. This implies
  that the $\mathcal{M}$ possesses privileged information that allows it to make a final
  decision, and again that it should not be able to learn anything about the
  user's real identity, or even be able to correlate or trace authentication runs
  from a given (unknown) user.

Definition 4. *Let $v = \{v_i\}_{i \in [0,s)}$ and $w = \{w_i\}_{i \in [0,s)}$ be two s-dimensional
vectors. Then the taxicab distance is defined as $T(v,w) = \sum_{i=0}^{s-1} |v_i - w_i|$. The
taxicab norm is defined as $T(v,0)$.*

The first step in having a useful authentication protocol is for it to be sound.
This requirement is formalized in Requirement 1. Requirements 2. and 3. are
concerned with the sensitive[4] relation between a user's identity and its biometric
characteristics. We want to guarantee that the only entity in the infrastructure
that knows information about this relation is the sensor.

Requirement 1. The matcher $\mathcal{M}$ can compute the taxicab distance $T(b_i, b_i')$,
where b_i is the reference biometric template and b_i' is the fresh biometric template
sent in the authentication request. Therefore, $\mathcal{M}$ can compare the distance to a
given threshold value d and the server $\mathcal{AS}$ can make the right decision.

Requirement 2. For any identity ID_{i_0}, two biometric templates b_{i_0}', b_{i_1}', where
$i_0, i_1 \geq 1$ and b_{i_0}' is the biometric template related to ID_{i_0}, it is infeasible for
any of $\mathcal{M}$, $\mathcal{DB}$ and $\mathcal{AS}$ to distinguish between (ID_{i_0}, b_{i_0}') and (ID_{i_0}, b_{i_1}').

Requirement 3. For any two users U_{i_0} and U_{i_1}, where $i_0, i_1 \geq 1$, if U_{i_β}, where
$\beta \xleftarrow{\$} \{0,1\}$ makes an authentication attempt, then the database $\mathcal{DB}$ can only
guess β with a negligible advantage. Suppose the database $\mathcal{DB}$ makes a guess
β', the advantage is $|Pr[b = b'] - 1/2|$.

---

[3] We further consider the binary string as a vector of fixed length blocks.
[4] In terms of the system's security.

3 A New Public Key Encryption Scheme

Inspired by the Joye-Libert scheme and wishing to obtain a meaningful generalization, we propose a new public key cryptosystem in Sect. 3.1 and analyze its security in Sect. 3.2. An implementation and performance analysis is provided in Sect. 3.3.

3.1 Description

Setup(λ): Set an integer $k \geq 1$. Randomly generate $\gamma + 1$ distinct large prime numbers $p_i, i \in [0, \gamma + 1)$ such that $p_i \geq 2^\lambda$ and $p_i \equiv 1 \bmod 2^k$. Let $n = p_0 \cdot \ldots \cdot p_\gamma$. Select $y_i \xleftarrow{\$} \mathbb{Z}_n^*, i \in [0, \gamma)$, such that the following conditions hold

1. $\left(\dfrac{y_i}{p_i}\right) = -1$

2. $\left(\dfrac{y_i}{p_\gamma}\right) = -1$

3. $\left(\dfrac{y_i}{p_j}\right)_{2^k} = 1$, where $j \neq i$

We denote by $y = \{y_i\}_{i \in [0, \gamma)}$ and $p = \{p_i\}_{i \in [0, \gamma)}$. Output the public key $pk = (n, y, k)$. The secret key is $sk = p$.

Encrypt(pk, m): To encrypt message $m \in [0, 2^k \gamma)$, first we divide it into γ blocks $m = m_0 \| \ldots \| m_{\gamma - 1}$. Then, we choose $x \xleftarrow{\$} \mathbb{Z}_n^*$ and compute $c \equiv x^{2^k} \cdot \prod_{i=0}^{\gamma-1} y_i^{m_i} \bmod n$. The output is ciphertext c.

Decrypt(sk, c): For each $i \in [0, \gamma)$, compute $m_i = Dec_{p_i}(p_i, y_i, c)$.

Algorithm 1: $Dec_{p_i}(p_i, y_i, c)$

Input: The secret prime p_i, the value y_i and the ciphertext c
Output: The message block m_i

1 $m_i \leftarrow 0, B \leftarrow 1$
2 **foreach** $s \in [1, k + 1)$ **do**
3 $\quad z \leftarrow \left(\dfrac{c}{p_i}\right)_{2^s}$
4 $\quad t \leftarrow \left(\dfrac{y_i}{p_i}\right)_{2^s}$
5 $\quad t \leftarrow t^{m_i} \bmod p_i$
6 $\quad$ **if** $t \neq z$ **then**
7 $\quad\quad \mid m_i \leftarrow m_i + B$
8 $\quad$ **end**
9 $\quad B \leftarrow 2B$
10 **end**
11 **return** m_i

Correctness. Let $m_i = \sum_{w=0}^{k-1} b_w 2^w$ be the binary expansion of block m_i. Note that

$$\left(\frac{c}{p_i}\right)_{2^s} = \left(\frac{x^{2^k} \cdot \prod_{v=0}^{\gamma-1} y_v^{m_v}}{p_i}\right)_{2^s} = \left(\frac{y_i^{m_i}}{p_i}\right)_{2^s} = \left(\frac{y_i}{p_i}\right)_{2^s}^{\sum_{w=0}^{s-1} b_w 2^w}$$

since

1. $\left(\dfrac{x^{2^k}}{p_i}\right)_{2^s} = 1$, where $1 \leq s \leq k$

2. $\left(\dfrac{y_j}{p_i}\right)_{2^k} = 1$, where $j \neq i$

3. $\sum_{w=0}^{k-1} b_w 2^w = \left(\sum_{w=0}^{s-1} b_w 2^w\right) + 2^s \cdot \left(\sum_{w=s}^{k-1} b_w 2^{w-s}\right)$

As a result, the message block m_i can be recovered bit by bit using p_i.

Remark 2. The case $\gamma = k = 1$ corresponds to the Goldwasser-Micali cryptosystem [9] and the case $\gamma = 1$ corresponds to the Joye-Libert PKE scheme [11].

Remark 3. In the *Setup* phase, we have to compute a special type of y_i. An efficient way to perform this step is to randomly select $y_{i,i} \xleftarrow{\$} \mathbb{Z}_{p_i}^*$, $y_{i,\gamma} \xleftarrow{\$} \mathbb{Z}_{p_\gamma}^*$ and $w_j \xleftarrow{\$} \mathbb{Z}_{p_j}^*$, compute $y_j \leftarrow w_j^{2^k} \bmod p_j$ and finally use the Chinese remainder theorem to compute an element $y_i \in \mathbb{Z}_n^*$ such that $y_i \equiv y_{i,\ell} \bmod p_\ell$.

3.2 Security Analysis

Theorem 1. *Assume that the* QR *and* SJS *assumptions hold. Then, the proposed scheme is* IND-CPA *secure in the standard model. Formally, let A be an efficient PPT adversary, then there exist two efficient PPT algorithms B_1 and B_2 such that*

$$ADV_A^{\text{IND-CPA}}(\lambda) \leq \frac{3}{2}\gamma\left(\left(k - \frac{1}{3}\right) \cdot ADV_{B_1}^{\text{QR}}(\lambda) + (k - 1) \cdot ADV_{B_2}^{\text{SJS}}(\lambda)\right).$$

Proof. To prove the statement, we simply replace the distribution of the public key y for the encryption query. Let $n_i = p_i p_\gamma$, $i \in [0, \gamma)$. Instead of choosing $y_i \in J_{n_i} \setminus QR_{n_i}$ we choose y_i from the multiplicative subgroup of 2^k residues modulo n_i. Under the GR assumption, the adversary does not detect the difference between the original scheme and the one with the modified y_is. In this case, the value c is not carrying any information about the message. Thus, the IND-CPA security of our proposed cryptosystem follows.

Remark 4. Note that in Theorem 1 is sufficient to consider the GR assumption modulo n_i instead of modulo n. To prove this, lets consider an efficient PPT distinguisher B for the GR assumption modulo n. Then we construct an efficient distinguisher C for the GR assumption modulo n_i.

Thus, on input (y_i, k, n_i), C first randomly selects $\gamma - 1$ primes $\{p_j\}_{j \in [0,\gamma) \setminus \{i\}}$ such that $p_j \equiv 1 \bmod 2^k$ and computes $n = n_i \cdot \prod_{j \in [0,\gamma) \setminus \{i\}} p_j$. Then, using the Chinese theorem, C computes a value $\bar{y}_i$ such that $\bar{y}_i \equiv y_i \bmod n_i$ and $\bar{y}_i \equiv 1 \bmod n/n_i$. Finally, C sends $(\bar{y}_i, k, n)$ to B and he outputs B answer. It is easy to see that C and B have the same success probability.

3.3 Implementation and Performance Analysis

Complexity Analysis. For simplicity, when computing the ciphertext expansion, the encryption and the decryption complexities, we consider the length of the prime numbers as being λ. Based on the complexities presented in Table 1, we obtain the results listed in Table 2.

Table 2. Performance analysis for an η-bit message

Scheme	Ciphertext size	Encryption Complexity
GM [9]	$2\lambda \cdot \eta$	$\mathcal{O}(2M(2\lambda)\eta)$
JL [11]	$2\lambda \cdot \lceil \frac{\eta}{k} \rceil$	$\mathcal{O}(2(k+1)M(2\lambda)\lceil \frac{\eta}{k} \rceil)$
This work	$(\gamma + 1) \cdot \lambda \cdot \lceil \frac{\eta}{\gamma k} \rceil$	$\mathcal{O}((\gamma+1)(k+1)M((\gamma+1)\lambda)\lceil \frac{\eta}{\gamma k} \rceil)$

Scheme	Decryption Complexity
GM [9]	$\mathcal{O}(\log(\lambda)M(\lambda)\eta)$
JL [11]	$\mathcal{O}((2k\lambda + \frac{k^2}{2})M(\lambda)\lceil \frac{\eta}{k} \rceil)$
This work	$\mathcal{O}(\gamma(2k\lambda + \frac{k^2}{2})M(\lambda)\lceil \frac{\eta}{\gamma k} \rceil)$

Implementation Details. We further provide the reader with benchmarks for our proposed PKE scheme.

We ran each of the three sub-algorithms on a CPU Intel i7-4790 4.00 GHz and used GCC to compile it (with the O3 flag activated for optimization). Note that for all computations we used the GMP library [2]. To calculate the running times we used the *omp_get_wtime()* function [1]. To obtain the average running time we chose to encrypt 100 128-bit messages.

For generating the primes needed in the *Setup* phase we used the naive implementation[5]. A more efficient method of generating primes is presented in [5,11].

We further list our results in Table 3 (running times in seconds). When analyzing Table 3, note that in the case $\gamma = 1$ we obtain the Goldwasser-Micali

---

[5] *i.e.* we randomly generated $r \xleftarrow{\$} [2^{\lambda-k}, 2^{\lambda-k+1})$ until the $2^k r + 1$ was prime.

scheme ($k = 1$) and the Joye-Libert scheme ($k = 2, 4, 8$). We stress that we considered $\lambda = 1536^6$.

For completeness, in Table 4 we also present the ciphertext size (in kilobytes $= 10^3$ bytes) for the previously mentioned parameters.

Table 3. Average running times for a 128-bit message

Algorithm	$\gamma = 1$				
	$k = 1$	$k = 2$	$k = 4$	$k = 8$	$k = 16$
Setup	0.680128	0.632187	0.647911	0.648035	0.606200
Encrypt	0.001062	0.000661	0.000457	0.000333	0.000232
Decrypt	0.091672	0.091081	0.093016	0.090269	0.081925

Algorithm	$\gamma = 2$			
	$k = 1$	$k = 2$	$k = 4$	$k = 8$
Setup	1.115970	1.186430	1.592270	15.27510
Encrypt	0.001050	0.000778	0.000570	0.000477
Decrypt	0.098191	0.096581	0.093230	0.094690

Algorithm	$\gamma = 4$			$\gamma = 8$	
	$k = 1$	$k = 2$	$k = 4$	$k = 1$	$k = 2$
Setup	3.215690	14.67540	762.1870	109.4590	12429.10
Encrypt	0.001287	0.001190	0.001052	0.001829	0.002174
Decrypt	0.098939	0.097237	0.099977	0.096664	0.092930

Table 4. Ciphertext size for a 128-bit message

	$k = 1$	$k = 2$	$k = 4$	$k = 8$	$k = 16$
$\gamma = 1$	49.152	24.576	12.288	6.1440	3.0720
$\gamma = 2$	36.864	18.432	9.2160	4.6080	–
$\gamma = 4$	30.720	15.360	7.6800	–	–
$\gamma = 8$	27.648	13.824	–	–	–

4　An Application to Biometric Authentication

In [6], the authors propose a biometric authentication protocol based on the Goldwasser-Micali scheme. A security flaw[7] of the protocol was indicated and fixed in [3]. A natural extension of Bringer *et al.*'s protocol can be obtained using the scheme proposed in Sect. 3.1. Thus, we describe our protocol in Sect. 4.1 and analyze its security in Sect. 4.2. A performance analysis is provided in Sect. 4.3.

---

[6] According to NIST this choice of λ offers a security strength of 128 bits.

[7] The running time is exponential in the number of users.

4.1   Description

Enrollment Phase. In the protocol we consider U_i's biometric template b_i as being a γM-dimensional vector $b_i = \{b_{i,j}\}_{j \in [0,M)}$, where $b_{i,j} = \{b_{i,j,\ell}\}_{\ell \in [0,\gamma)}$ and $b_{i,j,\ell} \in [0, 2^k)$.

In the enrollment phase, U_i registers (b_i, i) at the database $\mathcal{DB}$ and (ID_i, i) at the authentication server $\mathcal{AS}$, where ID_i is U_i's pseudonym and i is the index of record b_i in $\mathcal{DB}$. Let N denote the number of records in $\mathcal{DB}$. Note that the matcher $\mathcal{M}$ possesses a key pair (sk, pk) for the scheme presented in Sect. 3.1.

We further denote by $\mathcal{E}(pk, \cdot)$ and $\mathcal{E}_{JL}(pk, y_\ell, \cdot)$ the encryption algorithms for the scheme presented in Sect. 3.1 with $pk = (n, y, k)$ and the Joye-Libert scheme[8] with $pk = (n, y_\ell, k)$, where $\ell \in [0, \gamma)$.

Verification Phase. If a user U_i wishes to authenticate himself to $\mathcal{AS}$, the next procedure is followed:

1. $\mathcal{S}$ captures the user's biometric data b_i' and sends to $\mathcal{AS}$ the user's identity ID_i together with $\mathcal{E}(pk, b_i') = \{\mathcal{E}(pk, b_{i,j}')\}_{j \in [0,M)}$. Note that a *liveness link* is available between $\mathcal{S}$ and $\mathcal{AS}$ to ensure that data is coming from the sensor are indeed fresh and not artificial.
2. $\mathcal{AS}$ retrieves the index i using ID_i and then sends $\mathcal{E}_{JL}(pk, y_\ell, t_j)$ to the database, for $\ell \in [0, \gamma)$ and $j \in [0, N)$, where $t_j = 1$ if $j = i$, $t_j = 0$ otherwise.
3. For every $s \in [0, M)$, $\mathcal{DB}$ computes

$$\mathcal{E}(pk, b_{i,s}) = \prod_{j=0}^{N-1} \prod_{\ell=0}^{\gamma-1} \mathcal{E}_{JL}(pk, y_\ell, t_j)^{b_{j,s,\ell}} \bmod n.$$

To prevent $\mathcal{AS}$ from performing an exhaustive search of the profile space, $\mathcal{DB}$ re-randomizes the encryptions by calculating $\mathcal{E}(pk, b_{i,s}) = x_s^{2^k} \mathcal{E}(pk, b_{i,s})$, where $x_s \xleftarrow{\$} \mathbb{Z}_n^*$. Then, $\mathcal{DB}$ sends $\mathcal{E}(pk, b_{i,s})$, for $s \in [0, M)$ to the authentication server.
4. $\mathcal{AS}$ computes v_s, $s \in [0, M)$, where

$$v_s = \mathcal{E}(pk, b_{i,s}')/\mathcal{E}(pk, b_{i,s}) \bmod n = \mathcal{E}(pk, b_{i,s}' - b_{i,s}), \tag{1}$$

and $b_{i,s}' - b_{i,s} = \{b_{i,s,\ell}' - b_{i,s,\ell}\}_{\ell \in [0,\gamma)}$. Then, $\mathcal{AS}$ makes a random permutation among v_s, for $s \in [0, M)$, and sends the permuted vector w_s, for $s \in [0, M)$, to $\mathcal{M}$. Note that Item 4 will return a valid result with high probability, thus we do not explicitly require $\mathcal{E}(pk, b_{i,s})$ to be invertible.

---

[8] Note that in this case we consider n to be a product of $\gamma + 1$ primes.

5. $\mathcal{M}$ decrypts w_s to check that the taxicab norm of the corresponding plaintext vector

$$\sum_{s=0}^{M-1}\sum_{\ell=0}^{\gamma-1}|w_{s,\ell}|$$

is equal to or less than d and sends the result $\mathcal{AS}$.

6. $\mathcal{AS}$ accepts or rejects the authentication request accordingly.

Correctness (Requirement 1). We need to show that $v_s = \mathcal{E}(pk, b'_{i,s} - b_{i,s})$, for $s \in [0, M)$. First observe that

$$\mathcal{E}(pk, b_{i,s}) = \prod_{j=0}^{N-1}\prod_{\ell=0}^{\gamma-1}\mathcal{E}_{JL}(pk, y_\ell, t_j)^{b_{j,s,\ell}}$$

$$\equiv \prod_{j=0}^{N-1}\prod_{\ell=0}^{\gamma-1}(r_{j,\gamma}^{2^k}y_\ell^{t_j})^{b_{j,s,\ell}}$$

$$\equiv r_i^{2^k}\prod_{\ell=0}^{\gamma-1}y_\ell^{b_{i,s,\ell}} \bmod n.$$

Thus,

$$\mathcal{E}(pk, b'_{i,s})/\mathcal{E}(pk, b_{i,s}) \equiv \mathcal{E}(pk, b'_{i,s} - b_{i,s}) \bmod n.$$

It is obvious that the taxicab distance between b_i and b'_i

$$\sum_{s=0}^{M-1}\sum_{\ell=0}^{\gamma-1}|b'_{i,s,\ell} - b_{i,s,\ell}|$$

is equal to the taxicab norm of the plaintext vector corresponding to $\{v_s\}_{s\in[0,M)}$ and $\{w_s\}_{s\in[0,M)}$.

4.2   Security Analysis

The proofs of Theorems 2 and 3 are similar to the security proofs from [6] and, thus, are omitted. The only changes we have to make in the proofs of Theorems 2 and 3 is replacing Goldwasser-Micali with our scheme and, respectively, the Joye-Libert scheme.

Theorem 2 (Requirement 2). *For any identity ID_{i_0} and two biometric templates b'_{i_0}, b'_{i_1}, where $i_0, i_1 \geq 1$ and b'_{i_0} is the biometric template related to ID_{i_0}, any $\mathcal{M}$, $\mathcal{DB}$ and $\mathcal{AS}$ can distinguish between (ID_{i_0}, b'_{i_0}) and (ID_{i_0}, b'_{i_1}) with negligible advantage.*

Theorem 3 (Requirement 3). *For any two users U_{i_0} and U_{i_1}, where $i_0, i_1 \geq 1$, if U_{i_β}, where $\beta \xleftarrow{\$} \{0,1\}$ makes an authentication attempt, then the database $\mathcal{DB}$ can only guess β with a negligible advantage.*

4.3 Performance Analysis

It is easy to see that the sensor S and the matcher M perform only M encryptions and, respectively, decryptions. Comparing our proposed protocol's complexity with Bringer *et al.*'s, reduces to comparing the scheme from Sect. 3.1 with the Goldwasser-Micali cryptosystem.[9] On the authentication server's side, we perform γN Joye-Libert encryptions (which can be precomputed) and M divisions. Bringer *et al.*'s protocol, performs step 2 using the Goldwasser-Micali scheme and, thus, in step 4 they can use multiplications instead of divisions[10]. Since we took into consideration the fix from [3] when proposing our protocol, we have to perform M extra multiplications compared to the scheme in [6]. Since we have to assemble our scheme's ciphertexts from Joye-Libert's ciphertexts we have a blowout of γ multiplications on the database's side. Thus, we perform $\gamma MN/2$ multiplications on average.

5   Conclusions and Further Development

Based on the Joye-Libert scheme we proposed a new PKE scheme, proved its security in the standard model and analyzed its performance in a meaningful context. We also described an application of our cryptosystem to biometric authentication and presented its security analysis.

Future Work. An attractive research direction for the future is the construction of *lossy trapdoor functions* (based on the inherited homomorphic properties of our proposed cryptosystem). Another appealing future work idea is to propose a threshold variant of our scheme and to discuss security and efficiency matters.

A   Optimized Decryption Algorithms

In [12], the authors provide the reader with different versions of the decryption algorithm corresponding to the Joye-Libert cryptosystem. We present slightly modified versions of [12, Algorithm 3 and 4] in Algorithms 2 and 3. The authors also propose two other optimizations [12, Algorithm 5 and 6], but their complexity is similar with Algorithm 3 and 4's complexity. Note that these optimizations contain a typo: in line 5, Algorithm 5 and line 6, Algorithm 6 we should have $A^{k-j} \neq C[k-j] \bmod p$ instead of $A \neq C[k-j] \bmod p$.

For these algorithms to work we need to enhance the *Setup* algorithm of our proposed cryptosystem. More precisely, we generate the $\gamma + 1$ prime numbers p_i with the supplementary restriction $p_i \not\equiv 1 \bmod 2^{k+1}$. For $0 \leq i < \gamma$, let $p_i' = (p_i - 1)/2^k$. We precompute $D_i = y_i^{-p_i'}$ for Algorithm 2 and $D_i[j] = D_i^{2^{j-1}} \bmod p_i$, $1 \leq j \leq k - 1$, for Algorithm 3 and augment the private key with these values. Remark that Algorithm 3 requires more memory than Algorithm 2.

---

[9] See Sect. 3.3.
[10] In $\mathbb{Z}_2$ addition and subtraction are equivalent.

Algorithm 2: Fast decryption algorithm Version 1

Input: The secret values (p_i, p_i', D_i), the value y_i and the ciphertext c
Output: The message block m_i

1 $m_i \leftarrow 0, B \leftarrow 1$
2 $C \leftarrow c^{p_i'} \bmod p_i$
3 **foreach** $j \in [1, k-1]$ **do**
4 $\quad$ $z \leftarrow C^{2^{k-j}} \bmod p_i$
5 $\quad$ **if** $z \neq 1$ **then**
6 $\quad\quad$ $m_i \leftarrow m_i + B$
7 $\quad\quad$ $C \leftarrow C \cdot D_i \bmod p_i$
8 $\quad$ **end**
9 $\quad$ $B \leftarrow 2B, D \leftarrow D^2 \bmod p_i$
10 **end**
11 **if** $C \neq 1$ **then**
12 $\quad$ $m_i \leftarrow m_i + B$
13 **end**
14 **return** m_i

Correctness. Let $m_i = \sum_{w=0}^{k-1} b_w 2^w$ be the binary expansion of block m_i. We define $\alpha_i[s] = 2^{k-s} p_i'$. Note that

$$c^{\alpha_i[s]} \equiv (x^{2^k} \cdot \prod_{v=1}^{\gamma} y_v^{m_v})^{\alpha_i[s]}$$

$$\equiv y_i^{\alpha_i[s] \sum_{w=0}^{s-1} b_w 2^w}$$

$$\equiv y_i^{b_{s-1} 2^{k-1} p_i'} y^{\alpha_i[s] \sum_{w=0}^{s-2} b_w 2^w}$$

$$\equiv (-1)^{b_{s-1}} y^{\alpha_i[s] \sum_{w=0}^{s-2} b_w 2^w} \bmod p_i$$

since

1. $(x^{2^k})^{\alpha_i[s]} = x^{2^{k-s}(p_i-1)} = 1$
2. $\left(\dfrac{y_j}{p_i}\right)_{2^k} = 1$, where $j \neq i$
3. $\sum_{w=0}^{k-1} b_w 2^w = \left(\sum_{w=0}^{s-1} b_w 2^w\right) + 2^s \cdot \left(\sum_{w=s}^{k-1} b_w 2^{w-s}\right)$
4. $\left(\dfrac{y_i}{p_i}\right) = -1$

As a result, the message block m_i can be recovered bit by bit using the values p_i, p_i' and the vector D_i.

Implementation Details. The complexities of Algorithms 2 and 3 are $\mathcal{O}(\gamma(\lambda + \frac{k^2}{2} + \frac{3k}{2})M(\lambda)\lceil\frac{\eta}{\gamma k}\rceil)$ and $\mathcal{O}(\gamma(\lambda + \frac{k^2}{2} + \frac{k}{2})M(\lambda)\lceil\frac{\eta}{\gamma k}\rceil)$.

We further provide the reader with benchmarks for the optimized versions of our PKE scheme (Tables 5 and 6).

Algorithm 3: Fast decryption algorithm Version 2

Input: The secret values $(p_i, p_i', D_i[1], \ldots D_i[k-1])$, the value y_i and the ciphertext c

Output: The message block m_i

1 $m_i \leftarrow 0,\ B \leftarrow 1$
2 $C \leftarrow c^{p_i'} \bmod p_i$
3 **foreach** $j \in [1, k-1]$ **do**
4 $\quad z \leftarrow C^{2^{k-j}} \bmod p_i$
5 $\quad$ **if** $z \neq 1$ **then**
6 $\quad\quad m_i \leftarrow m_i + B$
7 $\quad\quad C \leftarrow C \cdot D_i[j] \bmod p_i$
8 $\quad$ **end**
9 $\quad B \leftarrow 2B$
10 **end**
11 **if** $C \neq 1$ **then**
12 $\quad m_i \leftarrow m_i + B$
13 **end**
14 **return** m_i

Table 5. Average running times for Algorithm 2.

| Algorithm | $\gamma = 1$ | | | | |
	$k = 1$	$k = 2$	$k = 4$	$k = 8$	$k = 16$
Setup	0.736027	0.691385	0.704239	0.673276	0.7184
Encrypt	0.001218	0.000787	0.000516	0.000383	0.000296
Decrypt	0.052399	0.026501	0.013326	0.006679	0.003577

| Algorithm | $\gamma = 2$ | | | |
	$k = 1$	$k = 2$	$k = 4$	$k = 8$
Setup	1.210450	1.334020	1.926020	15.35740
Encrypt	0.001137	0.000843	0.000638	0.000555
Decrypt	0.052409	0.026340	0.013168	0.007064

| Algorithm | $\gamma = 4$ | | | $\gamma = 8$ | |
	$k = 1$	$k = 2$	$k = 4$	$k = 1$	$k = 2$
Setup	3.662620	15.26860	828.9620	107.6630	14429.00
Encrypt	0.001423	0.001318	0.001058	0.002007	0.00244632
Decrypt	0.054294	0.026909	0.012723	0.052906	0.026168

Table 6. Average running times for Algorithm 3.

Algorithm	$\gamma = 1$				
	$k = 1$	$k = 2$	$k = 4$	$k = 8$	$k = 16$
Setup	0.702962	0.709076	0.684529	0.713416	0.711517
Encrypt	0.001117	0.000796	0.000499	0.000378	0.000287
Decrypt	0.048072	0.024782	0.012958	0.006617	0.003436

Algorithm	$\gamma = 2$			
	$k = 1$	$k = 2$	$k = 4$	$k = 8$
Setup	1.086650	1.181620	1.877680	13.54860
Encrypt	0.001177	0.000798	0.000600	0.000518
Decrypt	0.049691	0.025127	0.012281	0.006574

Algorithm	$\gamma = 4$			$\gamma = 8$	
	$k = 1$	$k = 2$	$k = 4$	$k = 1$	$k = 2$
Setup	3.354720	14.33620	847.9770	104.0870	12741.90
Encrypt	0.001323	0.001296	0.001087	0.001936	0.002280
Decrypt	0.050909	0.026515	0.012982	0.051005	0.024521

References

1. OpenMP. https://www.openmp.org/
2. The GNU Multiple Precision Arithmetic Library. https://gmplib.org/
3. Barbosa, M., Brouard, T., Cauchie, S., de Sousa, S.M.: Secure biometric authentication with improved accuracy. In: Mu, Y., Susilo, W., Seberry, J. (eds.) ACISP 2008. LNCS, vol. 5107, pp. 21–36. Springer, Heidelberg (2008). https://doi.org/10.1007/978-3-540-70500-0_3
4. Barker, E.: NIST SP800-57 Recommendation for Key Management, Part 1: General. Retrieved January (2016), 147 (2016)
5. Benhamouda, F., Herranz, J., Joye, M., Libert, B.: Efficient cryptosystems from 2^k-th power residue symbols. J. Cryptol. **30**(2), 519–549 (2017)
6. Bringer, J., Chabanne, H., Izabachène, M., Pointcheval, D., Tang, Q., Zimmer, S.: An application of the goldwasser-micali cryptosystem to biometric authentication. In: Pieprzyk, J., Ghodosi, H., Dawson, E. (eds.) ACISP 2007. LNCS, vol. 4586, pp. 96–106. Springer, Heidelberg (2007). https://doi.org/10.1007/978-3-540-73458-1_8
7. Cohen, J., Fischer, M.: A robust and verifiable cryptographically secure ellection scheme (extended abstract). In: FOCS 1985, pp. 372–382. IEEE Computer Society Press (1985)
8. Crandall, R., Pomerance, C.: Prime Numbers: A Computational Perspective. Number Theory and Discrete Mathematics, Springer, Heidelberg (2005). https://doi.org/10.1007/0-387-28979-8
9. Goldwasser, S., Micali, S.: Probabilistic encryption and how to play mental poker keeping secret all partial information. In: STOC 1982, pp. 365–377. ACM (1982)
10. Goldwasser, S., Micali, S.: Probabilistic encryption. J. Comput. Syst. Sci. **28**(2), 270–299 (1984)

11. Joye, M., Libert, B.: Efficient cryptosystems from 2^k-th power residue symbols. In: Johansson, T., Nguyen, P.Q. (eds.) EUROCRYPT 2013. LNCS, vol. 7881, pp. 76–92. Springer, Heidelberg (2013). https://doi.org/10.1007/978-3-642-38348-9_5
12. Joye, M., Libert, B.: Efficient Cryptosystems from 2^k-th Power Residue Symbols. IACR Cryptology ePrint Archive 2013/435 (2014)
13. Naccache, D., Stern, J.: A new public key cryptosytem based on higher residues. In: CCS 1998, pp. 59–66. ACM (1998)
14. Simoens, K., Bringer, J., Chabanne, H., Seys, S.: A framework for analyzing template security and privacy in biometric authentication systems. IEEE Trans. Inf. Foren. Secur. **7**(2), 833–841 (2012)
15. Yan, S.Y.: Number Theory for Computing. Theoretical Computer Science, Springer, Heidelberg (2002). https://doi.org/10.1007/978-3-662-04773-6

New Insights on Differential and Linear Bounds Using Mixed Integer Linear Programming

Anubhab Baksi[(✉)]

Nanyang Technological University, Singapore, Singapore
anubhab001@e.ntu.edu.sg

Abstract. Mixed Integer Linear Programming (MILP) is a very common method of modelling differential and linear bounds. The Convex Hull (CH) modelling, introduced by Sun et al. (Eprint 2013/Asiacrypt 2014), is a popular method in this regard, which can convert the conditions corresponding to a small (4-bit) SBox to MILP constraints efficiently. Our analysis shows, there are SBoxes for which the CH modelling can yield incorrect modelling. The problem arises from the observation that although the CH is generated for a certain set of points, there can be points outside this set which also satisfy all the inequalities of the CH. As apparently no variant of the CH modelling can circumvent this problem, we propose a new modelling for differential and linear bounds. Our modelling makes use of every points of interest individually. Additionally, we also explore the possibility of using redundant constraints, such that the run time for an MILP solver can be reduced while keeping the optimal result unchanged. With our experiments on round-reduced GIFT-128, we show it is possible to reduce the run time a few folds using a suitable choice of redundant constraints. We also present the optimal linear bounds for 11- and 12-rounds of GIFT-128, extending from the best-known result of 10-rounds.

Keywords: Differential cryptanalysis · Linear cryptanalysis · MILP · Heuristic

1 Introduction

Mixed Integer Linear Programming (MILP) is among the most frequently used tool in symmetric key cryptography, as evident from a large volume of research works [1,8,9,12,17,18,20,21]. More particularly, MILP is used to determine the bounds for differential cryptanalysis [5] and linear cryptanalysis [11] for a lot of modern ciphers. MILP aided techniques generally give an opportunity to cover more rounds with more precision. Since the differential and linear cryptanalytic methods are essential for any cipher design, MILP aided techniques are frequently used in cipher design and further cryptanalysis, such as design of GIFT [3] or the improved differential bounds on GIFT in [21].

In the process, the problem of differential/linear bounds for a (reduced round) cipher is converted to an MILP instance, which is then solved using a standard

© Springer Nature Switzerland AG 2021
D. Maimut et al. (Eds.): SecITC 2020, LNCS 12596, pp. 41–54, 2021.
https://doi.org/10.1007/978-3-030-69255-1_4

solver. It is to be noted that the modelling from a differential/linear bound to an MILP instance can be done in various ways. As the efficiency of such a solver greatly depends on the formulated MILP instance, the research community has been active to find out optimal way for modelling. For example, the authors of [9] experiment with heuristic techniques that can make the MILP solver can solve those instances in less time.

The full version of the paper can be found in [2]. This paper uses shorthand notations for the interest of conciseness. In particular, it uses the string notation for the SBox (instead of the more common table based notation), and $\sharp$ to denote the cardinality. Conversion of elements of $\mathbb{F}_2^n$ to-and-from $\mathbb{F}_{2^n}$ is assumed intrinsically.

Our Contributions

The authors of [18] have introduced a MILP modelling by incorporating the concept of *Convex Hull* (CH), which becomes quite popular in the literature [14,17,19,21]. It follows-up from Mouha et al.'s model [12].

We observe a problem related to this modelling which is not reported so far in the literature. We show the convex hull modelling only works when the SBox meets certain condition. Thus, applying the convex hull method to an arbitrary SBox may lead to incorrect results. The problem arises to due a property of the convex hull. That is, it may happen that a point may be inside the hyper-volume of the convex hull while the convex hull is generated excluding that point. Variations of the CH model, such as [17], are also affected by this problem. Eventually, this problem does not occur in common SBoxes, like GIFT (1A4C6F392DB7508E) [3] or PRESENT (C56B90AD3EF84712) [6]. In case the problem occurs, one may need to look for an alternate modelling; since apparently no variant of the convex hull modelling can properly work with such an SBox. To address this issue, i.e., to work with all SBoxes, we propose a different MILP modelling. This modelling works for both differential and linear cases, and can give the exact bound (similar to [17]). Further, this model can be fine-tuned to use with impossible differential cases (such as, [15]), or to find the minimum number of active SBoxes (used in the design of the GIFT family of block ciphers [3]), or iterative trails (like [21]). It is not explicitly tested though, this modelling will likely work for SBoxes with higher (>4) sizes (unlike the CH modelling of [18]).

On top of this, we propose heuristic methods to reduce the execution time. This is inspired from [9], where the authors experiment with various heuristics to improve run time of the MILP instances. These heuristics create a new MILP instance, but do not alter the actual MILP problem (thus, the optimal bound remains unchanged). Using suitable heuristic may help the MILP solver to return the optimal solution faster. We experiment with three main heuristics, along with its combinations. We show how one heuristic applies better to the differential cases, whereas the other applies better to the linear cases. We indeed show a few folds reduction of run time compared to the corresponding no heuristic cases. Interestingly, the idea for two of our main heuristics is actually taken from the convex hull modelling of [18]. The third idea makes use of the optimal bounds already available for smaller rounds.

For benchmark, we take the lightweight cipher GIFT-128 [3], and run the MILP differential and linear instances for reduced rounds. As mentioned, the problem associated with convex hull modelling does not appear for the GIFT SBox. Therefore, we are able to verify our results with existing MILP bounds on GIFT reported in the literature, namely [8,9,17,20]; and also with [10], which uses a Simple Theorem Prover (STP) based approach is used (instead of MILP). We also test with GIFT-64 [3] and PRESENT [6]; and report the optimal linear bounds for GIFT-128 for 11- and 12-rounds for the first time in the literature.

2   Background

As previously mentioned, the problem of differential or linear bounds is converted to an MILP instance through a proper modelling. After this, this MILP instance is solved by some state-of-the-art solver, like Gurobi[1].

This idea of using MILP is introduced by Mouha et al. [12]. The next major contribution comes from Sun et al. [18], where the convex hull (which is actually a concept in computation geometry [4,13]) is used to form the linear constraints. This is quite useful as the code to find convex hull is implemented in the open-source tool Sage[2]. The authors of [18] also propose a heuristic algorithm to reduce the number of constraints returned by the convex hull, so that the MILP instance thus constructed becomes faster to solve (but it does not change the underlying problem of differential/linear bound). However, this claim is apparently not backed-up by any experimental result.

It may be noted that, we actually model the *Difference Distribution Table* (DDT) [16, Chapter 3.4] (see see [Definition 2][2]) for the differential case, and the *Linear Approximation Table* (LAT) [16, Chapter 3.3] (see [Definition 2][2]) for the linear case. The convex hull method treats a given DDT/LAT as distinct points in a hyper-cube. Then, the hyper-dimensional convex hull of the desired points in the DDT/LAT is computed. Since a convex hull is represented by a set of linear inequalities, those can be directly used for the constraints for the MILP instance[3].

2.1   Sun et al. (Active SBox: Eprint'13/Asiacypt'14)

Convex Hull Based Modelling. The authors of [18] propose to use CH, which converts the input difference–output difference relations of the DDT into linear constraints. This modelling is particularly useful for bit-oriented ciphers like GIFT [3]. Since this model, similar to that of [12], uses the number of active SBoxes; it is not possible to get the exact bound, as the maximum transition probability for

---

[1] https://www.gurobi.com/.

[2] https://www.sagemath.org/.

[3] The inequalities are not strict, i.e., of the type $\leq$ or $\geq$ (but not of the type $<$ or $>$). The MILP solvers generally cannot handle strict inequalities, hence the inequalities representing CH suits well for forming the constraints of MILP instances.

each active SBox is assumed when computing the bound. Although not explored, a similar modelling would also work for the linear case.

Consider a $w \times v$ SBox where $(x_0, x_1, \ldots, x_{w-1})$ denotes the (non-zero) input difference vector, and $(y_0, y_1, \ldots, y_{v-1})$ denotes the (non-zero) output difference vector. A dummy variable A of type binary is created, which indicates whether the SBox is active $(A = 1)$ or not $(A = 0)$. The following constraints capture this property:

$$A - x_i \geq 0 \text{ for } i = 0, 1, \ldots, w - 1;$$

$$\sum_{i=0}^{w-1} x_i - A \geq 0.$$

Now the augmented vector $(x_0, x_1, \ldots, x_{w-1}, y_0, y_1, \ldots, y_{v-1})$ denote a (non-zero) input difference – (non-zero) output difference pattern in the DDT. Each of the vectors denote a point in the hyper-dimension. Then the concept of CH is applied on the set of all of the augmented vectors, to convert the set of hyper-dimensional points to non-strict linear inequalities.

In order to reduce the number of linear constraints, which in turn is expected to reduce the execution time for the MILP solver; the authors of [18] also discuss about a greedy algorithm. For example, the number of constraints for the GIFT SBox can be reduced to 21 [21, Section 4.2]. The basic idea of the greedy algorithm is to remove some of the linear constraints from the set of all linear constraints for the CH.

2.2 Sun et al. (Exact Bound: Eprint'14)

Extending the works of [18], the authors of [17] incorporate the individual transitions into the hyper-dimensional points (by increasing the dimension). After this, the convex hull is computed as in [18]. As the individual transitions of DDT are modelled, now it is possible to find the exact bound, thereby improving the modelling from [18]. The greedy algorithm proposed in [18] is used to reduce the number of linear constraints in the CH.

To see how this modelling works, we adopt (from [21, Section 4.2]) the example of the 4×4 SBox used in GIFT, 1A4C6F392DB7508E. There are 4 non-zero transitions in the DDT, namely $(16, 6, 4, 2)$. Those non-zero transitions are modelled by respectively a three-dimensional point. In particular, the 16 transition (corresponds to $2^{\log_2 16/16} = 1$-probability) is modelled by $(0, 0, 0)$; the 6 transition (corresponds to $2^{\log_2 6/16} \approx 2^{-1.415}$-probability) is modelled by $(0, 0, 1)$; the 4 transition (corresponds to $2^{\log_2 4/16} = 2^{-2}$-probability) is modelled by $(0, 1, 0)$; and finally the 2 transition (corresponds to $2^{\log_2 2/16} = 2^{-3}$-probability) is modelled by $(1, 0, 0)$. Now the eight-dimensional vectors $(x_0, x_1, x_2, x_3, y_0, y_1, y_2, y_3)$, which indicate the (non-zero) input difference – (non-zero) output difference relations of this SBox, are augmented with the corresponding three-dimensional vectors indicate the individual transitions. Thus now we have points over the binary eleven-dimensional space, on which the convex hull is computed. Finally, the objective function is set to minimize $\sum_{i=0,(p_0,p_1,p_2)=(2,4,6)}^{2} \left(\log_2 \frac{p_i}{16} \times q_i \right)$, where (q_0, q_1, q_2) is the augmented vector (denoting the individual transitions). The exact complexity for differential distinguisher is calculated by raising the result of the MILP solver to the power of 2.

2.3 Li et al. (Heuristic: Eprint'19)

On top of the MILP modelling proposed in [17], the authors of [9] experiment by altering the following parameters (in such a way that the solution to the MILP problem remains unchanged), as given next.

1. **Number of constraints.** Insert redundant constraint (i.e., this constraint is satisfied given other constraints) to the MILP instance. This will not change the solution, but will likely influence the solver's run time.
2. **Ordering of constraints.** The ordering of the constraints given by the code for convex hull can be altered. Similar to the previous case, the solution will not change.
3. **Ordering of variables.** The linear constraints can be written by changing the variables. For example, the constraint $a_0 x_0 + a_1 x_1 + \cdots + a_{n-1} x_{n-1} \geq b$ can be written as, $a_1 x_1 + \cdots + a_{n-1} x_{n-1} + a_0 x_0 \geq b$.

The authors show that, all three types of heuristics influence the search strategy of Gurobi. Thus, by carefully studying the effect of those heuristics on run time of Gurobi, it is possible to create a new instance of the MILP problem which is faster to solve (but has the same optimal solution).

3 Problem with Convex Hull Modelling

In this part, we describe our finding on the convex hull modelling used to find differential and linear bounds. For simplicity, we only consider the modelling from [18], i.e., without probability encoding for individual transitions.

As noted already, the convex hull method solves the problem of converting a DDT/LAT to MILP-compatible format. It maps a set of binary hyper-dimensional points to a system of non-strict linear inequalities with real coefficients. Thus, all the points will satisfy the corresponding linear constraints which describe the convex hull.

However, there is no check to ascertain a point not in the set of hyper-dimensional points does not satisfy all the linear constraints. As a convex hull has certain other properties, it may happen that a particular point which is not within the set of points (which is used to create the convex hull) still satisfies all the inequalities that govern the convex hull. In other words, the hyper-volume created by some other points includes this point. Thus, the convex hull model will take this point as a valid point (i.e., as if this point belongs to the set of points based on which the convex hull is generated). If used in the MILP instance, the solver will consider the point (which is outside the set of points for which the CH is generated, but inside the hyper-volume of the CH) as valid. This can lead to wrong results. Indeed, our experiments confirm that this actually occurs to a number of SBoxes. For a simple example, consider the 4×4 trivial SBox: 0123456789ABCDEF. There are 16 non-zero transitions in its DDT. Each being 16, are at the diagonal: $(0,0)$, $(1,1)$, $(2,2)$, $(3,3)$, $(4,4)$, $(5,5)$, $(6,6)$, $(7,7)$, $(8,8)$, $(9,9)$, (a,a), (b,b), (c,c), (d,d), (e,e), (f,f). Thus the convex hull is generated for the 16 eight-dimensional points. This is given by the following eight linear inequalities with dummy variables $z_0, z_1, \ldots, z_7$ (each of type binary), as returned by Sage: $1 - z_4 \geq 0, 1 - z_5 \geq 0, 1 - z_6 \geq 0, 1 - z_7 \geq 0, z_4 \geq 0, z_5 \geq 0, z_6 \geq 0, z_7 \geq 0$. Since the corner points of the eight-dimensional cube are used to create the CH, it inherently contains all other points, i.e., all 256 points $\in \mathbb{F}_2^8$ satisfy all the inequalities of the CH. This is due to the following property: For any two points u and v in convex hull, any linear combination of u and v is also in the convex hull. Out of those 256 points which satisfy the generated CH, 16 are of the form: $(0,0,0,0,y_0,y_1,y_2,y_3)$ or $(x_0,x_1,x_2,x_3,0,0,0,0)$. Hence those points can be caught by proper modelling; such as, $\sum_{i=0}^{3} x_i - 1 \geq 0, \sum_{i=0}^{3} y_i - 1 \geq 0$. The rest 240 points (none of which is at the diagonal of the DDT), correspond to zero transitions of the DDT; yet the convex hull model cannot capture it. As a result, the MILP instance will consider those points as non-zero transitions.

Here we present a few typical SBoxes with the same undesirable CH property: Some zero transitions in DDT or LAT lie within the hyper-volume of the convex hull (which is generated by points with non-zero transitions). We take the representatives of each of the 302 *Affine Equivalence* (AE) classes from [7, Chapter 5.4.2]. The results are summarized in Table 1 (Table 1(a) for differential and Table 1(b) for linear). Out of the 302 SBoxes tested, 49 show undesired property for differential and 13 for linear. For instance, with the AE representative #245 of [7] (40132567E8A9CDBF), the non-zero transitions in the DDT are $16, 6, 4, 2$. The number of points with non-zero transitions in its DDT is 86, the corresponding convex hull is given by 59 linear inequalities. Out of the 170 zero transitions in the DDT (ignoring the cases where either the input difference or the output difference is 0), 80 of those satisfy all the convex hull inequalities. Thus, for this SBox, the usual MILP modelling given in [18] could lead to incorrect results for the differential case.

It may be noted that the undesired property may also hold if each transition in DDT/LAT is modelled by separate convex hulls. It also appears that this characteristic of CH does not follow the affine equivalence property, therefore it is likely that more such SBoxes exist – finding which is left open for future research. See [2, Section 3] for more details.

Equality Constraints. Together with the inequality constraints, there is a Sage API which returns the equality constraints[4]. The problem mentioned here will likely not appear if both the equality and the inequality constraints are used,

---

[4] https://doc.sagemath.org/html/en/reference/discrete_geometry/sage/geometry/polyhedron/base.html#sage.geometry.polyhedron.base.Polyhedron_base.equations_list.

Table 1. Typical SBoxes with undesired zero transitions in respective convex hulls

(a) Differential												(b) Linear							
AE # representative	# Points for CH	# CH inequalities	# Zero transitions in CH	AE # representative	# Points for CH	# CH inequalities	# Zero transitions in CH	AE # representative	# Points for CH	# CH inequalities	# Zero transitions in CH	AE # representative	# Points for CH	# CH inequalities	# Zero transitions in CH	AE # representative	# Points for CH	# CH inequalities	# Zero transitions in CH
245	86	59	80	261	75	67	69	278	70	58	65	292	55	22	150	258	28	34	24
246	82	54	77	262	75	59	68	279	64	78	59	294	58	48	56	290	40	36	26
247	84	49	78	263	75	57	69	280	72	73	66	295	58	60	53	292	32	16	26
250	80	56	74	264	80	65	74	281	70	79	64	296	52	72	47	293	44	93	38
251	80	52	74	265	74	72	68	282	71	61	66	297	46	22	126	294	28	22	26
252	80	49	76	266	68	80	62	283	71	46	68	298	46	22	125	295	28	53	24
253	73	42	70	267	68	52	64	284	68	52	61	299	42	22	114	296	40	36	34
254	73	76	69	268	68	98	63	286	67	63	61	300	30	12	189	297	24	12	62
255	73	56	69	269	82	68	75	287	58	28	53	301	28	12	176	298	24	14	20
256	73	48	68	270	82	39	77	288	49	18	135	302	16	8	210	299	32	16	26
257	73	54	66	272	72	80	68	289	58	16	159					300	16	8	154
258	79	71	70	276	82	55	75	290	48	46	44					301	16	8	186
260	80	59	74	277	76	72	69	291	50	22	137					302	16	8	210

although it is not verified explicitly. Nonetheless, this is not mentioned in the literature to the best of our knowledge.

4   Automated Bounds with MILP: Our Proposal

In case the problem (described in Sect. 3) is observed for the given SBox, a new modelling different from that of [18] may be of interest since no variant of the CH based model can circumvent this problem, to the best of our knowledge. In this regard, we devise a new strategy for a Substitution-Permutation Network (SPN) permutation. We describe our modelling for 4×4 SBox only for simplicity, though it can be generalized if needed. We denote the state size and number of rounds as b (counting from 0) and η (counting from 1), respectively.

Our modelling is inspired from the MILP modelling proposed in [1] and the concept of *indicator constraint* (also known as the *big M* method) used in linear programming where the large constant, M, is chosen. In our case, it is sufficient to choose M = twice the SBox size (=8). Unlike [1], however, we do not rely on any Boolean function based optimization; the constraints are directly fed to the MILP instance instead.

To get the optimal differential probability, the result from the MILP solver is negated (assuming the maximization variation, see Sect. 4.1), and raised to the power of 2. So, if ϵ_d is the result from the MILP solver, the attacker will need at least $2^{\epsilon_d + 1}$ chosen inputs, following [16, Chapter 3.4]. For the linear case, if the result from the MILP solver (for the maximization variation) is ϵ_l, the attacker would need at least $2^{2\epsilon_l}$ known inputs [16, Chapter 3.3].

4.1 Modelling

In this part, we describe the MILP modelling for the differential case. The MILP formulation for the linear case is much alike, hence we skip the details for conciseness. For completeness, the main differences in the linear case are as follow. The absolute values for the biases are considered. Since $\pm\frac{1}{2}$ linear bias is equivalent to 1 differential probability, each $Q_{i,j}^p$ in the linear case are multiplied by 2 (the notations are described later).

Assume each of the p transitions (corresponds to $2^{\log_2 p/16}$ probability transition, $1 \geq p > 0$) has q_p frequency in the DDT. For example, there are fifty-seven 2 transitions (each corresponds to 2^{-3} probability transition) for the SBox 40132567E8A9CDBF, as can be seen from its DDT in [2, Table 2]; hence $q_2 = 57$.

First, for the ith SBox ($i = 0, 1, \ldots, b/4 - 1$) at the jth round ($j = 1, \ldots, \eta$); we create the binary variables:

$$
\begin{array}{ll}
Q_{i,j} & \text{to indicate if it is active;} \\
Q_{i,j}^p & \text{to indicate if it takes a } p \text{ transition;} \\
Q_{i,j,l}^p, \text{ for } l = 0, 1, \ldots, q_p - 1 & \text{to indicate which among the } q_p \text{ trails is chosen;} \\
\boldsymbol{x}_{i,j} = (x_{i,j}^0, x_{i,j}^1, x_{i,j}^2, x_{i,j}^3) & \text{to indicate the input difference;} \\
\boldsymbol{y}_{i,j} = (y_{i,j}^0, y_{i,j}^1, y_{i,j}^2, y_{i,j}^3) & \text{to indicate the output difference.}
\end{array}
$$

Next, we set the constraints for each SBoxes:

$$
\begin{array}{ll}
MQ_{i,j} \geq \sum_{l=0}^{3} x_{i,j}^l + \sum_{l=0}^{3} y_{i,j}^l & \text{to check if it is active;} \\
Q_{i,j} = \sum_p Q_{i,j}^p & \text{to ensure if active, it will take exactly} \\
& \text{one of the } q_p \text{ trails;}
\end{array}
$$

For each p transition, do:

$$
Q_{i,j,l}^p = \sum_{l=0}^{q_p-1} Q_{i,j}^l \qquad \text{to check which trail among all } q_p\text{-trails is chosen.}
$$

After this, each $Q_{i,j,l}^p$ for $l = 0, 1, \ldots, q_p - 1$ and for each p, is used to model respective transitions. For example, the $(6, 7)$ trail which is a 4 transition in the DDT for the SBox 40132567E8A9CDBF (see [2, Table 2] for its DDT) is modelled as: $MQ_{i,j}^4 \geq (x_{i,j}^0) + (1 - x_{i,j}^1) + (1 - x_{i,j}^2) + (x_{i,j}^3) + (y_{i,j}^0) + (1 - y_{i,j}^1) + (1 - y_{i,j}^2) + (1 - y_{i,j}^3)$. Basically, each negative literal is taken as is, and each positive literal is subtracted from 1; then added together.

Also, we have to give the initial input difference to at least one variable at the beginning ($j = 1$), i.e., $\sum_{i=0}^{b/4-1} \sum_{l=0}^{3} x_{i,1}^l \geq 1$.

There will be additional constraints representing the linear layer. For a bit-permutation based cipher like GIFT-128, 128 equality constraints are inserted for each round from 2 to η. For example, the second entry in the permutation ($1 \to 33$) is modelled as $x_{8,j}^1 = y_{0,j-1}^1$. If required, this can be generalized to other type of linear layers.

We fit the objective function: Minimize $\sum_{i=0}^{b/4-1} \sum_{j=1}^{\eta} \sum_{p<1} \log_2 \frac{p}{16} \times Q_{i,j}^p$. It is typically written as: Maximize $\sum_{i=0}^{b/4-1} \sum_{j=1}^{\eta} \sum_{p<1} \left(-\log_2 \frac{p}{16}\right) \times Q_{i,j}^p$.

4.2   Optimizations

Using the idea described earlier (in Sect. 4.1), we construct the MILP problems and attempt to solve them using the Gurobi solver. Being inspired from [9], we put redundant constraints in the MILP problem. Using redundant constraints together with the usual constraints does not change the optimal result, but could make the execution faster. Refer to [2, Section 4.2] for more discussion.

As for the choice of the heuristics, we reuse the idea of CH [18]/Sect. 2.1. Therefore, we put additional constraints in the MILP problem together with the usual constraints (described in Sect. 4.1). We basically employ three main heuristics and combinations of those heuristics. The main heuristics are termed as *All Convex Hull*, *Chosen Convex Hull* and *Previous Solutions* and are described next.

All Convex Hull (All-CH). In this heuristic, we use all the inequalities generated for the convex hull. The convex hull is generated with all points in the DDT/LAT the correspond to non-zero transitions. The choice of this heuristic is motivated by the observation that the claim made in [18] (i.e., having all the inequalities from the convex hull in the MILP instance will make the solver taking more time) is apparently not supported by any experimental result. Follow-up works, such as [17,21], seem to accept this claim without any apparent experimental result too. In fact, it is claimed in [14] that, increasing the size of the constraints that describe the DDT of an SBox may indeed reduce the run time.

Chosen Convex Hull (Chosen-CH). In this heuristic, we reduce the number of inequalities for the convex hull (which is generated with points corresponding to non-zero transitions of the DDT/LAT) by applying a randomized version of the greedy algorithm (the greedy algorithm is proposed in [18]). The randomization is applied in tie-breaking: When multiple inequalities are not satisfied by same number of zero transitions, we break time tie uniformly. This way, we run the algorithm few times to get the smallest number of constraints. Therefore, this heuristic can be thought as an improvement over that of [18], as it is non-deterministic in nature and chooses the smallest system of inequalities after a few runs.

Previous Solutions (Prev-Sol). Suppose, we want to know the optimal bound for round η and we already have optimal bounds (possibly by solving MILP instances) for rounds $0, 1, \ldots, \eta - 1$[5]. In this case, the solutions for the previous rounds can be fed to the MILP instance. Since we know the optimal bounds for smaller rounds, the objective functions can be assigned to those optimal bounds; thus creating new constraints. For example, suppose we have the

---

[5] Note that, this assumption is practical. As the run time for higher rounds take significantly longer than the smaller rounds, generally the solutions for the smaller rounds are available.

optimal solutions up to 3rd round: s_1, s_2, s_3; and want the optimal solution for the 4th (so, $\eta = 4$) round. We create the 1-round objective function for each round $\{(1), (2), (3), (4)\}$, and assign with s_1 to create 4 constraints. Next, we create the 2-round objective function by adding the 1-round objective functions for two consecutive rounds $\{(1, 2), (2, 3), (3, 4)\}$, and assign each with s_2 to create 3 constraints. Finally, we create the 3-round objective function by adding the 1-round objective functions for three consecutive rounds $\{(1, 2, 3), (2, 3, 4)\}$, and assign each with s_3 to create 2 constraints. More discussion is omitted here for the interest of brevity, an interested reader may refer to [2, Section 4.2].

4.3   Results

Here we present our experimental results for the differential and linear cases for GIFT-128, GIFT-64 and PRESENT for reduced rounds. Results are obtained from a workstation with $16\times$ Intel Xeon E7-8880 physical cores (shared among multiple users), running Gurobi 8.1 on 64-bit Ubuntu 18.04. It remains to see how those heuristics perform with a different solver and/or environment.

The experimental results for run time are summarized in Table 2. Here we present the average run time (in seconds) for the differential and linear MILP instances for reduced round (1 to 8) GIFT-128 corresponding to the cases where no heuristic is applied (only the usual constraints are used); usual constraints with all-CH constraints are used, usual constraints with chosen-CH constraints are used, usual constraints with previous solutions are used, usual constraints with previous solutions and all-CH constraints are used, usual constraints with previous solutions and chosen-CH constraints are used. The MILP instances with previous solutions as heuristic appear to slow down the solver for the differential case, particularly round 5 onward.

Table 2. Average run time for MILP instances for GIFT-128 with various heuristics

Round(s)		1	2	3	4	5	6	7	8
Differential	–	4.29	16.68	16.06	504.66	6698.07	914.91	1142.62	3142.78
	All-CH	0.25	3.47	15.05	63.15	931.07	607.34	754.12	2708.20
	Chosen-CH	0.69	6.23	25.56	173.39	1949.50	1148.18	1239.64	4671.95
	Prev-Sol	2.49	0.55	11.00	2097.36	12754.98	70514.22	122874.35	123434.43
	Prev-Sol + All-CH	0.89	1.21	12.94	2034.16	9841.02	47055.10	127680.92	200204.50
	Prev-Sol + Chosen-CH	0.38	1.06	10.51	1943.44	10867.38	40964.27	103575.79	229649.26
Linear	–	0.33	0.62	2.71	80.98	4546.46	2108.19	6814.77	38826.96
	All-CH	0.31	1.67	4.18	28.84	80.36	2698.96	3374.94	15166.05
	Chosen-CH	0.38	0.73	2.24	10.69	3205.41	1241.32	2649.87	13120.24
	Prev-Sol	0.15	0.49	1.40	32.87	2435.58	1110.57	2639.03	20523.93
	Prev-Sol + All-CH	0.22	0.61	2.01	19.46	52.88	1546.41	1750.24	9199.43
	Prev-Sol + Chosen-CH	0.21	1.35	2.56	16.42	50.77	1764.47	1992.35	7065.79

The relative (1.0×) run times for each of the heuristics, with respect to the cases where no heuristic is used; can be seen from Fig. 1. The differential case is shown in Fig. 1(a) (a zoomed in version till the 5th round is also shown), and the linear case is given in Fig. 1(b). As evident from the experimental results, it is generally difficult to find a general trend. Still, one may notice significant improvement in run time, generally by a few folds. For example, the all-CH heuristic is more suitable for the differential case; whereas the both the previous solutions with all-CH and the previous solutions with chosen-CH is more suitable for the linear case. Also, it appears that all three the previous solutions based heuristics model perform somewhat similarly for the differential case, and in general are slower than that of no heuristic. However, the same three heuristics perform faster than no heuristic for the linear case.

Table 3 shows the optimal bounds till round 12 for GIFT-128, GIFT-64 and PRESENT. We do not put the average run time corresponding to rounds 9 onward as those cases are not run sufficient times (as each of such cases takes a long time to run). These results are consistent with the existing literature [8–10, 17, 20]. Moreover, we present the optimal linear bounds of GIFT-128 for 11th and 12th rounds. For more information, one may refer to [2, Section 4.3, Section B].

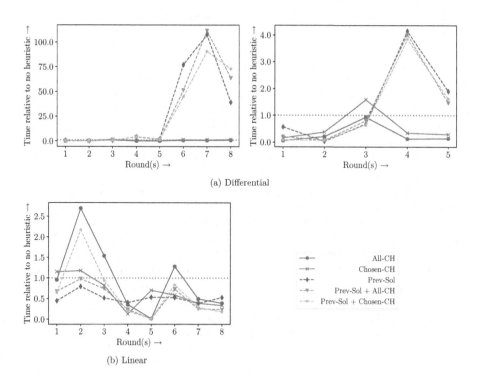

(a) Differential

(b) Linear

Fig. 1. Relative performance of MILP heuristics for GIFT-128

Table 3. Optimal bounds for GIFT-128, GIFT-64 and PRESENT

	Round(s)	1	2	3	4	5	6	7	8	9	10	11	12
GIFT-128	Differential	1.415	3.415	7.000	11.415	17.000	22.415	28.415	39.000	45.415	49.415	54.415	60.415
	Linear	1.000	2.000	3.000	5.000	7.000	10.000	13.000	17.000	22.000	26.000	31.000	36.000
GIFT-64	Differential	1.415	3.415	7.000	11.415	17.000	22.415	28.415	38.000	42.000	48.000	52.000	58.000
	Linear	1.000	2.000	3.000	5.000	7.000	10.000	13.000	16.000	20.000	25.000	29.000	31.000
PRESENT	Differential	2.000	4.000	8.000	12.000	20.000	24.000	28.000	32.000	36.000	41.000	46.000	52.000
	Linear	1.000	2.000	4.000	6.000	8.000	10.000	12.000	14.000	16.000	18.000	20.000	22.000

5 Conclusion

We attempt to study the problem of modelling differential and linear bounds using MILP in depth. In the process, we revisit the modelling proposed in [18], and explore a related shortcoming. It may happen for an SBox that the hypervolume of convex hull will contain some undesired points. Although this probably does not happen with the commonly used SBoxes, it can still be inferred that this model is not generic as it depends on specific properties of the SBox.

Therefore, we propose our new MILP modelling which works for any SBox and is partly inspired from [1]. Our modelling is simpler, and it does not require specialized library call like convex hull or Boolean logic minimization. At the same time, we also follow [9], where the authors observe that the number of constraints can influence the solution time taken by the MILP solver Gurobi. Being motivated by their research, we experiment with redundant constraints. The redundant constraints are inserted along with the usual constraints (which are enough to specify the MILP instance). Those constraints do not change the optimal solution, but can improve the run time. With our experiment, we observe significant speed-up with the redundant constraints, compared to the case with only usual constraints. We also show that one needs separate heuristic depending on the MILP instance is for differential or linear bound.

In the future scope, one may extend the search for heuristics. As we are always using our own constraints (described in Sect. 4.1), any other modelling can be used as a heuristic. This includes, the branch number based model [12] or that of [1]. One may also try to model the zero transitions (using an analogous modelling to ours), and use those as redundant constraints in a way that the MILP instance does not take those transitions. The effect of the heuristics is not straightforward, and more experiments are needed in this direction. Next, the problem with convex hull modelling can be more formally studied, and the SBoxes can be characterized with respect to this problem. Lastly, the effect of a different solver and/or environment can be studied.

References

1. Abdelkhalek, A., Sasaki, Y., Todo, Y., Tolba, M., Youssef, A.M.: MILP modeling for (large) s-boxes to optimize probability of differential characteristics. IACR Trans. Symmetric Cryptol. **2017**(4), 99–129 (2017). https://doi.org/10.13154/tosc. v2017.i4.99-129

2. Baksi, A.: New insights on differential and linear bounds using mixed integer linear programming (full version). Cryptology ePrint Archive, Report 2020/1414 (2020). https://eprint.iacr.org/2020/1414

3. Banik, S., Pandey, S.K., Peyrin, T., Sasaki, Y., Sim, S.M., Todo, Y.: Gift: a small present. Cryptology ePrint Archive, Report 2017/622 (2017). https://eprint.iacr. org/2017/622

4. de Berg, M., Cheong, O., van Kreveld, M., Overmars, M.: Computational Geometry. Springer, Heidelberg (2008). https://doi.org/10.1007/978-3-540-77974-2, https:// www.springer.com/gp/book/9783540779735

5. Biham, E., Shamir, A.: Differential cryptanalysis of DES-like cryptosystems. In: Menezes, A.J., Vanstone, S.A. (eds.) CRYPTO 1990. LNCS, vol. 537, pp. 2–21. Springer, Heidelberg (1991). https://doi.org/10.1007/3-540-38424-3_1

6. Bogdanov, A., et al.: PRESENT: an ultra-lightweight block cipher. In: Paillier, P., Verbauwhede, I. (eds.) CHES 2007. LNCS, vol. 4727, pp. 450–466. Springer, Heidelberg (2007). https://doi.org/10.1007/978-3-540-74735-2_31

7. De Cannière, C.: Analysis and Design of Symmetric Encryption Algorithms. Katholieke Universiteit Leuven, Belgium, Ph.D. thesis (2007). https://www.esat. kuleuven.be/cosic/publications/thesis-139.pdf

8. Ji, F., Zhang, W., Ding, T.: Improving matsui's search algorithm for the best differential/linear trails and its applications for des, desl and gift. Cryptology ePrint Archive, Report 2019/1190 (2019). https://eprint.iacr.org/2019/1190

9. Li, L., Wu, W., Zheng, Y., Zhang, L.: The relationship between the construction and solution of the milp models and applications. Cryptology ePrint Archive, Report 2019/049 (2019). https://eprint.iacr.org/2019/049

10. Liu, Y., Liang, H., Li, M., Huang, L., Hu, K., Yang, C., Wang, M.: STP models of optimal differential and linear trail for s-box based ciphers. Cryptology ePrint Archive, Report 2019/025 (2019). https://eprint.iacr.org/2019/025

11. Matsui, M.: Linear cryptanalysis method for DES cipher. In: Helleseth, T. (ed.) EUROCRYPT 1993. LNCS, vol. 765, pp. 386–397. Springer, Heidelberg (1994). https://doi.org/10.1007/3-540-48285-7_33

12. Mouha, N., Wang, Q., Gu, D., Preneel, B.: Differential and linear cryptanalysis using mixed-integer linear programming. In: Wu, C.-K., Yung, M., Lin, D. (eds.) Inscrypt 2011. LNCS, vol. 7537, pp. 57–76. Springer, Heidelberg (2012). https:// doi.org/10.1007/978-3-642-34704-7_5

13. Mount, D.M.: CMSC 754 - Computational Geometry (lecture notes) (2016). https://www.cs.umd.edu/class/fall2016/cmsc754/Lects/cmsc754-fall16-lects.pdf

14. Sasaki, Y., Todo, Y.: New algorithm for modeling S-box in MILP based differential and division trail search. In: Farshim, P., Simion, E. (eds.) SecITC 2017. LNCS, vol. 10543, pp. 150–165. Springer, Cham (2017). https://doi.org/10.1007/978-3-319-69284-5_11

15. Sasaki, Y., Todo, Y.: New impossible differential search tool from design and cryptanalysis aspects. In: Coron, J.-S., Nielsen, J.B. (eds.) EUROCRYPT 2017. LNCS, vol. 10212, pp. 185–215. Springer, Cham (2017). https://doi.org/10.1007/978-3-319-56617-7_7

16. Stinson, D.R.: Cryptography - Theory and Practice. Discrete Mathematics and its Applications Series. CRC Press (2006)
17. Sun, S., et al.: Towards finding the best characteristics of some bit-oriented block ciphers and automatic enumeration of (related-key) differential and linear characteristics with predefined properties. IACR Cryptol. ePrint Arch. 2014, 747 (2014). http://eprint.iacr.org/2014/747
18. Sun, S., Hu, L., Wang, P., Qiao, K., Ma, X., Song, L.: Automatic security evaluation and (related-key) differential characteristic search: Application to simon, present, lblock, des(l) and other bit-oriented block ciphers. Cryptology ePrint Archive, Report 2013/676 (2013). https://eprint.iacr.org/2013/676
19. Zhang, P., Zhang, W.: Differential cryptanalysis on block cipher skinny with MILP program. Security and Communication Networks 2018, 1–11 (10 2018). https://doi.org/10.1155/2018/3780407
20. Zhou, C., Zhang, W., Ding, T., Xiang, Z.: Improving the MILP-based security evaluation algorithm against differential/linear cryptanalysis using a divide-and-conquer approach. Cryptology ePrint Archive, Report 2019/019 (2019). https://eprint.iacr.org/2019/019
21. Zhu, B., Dong, X., Yu, H.: MILP-based differential attack on round-reduced gift. Cryptology ePrint Archive, Report 2018/390 (2018). https://eprint.iacr.org/2018/390

Secure Card-Based Cryptographic Protocols Using Private Operations Against Malicious Players

Yoshifumi Manabe$^{(\boxtimes)}$ (iD) and Hibiki Ono

Kogakuin University, Shinjuku, Tokyo 163–8677, Japan
manabe@cc.kogakuin.ac.jp

Abstract. This paper shows new card-based cryptographic protocols using private operations that are secure against malicious players. Physical cards are used in card-based cryptographic protocols instead of computers. Operations that a player executes in a place where the other players cannot see are called private operations. Using several private operations, calculations of two variable boolean functions and copy operations were realized with the minimum number of cards. Though the private operations are very powerful in card-based cryptographic protocols, there is a problem that it is very hard to prevent malicious actions during private operations. Though most card-based protocols are discussed in the semi-honest model, there might be cases when the semi-honest model is not enough. Thus, this paper shows new protocols that are secure against malicious players. We show logical XOR, logical AND, and copy protocols, since we can execute any logical computations with a combination of these protocols. We use envelopes as an additional tool that can be easily prepared and used by people.

Keywords: Multi-party secure computation · Card-based cryptographic protocols · Private operations · Logical computations · Copy · Malicious model

1 Introduction

Card-based cryptographic protocols [6,13,28] were proposed in which physical cards are used instead of computers to securely calculate values. They can be used when computers cannot be used or users cannot trust the software on the computer. Also, the protocols are easy to understand, thus the protocols can be used to teach the basics of cryptography [4,19,23]. den Boer [2] first showed a five-card protocol to securely calculate logical AND of two inputs. Since then, many protocols have been proposed to realize primitives to calculate any logical functions [1,12,14,16,29,33,39,40,48,49] and specific computations such as a specific class of logical functions [7,24,26,34,37,41,44,47,53], millionaires' problem [20,32,38], voting [25,31,35,54], random permutation [8,10,11], grouping [9], matching [19], ranking [51], proof of knowledge of a puzzle solution [3,5,18,21,22,42,43,45], and so on. This paper considers calculations of

© Springer Nature Switzerland AG 2021
D. Maimut et al. (Eds.): SecITC 2020, LNCS 12596, pp. 55–70, 2021.
https://doi.org/10.1007/978-3-030-69255-1_5

logical functions and a copy operation under the malicious model since any logical function can be realized with a combination of these calculations.

Operations that a player executes in a place where the other players cannot see are called private operations. These operations are considered to be executed under the table or in the back. Private operations are shown to be the most powerful primitives in card-based cryptographic protocols. They were first introduced to solve millionaires' problem [32]. Using three private operations shown later, committed-input and committed-output logical AND, logical XOR, and copy protocols can be achieved with the minimum number of cards [40]. Another class of private operations is private input operations that are used when a player inputs a private value [17, 38, 50]. These operations are not discussed in this paper since it is impossible to prevent false input from a malicious player. If the input values are honestly given, the players can use the protocols shown in this paper.

The biggest problem of protocols using private operations is malicious actions. Most of the card-based protocols assume the semi-honest model, in which the players obey the rule of the protocols but try to obtain private information. However, there are many cases when we must consider the malicious model. When we allow malicious actions, protocols using private operations are not secure. Since private operations are executed where the other player cannot see, any malicious operation is possible during the private operations, for example, watching the marks of face-down cards or changing the positions of cards.

One countermeasure to malicious actions is setting a watch person. When the protocols are executed by more than two players, it is possible to detect malicious actions by the following rule: whenever a player executes a private operation, another player watches the execution and reports incorrect behavior. The XOR, AND, and copy protocols can be executed securely against a malicious player when the protocols are executed by more than two players [40]. However, when the protocols are executed by two players, it is impossible to use the above method. If Bob watches Alice's private operations, Bob knows all operations, thus the relation between input data and output data is known to Bob. When the output card is opened, the secure input data are known to Bob using the relation between the input data and the output data.

Thus we need new protocols for the two-player case. Since Bob cannot watch Alice's private operations, some additional mechanism to prevent illegally watching the marks of face-down cards during private operations is necessary. This paper introduces envelopes to prevent illegally watching the marks of face-down cards. Cards that must not be seen are publicly put into an envelope. If the envelope is opened, it can be detected by anyone. Envelopes are used in [30] to realize cryptographic protocols that do not use physical cards. In card-based cryptographic protocols, envelopes are used in [8, 36, 44, 49] to realize some kind of shuffles that are not easy to execute by people.

This paper shows new card-based cryptographic protocols that are secure against malicious players using envelopes as an additional tool. The malicious actions during private operations are prevented by adding error-correction cards.

We show logical XOR, logical AND, and copy protocols since any logical functions can be obtained with a combination of these protocols.

As related works, protocols that use additional cards and prevent active attacks while a player executes a shuffle were shown [15]. Another type of active attack is inputting a false value that is not 0 or 1. A protocol to detect such injection attacks was discussed in [27]. Protocols that prevent revealing face-down cards were discussed in [52]. The protocol uses the technique of secret-sharing to prevent information leakage by opening some numbers of cards. The protocol cannot be applied to the problem discussed in this paper since a malicious player might reveal all cards. Another usage of private operations is realizing a public shuffle by multiple private shuffles [29]. Using the method, logical XOR, logical AND, and copy can be executed since there are no malicious actions in these private shuffles. Though the protocols are very simple, the private primitives used in the protocols is private shuffles. Preventing malicious actions for the new protocols that use private random bisection cuts and private reveals are not considered.

A protocol to detect malicious actions by executing two instances of a protocol and comparing the results was shown [46]. The protocol uses cases to prevent revealing face-down cards. The functionality of cases is just the same as the one of envelopes in this paper. The protocol uses twice as many cards as the original protocols and it is impossible to correct the malicious actions. This paper's protocols use fewer cards and can correct the result by malicious actions.

In Sect. 2, basic notations and the private operations introduced in [40] are shown. Section 3 shows XOR, AND, and copy protocols. Section 4 concludes the paper.

2   Preliminaries

2.1   Basic Notations

This section gives the notations and basic definitions of card-based protocols. This paper is based on a two-color card model. In the two-color card model, there are two kinds of marks, ♣ and ♥. Cards of the same marks cannot be distinguished. In addition, the back of both types of cards is ?. It is impossible to determine the mark in the back of a given card of ?.

One bit data is represented by two cards as follows: ♣♥ = 0 and ♥♣ = 1.

One pair of cards that represents one bit $x \in \{0, 1\}$, whose face is down, is called a commitment of x, and denoted as $commit(x)$. It is written as $\underbrace{?\ ?}_{x}$. Note that when these two cards are swapped, $commit(\bar{x})$ can be obtained. Thus, logical negation can be calculated without private operations.

A set of cards placed in a row is called a sequence of cards. A sequence of cards S whose length is n is denoted as $S = s_1, s_2, \ldots, s_n$, where s_i is i-th card of the sequence. . A sequence whose length is even is called an even sequence. $S_1 || S_2$ is a concatenation of sequence S_1 and S_2.

All protocols are executed by two players, Alice and Bob. The players might be malicious, that is, they might not obey the rule of the protocols. There is no collusion between Alice and Bob, otherwise private input data can be easily revealed.

2.2   Private Operations

We show three private operations introduced in [40]: private random bisection cuts, private reverse cuts, and private reveals.

Primitive 1 *(Private random bisection cut)*

A private random bisection cut is the following operation on an even sequence $S_0 = s_1, s_2, \ldots, s_{2m}$. *A player selects a random bit* $b \in \{0,1\}$ *and outputs*

$$S_1 = \begin{cases} S_0 & \text{if } b = 0 \\ s_{m+1}, s_{m+2}, \ldots, s_{2m}, s_1, s_2, \ldots, s_m & \text{if } b = 1 \end{cases}$$

The player executes this operation in a place where the other players cannot see. The player must not disclose the bit b.

Note that if the private random cut is executed when $m = 1$ and $S_0 = commit(x)$, given $S_0 = $,, the player's output $S_1 = $,, which is

or .

We sometimes write the result of the random bisection cut using bit b to a sequence $S_1 || S_2$ (where $|S_1| = |S_2|$) as $swap(b, S_1 || S_2)$. $swap(0, S_1 || S_2) = S_1 || S_2$ and $swap(1, S_1 || S_2) = S_2 || S_1$ are satisfied.

Primitive 2 *(Private reverse cut, Private reverse selection)*

A private reverse cut is the following operation on an even sequence $S_2 = s_1, s_2, \ldots, s_{2m}$ *and a bit* $b \in \{0,1\}$. *A player outputs*

$$S_3 = \begin{cases} S_2 & \text{if } b = 0 \\ s_{m+1}, s_{m+2}, \ldots, s_{2m}, s_1, s_2, \ldots, s_m & \text{if } b = 1 \end{cases}$$

The player executes this operation in a place where the other players cannot see. The player must not disclose b.

Note that the bit b is not newly selected by the player. This is the difference between the primitive in Primitive 1, where a random bit must be newly selected by the player.

Note that in some protocols below, selecting left m cards is executed after a private reverse cut. The sequence of these two operations is called a private reverse selection. A private reverse selection is the following procedure on an even sequence $S_2 = s_1, s_2, \ldots, s_{2m}$ and a bit $b \in \{0, 1\}$. A player outputs

$$S_3 = \begin{cases} s_1, s_2, \ldots, s_m & \text{if } b = 0 \\ s_{m+1}, s_{m+2}, \ldots, s_{2m} & \text{if } b = 1 \end{cases}$$

Primitive 3 *(Private reveal) A player privately opens a given committed bit. The player must not disclose the obtained value.*

Using the obtained value, the player privately sets a sequence of cards.

Consider the case when Alice executes a private random bisection cut on $commit(x)$ and Bob executes a private reveal on the bit. Since the committed bit is randomized by the bit b selected by Alice, the opened bit is $x \oplus b$. Even if Bob privately opens the cards, Bob obtains no information about x if b is randomly selected and not disclosed by Alice. Bob must not disclose the obtained value. If Bob discloses the obtained value to Alice, Alice knows the value of the committed bit.

2.3   Space and Time Complexities

The space complexity of card-based protocols is evaluated by the number of cards. Minimizing the number of cards is discussed in many works.

The number of rounds was proposed as a criterion to evaluate the time complexity of card-based protocols using private operations[39]. The first round begins from the initial state. The first round is (possibly parallel) local executions by each player using the cards initially given to each player. It ends at the instant when no further local execution is possible without receiving cards from another player. The local executions in each round include sending cards to some other players but do not include receiving cards. The result of every private execution is known to the player. For example, shuffling whose result is unknown to the player himself is not executed. Since the private operations are executed in a place where the other players cannot see, it is hard to force the player to execute such operations whose result is unknown to the player. The $i(> 1)$-th round begins with receiving all the cards sent during the $(i - 1)$-th round. Each player executes local executions using the received cards and the cards left to the player at the end of the $(i - 1)$-th round. Each player executes local executions until no further local execution is possible without receiving cards from another player. The number of rounds of a protocol is the maximum number of rounds necessary to output the result among all possible inputs and random values.

Let us show an example of a protocol execution and its space complexity and time complexity.

Protocol 1 *(AND protocol in [40])*
Input: $commit(x)$ and $commit(y)$.
Output: $commit(x \wedge y)$.

1. *Alice executes a private random bisection cut on commit(x). Let the output be commit(x'). Alice hands commit(x') and commit(y) to Bob.*
2. *Bob executes a private reveal on commit(x'). Bob sets*

$$S_2 = \begin{cases} commit(y)||commit(0) & \text{if } x' = 1 \\ commit(0)||commit(y) & \text{if } x' = 0 \end{cases}$$

   and hands S_2 to Alice.
3. *Alice executes a private reverse selection on S_2 using the bit b generated in the private random bisection cut. Let the obtained sequence be S_3. Alice outputs S_3.*

The correctness of the protocol is shown in [40]. The number of cards is four, since the cards of commit(x') is re-used to set commit(0).

The first round ends at the instant when Alice sends commit(x') and commit(y) to Bob. The second round begins at receiving the cards by Bob. The second round ends at the instant when Bob sends S_2 to Alice. The third round begins at receiving the cards by Alice. The number of rounds of this protocol is three.

Since each operation is relatively simple, the dominating time to execute protocols with private operations is the time to handing cards between players and setting up so that the cards are not seen by the other players. Thus the number of rounds is the criterion to evaluate the time complexity of card-based protocols with private operations.

2.4 Malicious Actions During Private Operations

We show examples of cheats by a malicious player for the AND protocol shown in Protocol 1. In the first round, Alice may open the cards of commit(x) and read the secret input value x. Alice might swap the two cards of commit(x) and use $\bar{x}$ as the input value. In the second round, Bob might open the cards of commit(y). Bob might set the cards incorrectly, for example, set

$$S_2 = \begin{cases} commit(1)||commit(y) & \text{if } x' = 1 \\ commit(y)||commit(1) & \text{if } x' = 0 \end{cases}$$

then the result becomes $x \vee y$ instead of $x \wedge y$. Bob can set any other card sequences to obtain other incorrect results. In the third round, Alice might execute a private reverse selection using a value $b'(\neq b)$. To make the protocol secure against malicious players, all of the above cheats must be prohibited or detected.

3   XOR, and and Copy Under Malicious Model

This section shows our new protocols for XOR, AND, and copy.

3.1 Additional Assumptions for Preventing Malicious Actions

Throughout this paper, we assume that each input is given as a committed value. The output must also be given as a committed value so that the output can be used as an input to further computations. Though some multi-party secure calculation protocols assume that each player knows his/her private input, there are some cases when we cannot assume that. For example, suppose that x_1, x_2 are Alice's private input values and y_1, y_2 are Bob's private input values and they want to securely calculate $(x_1 \vee y_1) \wedge (x_2 \vee y_2)$. After $commit(x_1 \vee y_1)$ and $commit(x_2 \vee y_2)$ are calculated, they need to calculate logical AND of two secret values. Thus, we need to calculate the logical functions of two committed inputs. If Alice knows an input value, she first commits her input and a committed input protocol can be used.

We add an assumption that for at least one input, say, x multiple copies of $commit(x)$ are given as input. The reason for this assumption is as follows. When a player, say, Alice is given $commit(x)$ and executes a private operation, there is no way for the other player to detect whether Alice maliciously executed swapping two cards of $commit(x)$ and made $commit(\bar{x})$. Since Bob does not know x, Bob cannot claim that $\bar{x}$ is used instead of x. To detect this type of malicious operation, another copy of $commit(x)$ must be given. Using the copy of $commit(x)$, Bob can detect that Alice used $commit(\bar{x})$ instead of $commit(x)$, as shown in the protocols in this paper. Note that a method to obtain multiple copies of inputs using envelopes is shown in Sect. 3.4.

Next, we need to prevent malicious reveal of committed input values. In the following protocols, we use envelopes as an additional tool. The cards can be put into an envelope and sealed. Opening the envelope can be easily detected by anyone. Thus a malicious player cannot irregularly open envelopes during private operations because it is detected by the other player. It is impossible to distinguish two envelopes. No player can prepare the same envelopes in his/her pocket and exchange them for the envelopes used in the protocol. Such envelopes are used in some card-based protocols [8, 36, 44, 49].

We show some basic operations and notations related to the envelopes. The order of the cards put into an envelope is preserved when the cards are removed. For example, a card sequence S is put into an envelope, the output card sequence from the envelope must also be S. In the following protocols, two envelopes, the left and the right envelope are used and the following two types of insertions are applied. The first one is putting each card of commitments to the left and right envelope. For example, put the left cards of $commit(x)$ and $commit(y)$ into the left envelope and put the right cards of $commit(x)$ and $commit(y)$ into the right envelope. When the players remove the cards from the envelopes, $commit(x)$ and $commit(y)$ are obtained. We write the state of the two envelopes as $[commit(x), commit(y)]$. When we swap the left and right envelopes, the output cards become $commit(\bar{x})$ and $commit(\bar{y})$. Thus we write the state of the swapped envelopes as $[commit(\bar{x}), commit(\bar{y})]$.

The second one is putting the left card of $commit(x)$ and the two cards of $commit(y)$ to the left envelope, and putting the right card of $commit(x)$ and the two cards of $commit(z)$ to the right envelope. We write the state of the two envelopes as $[commit(x), commit(y)||commit(z)]$. When we swap the two envelopes, we can obtain $[commit(\bar{x}), commit(z)||commit(y)]$.

In this paper, private random bisection cuts are executed to these two envelopes. When Alice executes a private random bisection cut to the two envelopes that have $[commit(x), commit(y)]$, $[commit(x \oplus b), commit(y \oplus b)]$ is obtained. When Alice executes a private random bisection cut to the two envelopes that have $[commit(x), commit(y)||commit(z)]$, $[commit(x \oplus b), swap(b, commit(y)||commit(z))]$ is obtained.

With the envelopes, the activities by a malicious player are as follows when the private primitives are private random bisection cuts, private reverse cuts, and private reveals on the envelopes.

Assumption 1 *(Operations by malicious players)*

- *When a malicious player executes a private operation, he/she can swap some envelopes even if it is not allowed in the protocol.*
- *When a malicious player executes a private random bisection cut to two sets of envelopes A and B using the same random bit, he/she can use different bits to A and B.*
- *When a malicious player executes a private reveal on envelope A, he/she can open another envelope B if it cannot be detected by the other player (for example, the number of cards in A and B are the same). Also, he/she might not place envelopes according to the opened cards.*
- *When a malicious player executes a private reverse cut using bit b, he/she might use $\bar{b}$ instead of b.*

3.2   XOR Protocol

Protocol 2 *(XOR protocol)*
   Input: two copies of $commit(x)$ and one copy of $commit(y)$.
   Output: $commit(x \oplus y)$.

1. *Alice and Bob publicly put cards of one $commit(x)$ and $commit(y)$ into two envelopes. The left(right) cards of $commit(x)$ and $commit(y)$ are put into the left(right) envelope. The two envelopes have $[commit(x), commit(y)]$.*
   The remaining two cards of $commit(x)$ are put into two new envelopes so that the left(right) card is put into the left(right) envelope. The two envelopes have $[commit(x)]$.
   The envelopes that have $[commit(x)]$ and $[commit(x), commit(y)]$ are handed to Alice.
2. *Alice executes a private random bisection cut on $[commit(x)]$ and $[commit(x), commit(y)]$ using the same random bit b. Let the output be $[S_1]$ and $[S_1', S_1'']$. $S_1 = commit(x \oplus b)$, $S_1' = commit(x \oplus b)$, and $S_1'' = commit(y \oplus b)$. Alice hands $[S_1]$ and $[S_1', S_1'']$ to Bob.*

3. *Bob first verifies that the envelopes are not opened. Then, Bob executes a private reveal on $[S_1 = commit(x')]$. Bob verifies that the numbers of cards in the envelopes are 1, otherwise Alice incorrectly handed envelopes. Bob privately swaps the two envelopes of $[S'_1, S''_1]$ if $x' = 1$, otherwise, does nothing. Bob makes the two envelopes public, which are denoted $[S'_2, S''_2]$.*

4. *Alice verifies that the envelopes are not opened. Alice and Bob open the envelopes together and obtain S'_2 and S''_2. They turns (that is, face-up) S'_2. If $S'_2 = 0$, S''_2 is the output of the protocol. If $S'_2 = 1$, swap the two cards of S''_2 and the result is the output of the protocol.*

The protocol is three rounds. The first round is the public execution by Alice and Bob. The second round is executed by Alice. The third round is executed by Bob. The last execution by Alice and Bob does not need handing cards or envelopes. Bob just makes the envelopes public and Bob can execute the operations in front of Alice. Thus no overhead is necessary for the public execution. Therefore, the number of rounds is considered to be three. The number of cards used in the protocol is six.

Theorem 1. *The output of the XOR protocol is correct even if Alice or Bob is malicious. The protocol does not reveal the input values to the players if no prohibited opening is executed.*

Proof. First, we show the correctness when both Alice and Bob are honest.

Alice hands $[S_1] = [commit(x \oplus b)]$ and $[S'_1, S''_1] = [commit(x \oplus b), commit(y \oplus b)]$ to Bob. Bob swaps the pair of $[S'_1, S''_1]$ if $x \oplus b = 1$. Thus $[S'_2, S''_2] = [commit((x \oplus b) \oplus (x \oplus b)), commit((y \oplus b) \oplus (x \oplus b))] = [commit(0), commit(x \oplus y)]$. Since $S'_2 = commit(0)$, S''_2 is not swapped and the output is $commit(x \oplus y)$. Therefore, the output is correct. The protocol is secure since Alice sees $S'_2 = 0$ and Bob sees $S'_2 = 0$ and $S_1 = x \oplus b$ but b is an unknown random value for Bob.

Next, consider the case when Alice is malicious and Bob is honest. If Alice opens an envelope during the private operation, Bob can detect the misbehavior. Next, consider the case when Alice does not execute the private random bisection cut correctly. Since the numbers of cards in $[S_1]$ and $[S'_1, S''_1]$ differs, the only cheat that cannot be detected by Bob is incorrectly swapping envelopes. Let b and b' be the random bits selected to swap the envelopes that have $[commit(x)]$ and $[commit(x), commit(y)]$, respectively. The output by Alice is $[S_1] = [commit(x \oplus b)]$ and $[S'_1, S''_1] = [commit(x \oplus b'), commit(y \oplus b')]$. After Bob opens $[S_1] = [commit(x \oplus b)]$, Bob swaps the envelopes if $x \oplus b = 1$, thus the result $[S'_2, S''_2] = [commit(x \oplus b' \oplus x \oplus b), commit(y \oplus b' \oplus x \oplus b)] = [commit(b \oplus b'), commit(y \oplus b' \oplus x \oplus b)]$. When the players open S'_2, they obtain no information about x since $S'_2 = commit(b \oplus b')$. In addition, if $b \oplus b' = 1$, the cards of S''_2 are swapped, thus the output is $commit(y \oplus b' \oplus x \oplus b \oplus (b \oplus b')) = commit(y \oplus x)$. The result is correct regardless of the selection of b and b'.

Next, consider the case Bob is also malicious. When Bob opens the envelopes of $[S'_1, S''_1]$, the cheat can be detected by Alice. Next, consider the case when Bob does not set the envelopes correctly. When Bob sees $x \oplus b$, Bob does not swap the envelopes correctly, that is, Bob selects some value $b''(\neq x \oplus b) \in \{0, 1\}$ and swaps the envelopes of $[S_1', S_1'']$ using b''. If $b'' = x \oplus b$, the result is correct as shown above. Thus the only cheat selection of b'' is $b'' = \overline{x \oplus b} = x \oplus b \oplus 1$.

In this case, the result is $[S_2', S_2''] = [commit(x \oplus b' \oplus b''), commit(y \oplus b' \oplus b'')] = [commit(b' \oplus b \oplus 1), commit(y \oplus b' \oplus x \oplus b \oplus 1)]$. When Alice and Bob open S_2', they do not obtain information about x since the value is independent of x. If $b' \oplus b \oplus 1 = 1$, the two envelopes of S_2'' is swapped. The result is correct since the output is $commit(y \oplus b' \oplus x \oplus b \oplus 1 \oplus (b' \oplus b \oplus 1)) = commit(y \oplus x)$. □

Note that the protocol achieves an error-correction. Even if Alice and/or Bob make mistakes in swapping envelopes, the mistakes are automatically corrected as shown above.

3.3 And Protocol

Protocol 3 *(AND protocol)*
Input: two copies of commit(x) and one copy of commit(y).
Output: commit($x \wedge y$).

1. *Alice and Bob publicly put cards into two envelopes. The left card of commit(x) and two new cards of commit(0) are put into the left envelope. The right card of commit(x) and the two cards of commit(y) are put into the right envelope. The envelopes have $[commit(x), commit(0)||commit(y)]$.*
   The remaining two cards of commit(x) are put into two envelopes so that the left(right) card is put into the left(right) envelope. The envelopes have $[commit(x)]$.
   The envelopes that have $[commit(x)]$ and $[commit(x), commit(0)||commit(y)]$ are handed to Alice.
2. *Alice executes a private random bisection cut on $[commit(x)]$ and $[commit(x), commit(0)||commit(y)]$ using the same random bit b. Let the output be $[S_1]$ and $[S_1', S_1'']$. $S_1 = commit(x')$, where $x' = x \oplus b$. $S_1' = commit(x')$ and $S_1'' = swap(b, commit(0)||commit(y))$. Alice hands $[S_1]$ and $[S_1', S_1'']$ to Bob.*
3. *Bob first verifies that the envelopes are not opened. Bob executes a private reveal on $[S_1 = commit(x')]$. Bob verifies that the numbers of cards in the envelopes are 1, otherwise Alice incorrectly handed the envelopes. Bob privately swaps two envelopes of $[S_1', S_1'']$ if $x' = 1$, otherwise, does nothing. Bob makes the two envelopes public, which are denoted $[S_2', S_2'']$.*
4. *Alice verifies that the envelopes that have $[S_2', S_2'']$ are not opened. Alice and Bob open the envelopes together and obtains S_2' and S_2''. They turn (that is, face-up) S_2'. If $S_2' = 0$, the left two cards of S_2'' is the output of the protocol. If $S_2' = 1$, the right two cards of S_2'' is the output of the protocol.*

The protocol is three rounds. The protocol uses eight cards since two new cards are used to set $commit(0)$.

Theorem 2. *The output of the AND protocol is correct even if Alice or Bob is malicious. The protocol does not reveal the input values to the players if no prohibited opening is executed.*

Proof. The desired output can be represented as follows.

$$x \wedge y = \begin{cases} y \text{ if } x = 1 \\ 0 \text{ if } x = 0 \end{cases}$$

First, we show the correctness when both Alice and Bob are honest.

Alice hands $[S_1] = [commit(x \oplus b)]$ and $[S'_1, S''_1] = [commit(x \oplus b), swap(b, commit(0)||commit(y))]$ to Bob. Bob swaps the pair of $[S'_1, S''_1]$ if $x \oplus b = 1$. Thus $[S'_2, S''_2] = [commit((x \oplus b) \oplus (x \oplus b)), swap(x \oplus b, swap(b, commit(0)|| commit(y)))] = [commit(0), swap(x, commit(0)||commit(y))]$. Thus the players select the left two cards of $swap(x, commit(0)||commit(y))$. The selected cards are $commit(y)$ if $x = 1$ and $commit(0)$ if $x = 0$. Thus, the output is correct.

The protocol is secure since Alice sees $S'_2 = 0$ and Bob sees $S'_2 = 0$ and $S_1 = x \oplus b$ but b is an unknown random value for Bob.

Next, consider the case when Alice is malicious and Bob is honest. If Alice opens an envelope during the private operation, Bob can detect the misbehavior. Next, consider the case when Alice does not execute the private random bisection cut correctly. Since the numbers of cards in the envelopes for $[S_1]$ and $[S'_1, S''_1]$ differs, the only cheat that cannot be detected by Bob is incorrectly swapping envelopes. Let b and b' be the random bits selected to swap the envelopes that have $[commit(x)]$ and $[commit(x), commit(0)||commit(y)]$, respectively. The output by Alice is $[commit(x \oplus b)]$ and $[commit(x \oplus b'), swap(b', commit(0)||commit(y))]$. After Bob opens $[commit(x \oplus b)]$, Bob swaps the envelopes if $x \oplus b = 1$, thus the result $[S'_2, S''_2] = [commit(x \oplus b' \oplus x \oplus b), swap(x \oplus b, swap(b', commit(0)||commit(y)))] = [commit(b \oplus b'), swap(x \oplus b \oplus b', commit(0)||commit(y))]$. When the players open S'_2, they obtain no information about x since $S'_2 = commit(b \oplus b')$. In addition, if $b \neq b'$, the right two cards of S''_2 are used as the output otherwise, the left two cards of S''_2 are used as the output. This is equivalent to execute $swap(b \oplus b', S''_2)$ and select the left two cards. Since $swap(b \oplus b', S''_2) = swap(b \oplus b', swap(x \oplus b \oplus b', commit(0)||commit(y))) = swap(x, commit(0)||commit(y))$, the output is $commit(0)$ if $x = 0$, otherwise the output is $commit(y)$. Therefore, the output is correct regardless of the selection of b and b'.

Next, consider the case Bob is also malicious. When Bob opens the envelopes of $[S'_1, S''_1]$, the cheat can be detected by Alice. Next, consider the case when Bob does not set the envelopes correctly. When Bob sees $x \oplus b$, Bob does not swap the envelopes correctly, that is, Bob selects some value $b''(\neq x \oplus b) \in \{0, 1\}$ and swaps the envelopes of $[S'_1, S''_1]$ using b''. When $b'' = x \oplus b$, the output is correct since it is the correct value. Thus the only cheat selection of b'' is $b'' = \overline{x \oplus b} = x \oplus b \oplus 1$.

In this case, the result is $[S'_2, S''_2] = [commit(x \oplus b' \oplus b''), swap(b'', swap(b, commit(0)||commit(y)))] = [commit(b \oplus b' \oplus 1), swap(x \oplus b \oplus b' \oplus 1, commit(0)||commit(y))]$. When Alice and Bob open S'_2, they do not obtain information about x since the value is independent of x.

In addition, if $b \oplus b' \oplus 1 = 1$, the right two cards of S''_2 are used as the output otherwise, the left two cards of S''_2 are used as the output. This is equivalent to execute $swap(b \oplus b' \oplus 1, S'_2)$ and select the left two cards. Since $swap(b \oplus$

$b' \oplus 1, S_2'') = swap(b \oplus b' \oplus 1, swap(x \oplus b \oplus b' \oplus 1, commit(0)||commit(y))) = swap(x, commit(0)||commit(y))$, the output is $commit(0)$ if $x = 0$, otherwise the output is $commit(y)$. Therefore, the output is correct regardless of the selection of b and b'. $\square$

Note that even if Alice and/or Bob make mistakes in swapping envelopes, the mistakes are automatically corrected as shown above.

3.4 COPY Protocol

Next, we show a copy protocol. Multiple copies of output data of computation might be needed in some cases, for example, use the output result to a further computation. A method to obtain $m(> 1)$ copies of the output is preparing m copies of $commit(y)$.

In the XOR protocol, at the first step of the protocol, they put cards into two envelopes so that $[commit(x), commit(y), commit(y), \ldots, commit(y)]$ is obtained. At the last step, S_2'' is m pairs of cards. When they need to swap the cards, each pair of S_2'' is swapped. Then we can obtain m copies of $commit(x \oplus y)$.

In the AND protocol, at the first step of the protocol, they put cards into two envelopes so that $[commit(x), (commit(0), \ldots, commit(0))||(commit(y), \ldots, commit(y))]$ is obtained, that is, put m copies of $commit(0)(commit(y))$ to the left(right) envelope. At the last step, if $S_2' = 0$, the output is the left m pairs of cards. Otherwise, the output is the right m pairs of cards.

We can obtain another protocol that directly increases the number of copies of input data using the XOR protocol. Two copies of $commit(x)$ are given as input. Execute the XOR protocol with two copies of $commit(x)$ and m copies of $commit(0)$. Then the players obtain m copies of $commit(x)$ as the output since $x \oplus 0 = x$.

Last, we show a method to obtain multiple copies of input x using two envelopes. For any number n, n ♣ (♥) cards are publicly put into the left(right) envelope and the envelopes are sealed. The two envelopes are given to the input player. The input player privately sets the two envelopes according to the private input value x. Then all players publicly open the seals of the envelopes and two piles of cards are obtained. When the players select one card from each of the piles, a copy of $commit(x)$ can be obtained, thus n copies of $commit(x)$ can be obtained.

When we calculate general logical functions using the above primitives, we need to prepare two copies of each input. Any number of copies of a value can be obtained by using the copy protocol at any time, if there are two copies of the value. Obtaining two copies of an output value can be realized by the above protocols, thus any logical functions can be calculated securely using these protocols.

4 Conclusion

This paper proposed new protocols using private operations that are secure against malicious players. We show logical XOR, logical AND, and copy protocols that use envelopes for an additional tool. Since the envelopes are a very powerful tool to restrict shuffle executions, malicious executions are corrected in the protocols.

We can consider weak tools for preventing illegal opening face-down cards, for example, seals on the marks of the cards. They cannot restrict shuffle executions. One of the open problems is considering secure protocols with such tools.

References

1. Abe, Y., Hayashi, Y., Mizuki, T., Sone, H.: Five-card and protocol in committed format using only practical shuffles. In: Proceedings of the 5th ACM International Workshop on Asia Public-Key Cryptography (APKC 2018). pp. 3–8 (2018)
2. den Boer, B.: More efficient match-making and satisfiability *The Five Card Trick*. In: Quisquater, J.-J., Vandewalle, J. (eds.) EUROCRYPT 1989. LNCS, vol. 434, pp. 208–217. Springer, Heidelberg (1990). https://doi.org/10.1007/3-540-46885-4_23
3. Bultel, X., et al.: Physical Zero-knowledge proof for Makaro. In: Izumim, T., Kuznetsov, P. (eds) Stabilization, Safety, and Security of Distributed Systems. SSS 2018. Lecture Notes in Computer Science, vol 11201. Springer, Cham (2018). https://doi.org/10.1007/978-3-030-03232-6_8
4. Cheung, E., Hawthorne, C., Lee, P.: Cs 758 project: Secure computation with playing cards (2013), http://cdchawthorne.com/writings/secure_playing_cards.pdf
5. Dumas, J.-G., Lafourcade, P., Miyahara, D., Mizuki, T., Sasaki, T., Sone, H.: Interactive physical zero-knowledge proof for norinori. In: Du, D.-Z., Duan, Z., Tian, C. (eds.) COCOON 2019. LNCS, vol. 11653, pp. 166–177. Springer, Cham (2019). https://doi.org/10.1007/978-3-030-26176-4_14
6. Dvořák, P., Koucký, M.: Barrington plays cards: The complexity of card-based protocols. arXiv preprint arXiv:2010.08445 (2020)
7. Francis, D., Aljunid, S.R., Nishida, T., Hayashi, Y., Mizuki, T., Sone, H.: Necessary and sufficient numbers of cards for securely computing two-bit output functions. In: Phan, R.C.-W., Yung, M. (eds.) Mycrypt 2016. LNCS, vol. 10311, pp. 193–211. Springer, Cham (2017). https://doi.org/10.1007/978-3-319-61273-7_10
8. Hashimoto, Y., Nuida, K., Shinagawa, K., Inamura, M., Hanaoka, G.: Toward finite-runtime card-based protocol for generating hidden random permutation without fixed points. IEICE Trans. Fund. Electron, Commun. Comput. Sci. **101**(9), 1503–1511 (2018)
9. Hashimoto, Y., Shinagawa, K., Nuida, K., Inamura, M., Hanaoka, G.: Secure grouping protocol using a deck of cards. In: Proc. of 10th International Conference on Information Theoretic Security(ICITS 2017), LNCS Vol. 10681. pp. 135–152 (2017)
10. Ibaraki, T., Manabe, Y.: A more efficient card-based protocol for generating a random permutation without fixed points. In: Proceedings of 3rd International Conference on Mathematics and Computers in Sciences and in Industry (MCSI 2016). pp. 252–257 (2016)
11. Ishikawa, R., Chida, E., Mizuki, T.: Efficient card-based protocols for generating a hidden random permutation without fixed points. In: Proceedings of 14th International Conference on Unconventional Computation and Natural Computation(UCNC 2015), LNCS Vol. 9252. pp. 215–226 (2015)

12. Kastner, J., et al.: The minimum number of cards in practical card-based protocols. In: Proceedings of Asiacrypt 2017, Part III, LNCS Vol. 10626. pp. 126–155 (2017)
13. Koch, A.: The landscape of optimal card-based protocols. IACR Cryptology ePrint Archive, Report 2018/951 (2018)
14. Koch, A., Schrempp, M., Kirsten, M.: Card-based cryptography meets formal verification. In: Galbraith, S.D., Moriai, S. (eds.) ASIACRYPT 2019. LNCS, vol. 11921, pp. 488–517. Springer, Cham (2019). https://doi.org/10.1007/978-3-030-34578-5_18
15. Koch, A., Walzer, S.: Foundations for actively secure card-based cryptography. In: 10th International Conference on Fun with Algorithms (FUN 2020). Schloss Dagstuhl-Leibniz-Zentrum für Informatik (2020)
16. Koch, A., Walzer, S., Härtel, K.: Card-based cryptographic protocols using a minimal number of cards. In: Proceedings of Asiacrypt 2015, LNCS Vol. 9452. pp. 783–807 (2015)
17. Kurosawa, K., Shinozaki, T.: Compact card protocol. In: Proceedings of 2017 Symposium on Cryptography and Information Security(SCIS 2017). pp. 1A2–6 (2017), (In Japanese)
18. Lafourcade, P., Miyahara, D., Mizuki, T., Sasaki, T., Sone, H.: A Physical zkp for slitherlink: how to perform physical topology-preserving computation. In: Heng, S.-H., Lopez, J. (eds.) ISPEC 2019. LNCS, vol. 11879, pp. 135–151. Springer, Cham (2019). https://doi.org/10.1007/978-3-030-34339-2_8
19. Marcedone, A., Wen, Z., Shi, E.: Secure dating with four or fewer cards. IACR Cryptology ePrint Archive, Report 2015/1031 (2015)
20. Miyahara, D., Hayashi, Y.i., Mizuki, T., Sone, H.: Practical card-based implementations of yao's millionaire protocol. Theor. Comput. Sci. **803**, 207–221 (2020)
21. Miyahara, D., et al.: Card-based zkp protocols for takuzu and juosan. In: 10th International Conference on Fun with Algorithms (FUN 2020). Schloss Dagstuhl-Leibniz-Zentrum für Informatik (2020)
22. Miyahara, D., Sasaki, T., Mizuki, T., Sone, H.: Card-based physical zero-knowledge proof for kakuro. IEICE Trans. Fund. Electron. Commun. Comput. Sci. **102**(9), 1072–1078 (2019)
23. Mizuki, T.: Applications of card-based cryptography to education. In: IEICE Technical Report ISEC2016-53. pp. 13–17 (2016), (In Japanese)
24. Mizuki, T.: Card-based protocols for securely computing the conjunction of multiple variables. Theoret. Comput. Sci. **622**, 34–44 (2016)
25. Mizuki, T., Asiedu, I.K., Sone, H.: Voting with a logarithmic number of cards. In: Proceedings of International Conference on Unconventional Computing and Natural Computation (UCNC 2013), LNCS Vol. 7956. pp. 162–173 (2013)
26. Mizuki, T., Kumamoto, M., Sone, H.: The five-card trick can be done with four cards. In: Proceedings of Asiacrypt 2012, LNCS Vol. 7658 pp. 598–606 (2012)
27. Mizuki, T., Shizuya, H.: Practical card-based cryptography. In: Proceedings of 7th International Conference on Fun with Algorithms(FUN2014), LNCS Vol. 8496. pp. 313–324 (2014)
28. Mizuki, T., Shizuya, H.: Computational model of card-based cryptographic protocols and its applications. IEICE Trans. Fund. Electron. Commun. Comput. Sci. **100**(1), 3–11 (2017)
29. Mizuki, T., Sone, H.: Six-card secure and and four-card secure xor. In: Proceedings of 3rd International Workshop on Frontiers in Algorithms(FAW 2009), LNCS Vol. 5598. pp. 358–369 (2009)

30. Moran, T., Naor, M.: Polling with physical envelopes: a rigorous analysis of a human-centric protocol. In: Vaudenay, S. (ed.) EUROCRYPT 2006. LNCS, vol. 4004, pp. 88–108. Springer, Heidelberg (2006). https://doi.org/10.1007/11761679_7

31. Nakai, T., Shirouchi, S., Iwamoto, M., Ohta, K.: Four cards are sufficient for a card-based three-input voting protocol utilizing private sends. In: Proceedings of 10th International Conference on Information Theoretic Security (ICITS 2017), LNCS Vol. 10681. pp. 153–165 (2017)

32. Nakai, T., Tokushige, Y., Misawa, Y., Iwamoto, M., Ohta, K.: Efficient card-based cryptographic protocols for millionaires' problem utilizing private permutations. In: Proceedings of International Conference on Cryptology and Network Security(CANS 2016), LNCS vol. 10052. pp. 500–517 (2016)

33. Nishida, T., Hayashi, Y., Mizuki, T., Sone, H.: Card-based protocols for any boolean function. In: Proc. of 15th International Conference on Theory and Applications of Models of Computation(TAMC 2015), LNCS Vol. 9076. pp. 110–121 (2015)

34. Nishida, T., Hayashi, Y., Mizuki, T., Sone, H.: Securely computing three-input functions with eight cards. IEICE Trans. Fund. Electron. Commun. Comput. Sci. **98**(6), 1145–1152 (2015)

35. Nishida, T., Mizuki, T., Sone, H.: Securely computing the three-input majority function with eight cards. In: 2nd International Conference on Theory and Practice of Natural Computing(TPNC 2013), LNCS Vol. 8273. pp. 193–204 (2013)

36. Nishimura, A., Hayashi, Y.i., Mizuki, T., Sone, H.: Pile-shifting scramble for card-based protocols. IEICE Trans. Fund. Electron. Commun. Comput. Sci. **101**(9), 1494–1502 (2018)

37. Nishimura, A., Nishida, T., Hayashi, Y., Mizuki, T., Sone, H.: Card-based protocols using unequal division shuffles. Soft. Comput. **22**(2), 361–371 (2018)

38. Ono, H., Manabe, Y.: Efficient card-based cryptographic protocols for the millionaires' problem using private input operations. In: Proceedings of 13th Asia Joint Conference on Information Security(AsiaJCIS 2018). pp. 23–28 (2018)

39. Ono, H., Manabe, Y.: Card-based cryptographic protocols with the minimum number of rounds using private operations. In: Proceedings of 14th International Workshop on Data Privacy Management (DPM 2019) LNCS Vol. 11737. pp. 156–173 (2019)

40. Ono, H., Manabe, Y.: Card-based cryptographic logical computations using private operations. New Generation Computing pp. 1–22 (2020)

41. Ruangwises, S., Itoh, T.: And protocols using only uniform shuffles. In: Proceedings of 14th International Computer Science Symposium in Russia(CSR 2019), LNCS Vol. 11532. pp. 349–358 (2019)

42. Ruangwises, S., Itoh, T.: Physical zero-knowledge proof for numberlink. arXiv preprint arXiv:2002.01143 (2020)

43. Ruangwises, S., Itoh, T.: Physical zero-knowledge proof for ripple effect. arXiv preprint arXiv:2009.09983 (2020)

44. Ruangwises, S., Itoh, T.: Securely computing the n-variable equality function with 2n cards. In: International Conference on Theory and Applications of Models of Computation. pp. 25–36. Springer (2020)

45. Sasaki, T., Miyahara, D., Mizuki, T., Sone, H.: Efficient card-based zero-knowledge proof for sudoku. Theoretical Computer Science (2020)

46. Shimizu, Y., Kishi, Y., Sasaki, T., Fujioka, A.: Card-based cryptographic protocols with private operations which can prevent malicious behaviors. In: IEICE Techinical Report ISEC2017-113. pp. 129–135 (2018), (In Japanese)

47. Shinagawa, K., Mizuki, T.: The six-card trick:secure computation of three-input equality. In: Proc. of 21st International Conference on Information Security and Cryptology (ICISC 2018), LNCS Vol. 11396. pp. 123–131 (2018)
48. Shinagawa, K., Mizuki, T.: Secure computation of any boolean function based on any deck of cards. In: Chen, Y., Deng, X., Lu, M. (eds.) FAW 2019. LNCS, vol. 11458, pp. 63–75. Springer, Cham (2019). https://doi.org/10.1007/978-3-030-18126-0_6
49. Shinagawa, K., Nuida, K.: A single shuffle is enough for secure card-based computation of any boolean circuit. Discr. Appl. Math. **289**, 248–261 (2021)
50. Shirouchi, S., Nakai, T., Iwamoto, M., Ohta, K.: Efficient card-based cryptographic protocols for logic gates utilizing private permutations. In: Proc. of 2017 Symposium on Cryptography and Information Security(SCIS 2017). pp. 1A2–2 (2017), (In Japanese)
51. Takashima, K., Abe, Y., Sasaki, T., Miyahara, D., Shinagawa, K., Mizuki, T., Sone, H.: Card-based protocols for secure ranking computations. Theoret. Comput. Sci. **845**, 122–135 (2020)
52. Takashima, K., Miyahara, D., Mizuki, T., Sone, H.: Card-based protocol against actively revealing card attack. In: Martín-Vide, C., Pond, G., Vega-Rodríguez, M.A. (eds.) TPNC 2019. LNCS, vol. 11934, pp. 95–106. Springer, Cham (2019). https://doi.org/10.1007/978-3-030-34500-6_6
53. Toyoda, K., Miyahara, D., Mizuki, T., Sone, H.: Six-card finite-runtime xor protocol with only random cut. In: Proceedings of the 7th ACM Workshop on ASIA Public-Key Cryptography. pp. 2–8 (2020)
54. Watanabe, Y., Kuroki, Y., Suzuki, S., Koga, Y., Iwamoto, M., Ohta, K.: Card-based majority voting protocols with three inputs using three cards. In: 2018 International Symposium on Information Theory and Its Applications (ISITA). pp. 218–222. IEEE (2018)

Decentralized Multi-authority Anonymous Credential System with Bundled Languages on Identifiers

Hiroaki Anada$^{(\boxtimes)}$ (iD)

Department of Information Security, University of Nagasaki,
W408, 1-1-1, Manabino, Nagayo-cho, Nishisonogi-gun, Nagasaki 851-2195, Japan
anada@sun.ac.jp

Abstract. We propose an anonymous credential system equipped with independent decentralized authorities who issue credentials. In our system, the number of authorities can dynamically increase or decrease. A credential is a private secret key issued by an authority, and it is given to an entity distinguished by an identifier. In the issuing phase, an authority only has to sign identifiers. In the proving phase, under a principle of "commit-to-id", an entity proves to a verifier the knowledge of his/her identifier and private secret keys by generating a unified proof. The verifier should resist against collusion attacks executed by adversaries who bring together the private secret keys issued to different identifiers. To construct our system, we employ two building blocks; the structure-preserving signature scheme and the Groth-Sahai non-interactive proof system. Both blocks work in the setting of bilinear groups. To attain the collusion resistance, we propose a notion of "bundled language" that is abstraction of simultaneous pairing-product equations which include an identifier as a variable.

Keywords: Anonymous credential system · Attribute · Decentralized · Collusion resistance · Identifier

1 Introduction

Global identifiers are useful digital-identity data on our connected networks. Legitimately issued e-mail addresses and e-passports can be global identifiers, which are used in registration phase of our activity on networks. Universally unique identifiers (UUID) stipulated by ISO/IEC 11578:1996 are global identifiers for devices with MAC addresses. Once a global identifier is linked to an entity, the *attribute credentials* of the entity can be issued to the identifier by authorities. In the proving phase, the entity proves its possession of authorized attribute credentials.

Privacy protection on connected networks is a demand arising from the trend that governments and platform-enterprises collect much information of individuals. This trend is because public monitoring is critical in cyber-physical societies. Another reason is because data-driven decision-making becomes important

© Springer Nature Switzerland AG 2021
D. Maimut et al. (Eds.): SecITC 2020, LNCS 12596, pp. 71–90, 2021.
https://doi.org/10.1007/978-3-030-69255-1_6

for corporate entrepreneurship. Under the demand, we should distinguish cases where identity information of entities is not needed. In the cases, the entities should be authenticated and authorized by their attributes without identity data. Cryptography can provide the solution for the cases, which is called anonymous credential systems [5,7,8]. The entity is able to prove to a verifier the possession of authorized attribute credentials anonymously.

There arises another trend that an individual is registered and authenticated by independent decentralized authorities the number of which dynamically increases or decreases in the world. For example, Single-Sign-On at "social-login" has already become popular in cyber-physical space. Thus, we need to seek a privacy protecting cryptographic primitive that can treat independent decentralized multi-authorities. An ingredient is to develop a decentralized multi-authority anonymous credential system (DMA-ACS), in which attribute credentials are attached to a global identifier. We note that "global" is useful in the case of decentralized multi-authorities. However, there is a challenging task; attaining *collusion resistance*. That is, in the case of DMA-ACS for which we will try, the verifier should resist against collusion attacks by adversaries who bring together the attribute credentials issued to *different* identifiers. Note that the collusion resistance has been already pursued in attribute-based cryptographic primitives such as attribute-based encryption [14] and signatures [15], but in the case of DMA-ACS, it has not been studied yet.

1.1 Our Contribution and Related Work

Our Contribution. In this paper, we define syntax and security definitions of DMA-ACS with collusion resistance in scope. Especially we give three security definitions. One is existential unforgeability (EUF) against collusion attacks that cause mis-authorization. Note that in a real scenario the number of authorities is increasing/decreasing, and hence an adversary can *corrupt* some of the authorities and get the master secret keys of them. We will reflect the corrupted authorities in the definition.

The other two security definitions are anonymity and unlinkability. Here we should distinguish the two types of anonymity; anonymity at the issuing phase and anonymity of the proofs generated by entities. The former anonymity means that the issuer is blinded under mechanisms such as a blind signature scheme. On the other hand, the latter anonymity means that even the issuer cannot get any information on identifiers from given proofs. The anonymity defined and proved in this paper is the latter one. As for unlinkability, it is security notion on the proofs; if any PPT adversary cannot distinguish whether two given proofs are generated by an entity having a single identifier or by two entities having different identifiers, ACS is said to have unlinkability of proofs. In our definitions, the unlinkability of proofs implies the anonymity of proofs, and we will prove the relation.

Then, we propose a generic construction of DMA-ACS. A functional feature is that an attribute authority who issues a private secret key to a prover only has to sign prover's identifier. We remark that the authorities use a set of common public parameters. This is a natural scenario under a standard like NIST FIPS 186-4. The prover who has private secret keys as authorized attributes generates a proof under a principle of "commit-to-identifier". The verifier who has to check the validity of the proof downloads the public keys of the authorities from nearest repository servers, and executes verification.

We give the generic construction by employing two building blocks; the structure-preserving signature scheme (SPS) [3] and the Groth-Sahai non-interactive proof system [9,13]. The both blocks are based on asymmetric bilinear groups. A constructional feature is that we use the notion of "bundled language" which was proposed by [4]. That is, the above principle corresponds to *simultaneous* pairing-product equations that are in the verification phase of the structure-preserving signatures. More precisely, a prover first generates a commitment c_0 to her identifier i. Then for each authority index 'a', she also generates commitments $(c_i^a)_i$ to the components of the structure-preserving signature $\sigma^a = (\sigma_i^a)_i$ in the componentwise way (i.e. for each i separately). Then, she computes proofs π^a for each 'a' by using the pairing-product equation for verification of the message-signature pair (i, σ^a). She merges all the commitments and proofs as a whole proof $\pi = (c_0, ((c_i^a)_i, \pi^a)^a)$.

We prove that our construction satisfies the above three security definitions. As for EUF against collusion attacks, collusion resistance is a direct consequence of the binding property of the commitment c_0 to i because c_0 is common in the generation of proofs $(\pi^a)^a$. EUF is due to the knowledge extraction property of the Groth-Sahai proofs and the EUF property of the structure-preserving signatures. As for anonymity and unlinkability of proofs, we first prove that our unlinkability implies anonymity. Then, unlinkability is derived from the two properties; the perfectly hiding property of commitments and the perfect witness-indistinguishability of proofs. We must note that these two properties hold in the simulation mode of the commitments, which is due to the simulation-mode commitment key that is in the common-reference string. This notion is known as the dual-mode commitment [9,13]).

Related Work. We briefly compare the related work on ACS with our proposed DMA-ACS. Table 1 shows the comparison. dACS₁ is our DMA-ACS that employs the SPS scheme of [1], and dACS₂ is our DMA-ACS that employs the SPS scheme of [3]. $|A'|$ is the number of attribute credentials involved in a proof (see Sect. 4.1). Note that, in our DMA-ACS, each attribute credential is issued by an possibly independent authority.

Camenisch et al. [5] proposed ACS with the universal composability property. Fuchsbauer et al. [11] proposed ACS with addtional anonymity at issuing phase. Both [5] and [11] are capable of proving satisfiability of all-AND formulas. Okishima-Nakanishi [16] proposed ACS with expressiveness; that is, it is capable of proving satisfiability of CNF formulas in which each clause may have negations. Note that all the three ACSs [5,10,16] are single-authority systems and attain the property of constant-size proof. However, they do not have collusion resistance. In contrast, our DMA-ACS is multi-authority system, and it attains

Table 1. Feature comparison of aonymous cedential sstems

Scheme	Decentra. Auth.	Collus. Resist.	Formula of Proof	Ano. Iss.	Ano. Proof	Unlink Proof	Unforge. Assump.	Length of Proof
CDHK [5]	No	-	All-AND	-	✓	✓	SXDH, J-RootDH, q-SFP	$O(1)$
FHS [11]	No	-	All-AND	✓	✓	✓	t-co-DL, GGM	$O(1)$
ON [16]	No	-	CNF w.¬	-	✓	✓	DLIN, q-SFP, n-DHE	$O(1)$
Our dACS$_1$	✓	✓	All-AND	No	✓	✓	SXDH, q-SFP	$O(|A'|)$
Our dACS$_2$	✓	✓	All-AND	No	✓	✓	SXDH	$O(|A'|)$

Note. "Formula of Proof" means the type of boolean formulas attached to the proofs. "all-AND" means a formula in which all the boolean connectives are AND. "CNF w.¬" means a CNF formula in which each clause may have negations. "Anonym. Iss." means whether anonymity at the issuing phase is attained or not. "Unforge. Assump." means the assumptions needed for unforgeability. '✓' means "attained" and "no" means "not attained". $|A'|$ is the number of attribute credentials involved. For each "Unforgeability Assumption", see the cited references.

collusion resistance. Its proof-size is linear to the number of proven attribute credentials. We must say that it is a drawback of our proposed DMA-ACS. Instead, in our DMA-ACS, an individual can be registered by independent decentralized authorities the number of which dynamically increases or decreases. As for non-transferability [6], our DMA-ACS *suppresses* transferring one's credentials to another. This is because, in the proving phase, the prover must use her global identifier which is better to be kept secret within her. Finally, the anonymous credential systems including our DMA-ACS have *universal composability* when their proofs are generated by the Groth-Sahai proof system [9,13].

2 Preliminaries

The set of natural numbers is denoted by $\mathbb{N}$. The residue class ring of integers modulo a prime number p is denoted by $\mathbb{Z}_p$. The security parameter is denoted by λ, where $\lambda \in \mathbb{N}$. A probability P is said to be negligible in λ if for any given positive polynomial poly($\cdot$) $P < 1/\text{poly}(\lambda)$ for sufficiently large $\lambda \in \mathbb{N}$. Two probabilities P and Q are said to be computationally indistinguishable if $|P - Q|$ is negligible in λ, which is denoted as $P \approx_c Q$. A uniform random sampling of an element a from a set S is denoted as $a \in_R S$. When a probabilistic algorithm A with an input a and a randomness r on a random tape returns z, we denote it as $z \leftarrow A(a; r)$. We denote the inner state of an algorithm by St. A vector $c = (c_i)_{i \in I}$ whose components are with subscripts is abbreviated as

$(c_i)_i$. Simmilarly, a vector $c = (c^a)^{a \in A}$ is abbreviated as $(c^a)^a$, and a vector $c = (c_i^a)_{i \in I}^{a \in A}$ is abbreviated as $(c_i^a)_i^a$.

2.1 Bilinear Groups [9,12]

Let $\mathcal{BG}$ be a bilinear group generator algorithm [12]: $\mathcal{BG}(1^\lambda) \rightarrow (p, \hat{G}, \breve{H}, \mathbb{T}, e, \hat{G}, \breve{H})$. Here p is a prime number of bit-length λ, $\hat{G}, \breve{H}$ and $\mathbb{T}$ are cyclic groups of order p, and $\hat{G}$ and $\breve{H}$ are generators of $\hat{G}$ and $\breve{H}$, respectively. We denote operations in $\hat{G}$, $\breve{H}$ and $\mathbb{T}$ multiplicatively. e is the bilinear map of $\hat{G} \times \breve{H}$ to $\mathbb{T}$. e should have the following two properties: Non-degeneracy : $e(\hat{G}, \breve{H}) \neq 1_{\mathbb{T}}$, and Bilinearity : $\forall a \in \mathbb{Z}_p, \forall b \in \mathbb{Z}_p, \forall \hat{X} \in \hat{G}, \forall \breve{Y} \in \breve{H}, e(\hat{X}^a, \breve{Y}^b) = e(\hat{X}, \breve{Y})^{ab}$. Hereafter we denote an element in $\hat{G}$ and $\breve{H}$ with hat ' ˆ ' and check ' ˘ ', respectively.

2.2 Structure-Preserving Signature Scheme [1,3]

The structure-preserving signature scheme Sig consists of four PPT algorithms: Sig = (Sig.Setup, Sig.KG$_{pp}$, Sig.Sign$_{pp}$, Sig.Vrf$_{pp}$).

Sig.Setup$(1^\lambda) \rightarrow pp$. On input the security parameter 1^λ, this PPT algorithm executes the bilinear-group generator algorithm, and it puts the output as a set of public parameters: $\mathcal{BG}(1^\lambda) \rightarrow (p, \hat{G}, \breve{H}, \mathbb{T}, e, \hat{G}, \breve{H}) =: pp$. It returns pp.

Sig.KG$_{pp}() \rightarrow$ (PK, SK). Based on the set of public parameters pp, this PPT algorithm generates a signing key SK and the corresponding public key PK. It returns (PK, SK).

Sig.Sign$_{pp}$(PK, SK, $m) \rightarrow \sigma$. On input the public key PK, the secret key SK and a message $m \in \hat{G}$ or $\breve{H}$, this PPT algorithm generates a signature σ. In the case of SPS, σ consists of elements $(V_i)_i$ where V_i is in either $\hat{G}$ or $\breve{H}$. It returns $\sigma := (V_i)_i$.

Sig.Vrf$_{pp}$(PK, $m, \sigma) \rightarrow d$. On input the public key PK, a message $m \in \hat{G}$ or $\breve{H}$ and a signature $\sigma = (V_i)_i$, this deterministic algorithm returns a boolean decision d.

The correctness should hold for the scheme Sig: For any security parameter 1^λ, any set of public parameters $pp \leftarrow$ Sig.Setup(1^λ) and any message m, $\Pr[d = 1 \mid (PK, SK) \leftarrow$ Sig.KG$_{pp}(), \sigma \leftarrow$ Sig.Sign$_{pp}$(PK, SK, $m), d \leftarrow$ Sig.Vrf$_{pp}$(PK, $m, \sigma)] = 1$.

Adaptive chosen-message attack of an existential forgery on the scheme Sig by a forger algorithm **F** is defined by the following algorithm of experiment.

$$\mathsf{Exp}_{\mathsf{Sig},\mathbf{F}}^{\mathsf{euf\text{-}cma}}(1^\lambda):$$

$$pp \leftarrow \mathsf{Sig.Setup}(1^\lambda), (PK, SK) \leftarrow \mathsf{Sig.KG}_{pp}()$$

$$(m^*, \sigma^*) \leftarrow \mathbf{F}^{\mathsf{SignO}_{pp}(PK,SK,\cdot)}(pp, PK)$$

$$\text{If } m^* \notin \{m_j\}_{1 \leq j \leq q_s} \text{ and } \mathsf{Sig.Vrf}_{pp}(PK, m^*, \sigma^*) = 1,$$

$$\text{then Return WIN else Return LOSE}$$

In the experiment, **F** issues a signing query to its signing oracle **SignO**$_{pp}$(PK, SK, ·) by sending a message m_j at most q_s times ($1 \leq j \leq q_s$). As a reply, **F** receives a valid signature σ_j. Here q_s is bounded by a polynomial in λ. Then **F** returns a pair of a message and a signature (m^*, σ^*). A restriction on **F** is that the set of queried messages $\{m_j\}_{1 \leq j \leq q_s}$ should not contain the message m^*. The advantage of **F** over Sig is defined as **Adv**$_{\mathsf{Sig},\mathbf{F}}^{\text{euf-cma}}(\lambda) := \Pr[\mathsf{Exp}_{\mathsf{Sig},\mathbf{F}}^{\text{euf-cma}}(1^\lambda)$ returns WIN]. The scheme Sig is said to be *existentially unforgeable against adaptive chosen-message attacks (EUF-CMA)* if for any PPT algorithm **F** the advantage **Adv**$_{\mathsf{Sig},\mathbf{F}}^{\text{euf-cma}}(\lambda)$ is negligible in λ.

2.3 Non-interactive Commit-and-Prove Scheme for Structure-Preserving Signatures

According to the fine-tuned Groth-Sahai proof system [9], we survey here the non-interactive commit-and-prove scheme on pairing-product equations. A commit-and-prove scheme CmtPrv consists of six PPT algorithms: CmtPrv = (CmtPrv.Setup, Cmt.KG$_{pp}$, Cmt$_{pp}$ = (Cmt.Com$_{pp}$, Cmt.Vrf$_{pp}$), Prv$_{pp}$ = (P$_{pp}$, V$_{pp}$)).

Language. We first describe the language for which our scheme will work. The language is dependent on the type of verification equations of the Groth-Sahai proofs (group-dependent languages [13]). For this purpose, we first fix the set of public parameters and the commitment key, which are common reference string in the term of non-interactive proof systems [9, 13].

- CmtPrv.Setup(1^λ) → pp. On input the security parameter 1^λ, this PPT algorithm executes a bilinear-group generator algorithm $\mathcal{BG}$, and it puts the output as the public parameters pp: $\mathcal{BG}(1^\lambda) \rightarrow (p, \hat{\mathbb{G}}, \check{\mathbb{H}}, \mathbb{T}, e, \hat{G}, \check{H}) =: pp$. It returns pp.
- Cmt.KG$_{pp}$(mode) → key. On input a string mode, this PPT algorithm generates a key. If mode = nor, then $key = ck$ which is a commitment key. If mode = ext, then $key = (ck, xk)$ which is a pair of ck and an extraction key xk. If mode = sim, then $key = (ck, tk)$ which is a pair of ck and a trapdoor key tk. It returns key.

We put $pp := (pp, ck)$. Note here that the commitment key ck is treated as one of the public parameters.

Let $n \in \mathbb{N}$ be a constant. Suppose that we are given a pairing-product equation system with n equations and with variables $(\hat{X}_i)_i$ and $(\check{Y}_j)_j$:

$$\begin{cases} \prod_i e(\hat{X}_i, \check{B}_{1i}) \prod_j e(\hat{A}_{1j}, \check{Y}_j) \prod_i \prod_j e(\hat{X}_i, \check{Y}_j)^{\gamma_{1ij}} = t_{\mathbb{T}1}, \\ \cdots \\ \prod_i e(\hat{X}_i, \check{B}_{ni}) \prod_j e(\hat{A}_{nj}, \check{Y}_j) \prod_i \prod_j e(\hat{X}_i, \check{Y}_j)^{\gamma_{nij}} = t_{\mathbb{T}n}. \end{cases} \quad (1)$$

Let L_{pp} denote the set of coefficients of the pairing-product equation system (1) and $W_{pp}(x)$ denote the set of solutions for $x \in L_{pp}$:

$$L_{pp} := \{x \in (\prod_i \hat{\mathbb{G}} \times \prod_j \check{\mathbb{H}} \times \prod_i \prod_j \mathbb{Z}_p)^n \mid x = ((\check{B}_{ki})_i, (\hat{A}_{kj})_j, (\gamma_{kij})_{i,j})_{k=1}^n\},$$
(2)

$$W_{pp}(x) := \{w \in \prod_i \hat{\mathbb{G}} \times \prod_j \check{\mathbb{H}} \mid w = ((\hat{W}_i)_i, (\check{W}_j)_j) \text{ satisfies } (1) \text{ for } x\},$$
(3)

$$R_{pp} := \{(x, w) \in (\prod_i \hat{\mathbb{G}} \times \prod_j \check{\mathbb{H}} \times \prod_i \prod_j \mathbb{Z}_p)^n \times \prod_i \hat{\mathbb{G}} \times \prod_j \check{\mathbb{H}}$$

$$\mid (x, w) = (((\check{B}_{ki})_i, (\hat{A}_{kj})_j, (\gamma_{kij})_{i,j})_{k=1}^n, ((\hat{W}_i)_i, (\check{W}_j)_j)) \text{ satisfies } (1)\}.$$
(4)

For a fixed parameter set pp, we call L_{pp}, $W_{pp}(x)$ and R_{pp} the group-dependent language with pp, the witness space of x with pp and the relation with pp, respectively.

Commitment Part [9,13]. The commitment part $\mathsf{Cmt}_{pp} = (\mathsf{Cmt.Com}_{pp}, \mathsf{Cmt.Vrf}_{pp})$ is described as follows.

- $\mathsf{Cmt.Com}_{pp}(w; r) \to (c, r)$. On input a message w (which will be a witness in the proof part), this PPT algorithm generates a commitment c with a randomness r. r will also be a verification key. It returns (c, r). When w is a vector $w = (w_i)_i$, c and r are also vectors of the same number of components: $c = (c_i)_i$ and $r = (r_i)_i$. Note that computation is executed in the *componentwise way*; $\mathsf{Cmt.Com}_{pp}(w_i; r_i) \to (c_i, r_i)$.
- $\mathsf{Cmt.Vrf}_{pp}(c, w, r) \to d$. On input a commitment c, a message w and a verification key r, this deterministic algorithm generates a boolean decision d. It returns d.

The commitment part Cmt_{pp} of the Groth-Sahai proof system has the four properties [9]: *(1) perfect correctness, (2) dual mode, (3) perfectly binding and (4) perfectly hiding*. The detailed definitions are given in Appendix A.

Proof Part [9,13]. The proof part $\mathsf{Prv}_{pp} = (\mathsf{P}_{pp}, \mathsf{V}_{pp})$ is described as follows.

- $\mathsf{P}_{pp}(x, c, w, r) \to \pi$. On input a statement x, a commitment c, a witness w and a randomness r which was used to generate a commitment c, this PPT algorithm executes the proof-generation algorithm of the Groth-Sahai proof system to obtain a proof π (see [9] for the details and [2,3] for instantiations). It returns π.
- $\mathsf{V}_{pp}(x, c, \pi) \to d$. On input a statement x, a commitment c and a proof π, this deterministic algorithm executes the verification algorithm of the Groth-Sahai proof system to obtain a boolean decision d (see [9] for the details). It returns d.

The proof part $(\mathsf{CmtPrv.Setup}, \mathsf{Prv}_{pp})$ of the Groth-Sahai proof system has the four properties [9]: *(1) perfect correctness, (2) perfect soundness, (3) perfect F-knowledge and (4) composable witness-indistinguishability (especially (4) means perfect witness-indistinguishability)*. The detailed definitions are given in Appendix B.

3   Our Bundled Language

In this section, we describe bundled languages [4] in the case of our group-dependent languages. Intuitively, the notion determines a subset of a Cartesian product of a language when the pairing-product equations are a *simultaneous equation system*.

For a polynomially bounded integer q, we prepare q copies of the equation system as (5). Then the equation systems are with variables $(\hat{X}_i^a)_i$ and $(\check{Y}_j^a)_j$ (We remark that ^{a} is not an exponent but an index.):

For $a \in \{1, \dots, q\}$,
$$\begin{cases} \prod_i e(\hat{X}_i^a, \check{B}_{1i}^a) \prod_j e(\hat{A}_{1j}^a, \check{Y}_j^a) \prod_i \prod_j e(\hat{X}_i^a, \check{Y}_j^a)^{\gamma_{1ij}^a} = t_{\mathbb{T}1}^a, \\ \cdots \\ \prod_i e(\hat{X}_i^a, \check{B}_{ni}^a) \prod_j e(\hat{A}_{nj}^a, \check{Y}_j^a) \prod_i \prod_j e(\hat{X}_i^a, \check{Y}_j^a)^{\gamma_{nij}^a} = t_{\mathbb{T}n}^a. \end{cases} \quad (5)$$

Now we impose a constraint that the above q equation systems have a common variable. For simplicity, we enforce that
$$\hat{X}_1^1 = \cdots = \hat{X}_1^q = \hat{X}_1. \quad (6)$$

Definition 1 (Bundled language (Group-Dependent)). *Let L_{pp} be the language (2). For a polynomially bounded integer q, put $A := \{1, \dots, q\}$. The q-bundled language $\prod_{a \in A}^{bnd} L_{pp}$ of the languages L_{pp} is the subset of the q-Cartesian product of L_{pp} with the constraint (6):*

$$\prod_{a \in A}^{bnd} L_{pp} \stackrel{def}{=} \{(x^a)^{a \in A} \in \prod_{a \in A} L_{pp} \mid \hat{X}_1^1 = \cdots = \hat{X}_1^q = \hat{X}_1\}. \quad (7)$$

The bundled language is a special case of simultaneous equation system (5) for all $a \in A$ with the constraint (6). It would be natural to consider a generalization into the case of more than one common variable. The study of this direction is of independent interest.

4   Our Decentralized Multi-authority Anonymous Credential System

In this section, we give syntax and security definitions of our decentralized multi-authority anonymous credential system dACS. We introduce three security definitions. One is existential unforgeability (EUF) against collusion attacks that cause mis-authorization. The other two is anonymity and unlinkability of proofs. For convenience, we hereafter denote $\mathbf{i} \in \mathbb{G}$, where $\mathbb{G}$ is either $\hat{\mathbb{G}}$ or $\check{\mathbb{H}}$ depending on an instantiation of the structure-preserving signature scheme.

4.1   Syntax

Our dACS consists of five PPT algorithms, (Setup, AuthKG_{pp}, PrivKG_{pp}, Prover_{pp}, $\mathsf{Verifier}_{pp}$).

- $\mathsf{Setup}(1^\lambda) \rightarrow pp$. This PPT algorithm is needed to generate a set of public parameters pp. On input the security parameter 1^λ, it generates the set pp. It returns pp.
- $\mathsf{AuthKG}_{pp}(a) \rightarrow (\mathrm{PK}^a, \mathrm{MSK}^a)$. This PPT algorithm is executed by a key-issuing authority indexed by a. On input the authority index a, it generates the a-th public key PK^a of the authority and the corresponding a-th master secret key MSK^a. It returns $(\mathrm{PK}^a, \mathrm{MSK}^a)$.
- $\mathsf{PrivKG}_{pp}(\mathrm{PK}^a, \mathrm{MSK}^a, \mathtt{i}) \rightarrow \mathrm{sk}_{\mathtt{i}}^a$. This PPT algorithm is executed by the a-th key-issuing authority. On input the a-th public and master secret keys $(\mathrm{PK}^a, \mathrm{MSK}^a)$ and an element $\mathtt{i} \in \mathbb{G}$ (that is an identifier of a prover), it generates a private secret key $\mathrm{sk}_{\mathtt{i}}^a$ of a prover. It returns $\mathrm{sk}_{\mathtt{i}}^a$.
- $\mathsf{Prover}_{pp}((\mathrm{PK}^a, \mathrm{sk}_{\mathtt{i}}^a)^{a\in A'}) \rightarrow \pi$. This PPT algorithm is executed by a prover who is to be authenticated, where A' denotes a subset of the set A of all the authority indices. On input the public keys $(\mathrm{PK}^a)^{a\in A'}$ and the corresponding private secret keys $(\mathrm{sk}_{\mathtt{i}}^a)^{a\in A'}$, it returns a proof π.
- $\mathsf{Verifier}_{pp}((\mathrm{PK}^a)^{a\in A'}, \pi) \rightarrow d$. This deterministic polynomial-time algorithm is executed by a verifier who confirms that the prover certainly knows the secret keys for indices $a \in A'$. On input the public keys $(\mathrm{PK}^a)^{a\in A'}$ and the proof π, it returns $d := 1$ ("accept") or $d := 0$ ("reject").

4.2   Security Definitions

We define three security notions for our anonymous credential system dACS; EUF against collusion attacks, anonymity and unlinkability of proofs.

EUF Against Collusion Attack. Formally we define the following experiment on dACS and an adversary algorithm $\mathbf{A}$.

$\mathrm{Exp}_{\mathsf{dACS},\mathbf{A}}^{\mathrm{euf\text{-}coll}}(1^\lambda, 1^\mu)$:

$\quad pp \leftarrow \mathsf{Setup}(1^\lambda), A := \{1, \ldots, \mu\}, \text{For } a \in A : (\mathrm{PK}^a, \mathrm{MSK}^a) \leftarrow \mathsf{AuthKG}_{pp}(a)$

$\quad (\tilde{A}, St) \leftarrow \mathbf{A}(pp, (\mathrm{PK}^a)^{a\in A}), \bar{\tilde{A}} := A \backslash \tilde{A}$

$\quad (\pi^*, A^*) \leftarrow \mathbf{A}^{\mathbf{PrivKO}_{pp}(\mathrm{PK}^{\cdot}, \mathrm{MSK}^{\cdot}, \cdot)}(St, (\mathrm{MSK}^a)^{a\in\tilde{A}})$

$\quad \mathsf{Verifier}_{pp}((\mathrm{PK}^a)^{a\in A^*}, \pi^*) \rightarrow d$

$\quad$ If $d = 1$ then return WIN else return LOSE

Intuitively, the above experiment describes the attack as follows. On input the public keys $(\mathrm{PK}^a)^{a\in A}$, $\mathbf{A}$ outputs a set of indices of corrupted authorities $\tilde{A}$. $\mathbf{A}$ collects at most q_{sk} private secret keys by issuing queries to the private secret key oracle $\mathbf{PrivKO}_{pp}(\mathrm{PK}^{\cdot}, \mathrm{MSK}^{\cdot}, \cdot)$ with an authority index $a \in \bar{\tilde{A}} := A \backslash \tilde{A}$ and an identifier element $\mathbf{i}_j \in \mathbb{G}$ for $j = 1, \ldots, q_{\mathsf{sk}}$. We denote by A_j the set of authority indices for which the private secret key queries were issued with $\mathbf{i}_j$. That is, $A_j := \{a \in A \mid \mathbf{A} \text{ is given } \mathsf{sk}_{\mathbf{i}_j}^a\} \subset \tilde{\bar{A}}$. Note that the maximum number of private secret key queries is $\mu \cdot q_{\mathsf{sk}}$. We require that the numbers μ and q_{sk} are bounded by a polynomial in λ. At the end $\mathbf{A}$ returns a forgery proof π^* together with the target set of authority indices A^* that is a subset of $\tilde{\bar{A}}$: $A^* \subset \tilde{\bar{A}}$. If the decision d on π^* by $\mathsf{Verifier}_{pp}$ is 1 under $(\mathrm{PK}^a)^{a \in A^*}$, then the experiment returns WIN; otherwise it returns LOSE.

A restriction is imposed on the adversary $\mathbf{A}$: The queried $\mathbf{i}_j$s are pairwise different, and any A_j is a proper subset of the target set A^*:

$$\mathbf{i}_{j_1} \neq \mathbf{i}_{j_2} \text{ for } j_1, j_2 \in \{1, \ldots, q_{\mathsf{sk}}\}, j_1 \neq j_2, \tag{8}$$

$$A_j \subsetneq A^*, \quad j = 1, \ldots, q_{\mathsf{sk}}. \tag{9}$$

These restrictions are because, otherwise, the adversary $\mathbf{A}$ can trivially succeed in causing forgery.

The advantage of an adversary $\mathbf{A}$ over an anonymous credential system dACS in the experiment is defined as: $\mathbf{Adv}_{\mathsf{dACS},\mathbf{A}}^{\mathsf{euf\text{-}coll}}(\lambda, \mu) \overset{\mathrm{def}}{=} \Pr[\mathsf{Exp}_{\mathsf{dACS},\mathbf{A}}^{\mathsf{euf\text{-}coll}}(1^\lambda, 1^\mu) = $ WIN]. A scheme dACS is called existentially unforgeable against collusion attacks that cause mis-authorization. if, for any PPT algorithm $\mathbf{A}$, the advantage $\mathbf{Adv}_{\mathsf{dACS},\mathbf{A}}^{\mathsf{euf\text{-}coll}}(\lambda, \mu)$ is negligible in λ.

Anonymity of Proofs. Formally we define the following experiment on dACS and an adversary algorithm $\mathbf{A}$.

$\mathsf{Exp}_{\mathsf{dACS},\mathbf{A}}^{\mathsf{ano\text{-}prf}}(1^\lambda, 1^\mu) :$

   $pp \leftarrow \mathsf{Setup}(1^\lambda), A := \{1, \ldots, \mu\}, \text{For } a \in A : (\mathrm{PK}^a, \mathrm{MSK}^a) \leftarrow \mathsf{AuthKG}_{pp}(a)$

   $(\mathbf{i}_0, \mathbf{i}_1, St) \leftarrow \mathbf{A}(pp, (\mathrm{PK}^a)^{a \in A})$

   $\text{For } a \in A : \text{For } i = 0, 1 : \mathsf{sk}_{\mathbf{i}_i}^a \leftarrow \mathsf{PrivKG}_{pp}(\mathrm{PK}^a, \mathrm{MSK}^a, \mathbf{i}_i)$

   $b \in_R \{0, 1\}, b' \leftarrow \mathbf{A}^{\mathsf{Prover}_{pp}((\mathrm{PK}^a, \mathsf{sk}_{\mathbf{i}_b}^a)^{a \in A})}(St, (\mathrm{MSK}^a, \mathsf{sk}_{\mathbf{i}_0}^a, \mathsf{sk}_{\mathbf{i}_1}^a)^{a \in A})$

   $\text{If } b = b' \text{ then return WIN, else return LOSE}$

Intuitively, the above experiment describes the attack as follows. On input the set of public parameters pp and the issued public keys $(\mathrm{PK}^a)^{a \in A}$, $\mathbf{A}$ designates two identity elements $\mathbf{i}_0$ and $\mathbf{i}_1$, and $\mathbf{A}$ is given two kinds of private secret keys $(\mathsf{sk}_{\mathbf{i}_0}^a, \mathsf{sk}_{\mathbf{i}_1}^a)$ for all $a \in A$. Next, for randomly chosen $b \in \{0, 1\}$, which is hidden from $\mathbf{A}$, $\mathbf{A}$ does oracle-access to a prover Prover_{pp} that is on input the private secret keys $(\mathsf{sk}_{\mathbf{i}_b}^a)^{a \in A}$. If the decision b' of $\mathbf{A}$ is equal to b, then the experiment returns WIN; otherwise it returns LOSE.

The advantage of an adversary $\mathbf{A}$ over an anonymous credential system dACS in the experiment is defined as: $\mathbf{Adv}_{\mathsf{dACS},\mathbf{A}}^{\mathsf{ano\text{-}prf}}(\lambda, \mu) \overset{\mathrm{def}}{=} \left| \Pr[\mathsf{Exp}_{\mathsf{dACS},\mathbf{A}}^{\mathsf{ano\text{-}prf}}(1^\lambda, 1^\mu) = \right.$ WIN$] - (1/2) \left. \right|$. An anonymous credential system dACS is called to have anonymity of proofs if, for any PPT algorithm $\mathbf{A}$, the advantage $\mathbf{Adv}_{\mathsf{dACS},\mathbf{A}}^{\mathsf{ano\text{-}prf}}(\lambda, \mu)$ is negligible in λ.

Unlinkability of Proofs. Formally we define the following experiment on dACS and an adversary algorithm **A**.

$\mathsf{Exp}^{\text{unlink-prf}}_{\text{dACS},\mathbf{A}}(1^\lambda, 1^\mu)$:

$pp \leftarrow \mathsf{Setup}(1^\lambda), A := \{1, \ldots, \mu\}, \text{For } a \in A : (\text{PK}^a, \text{MSK}^a) \leftarrow \mathsf{AuthKG}_{pp}(a)$

$(\mathtt{i}_0, \mathtt{i}_1, St) \leftarrow \mathbf{A}(pp, (\text{PK}^a)^{a \in A})$

For $a \in A$: For $i = 0, 1 : \text{sk}^a_{\mathtt{i}_i} \leftarrow \mathsf{PrivKG}_{pp}(\text{PK}^a, \text{MSK}^a, \mathtt{i}_i)$

$b \in_R \{0, 1\}$

If $b = 0$ then $St \leftarrow \mathbf{A}^{\mathsf{Prover}_{pp}((\text{PK}^a, \text{sk}^a_{\mathtt{i}_0})^{a \in A})}(St, (\text{MSK}^a, \text{sk}^a_{\mathtt{i}_0}, \text{sk}^a_{\mathtt{i}_1})^{a \in A})$

$\qquad\qquad\qquad d \leftarrow \mathbf{A}^{\mathsf{Prover}_{pp}((\text{PK}^a, \text{sk}^a_{\mathtt{i}_1})^{a \in A})}(St)$

else $\qquad\qquad St \leftarrow \mathbf{A}^{\mathsf{Prover}_{pp}((\text{PK}^a, \text{sk}^a_{\mathtt{i}_0})^{a \in A})}(St, (\text{MSK}^a, \text{sk}^a_{\mathtt{i}_0}, \text{sk}^a_{\mathtt{i}_1})^{a \in A})$

$\qquad\qquad\qquad d \leftarrow \mathbf{A}^{\mathsf{Prover}_{pp}((\text{PK}^a, \text{sk}^a_{\mathtt{i}_0})^{a \in A})}(St)$

If $b = d$ then return WIN, else return LOSE

Intuitively, the above experiment resembles the experiment of anonymity $\mathsf{Exp}^{\text{ano-prf}}_{\text{dACS},\mathbf{A}}(1^\lambda, 1^\mu)$. The difference is that, in the above experiment, the adversary **A** has to distinguish whether the proofs (π) are of the same user or of the other user.

The advantage of an adversary **A** over an anonymous credential system dACS in the experiment is defined as: $\mathbf{Adv}^{\text{unlink-prf}}_{\text{dACS},\mathbf{A}}(\lambda, \mu) \overset{\text{def}}{=} \left| \Pr[\mathsf{Exp}^{\text{unlink-prf}}_{\text{dACS},\mathbf{A}}(1^\lambda, 1^\mu) = \text{WIN}] - (1/2) \right|$. An anonymous credential system dACS is called to have unlinkability of proofs if, for any PPT algorithm **A**, the advantage $\mathbf{Adv}^{\text{unlink-prf}}_{\text{dACS},\mathbf{A}}(\lambda, \mu)$ is negligible in λ.

Proposition 1 (Unlinkability Implies Anonymity). *For any PPT algorithm* **A** *that is in accordance with the experiment* $\mathsf{Exp}^{\text{ano-prf}}_{\text{dACS},\mathbf{A}}(1^\lambda, 1^\mu)$, *there exists a PPT algorithm* **B** *that is in accordance with the experiment* $\mathsf{Exp}^{\text{unlink-prf}}_{\text{dACS},\mathbf{B}}(1^\lambda, 1^\mu)$ *and the following inequality holds.*

$$\mathbf{Adv}^{\text{ano-prf}}_{\text{dACS},\mathbf{A}}(\lambda, \mu) \leq \mathbf{Adv}^{\text{unlink-prf}}_{\text{dACS},\mathbf{B}}(\lambda, \mu).$$

(For a proof, see Appendix D.)

5   Construction and Security Proofs

In this section, we give a generic construction of our scheme of dACS. We employ two building blocks. One is the structure-preserving signature scheme [1,3]. Each decentralized authority indexed by 'a' issues a private secret key $\text{sk}^a_{\mathtt{i}}$ for an identifier element $\mathtt{i}$. The other building block is the commit-and-prove scheme of the fine-tuned Groth-Sahai proof system [9,13] on pairing-product equations. In the commit-phase a prover generates commitments to the identifier element $\mathtt{i}$ and all the components of the structure-preserving signatures $(\sigma^a_k)^a_k$. In the proof phase the prover generates a proof π by putting $w_0 := \mathrm{i}$ as the common component and $(w_k^a)_k := (\sigma_k^a)_k$ for each authority index a. Then w_0 is the value which satisfies equation (6) in Sect. 3, and $(w_0, (w_k^a)_k)$ are the values which satisfy 5. That is, the proof π will be a proof for our *bundled language*.

5.1 Construction

According to the syntax in Sect. 4, the scheme dACS consists of five PPT algorithms: dACS = (Setup, AuthKG$_{pp}$, PrivKG$_{pp}$, Prover$_{pp}$, Verifier$_{pp}$).

- Setup$(1^\lambda) \rightarrow pp$. On input the security parameter 1^λ, it runs the bilinear group generator algorithm, and it puts the output as a set of public parameters: $\mathcal{BG}(1^\lambda) \rightarrow (p, \hat{\mathbb{G}}, \check{\mathbb{H}}, \mathbb{T}, e, \hat{G}, \check{H}) =: pp$. Note that pp is a common for both the structure-preserving signature scheme Sig and the commit-and-prove scheme CmtPrv. Besides, it runs the generation algorithm of commitment key: Cmt.KG$_{pp}(\mathrm{nor}) \rightarrow ck$. It returns $pp := (pp, ck)$.
- AuthKG$_{pp}(a) \rightarrow (\mathrm{PK}^a, \mathrm{MSK}^a)$. On input an authority index a, it executes the key-generation algorithm Sig.KG$_{pp}()$ to obtain $(\mathrm{PK}, \mathrm{SK})$. It puts $\mathrm{PK}^a := \mathrm{PK}$ and $\mathrm{MSK}^a := \mathrm{SK}$. It returns $(\mathrm{PK}^a, \mathrm{MSK}^a)$.
- PrivKG$_{pp}(\mathrm{PK}^a, \mathrm{MSK}^a, \mathrm{i}) \rightarrow \mathrm{sk}_\mathrm{i}^a$. On input PK^a, MSK^a and an element $\mathrm{i} \in \mathbb{G}$, it puts $\mathrm{PK}^a := \mathrm{PK}^a$ and $\mathrm{SK}^a := \mathrm{MSK}^a$ and $m := \check{M} := \mathrm{i}$. It executes the signing algorithm Sig.Sign$_{pp}(\mathrm{PK}^a, \mathrm{SK}^a, m)$ to obtain a signature σ^a. It puts $\mathrm{sk}_\mathrm{i}^a := (\mathrm{i}, \sigma^a)$. It returns sk_i^a.
- Prover$_{pp}((\mathrm{PK}^a, \mathrm{sk}_\mathrm{i}^a)^{a \in A'}) \rightarrow \pi$. On input $(\mathrm{PK}^a, \mathrm{sk}_\mathrm{i}^a)^{a \in A'}$, first, it commits to i:

$$c_0 \leftarrow \mathsf{Cmt.Com}_{pp}(\mathrm{i}; r_0).$$

Second, for each $a \in A'$, it commits to the components $(\sigma_k^a)_k$ of the signature σ^a in the componentwise way.

$$(c_k^a)_k \leftarrow \mathsf{Cmt.Com}_{pp}((\sigma_k^a)_k; (r_k^a)_k).$$

Then, for each authority index a it puts $x^a := \mathrm{PK}^a$. It also puts $c^a := (c_0, (c_k^a)_k)$, $w^a := (w_0, (w_k^a)_k) := (\mathrm{i}, (\sigma_k^a)_k)$ and $r^a := (r_0, (r_k^a)_k)$. It executes the prove-algorithm to obtain a proof:

$$\pi^a \leftarrow \mathsf{P}_{pp}(x^a, c^a, w^a, r^a), a \in A'.$$

It puts $\bar{\pi}^a := ((c_k^a)_k, \pi^a)$ for each $a \in A'$, and it merges all the $\bar{\pi}^a$s and the commitment c_0 as $\pi := (c_0, (\bar{\pi}^a)^{a \in A'})$. It returns π.

- Verifier$_{pp}((\mathrm{PK}^a)^{a \in A'}, \pi) \rightarrow d$. On input $((\mathrm{PK}^a)^{a \in A'}, \pi)$, it puts $x^a := \mathrm{PK}^a$ and it puts $c^a := (c_0, (c_k^a))$ for each $a \in A'$. Then it executes the verify-algorithm for each $a \in A'$ to obtain the decisions:

$$d^a \leftarrow \mathsf{V}_{pp}(x^a, c^a, \pi^a), a \in A'.$$

If all the decisions d^as are 1, then it returns $d := 1$; otherwise it returns $d := 0$.

5.2   Security Proofs

Theorem 1 (EUF against Collision Attacks). *For any* PPT *algorithm* **A** *that is in accordance with the experiment* $\mathsf{Exp}_{dACS,\mathbf{A}}^{euf\text{-}coll}(1^\lambda, 1^\mu)$, *there exists a* PPT *algorithm* **F** *that is in accordance with the experiment* $\mathsf{Exp}_{Sig,\mathbf{F}}^{euf\text{-}cma}(1^\lambda)$ *and the following inequality holds.*

$$\mathbf{Adv}_{dACS,\mathbf{A}}^{euf\text{-}coll}(\lambda, \mu) = \mu \cdot \mathbf{Adv}_{Sig,\mathbf{F}}^{euf\text{-}cma}(\lambda).$$

(For a proof, see Appendix E).

This theorem means that, if the structure-preserving signature scheme Sig is existentially unforgeable against adaptive chosen-message attacks, then our dACS is EUF against collision attacks.

To state the theorem of anonymity and unlinkability below, we need to see Definition 3 in Appendix.

Theorem 2 (Unlinkability of Proofs). *For any* PPT *algorithm* **A** *that is in accordance with the experiment* $\mathsf{Exp}_{dACS,\mathbf{A}}^{unlink\text{-}prf}(1^\lambda, 1^\mu)$, *there exists a* PPT *algorithm* **D** *and the following inequality holds.*

$$\mathbf{Adv}_{dACS,\mathbf{A}}^{unlink\text{-}prf}(\lambda, \mu) \leq \mathbf{Adv}_{Cmt_{pp},\mathbf{D}}^{ind\text{-}dual}(\lambda).$$

(For the definition of $\mathbf{Adv}_{Cmt_{pp},\mathbf{D}}^{ind\text{-}dual}(\lambda)$, *see Definition 3 in Appendix A).*

(For a proof, see Appendix F).

This theorem means that, if the dual-mode commitment keys are indistinguishable, then our dACS has unlinkability.

6   Conclusion

We proposed DMA-ACS, a decentralized multi-authority anonymous credential system. In our generic construction that is based on bilinear groups, an authority only has to sign identifiers. In the proving phase, a prover generates a unified proof under a principle of "commit-to-id". In the term of the Groth-Sahai proof system, The principle corresponds to simultaneous pairing-product equations which include an identifier as a variable. Due to the principle, collusion resistance is attained. A drawback is that the proof-size is linear to the number of proven attribute credentials. Hence, to attain a constant-size proof should be our future work.

Appendix

A   Four Properties of Commitment Part

Definition 2 (Correctness [9,13]). *A commitment scheme* Cmt_{pp} *is said to be correct if it satisfies the following condition: For any security parameter* 1^λ, *any set of public parameters* $pp \leftarrow CmtPrv.Setup(1^\lambda)$, *any commitment key* $ck \leftarrow Cmt.KG_{pp}(\textbf{mode})$ *where* $\textbf{mode} = \textbf{nor}$ *or* $\textbf{ext}$ *or* $\textbf{sim}$, *and any message* w,

$$\Pr[d = 1 \mid (c, r) \leftarrow Cmt.Com_{pp}(w), d \leftarrow Cmt.Vrf_{pp}(c, w, r)] = 1.$$

Definition 3 (Dual Mode [13]). *A commitment scheme* Cmt_{pp} *is said to be dual mode if it satisfies the following condition: For any security parameter* 1^λ, *any set of public parameters* $pp \leftarrow CmtPrv.Setup(1^\lambda)$ *and any* PPT *algorithm* $\textbf{A}$,

$$\Pr[\textbf{A}(pp, ck) = 1 \mid ck \leftarrow Cmt.KG_{pp}(\textbf{nor})]$$
$$= \Pr[\textbf{A}(pp, ck) = 1 \mid (ck, xk) \leftarrow Cmt.KG_{pp}(\textbf{ext})], \tag{10}$$
$$\Pr[\textbf{A}(pp, ck) = 1 \mid ck \leftarrow Cmt.KG_{pp}(\textbf{nor})]$$
$$\approx_c \Pr[\textbf{A}(pp, ck) = 1 \mid (ck, tk) \leftarrow Cmt.KG_{pp}(\textbf{sim})]. \tag{11}$$

The computational indistinguishability (11) is equivalent to the following: For any security parameter 1^λ, for any set of public parameters $pp \leftarrow CmtPrv.Setup(1^\lambda)$ and any PPT algorithm $\textbf{A}$, the advantage $\textbf{Adv}_{Cmt_{pp}, \textbf{A}}^{\text{ind-dual}}(\lambda)$ of $\textbf{A}$ over Cmt_{pp} defined by the difference below is negligible in λ:

$$\textbf{Adv}_{Cmt_{pp}, \textbf{A}}^{\text{ind-dual}}(\lambda) \overset{\text{def}}{=} |\Pr[\textbf{A}(pp, ck) = 1 \mid ck \leftarrow Cmt.KG_{pp}(\textbf{nor})]$$
$$- \Pr[\textbf{A}(pp, ck) = 1 \mid (ck, tk) \leftarrow Cmt.KG_{pp}(\textbf{sim})]|. \tag{12}$$

The indistinguishability holds, for example, for an instance of the Groth-Sahai proof system under the SXDH assumption [9,13].

Definition 4 (Perfectly Binding [13]). *A commitment scheme* Cmt_{pp} *is said to be perfectly binding if it satisfies the following condition for some unbounded algorithm* $Cmt.Open_{pp}$: *For any security parameter* 1^λ, *any set of public parameters* $pp \leftarrow CmtPrv.Setup(1^\lambda)$, *any commitment key* $ck \leftarrow Cmt.KG_{pp}(\textbf{nor})$ *and any message* w,

$$\Pr[w = w' \mid (c, r) \leftarrow Cmt.Com_{pp}(w; r), w' \leftarrow Cmt.Open_{pp}(c)] = 1.$$

Definition 5 (Perfectly Hiding [13]). *A commitment scheme* Cmt_{pp} *is said to be perfectly hiding if it satisfies the following condition: For any security parameter* 1^λ, *any set of public parameters* $pp \leftarrow CmtPrv.Setup(1^\lambda)$, *any commitment key* ck *s.t.* $(ck, tk) \leftarrow Cmt.KG_{pp}(\textbf{sim})$ *and any* PPT *algorithm* $\textbf{A}$,

$$\Pr[\textbf{A}(St, c) = 1 \mid (w, w', St) \leftarrow \textbf{A}(pp, ck, tk), (c, r) \leftarrow Cmt.Com_{pp}(w)]$$
$$= \Pr[\textbf{A}(St, c') = 1 \mid (w, w', St) \leftarrow \textbf{A}(pp, ck, tk), (c', r') \leftarrow Cmt.Com_{pp}(w')]. \tag{13}$$

B   Four Properties of Proof Part

Definition 6 (Perfect Correctness [13]). *A commit-and-prove scheme* $CmtPrv$ *is said to be perfectly correct if it satisfies the following condition: For* *any security parameter* 1^λ, *any set of public parameters* $pp \leftarrow \mathsf{CmtPrv.Setup}(1^\lambda)$, *any commitment key* $ck \leftarrow \mathsf{Cmt.KG}_{pp}(\mathsf{mode})$ *where* $\mathsf{mode} = \mathsf{nor}$ *or* ext *or* sim *with* $pp := (pp, ck)$, *and any* PPT *algorithm* $\mathbf{A}$,

$$\Pr[V_{pp}(x, c, \pi) = 1 \ \textit{if} \ (ck, x, w) \in R_{pp} \ | $$
$$(x, w) \leftarrow \mathbf{A}(pp), (c, r) \leftarrow \mathsf{Cmt.Com}_{pp}(w), $$
$$\pi \leftarrow P_{pp}(x, c, w, r)] = 1.$$

Definition 7 (Perfect Soundness [13]). *A commit-and-prove scheme* CmtPrv *is said to be perfectly sound if it satisfies the following condition for some unbounded algorithm* $\mathsf{Cmt.Open}_{pp}$: *For any security parameter* 1^λ, *any set of public parameters* $pp \leftarrow \mathsf{CmtPrv.Setup}(1^\lambda)$, *any commitment key* $ck \leftarrow \mathsf{Cmt.KG}_{pp}(\mathsf{nor})$ *and any* PPT *algorithm* $\mathbf{A}$,

$$\Pr[V_{pp}(x, c, \pi) = 0 \ \textit{or} \ (ck, x, w) \in R_{pp} \ | $$
$$(x, c, \pi) \leftarrow \mathbf{A}(pp), w \leftarrow \mathsf{Cmt.Open}_{pp}(c)] = 1.$$

Let $\mathcal{C}_{ck}$ be the set of commitments under ck to some message w.

Definition 8 (Perfect Knowledge Extraction[13]). *A commit-and-prove scheme* CmtPrv *is said to be perfectly knowledge extractable if it satisfies the following condition for some* PPT *algorithm* $\mathsf{Cmt.Ext}_{pp}$: *For any security parameter* 1^λ, *any set of public parameters* $pp \leftarrow \mathsf{CmtPrv.Setup}(1^\lambda)$, *any commitment key* $(ck, xk) \leftarrow \mathsf{Cmt.KG}_{pp}(\mathsf{ext})$ *and any* PPT *algorithm* $\mathbf{A}$,

$$\Pr[c \notin \mathcal{C}_{ck} \ \textit{or} \ \mathsf{Cmt.Ext}_{pp}(xk, c) = \mathsf{Cmt.Open}_{pp}(c) \ | \ c \leftarrow \mathbf{A}(pp, ck, xk)] = 1.$$

Definition 9 (Composable Witness-Indistinguishability [13]). *A commit-and-prove scheme* CmtPrv *is said to be composably witness-indistinguishable if it satisfies the following condition: For any security parameter* 1^λ, *any set of public parameters* $pp \leftarrow \mathsf{CmtPrv.Setup}(1^\lambda)$ *and any* PPT *algorithm* $\mathbf{A}$,

$$\Pr[\mathbf{A}(pp, ck) = 1 \ | \ ck \leftarrow \mathsf{Cmt.KG}_{pp}(\mathsf{nor})]$$
$$\approx_c \Pr[\mathbf{A}(pp, ck) = 1 \ | \ (ck, tk) \leftarrow \mathsf{Cmt.KG}_{pp}(\mathsf{sim})], \ \textit{and}$$
$$\Pr[(ck, x, w), (ck, x, w') \in R_{pp} \ \textit{and} \ \mathbf{A}(St, \pi) = 1 \ | \ (ck, tk) \leftarrow \mathsf{Cmt.KG}_{pp}(\mathsf{sim}), pp := (pp, ck),$$
$$(x, w, w', St) \leftarrow \mathbf{A}^{\mathsf{Cmt.Com}_{pp}(\cdot)}(pp, ck, tk), (c, r) \leftarrow \mathsf{Cmt.Com}_{pp}(w), \pi \leftarrow P_{pp}(x, c, w, r)]$$
$$= \Pr[(ck, x, w), (ck, x, w') \in R_{pp} \ \textit{and} \ \mathbf{A}(St, \pi') = 1 \ | \ (ck, tk) \leftarrow \mathsf{Cmt.KG}_{pp}(\mathsf{sim}), pp := (pp, ck),$$
$$(x, w, w', St) \leftarrow \mathbf{A}^{\mathsf{Cmt.Com}_{pp}(\cdot)}(pp, ck, tk), (c', r') \leftarrow \mathsf{Cmt.Com}_{pp}(w'), \pi' \leftarrow P_{pp}(x, c', w', r')].$$
$$(14)$$

Especially, perfect witness-indistinguishability holds from (14).

C   Instantiation of Structure-Preserving Signature Scheme [1, 2]

We concretely describe an instantiation of the SPS scheme [1,2], which is known to be EUF-CMA under the q-SFP assumption.

Sig.Setup(1^λ) $\to$ pp. On input the security parameter 1^λ, this PPT algorithm executes the bilinear group generator algorithm, and it puts the output as a set of public parameters: $\mathcal{BG}(1^\lambda) \to (p, \hat{\mathbb{G}}, \check{\mathbb{H}}, \mathbb{T}, e, \hat{G}, \check{H}) =: pp$. It returns pp.

Sig.KG$_{pp}$() $\to$ (PK, SK). Based on the set of public parameters pp, this PPT algorithm generates a signing key SK and the corresponding public key PK as follows: $\hat{G}_u \in_R \hat{\mathbb{G}}$, $\gamma_1, \delta_1 \in_R \mathbb{Z}_p^*$, $\hat{G}_1 := \hat{G}^{\gamma_1}, \hat{G}_{u,1} := \hat{G}_u^{\delta_1}$. $\gamma_z, \delta_z \in_R \mathbb{Z}_p^*$, $\hat{G}_z := \hat{G}^{\gamma_z}, \hat{G}_{u,z} := \hat{G}_u^{\delta_z}$. $\alpha, \beta \in_R \mathbb{Z}_p^*$, $(\hat{A}_i, \check{A}_i)_{i=0}^1 \leftarrow$ Extend($\hat{G}, \check{H}^\alpha$), $(\hat{B}_i, \check{B}_i)_{i=0}^1 \leftarrow$ Extend($\hat{G}_u, \check{H}^\beta$) (for Extend, see [1,2]). It puts PK $:= (\hat{G}_z, \hat{G}_{u,z}, \hat{G}_u, \hat{G}_1, \hat{G}_{u,1}, (\hat{A}_i, \check{A}_i, \hat{B}_i, \check{B}_i)_{i=0}^1)$ and SK $:= (\alpha, \beta, \gamma_z, \delta_z, \gamma_1, \delta_1)$. It returns (PK, SK).

Sig.Sign$_{pp}$(PK, SK, m) $\to$ σ. On input the public key PK, the secret key SK and a message $m = \check{M} \in \check{\mathbb{H}}$, this PPT algorithm generates a signature σ as follows.

$$\zeta, \rho, \tau, \phi, \omega \in_R \mathbb{Z}_p, \quad \check{Z} := \check{H}^\zeta, \check{R} := \check{H}^{\alpha - \rho\tau - \gamma_z\zeta} \check{M}^{-\gamma_1}, \hat{S} := \hat{G}^\rho, \check{T} := \check{H}^\tau,$$
$$\check{U} := \check{H}^{\beta - \phi\omega - \delta_z\zeta} \check{M}^{-\delta_1}, \hat{V} := \hat{G}_u^\phi, \check{W} := \check{H}^\omega.$$

It returns $\sigma := (\check{Z}, \check{R}, \hat{S}, \check{T}, \check{U}, \hat{V}, \check{W})$.

Sig.Vrf$_{pp}$(PK, m, σ) $\to$ d. On input the public key PK, a message $m = \check{M} \in \check{\mathbb{H}}$ and a signature $\sigma = (\check{Z}, \check{R}, \hat{S}, \check{T}, \check{U}, \hat{V}, \check{W})$, this deterministic algorithm checks whether the following verification equation system holds or not.

$$e(\hat{G}_z, \check{Z})e(\hat{G}, \check{R})e(\hat{S}, \check{T})e(\hat{G}_1, \check{M})e(\hat{A}_0, \check{A}_0)^{-1}e(\hat{A}_1, \check{A}_1)^{-1} = 1_\mathbb{T}, \text{ and} \quad (15)$$
$$e(\hat{G}_{u,z}, \check{Z})e(\hat{G}_u, \check{U})e(\hat{V}, \check{W})e(\hat{G}_{u,1}, \check{M})e(\hat{B}_0, \check{B}_0)^{-1}e(\hat{B}_1, \check{B}_1)^{-1} = 1_\mathbb{T}. \quad (16)$$

It returns a boolean decision d.

D   Proof of Proposition 1

Proof (Sketc.h). Suppose that any PPT algorithm **A** that is in accordance with the experiment $\mathsf{Exp}^{\text{ano-prf}}_{\text{dACS,A}}(1^\lambda, 1^\mu)$ is given. Then we construct a PPT algorithm **A** that is in accordance with the experiment $\mathsf{Exp}^{\text{unlink-prf}}_{\text{dACS,B}}(1^\lambda, 1^\mu)$ as follows. **B** employs A as a subroutine. **B** is able to generate **A**'s input by using **B**'s input and **A**'s output. Also, **B** is able to answer to **A**'s queries by issuing queries to **B**'s oracle and using the answers. Finally, when **A** outputs b', **B** puts $d := b'$. $\square$

E   Proof of Theorem 1

Proof. Given any PPT algorithm **A** that is in accordance with the experiment $\mathsf{Exp}^{\text{euf-coll}}_{\text{dACS,A}}(1^\lambda, 1^\mu)$, we construct a PPT algorithm **F** that generates an existential forgery of Sig according to the experiment $\mathsf{Exp}^{\text{euf-cma}}_{\text{Sig,F}}(1^\lambda)$. **F** is given as input the set of public parameters pp and a public key PK$_{\text{Sig}}$. **F** is also given an auxiliary input μ. **F** executes Cmt.KG$_{pp}$(ext) to obtain a pair (ck, xk). **F** puts $pp := (pp, ck)$. **F** invokes the algorithm **A** with 1^λ to obtain the number μ and St.

$\mathbf{F}$ chooses a *target index* $a^\dagger$ from the set $A := \{1, \ldots, \mu\}$ *uniformly at random*. $\mathbf{F}$ executes the authority key generation algorithm honestly for $a \in A$ *except* the target index $a^\dagger$. As for $a^\dagger$, $\mathbf{F}$ uses the input public key:

$$\text{For } a \in A, a \neq a^\dagger : (\text{PK}^a, \text{MSK}^a) \leftarrow \text{AuthKG}_{pp}(a),$$

$$\text{For } a = a^\dagger : \text{PK}^{a^\dagger} := \text{PK}_{\text{Sig}}.$$

$\mathbf{F}$ inputs St and the public keys $(\text{PK}^a)^{a \in A}$ into $\mathbf{A}$. Then $\mathbf{F}$ obtains a set of corrupted authority indices $\tilde{A}$ from $\mathbf{A}$. $\mathbf{F}$ puts $\bar{\tilde{A}} := A \backslash \tilde{A}$. If $a^\dagger \in \bar{\tilde{A}}$ (the case TGTIDX$_1$), then $a^\dagger$ is not in $\tilde{A}$ and $\mathbf{F}$ is able to input $(St, (\text{MSK}^a)^{a \in \tilde{A}})$ into $\mathbf{A}$. Otherwise $\mathbf{F}$ aborts.

Simulation of Private Secret Key Oracle. When $\mathbf{A}$ issues a private secret key query with $a \in A_j \subsetneq \bar{\tilde{A}}$ and $\mathbf{i}_j \in \mathbb{Z}_p (j = 1, \ldots, q_{\text{sk}})$, $\mathbf{F}$ executes the private secret key generation algorithm with $\mathbf{i}_j$ honestly for $a \in \bar{\tilde{A}}$ such that $a \neq a^\dagger$. As for $a = a^\dagger$, $\mathbf{F}$ issues a signing query to its oracle with $\mathbf{i}_j$:

$$\text{For } a \in \bar{\tilde{A}} \text{ s.t. } a \neq a^\dagger : \text{sk}^a_{\mathbf{i}_j} \leftarrow \text{PrivKG}_{pp}(\text{PK}^a, \text{MSK}^a, \mathbf{i}_j),$$

$$\text{For } a = a^\dagger, \text{sk}^{a^\dagger}_{\mathbf{i}_j} \leftarrow \mathbf{SignO}_{pp}(\text{PK}, \text{SK}, \mathbf{i}_j).$$

$\mathbf{F}$ replies to $\mathbf{A}$ with the secret key $\text{sk}^a_{\mathbf{i}_j}$. This is a perfect simulation.

At the end $\mathbf{A}$ returns a forgery proof and the target set of authority indices (π^*, A^*). Note here that $A^* \subset \bar{\tilde{A}}$ as in the definition.

Generating Existential Forgery. Next, $\mathbf{F}$ runs a Verifier$_{pp}$ with an input $((\text{PK}^a)^{a \in A^*}, \pi^*)$. If the decision d of Verifier$_{pp}$ is 1, then $\mathbf{F}$ executes for each $a \in A^*$ the extraction algorithm $\text{Cmt.Ext}_{pp}(xk, c^a)$ to obtain a committed message $(w^a)^* = ((w_0^a)^*, ((w_k^a)^*)_k)$ (see Definition 8 in Appendix). Note here that, for all $a \in A^*$, $(w_0^a)^*$ is equal to a single element $(w_0)^*$ in $\mathbb{G}$. This is because of the *perfectly binding property* of Cmt_{pp}. Then $\mathbf{F}$ puts $\mathbf{i}^* := (w_0)^*$. Here the restriction (8)(9) assures that, if $q_{\text{sk}} > 0$, then there exists at least one $\hat{a} \in (A^* \backslash A_j)$ for some $j \in \{1, \ldots, q_{\text{sk}}\}$. If $q_{\text{sk}} = 0$, then there exists at least one $\hat{a} \in A^*$. $\mathbf{F}$ chooses one such $\hat{a}$ and puts $\sigma^* := (\sigma^{\hat{a}})^* := ((w_k^{\hat{a}})^*)_k$. $\mathbf{F}$ returns a forgery pair of a message and a signature $(\mathbf{i}^*, \sigma^*)$. This completes the description of $\mathbf{F}$.

Probability Evaluation. The probability that the returned value $(\mathbf{i}^*, \sigma^*)$ is actually an existential forgery is evaluated as follows. We name the events in the above $\mathbf{F}$ as:

$$\text{ACC} : d = 1,$$

$$\text{EXT} : \text{Cmt.Ext}_{pp} \text{ returns a witness } (w^a)^*$$

$$\text{TGTIDX} : \hat{a} = a^\dagger,$$

$$\text{FORGE} : (\mathbf{i}^*, \sigma^*) \text{ is an existential forgery on Sig.}$$

We have the following equalities.

$$\mathbf{Adv}_{\mathsf{dACS},\mathbf{A}}^{\text{euf-coll}}(\lambda,\mu) = \Pr[\textsc{Acc}], \tag{17}$$

$$\Pr[\textsc{Acc}, \textsc{Ext}, \textsc{TgtIdx}] = \Pr[\textsc{Forge}], \tag{18}$$

$$\Pr[\textsc{Forge}] = \mathbf{Adv}_{\mathsf{Sig},\mathbf{F}}^{\text{euf-cma}}(\lambda). \tag{19}$$

The left-hand side of the equality (18) is expanded as follows.

$$\Pr[\textsc{Acc}, \textsc{Ext}, \textsc{TgtIdx}] = \Pr[\textsc{TgtIdx}] \cdot \Pr[\textsc{Acc}, \textsc{Ext}]$$
$$= \Pr[\textsc{TgtIdx}] \cdot \Pr[\textsc{Acc}] \cdot \Pr[\textsc{Ext} \mid \textsc{Acc}]. \tag{20}$$

Claim 1

$$\Pr[\textsc{TgtIdx}] = 1/|A| = 1/\mu. \tag{21}$$

Proof. $\hat{a}$ coincides with $a^\dagger$ with probability $1/|A|$ because $a^\dagger$ is chosen uniformly at random from A by $\mathbf{F}$ and no information of $a^\dagger$ is leaked to $\mathbf{A}$. $\qquad\square$

Claim 2. *If* $\textsc{TgtIdx}$ *occurs, then* i^* *is not queried by* $\mathbf{F}$ *to its oracle* $\mathbf{SignO}_{pp}$.

Proof. This is because of the restriction (8)(9). $\qquad\square$

Claim 3

$$\Pr[\textsc{Ext} \mid \textsc{Acc}] = 1. \tag{22}$$

Proof. This is because of the perfect knowledge extraction of Prv_{pp} (see Definition 8 in Appendix). $\qquad\square$

Combining (17), (18), (19), (20), (21) and (22) we have:

$$\mathbf{Adv}_{\mathsf{dACS},\mathbf{A}}^{\text{euf-coll}}(\lambda,\mu) = \mu \cdot \mathbf{Adv}_{\mathsf{Sig},\mathbf{F}}^{\text{euf-cma}}(\lambda). \tag{23}$$

$\qquad\square$

F   Proof of Theorem 2

Proof. Suppose that any PPT algorithm $\mathbf{A}$ that is in accordance with the experiment $\mathsf{Exp}_{\mathsf{dACS},\mathbf{A}}^{\text{unlink-prf}}(1^\lambda, 1^\mu)$ is given. We set a sequence of games, Game_0 and Game_1, as follows. Game_0 is exactly the same as $\mathsf{Exp}_{\mathsf{dACS},\mathbf{A}}^{\text{unlink-prf}}(1^\lambda, 1^\mu)$. Note that when a set of public parameters $pp = (pp', ck)$ is given to $\mathbf{A}$ where pp' is for bilinear groups, the commitment key ck is chosen as a commitment key ck of the mode nor. We denote the probability that Game_0 returns WIN as $\Pr[\textsc{Win}_0]$.

Game_1 is the same as Game_0 except that, when a set of public parameters $pp = (pp', ck)$ is given to $\mathbf{A}$, the commitment key ck is chosen as a commitment key ck of the mode sim. We denote the probability that Game_1 returns WIN as $\Pr[\textsc{Win}_1]$. The values in Game_1 distribute identically for both i_0 and i_1 due to the perfectly hiding property (13) and the perfect witness-indistinguishability (14). Therefore, $\Pr[\text{WIN}_1] = 1/2$.

Employing $\mathbf{A}$ as a subroutine, we construct a PPT distinguisher algorithm $\mathbf{D}$ as follows. Given an input pp, ck, $\mathbf{D}$ reads out the security parameter. $\mathbf{D}$ simulates the environment of $\mathbf{A}$ in Game_0 or Game_1 honestly except that $\mathbf{D}$ puts $pp := (pp, ck)$ instead of executing $\mathsf{Setup}(1^\lambda)$. If $b = b'$, then $\mathbf{D}$ returns 1, and otherwise, 0. By the definition of (12) (see Definition 3 in Appendix), $\Pr[\mathbf{D}(pp, ck) = 1 \mid ck \leftarrow \mathsf{Cmt.KG}_{pp}(\mathtt{nor})] = \Pr[\text{WIN}_0]$ and $\Pr[\mathbf{D}(pp, ck) = 1 \mid (ck, tk) \leftarrow \mathsf{Cmt.KG}_{pp}(\mathtt{sim})] = \Pr[\text{WIN}_1]$, and

$$\mathbf{Adv}^{\text{ind-dual}}_{\mathsf{Cmt}_{pp},\mathbf{D}}(\lambda) = |\Pr[\text{WIN}_0] - \Pr[\text{WIN}_1]|. \tag{24}$$

Therefore,

$$\begin{aligned}
\mathbf{Adv}^{\text{unlink-prf}}_{\mathsf{dACS},\mathbf{A}}(\lambda, \mu) &= |\Pr[\text{WIN}_0] - (1/2)| \\
&\leq |\Pr[\text{WIN}_0] - \Pr[\text{WIN}_1]| + |\Pr[\text{WIN}_1] - (1/2)| \\
&= \mathbf{Adv}^{\text{ind-dual}}_{\mathsf{Cmt}_{pp},\mathbf{D}}(\lambda) + 0 = \mathbf{Adv}^{\text{ind-dual}}_{\mathsf{Cmt}_{pp},\mathbf{D}}(\lambda). \tag{25}
\end{aligned}$$

$\square$

References

1. Abe, M., Fuchsbauer, G., Groth, J., Haralambiev, K., Ohkubo, M.: Structure-preserving signatures and commitments to group elements. In: Rabin, T. (ed.) CRYPTO 2010. LNCS, vol. 6223, pp. 209–236. Springer, Heidelberg (2010). https://doi.org/10.1007/978-3-642-14623-7_12
2. Abe, M., Fuchsbauer, G., Groth, J., Haralambiev, K., Ohkubo, M.: Structure-preserving signatures and commitments to group elements. J. Cryptol. **29**(2), 363–421 (2016)
3. Abe, M., Hofheinz, D., Nishimaki, R., Ohkubo, M., Pan, J.: Compact structure-preserving signatures with almost tight security. In: Katz, J., Shacham, H. (eds.) CRYPTO 2017. LNCS, vol. 10402, pp. 548–580. Springer, Cham (2017). https://doi.org/10.1007/978-3-319-63715-0_19
4. Anada, H., Arita, S.: Witness-indistinguishable arguments with Σ-protocols for bundled witness spaces and its application to global identities. In: Proceedings of 20th International Conference on Information and Communications Security (ICICS 2018), pp. 530–547, Lille, France, October 29–31 (2018)
5. Camenisch, J., Dubovitskaya, M., Haralambiev, K., Kohlweiss, M.: Composable and modular anonymous credentials: definitions and practical constructions. In: Iwata, T., Cheon, J.H. (eds.) ASIACRYPT 2015. LNCS, vol. 9453, pp. 262–288. Springer, Heidelberg (2015). https://doi.org/10.1007/978-3-662-48800-3_11
6. Camenisch, J., Lysyanskaya, A.: An efficient system for non-transferable anonymous credentials with optional anonymity revocation. In: Pfitzmann, B. (ed.) EUROCRYPT 2001. LNCS, vol. 2045, pp. 93–118. Springer, Heidelberg (2001). https://doi.org/10.1007/3-540-44987-6_7
7. Camenisch, J., Lysyanskaya, A.: A signature scheme with efficient protocols. In: Cimato, S., Persiano, G., Galdi, C. (eds.) SCN 2002. LNCS, vol. 2576, pp. 268–289. Springer, Heidelberg (2003). https://doi.org/10.1007/3-540-36413-7_20

8. Camenisch, J., Lysyanskaya, A.: Signature schemes and anonymous credentials from bilinear maps. In: Franklin, M. (ed.) CRYPTO 2004. LNCS, vol. 3152, pp. 56–72. Springer, Heidelberg (2004). https://doi.org/10.1007/978-3-540-28628-8_4

9. Escala, A., Groth, J.: Fine-Tuning Groth-Sahai Proofs. In: Krawczyk, H. (ed.) PKC 2014. LNCS, vol. 8383, pp. 630–649. Springer, Heidelberg (2014). https://doi.org/10.1007/978-3-642-54631-0_36

10. Fuchsbauer, G.: Commuting signatures and verifiable encryption. In: Paterson, K.G. (ed.) EUROCRYPT 2011. LNCS, vol. 6632, pp. 224–245. Springer, Heidelberg (2011). https://doi.org/10.1007/978-3-642-20465-4_14

11. Fuchsbauer, G., Hanser, C., Slamanig, D.: Structure-preserving signatures on equivalence classes and constant-size anonymous credentials. J. Cryptol. $32(2)$, 498–546 (2019)

12. Galbraith, S.D., Paterson, K.G., Smart, N.P.: Pairings for cryptographers. Discrete Appl. Math. $156(16)$, 3113–3121 (2008)

13. Groth, J., Sahai, A.: Efficient non-interactive proof systems for bilinear groups. In: Smart, N. (ed.) EUROCRYPT 2008. LNCS, vol. 4965, pp. 415–432. Springer, Heidelberg (2008). https://doi.org/10.1007/978-3-540-78967-3_24

14. Lewko, A., Waters, B.: Decentralizing attribute-based encryption. In: Paterson, K.G. (ed.) EUROCRYPT 2011. LNCS, vol. 6632, pp. 568–588. Springer, Heidelberg (2011). https://doi.org/10.1007/978-3-642-20465-4_31

15. Okamoto, T., Takashima, K.: Decentralized attribute-based signatures. In: Kurosawa, K., Hanaoka, G. (eds.) PKC 2013. LNCS, vol. 7778, pp. 125–142. Springer, Heidelberg (2013). https://doi.org/10.1007/978-3-642-36362-7_9

16. Okishima, R., Nakanishi, T.: An anonymous credential system with constant-size attribute proofs for CNF formulas with negations. In: Attrapadung, N., Yagi, T. (eds.) IWSEC 2019. LNCS, vol. 11689, pp. 89–106. Springer, Cham (2019). https://doi.org/10.1007/978-3-030-26834-3_6

A Scalable Simulation of the BB84 Protocol Involving Eavesdropping

Mihai-Zicu Mina[1]([⊠])[iD] and Emil Simion[2][iD]

[1] Faculty of Automatic Control and Computers, University Politehnica of Bucharest,
Bucharest, Romania
`mihai_zicu.mina@stud.acs.upb.ro`

[2] Center for Research and Training in Innovative Techniques of Applied Mathematics
in Engineering – "Traian Lalescu", University Politehnica of Bucharest,
Bucharest, Romania
`emil.simion@upb.ro`

Abstract. In this article we present the BB84 quantum key distribution scheme from two perspectives. First, we provide a theoretical discussion of the steps Alice and Bob take to reach a shared secret using this protocol, while an eavesdropper Eve is either involved or not. Then, we offer and discuss two distinct implementations that simulate BB84 using IBM's Qiskit framework, the first being an exercise solved during the "IBM Quantum Challenge" event in early May 2020, while the other was developed independently to showcase the intercept-resend attack strategy in detail. We note the latter's scalability and increased output verbosity, which allow for a statistical analysis to determine the probability of detecting the act of eavesdropping.

Keywords: Quantum key distribution · BB84 · Intercept-resend attack · Qiskit · Simulation

1 Introduction

The process of establishing a shared key for secure communication between parties is an essential operation in modern cryptographic tasks and it can be ensured by using the Diffie-Hellman protocol or RSA. However, the underlying security of these schemes is conditioned by the intractability of certain mathematical problems, an aspect that advanced quantum computers can overcome. We would need another approach to the key sharing problem, one that is provably secure. Fortunately, quantum theory offers a solution that fits this criterion, *quantum key distribution* (QKD). The inherent features of quantum information make quantum key distribution secure from an information-theoretic perspective [1–3]. However, flaws in practical implementations could actually be exploited by attackers. The downside of quantum key distribution is represented precisely by such challenges in its practical deployment. The first QKD protocol is BB84 [4],

© Springer Nature Switzerland AG 2021
D. Maimut et al. (Eds.): SecITC 2020, LNCS 12596, pp. 91–109, 2021.
https://doi.org/10.1007/978-3-030-69255-1_7

devised in 1984 and first implemented in 1989 over 32 cm [5], a modest achievement in terms of distribution distance that has been impressively exceeded ever
since [6–8].

We take a closer look at the core idea behind this scheme by discussing the
operations performed by parties when an eavesdropper is absent and then when
tampering indeed occurs, which is of practical interest. For the second case,
we analyze the *intercept-resend attack* to which the intruder Eve resorts in her
attempt to acquire information. We give two examples to illustrate those cases
and emphasize the statistical aspect regarding Alice and Bob's chances to detect
Eve. We then present two Qiskit simulations of the protocol, an exercise from
the "IBM Quantum Challenge" and a separate program demonstrating how the
scheme is executed in a scenario featuring Eve. We refer to the second implementation as being "scalable", in that the program can be run for an arbitrary
number of qubits, this aspect being limited only by the capability of Qiskit's
built-in simulator. The program we designed details relevant information about
each party's actions and the factors that lead to the conclusion. Furthermore, we
explored the end result of the simulation from a statistical perspective by running
multiple instances of the program, observing how many times eavesdropping is
detected and correlating the associated probability with the analytical one.

2   BB84 Protocol

Charles Bennett and Gilles Brassard pioneered the first quantum key distribution protocol in 1984, which relies on the *uncertainty principle*, a central aspect
of quantum theory. This phenomenon essentially shows that extracting information about one property from a quantum state will introduce an indeterminacy
in the information we can access about another property. Using BB84, Alice and
Bob can arrive at a shared key, which they can use afterwards with a symmetric encryption scheme, such as a one-time pad. The original formulation of the
protocol uses photons as qubits, the information being encoded in their polar-
ization. We will start our discussion of the protocol with the case that does not
involve any eavesdropping.

2.1   No Eavesdropping

Initially, Alice randomly generates an n-bit string **k**, from which the shared key
will be eventually derived. The protocol requires that she and Bob agree on two
distinct encodings of a classical bit using a qubit. For example, 0 can be encoded
by a photon that is polarized horizontally ($\rightarrow$) and at an angle of 45° ($\nearrow$), while
1 is then encoded by photon polarized vertically ($\uparrow$) and at an angle of 135°
($\nwarrow$). Thus, we have two bases in which a photon can be prepared in order to
represent one bit of information. The *rectilinear basis* is given by $\{|\rightarrow\rangle, |\uparrow\rangle\}$,
while the *diagonal basis* is $\{|\nearrow\rangle, |\nwarrow\rangle\}$. They are *conjugate bases*, because a
measurement of a state from one of the bases performed in the other basis is
equally likely to return either state. In other words, an element from one basis

is a uniform superposition of the elements from the other basis. These bases are in fact "practical" representations of the computational and Hadamard basis. Thus, the encodings for the protocol are the following.

$$R: \quad 0 \mapsto |\rightarrow\rangle, \quad 1 \mapsto |\uparrow\rangle, \qquad D: \quad 0 \mapsto |\nearrow\rangle, \quad 1 \mapsto |\nwarrow\rangle \qquad (1)$$

After agreeing on the bases that are to be used, Alice generates again a random sequence of n bits $\mathbf{a}$, where each bit a_i in turn indicates the encoding (R or D) she will choose for the i-th bit of $\mathbf{k}$. Both parties must again establish a convention here, for example $a_i = 0$ means that the corresponding qubit will be prepared in the rectilinear basis. After encoding each bit k_i into a qubit, Alice sends the photon to Bob, who then measures it in his own basis. Since he does not know what basis was chosen by Alice, Bob randomly picks a basis for measuring the i-th qubit. According to the previous convention for denoting the basis, his choice is given by a bit b_i. Therefore, the bases he chooses for the total n qubits that are transmitted constitute another bit sequence $\mathbf{b}$.

Given the uncertainty revolving around Bob's measurements, the next step for the parties is to publicly announce the bases each of them picked, information stored in bitstrings $\mathbf{a}$ and $\mathbf{b}$. Following this phase, bit k_i will be kept as valid only if Alice's and Bob's choices coincided, i.e. $a_i = b_i$, a process referred to as *sifting* [3]. The new bitstring $\tilde{\mathbf{k}}$ composed of all these k_i is the shared key. Of course, Bob could obtain the correct state even though he chose the wrong basis, but this only happens probabilistically. On average, he chooses right 50% of the time, making the length of $\tilde{\mathbf{k}}$ half the length of the initial $\mathbf{k}$.

To illustrate an example, we consider the following sequences and then examine Table 1.

$$\mathbf{k} = 11000100, \quad \mathbf{a} = 11010011, \quad \mathbf{b} = 01011001 \qquad (2)$$

Table 1. Example of BB84 protocol without eavesdropping

Initial bit sequence $\mathbf{k}$	1	1	0	0	0	1	0	0
Alice encodes:	$\nwarrow$	$\nwarrow$	$\rightarrow$	$\nearrow$	$\rightarrow$	$\uparrow$	$\nearrow$	$\nearrow$
Bob measures:	$\uparrow$	$\nwarrow$	$\rightarrow$	$\nearrow$	$\nwarrow$	$\uparrow$	$\rightarrow$	$\nearrow$
Bases comparison:	✗	✓	✓	✓	✗	✓	✗	✓
Shared key $\tilde{\mathbf{k}}$		1	0	0		1		0

When Bob performs his measurement, the result is colored blue to indicate that it is probabilistic. As it can be noticed, out of all three wrong guesses he took, the first and last states he observes are indeed the correct encodings of the bits in the rectangular basis, but he only owes this to chance. In the end, they arrive at a 5-bit shared key.

2.2   Intercept-Resend Attack

It is natural to ask how the derivation of the key is impacted by the presence of an eavesdropper Eve. The type of attack we consider for this case is called "intercept-resend", a strategy that implies capturing the photons, measuring them and then sending them to Bob, their intended recipient. Once she intercepts a photon, Eve cannot do anything more than just pick a random basis e_i in which to measure it, as Bob does. Inevitably, her action will alter the state of the qubit. It is noteworthy that she has to resort to this kind of technique because she has to send the photons to Bob, otherwise she would compromise her presence. Ideally, she would copy each qubit and wait for the transmission to end in order to find out the bases used by Alice and Bob, so she could know the correct ones. Unfortunately for her, copying arbitrary qubits is forbidden by the *no-cloning theorem* [9,10], a fundamental result that sets quantum information apart from classical information, where we take this operation for granted.

Before looking at another example that involves Eve this time, it is important to identify several scenarios that are possible when she is present. Specifically, we analyze how the correlation between Alice's basis and Eve's basis determines what Bob will measure on his side.

Eve Chooses the Wrong Basis: $e_i = \overline{a_i} \longrightarrow$ qubit is altered.

Bob chooses correctly: $b_i = a_i \longrightarrow$ an error is introduced with 50% probability.

Bob chooses incorrectly: $b_i = \overline{a_i} \longrightarrow$ random outcome, Eve is undetected.

Eve Chooses the Correct Basis: $e_i = a_i \longrightarrow$ qubit is unaltered.

Bob chooses correctly: $b_i = a_i \longrightarrow$ Eve is undetected, has one bit of information.

Bob chooses incorrectly: $b_i = \overline{a_i} \longrightarrow$ random outcome, Eve is undetected.

These possibilities reveal that for each transmitted qubit, there is 75% probability that Eve's action goes undetected. The remaining 25% probability is due to Bob's correct choice when Eve chooses incorrectly: he obtains the wrong state after his measurement and therefore decodes the wrong bit. Considering that Alice's and Bob's sequences of bits do not match exactly in such situation, they take an additional step to test against eavesdropping. They decide to select a subset of the remaining bits and compare them. If they do not match, they know for sure that Eve interfered. Of course, there is a compromise between the number of bits they want to "sacrifice" to discover Eve with a high probability and the length of the shared key, which decreases as they discard those bits that were compared.

Table 2 shows an example. Sequences $\mathbf{k}_A$ and $\mathbf{k}_B$ represent Alice's original $\mathbf{k}$ and the bits decoded by Bob, respectively, both after the sifting phase. Eve's bases are represented by $\mathbf{e}$.

$$\mathbf{k}_A = 11000100, \quad \mathbf{a} = 11010011, \quad \mathbf{b} = 01011001, \quad \mathbf{e} = 10001001 \qquad (3)$$

Table 2. Example of BB84 protocol with eavesdropping

Initial bit sequence **k**	1	1	0	0	0	1	0	0
Alice encodes:	↖	↖	→	↗	→	↑	↗	↗
Eve measures:	↖	↑	→	→	↗	↑	→	↗
Bob measures:	↑	↗	→	↗	↗	↑	→	↗
Bases comparison:	✗	✓	✓	✓	✗	✓	✗	✓
Alice's bit sequence $\mathbf{k}_A$		1	0	0		1		0
Eve's information:		0				1		0
Eve introduces error?	N	**Y**	N	N	N	N	N	N
Bob's bit sequence $\mathbf{k}_B$		**0**	**0**	**0**		**1**		**0**

From Eve's choices, we notice that her correct bases agreed with Bob's bases three out of eight times, thus allowing her to gain information about three bits from the initial bit sequence. She introduces an error in the second bit, making Bob decode 0 instead of 1. The example illustrates the idea of this attack, but it is rather impractical because the length of $\mathbf{k}$ is short. In a real scenario, Alice and Bob would need to compare many bits from $\mathbf{k}_A$ and $\mathbf{k}_B$, which have a length of $n_s \approx n/2$ bits on average. If they choose to compare one bit from their respective strings, the probability of them being the same is 0.75. For a selection of $\tilde{n}$ bits, the probability of having all of them match represents Eve's chance of evading detection, which decreases exponentially with $\tilde{n}$. Therefore, the probability of detection p_d that Alice and Bob wish to have above a confident threshold is given by

$$p_d = 1 - p_e = 1 - \left(\frac{3}{4}\right)^{\tilde{n}}, \quad \tilde{n} < n_s, \quad n_s = |\mathbf{k}_A| = |\mathbf{k}_B| \approx \frac{n}{2}. \qquad (4)$$

For example, $\tilde{n} = 20$ determines $p_e \approx 32 \times 10^{-4}$, making the probability of finding the eavesdropper $p_d \approx 0.997$. The dependence of this probability on the number of compared bits is depicted in Fig. 1.

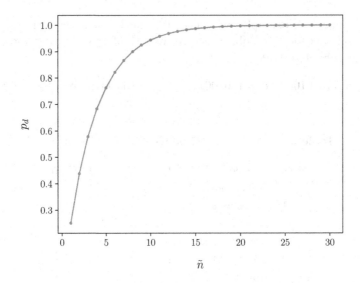

Fig. 1. Probability of detecting Eve increases with $\tilde{n}$

In a scenario involving such an attack, establishing a shared key becomes a lengthier process. Alice and Bob may agree on a certain acceptable number of bit errors that makes them continue the protocol, otherwise they abort and try again. When they decide to continue, additional measures are taken in order to correct the unmatched bits due to Eve's interference and also ensure that the information she gains following their actions is kept to a minimum. These steps are called *information reconciliation* and *privacy amplification*, respectively [11]. Even in the unlikely event when all of their compared bits are equal, Alice and Bob cannot conclude that the transmission was free of any eavesdropping and they must still perform these actions. Hypothetically, when no eavesdropping occurs, Alice and Bob would possess a shared key after comparing their selections and discarding those bits, since the remaining ones are sure to match.

2.3 "IBM Quantum Challenge"

In May 2020, IBM celebrated the fourth anniversary of their *Quantum Experience* cloud platform by organizing an event called "IBM Quantum Challenge" [12]. It lasted from May 4 to May 8, inviting users of the platform to solve four exercises using the Qiskit framework [13]. Among the topics of the exercises was a simulation of the BB84 protocol [14], whose co-designer Charles H. Bennett is an IBM Fellow. The implementation considers $n = 100$ bits and the goal sought by Alice and Bob is to obtain a shared key that is later used to encrypt a message using a one-time pad scheme. There is no eavesdropping and the user is given Bob's role of performing the following operations:

- measure each qubit sent by Alice;
- compare bases with Alice and extract the 50-bit key;
- decrypt Alice's 200-bit message by concatenating the key with itself;
- decode Alice's binary message that "disguises" a message in Morse code:

0	character separator
1	.
00	letter separator
11	-
000	word separator

- discover the original message.

The source code for the completed exercise is given in Listing 1. Considering its dependence on several dedicated modules, the webpage of the repository [15] should be visited for instructions on how to get the program running properly. Variables alice_bases and bob_bases are binary strings that represent parameters **a** and **b** we used thus far, respectively. Their bits match exactly 50 times, thus determining the 50-bit shared key

$$\tilde{\mathbf{k}} = 10000010001110010011101001010000110000110011100000. \tag{5}$$

Alice then uses this key with a one-time pad to encrypt a 200-bit message **p**, whose ciphertext can be found in the source code (variable m). Since the key is much shorter than the plaintext, she pads the key with itself three more times until it reaches 200 bits. Of course, the security of the scheme is weakened because of this practice, but that is not the focus of the exercise.

$$\mathbf{m} = \mathbf{p} \oplus 4\tilde{\mathbf{k}} \tag{6}$$

Bob undoes the operation to find the plaintext, which is further decoded into a Morse code sequence, according to the previous mappings.

$$\mathbf{p}_M = \text{.-..-..-....-.-.-.--.-.------..-..-.-..--.--.--....---.-..-.--.-..---} \tag{7}$$

Based on a dictionary that maps the letters of the Latin alphabet, digits and other characters to symbols of the Morse code, the intelligible message is found to be a nice reward "key" to a dedicated webpage, as pictured in Fig. 2.

$$\mathbf{p}_L = \texttt{reddit.com/r/may4quantum} \tag{8}$$

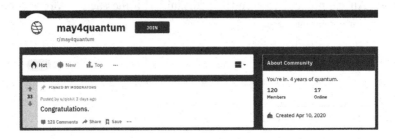

Fig. 2. A snapshot of the webpage to which users are taken after finding the solution

2.4   Simulation with Eavesdropping

The implementation of the protocol for the proposed exercise used a module given by IBM specifically for the purpose of the event, providing already defined functions for certain operations. We now present a distinct implementation that was written from scratch, taking into account the intercept-resend attack we discussed earlier. As mentioned in the source code found in Listing 2, we choose the length of **k** by passing the value as argument to the script, which is stored in variable **n**. For convenience and practical significance, this number should be large enough. Several functions are defined, some representing subcircuits, while others test the choices the parties made for their bases. One function actually implements a simple quantum random number generator, which can be used to substitute that functionality from the **random** module. Running the program will output information about the bases that were chosen by Alice, Eve and Bob, when their choices coincided (Y), the bits obtained after measurements and whether some of them are correct by chance (R). The errors introduced by Eve are also highlighted (!), while Alice and Bob choose a subset of their presumably correct key bits to test for eavesdropping. In order to simulate their agreement, the lists of bits are randomly sampled using the same seed. The size of this selection can be specified and a conclusion message is displayed at the end. If they discover that at least one error in the string of compared bits, they abort and start the protocol over again, which is very likely to happen, based on the previous analysis.

The output of an execution for **n = 100** is given in Listing 3, a case where eavesdropping is detected. We notice that bases chosen by Bob and Eve agree with those picked by Alice for roughly half the qubits. In 34 instances, Eve chose the wrong basis, while Bob's choice agreed with Alice's, making him decode a random bit, as the qubit state was changed by Eve's measurement. Still, he randomly got the right bit 14 times out of those 34, leaving 20 unmatched bits that confirm Eve's presence. She can only hope that the random subset of bits Alice and Bob decide to compare will not contain any of those, otherwise her tampering will be revealed. As per the authors' suggestion in [4], the length of the subset is the integer part of a third of the length of the bit sequences sifted by Alice and Bob following the public disclosure of their bases. Since these sequences have 53 bits in this example, our parties compare 17 randomly selected bits and find 9 disagreements, which is the signal that makes them abort and restart the procedure.

Choosing a smaller value for **n** makes it more likely to have a simulation where the errors introduced by Eve are not found by Alice and Bob. An output fragment for such a scenario with **n = 30** is displayed in Listing 4.

Finally, we wish to validate the previous relation that determines the probability of detecting Eve based on the number of sacrificed bits. We keep the length of the random selection at the same value

$$\tilde{n} = \left\lfloor \frac{n_s}{3} \right\rfloor \approx \left\lfloor \frac{n}{6} \right\rfloor \tag{9}$$

and choose $n = 40$, such that $p_d \approx 0.822$. We use the script in Listing 5 to simulate the protocol **s = 100** times for **n = 40**, in order to find out how many times Eve has evaded detection. As the results in Listing 6 indicate, eavesdropping goes unnoticed **s - d = 18** times, such that Alice and Bob have a chance of **d/s = 0.82** to catch Eve, as expected. Certainly, given that the actions performed by parties yield random outcomes, this probability varies between runs, but it remains close to the analytical result. We can go further and test how this probability increases indeed with the number of bits that Alice and Bob compare. The plot we intend to observe is actually an indirect relation between those two parameters, since the number of bits selected to be compared is exactly or close to a sixth of the number of qubits **n** we are using as argument to run the simulation. To acquire the necessary data, we ran 100 simulations for each even value of **n** between 10 and 120. The graph that resulted following this experiment is displayed in Fig. 3 and we notice that it resembles the one from Fig. 1.

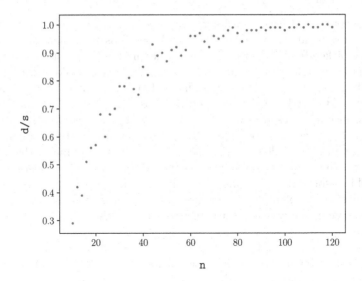

Fig. 3. The statistical chance d/s of detecting Eve increases with n, which is roughly six times the number of bits they end up comparing

3   Conclusion

Quantum key distribution has emerged as a promising direction within the field of quantum information science and it has repeatedly broken new ground as quantum technologies continue to advance at a remarkable pace. Here we have focused on the BB84 protocol, the early result that revealed the fundamental implications of quantum information on cryptography. Throughout this article, we presented the operational aspects of the protocol when a type of eavesdropping happens or not, with some examples alongside the theoretical discussion, and we provided two implementations of it using Qiskit, the quantum computing framework from IBM. The first program represents a solved exercise that was part of the "IBM Quantum Challenge" held in May 2020, while the second one is a simulation we developed to show how the intercept-resend attack impacts Alice and Bob's plan to establish a shared key. We exploited the capability of the program to run for any number of qubits and we conducted experiments to determine the probability of having Alice and Bob detect Eve. Our results indicate that her presence is discovered with a high degree of certainty when enough bits from their sequences are spared and the statistical analysis we performed underlines that simulation data follows the theoretical model.

Acknowledgements. We acknowledge the use of IBM Quantum services for this work. The views expressed are those of the authors, and do not reflect the official policy or position of IBM or the IBM Quantum team.

A   Qiskit Source Code and Output

A.1   "IBM Quantum Challenge"

Listing 1: QKD exercise from "IBM Quantum Challenge"

```python
%matplotlib inline

# Importing standard Qiskit libraries
import random
from qiskit import execute, Aer, IBMQ
from qiskit.tools.jupyter import *
from qiskit.visualization import *
from may4_challenge.ex3 import alice_prepare_qubit, check_bits, check_key,
    check_decrypted, show_message

# Configuring account
provider = IBMQ.load_account()
backend = provider.get_backend('ibmq_qasm_simulator')  # with this simulator it wouldn't
    work \

# Initial setup
random.seed(84)  # do not change this seed, otherwise you will get a different key

# This is your 'random' bit string that determines your bases
numqubits = 100
bob_bases = str('{0:0100b}'.format(random.getrandbits(numqubits)))

def bb84():
    print('Bob\'s bases:', bob_bases)

    # Now Alice will send her bits one by one...
    all_qubit_circuits = []
    for qubit_index in range(numqubits):

        # This is Alice creating the qubit
        thisqubit_circuit = alice_prepare_qubit(qubit_index)

        # This is Bob finishing the protocol below
        bob_measure_qubit(bob_bases, qubit_index, thisqubit_circuit)

        # We collect all these circuits and put them in an array
        all_qubit_circuits.append(thisqubit_circuit)

    # Now execute all the circuits for each qubit
    results = execute(all_qubit_circuits, backend=backend, shots=1).result()

    # And combine the results
    bits = ''
    for qubit_index in range(numqubits):
        bits += [measurement for measurement in results.get_counts(qubit_index)][0]

    return bits

# Here is your task
def bob_measure_qubit(bob_bases, qubit_index, qubit_circuit):
    if int(bob_bases[qubit_index]) == 1:
        qubit_circuit.h(0)
    qubit_circuit.measure(0,0)

bits = bb84()
print('Bob\'s bits: ', bits)
check_bits(bits)

#=== KEY EXTRACTION ===#

alice_bases = '10000000001000111111100110110010100011111101001101'\
              '11111000110000011000001001100011100111010010000110'  # Alice's bases bits

key = ''

for i in range(numqubits):
    if alice_bases[i] == bob_bases[i]:
        key += bits[i]
```

```
67
68  check_key(key)
69
70  #=== MESSAGE DECRYPTION ===#
71
72  m = '0011011010100011101000001100010000001000011000101011'\
73      '1011011110011111111000111110001110010101101011101'\
74      '1110100011101010010111111001010000110100110110110'\
75      '1110111101011100010111111100101010100110010111011' # encrypted message
76
77  key = 4*key
78  decrypted = ''
79
80  for i in range(len(m)):
81      s = int(m[i]) + int(key[i])
82      decrypted += str(s % 2)
83
84  check_decrypted(decrypted)
85
86  #=== MESSAGE DECODING ===#
87
88  symbols = []
89  i = 0
90  while i < len(decrypted)-1:
91      if decrypted[i] + decrypted[i+1] == "11":
92          symbols.append("11")
93          i = i+2
94      elif decrypted[i] + decrypted[i+1] == "00":
95          symbols.append("00")
96          i = i+2
97      else:
98          symbols.append(decrypted[i])
99          i = i+1
100
101 d = {'1':'.', '11':'-', '0':'', '00':2* ' ', '000':3* ' '}
102 morse_message = [d[i] for i in symbols]
103 morse_message = ''.join(morse_message).split("   ")
104
105 MORSE_CODE_DICT = { 'a':'.-', 'b':'-...',
106                     'c':'-.-.', 'd':'-..', 'e':'.',
107                     'f':'..-.', 'g':'--.', 'h':'....',
108                     'i':'..', 'j':'.---', 'k':'-.-',
109                     'l':'.-..', 'm':'--', 'n':'-.',
110                     'o':'---', 'p':'.--.', 'q':'--.-',
111                     'r':'.-.', 's':'...', 't':'-',
112                     'u':'..-', 'v':'...-', 'w':'.--',
113                     'x':'-..-', 'y':'-.--', 'z':'--..',
114                     '1':'.----', '2':'..---', '3':'...--',
115                     '4':'....-', '5':'.....', '6':'-....',
116                     '7':'--...', '8':'---..', '9':'----.',
117                     '0':'-----', ',':'--..--', '.':'.-.-.-',
118                     '?':'..--..', '/':'-..-.', '-':'-....-',
119                     '(':'-.--.', ')':'-.--.-'}
120
121 keys = list(MORSE_CODE_DICT.keys())
122 values = list(MORSE_CODE_DICT.values())
123 solution = []
124
125 for c in morse_message:
126     if c in values:
127         index = values.index(c)
128         solution.append(keys[index])
129
130 solution = ''.join(solution)
131
132 show_message(solution)
```

A.2   Simulation of Intercept-Resend Attack

Listing 2: BB84 protocol with eavesdropping

```python
#!/usr/bin/python

#================================================
# BB84 PROTOCOL WITH EAVESDROPPING
# USAGE: ./bb84_eavesdropping.py <num_qubits>
#================================================

from sys import argv, exit
from qiskit import *
from random import randrange, seed, sample

# local simulation
backend = Aer.get_backend('qasm_simulator')

#================================================
#=== FUNCTION DEFINITIONS #======================

# n-bit binary representation of integer
def bst(n,s):
    return str(bin(s)[2:].rjust(n,'0'))

# generate n-bit string from measurement on n qubits
def qrng(n):
    qc = QuantumCircuit(n,n)
    for i in range(n):
        qc.h(i)
    qc.measure(list(range(n)),list(range(n)))
    result = execute(qc,backend,shots=1).result()
    bits = list(result.get_counts().keys())[0]
    bits = ''.join(list(reversed(bits)))
    return bits

# qubit encodings in specified bases
def encode_qubits(n,k,a):
    qc = QuantumCircuit(n,n)
    for i in range(n):
        if a[i] == '0':
            if k[i] == '1':
                qc.x(i)
        else:
            if k[i] == '0':
                qc.h(i)
            else:
                qc.x(i)
                qc.h(i)
    qc.barrier()
    return qc

# capture qubits, measure and send to Bob
def intercept_resend(qc,e):
    backend = Aer.get_backend('qasm_simulator')
    l = len(e)

    for i in range(l):
        if e[i] == '1':
            qc.h(i)

    qc.measure(list(range(l)),list(range(l)))
    result = execute(qc,backend,shots=1).result()
    bits = list(result.get_counts().keys())[0]
    bits = ''.join(list(reversed(bits)))

    qc.reset(list(range(l)))

    for i in range(l):
        if e[i] == '0':
            if bits[i] == '1':
                qc.x(i)
        else:
            if bits[i] == '0':
                qc.h(i)
```

```
72              else:
73                  qc.x(i)
74                  qc.h(i)
75
76      qc.barrier()
77      return [qc,bits]
78
79   # qubit measurements in specified bases
80   def bob_measurement(qc,b):
81      backend = Aer.get_backend('qasm_simulator')
82      l = len(b)
83
84
85      for i in range(l):
86          if b[i] == '1':
87              qc.h(i)
88
89      qc.measure(list(range(l)),list(range(l)))
90      result = execute(qc,backend,shots=1).result()
91      bits = list(result.get_counts().keys())[0]
92
93      bits = ''.join(list(reversed(bits)))
94
95
96      qc.barrier()
97      return [qc,bits]
98
99
100  # check where bases matched
101  def check_bases(b1,b2):
102          check = ''
103          matches = 0
104          for i in range(len(b1)):
105              if b1[i] == b2[i]:
106                  check += "Y"
107                  matches += 1
108              else:
109                  check += "-"
110          return [check,matches]
111
112  # check where measurement bits matched
113  def check_bits(b1,b2,bck):
114      check = ''
115      for i in range(len(b1)):
116          if b1[i] == b2[i] and bck[i] == 'Y':
117              check += 'Y'
118          elif b1[i] == b2[i] and bck[i] != 'Y':
119              check += 'R'
120          elif b1[i] != b2[i] and bck[i] == 'Y':
121              check += '!'
122          elif b1[i] != b2[i] and bck[i] != 'Y':
123              check += '-'
124      return check
125
126
127  #================================================
128  #=== INITIAL PARAMETER #=====================
129
130  if len(argv) != 2:
131              print("USAGE:   " + argv[0] + " <num_qubits>")
132              exit(1)
133  else:
134          try:
135              # size of quantum and classical registers
136              n = int(argv[1])
137
138              if n < 10:
139                      print("[!] Number of qubits should be at least 10.")
140                      exit(1)
141
142          except ValueError:
143                  print("[!] Argument must be an integer.")
144                  exit(1)
145
```

```
146   print("\nAlice prepares " + str(n) + " qubits.\n")
147
148   N = 2**n
149
150   #===============================================
151   #=== BIT SEQUENCE AND BASES #==================
152
153   #seed(81)
154   #alice_bits = bst(n,randrange(N))
155   alice_bits = qrng(n)
156
157   #seed(147)
158   #a = bst(n,randrange(N))
159   a = qrng(n)
160
161   #seed(875)
162   #e = bst(n,randrange(N))
163   e = qrng(n)
164
165   #seed(316)
166   #b = bst(n,randrange(N))
167   b = qrng(n)
168
169   #===============================================
170
171   bb84 = QuantumCircuit(n,n)
172   bb84 += encode_qubits(n,alice_bits,a)
173
174   bb84, eve_bits = intercept_resend(bb84,e)
175   ae_bases, ae_matches = check_bases(a,e)
176   ae_bits = check_bits(alice_bits,eve_bits,ae_bases)
177
178   bb84, bob_bits = bob_measurement(bb84,b)
179   eb_bases, eb_matches = check_bases(e,b)
180   eb_bits = check_bits(eve_bits,bob_bits,eb_bases)
181
182   ab_bases, ab_matches = check_bases(a,b)
183   ab_bits = check_bits(alice_bits,bob_bits,ab_bases)
184
185   altered_qubits = 0
186   err_num = 0
187   err_str = ''
188   key = ''
189   ka = ''
190   ke = ''
191   kb = ''
192
193   for i in range(n):
194       if ae_bases[i] != 'Y' and ab_bases[i] == 'Y':
195           altered_qubits += 1
196       if ab_bases[i] == 'Y':
197           ka += alice_bits[i]
198           kb += bob_bits[i]
199       else:
200           ka += '-'
201           kb += '-'
202       if ae_bases[i] == 'Y' and ab_bases[i] == 'Y':
203           ke += eve_bits[i]
204       else:
205               ke += '-'
206       if ab_bits[i] == '!':
207           err_num += 1
208
209   err_str = ''.join(['!' if ka[i] != kb[i] else ' ' for i in range(len(ka))])
210
211   print("Alice's bases:          " + a)
212   print("Eve's bases:            " + e)
213   print("Alice-Eve bases match:  " + ae_bases)
214   print("")
215   print("Eve guessed correctly " + str(ae_matches) + " times.")
216   print("")
217   print("Alice's bits:           " + alice_bits)
218   print("Eve's bits:             " + eve_bits)
219   print("Alice-Eve bits match:   " + ae_bits)
```

```python
220    print("")
221
222    print("Eve's bases:            " + e)
223    print("Bob's bases:            " + b)
224    print("Eve-Bob bases match:    " + eb_bases)
225    print("")
226    print("Eve and Bob chose the same basis " + str(eb_matches) + " times.")
227    print("")
228    print("Eve's bits:             " + eve_bits)
229    print("Bob's bits:             " + bob_bits)
230    print("Eve-Bob bits match:     " + eb_bits)
231    print("")
232
233    print((len("Alice's remaining bits: ") + n)*'=')
234    print("")
235
236    print("Alice-Bob bases match:  " + ab_bases)
237    print("Alice's bits:           " + alice_bits)
238    print("Bob's bits:             " + bob_bits)
239    print("Alice-Bob bits match:   " + ab_bits)
240    print("")
241    print("Bob guessed correctly " + str(ab_matches) + " times.")
242    print("Eve altered " + str(altered_qubits) + " qubits (she chose wrong and Bob chose
    ↪ right).")
243    print("Eve got lucky " + str(altered_qubits - err_num) + " times (Bob measured the right
    ↪ state by chance).")
244    print("Alice and Bob keep only the bits for which their bases matched.")
245    print("Eve successfully gains information when her basis was also Bob's correct basis.")
246    print("")
247    print("Alice's remaining bits: " + ka)
248    print("Error positions:        " + err_str)
249    print("Bob's remaining bits:   " + kb)
250    print("Number of errors: " + str(err_num))
251    print("")
252    print("Eve's information:      " + ke)
253    print("")
254
255    ka = ka.replace('-','')
256    kb = kb.replace('-','')
257
258    selection_size = int(ab_matches/3)
259
260    seed(63)
261    selection_alice = [list(pair) for pair in sample(list(enumerate(ka)),selection_size)]
262    indices_alice = [pair[0] for pair in selection_alice]
263    substring_alice = ''.join([pair[1] for pair in selection_alice])
264
265    seed(63)
266    selection_bob = [list(pair) for pair in sample(list(enumerate(kb)),selection_size)]
267    indices_bob = [pair[0] for pair in selection_bob]
268    substring_bob = ''.join([pair[1] for pair in selection_bob])
269
270    print("Alice and Bob compare " + str(selection_size) + " of the " + str(ab_matches) + "
    ↪ bits (indices: " + ', '.join([str(i) for i in indices_alice]) + ').')
271    print("Alice's substring: " + substring_alice)
272    print("Bob's substring:   " + substring_bob)
273
274    err_found = 0
275
276    for i in range(len(substring_alice)):
277        if substring_alice[i] != substring_bob[i]:
278            err_found += 1
279
280    if err_found > 0:
281        conclusion = "They find " + str(err_found) + " error(s) and realize that Eve
    ↪ interfered. "
282        conclusion += "They abort and start over.\n"
283    else:
284        conclusion = "Their selections match and Eve is not detected.\n"
285        ka = list(ka)
286        kb = list(kb)
287        for pos in list(reversed(sorted(indices_alice))):
288            ka.pop(pos)
289            kb.pop(pos)
290        ka = ''.join(ka)
291        kb = ''.join(kb)
292        conclusion += "When no eavesdropping occurs, they would have a " +
    ↪ str(ab_matches-len(substring_alice)) + "-bit shared key at this point, " + ka +
    ↪ ".\n"
293        conclusion += "Here, they must correct the erroneous bits and make sure Eve gains
    ↪ minimal information during the process.\n"
294
295    print(conclusion)
```

Listing 3: A complete output example for n = 100

```
$ ./bb84_eavesdropping.py 100

Alice prepares 100 qubits.

Alice's bases:          0101110011111110000101010011011111010010010110110000011001101110000010110000110000010010111111111010110
Eve's bases:            1000100110110011010010101001001111010110101010110110011110001111100111100101000111011101110111000010001
Alice-Eve bases match:  --Y-Y-Y-Y-YY----Y--YYYYY--Y---Y-YY--YY---Y---YY--YYY-Y-YY----------YYY--YYY--YY--Y-YY-Y-YYY---YYY---

Eve guessed correctly 45 times.

Alice's bits:           1001100001110100110110011110111101000110110011110111100111110110111110000111010110100100100100100
Eve's bits:             1100100000111100110110001111011100100001100011110111110010111110110111000010001111110110100101100000
Alice-Eve bits match:   R-Y-YRYRYRYYR-RRYRRYYYYY-RYR--YRYY---YY---Y-RRYYRAYYYRYRYY-RRR-R--R-YYYRRYYY--YY-RY-YY-YRYYYRR-YYY-RR

Eve's bases:            1000100110110011010010101001001111010110101010110110011110001111100111100101000110010100100100100010001
Bob's bases:            0110101001001010111100010011011000010010010001111001110001001101010110111100100110010000110100110100110
Eve-Bob bases match:    ---YYY-------YY--YY---Y---YYYY-YYY-Y-------YY-Y----YYYY-Y----YY-Y-Y--YY---Y--YYYY---YYY----Y--Y--Y---

Eve and Bob chose the same basis 40 times.

Eve's bits:             1100100000111100110110001111011100100001100011110111110010111110110111000010001111110110100101100000
Bob's bits:             0000100111100110111111111101111011110111101110010001110101111011011100010011111110100010111100111
Eve-Bob bits match:     --RYYYR---R--YY-RYR-RY--RYYYYRYYY-YR--RRR-YY-YR-RRYYYY-YR--RYYRY-Y--YYR-RY--YYYYRRRYYY-R--YR-YRRY---

==============================================================================================================

Alice-Bob bases match:  YY--Y--Y-Y--Y--Y--Y--Y-Y--Y-Y--YY-Y--Y--YYY---YY-YY-YY-YYY-YYY--Y-Y-Y-YYYY-Y-Y-YY-Y-YYY--Y--YYY---YYYY
Alice's bits:           1001100000111010011011001111011110100011011001111011110011111011011111000011101011010010010010010010
Bob's bits:             0000100111100110111111111101111011110111101110010001110101111011011100010011111110100010111100111
Alice-Bob bits match:   !YR-YRR!-!R-!-R!RRY-RY--!RYR-!YRY--!--!!!--R!YR!YRYYRY!YRY!YR-Y-YRY-YYY!RY-Y-YY-YR!YY--Y--YY!-RRYY!!

Bob guessed correctly 53 times.
Eve altered 34 qubits (she chose wrong and Bob chose right).
Eve got lucky 14 times (Bob measured the right state by chance).
Alice and Bob keep only the bits for which their bases matched.
Eve successfully gains information when her basis was also Bob's correct basis.

Alice's remaining bits: 10--1--0-0--1--0--1--1-1--11-1--0--110---01-11-11-100-111--1-0-1-1100-0-1-01-1-010--0--010---0100
Error positions:        !    !! ! !        !   !    ! !!! ! !       ! !           !          !         !       ! !!
Bob's remaining bits:   00--1--1-1--0--1--1--1--0-1--01-1--1--001---11-01-11-110-101--1-0-1-1101-0-1-01-1-110--0--011---0111
Number of errors: 20

Eve's information:      ----1----------------1----1---1-1------------1----11-1-0-----------11---0---01----10-----0-----0---

Alice and Bob compare 17 of the 53 bits (indices: 28, 52, 18, 16, 30, 42, 5, 24, 46, 4, 47, 12, 50, 43, 19, 3, 14).
Alice's substring: 10011011001111100
Bob's substring:   01101101011111111
They find 9 error(s) and realize that Eve interfered. They abort and start over.
```

Listing 4: A partial output example for n = 30

```
$ ./bb84_eavesdropping.py 30

Alice prepares 30 qubits.
.
.
.
Alice's remaining bits: -10-0-----10--11100--1011--0--
Error positions:                   !
Bob's remaining bits:   -10-0-----00--11100--1011--0--
Number of errors: 1

Eve's information:      ----0------0--1-0---0-1--0--

Alice and Bob compare 5 of the 15 bits (indices 7, 14, 4, 12, 13).
Alice's substring: 10011
Bob's substring:   10011
Their selections match and Eve is not detected.
When no eavesdropping occurs, they would have a 10-bit shared key at this point, 1001110010.
Here, they must correct the erroneous bits and make sure Eve gains minimal information during the process.
```

Listing 5: Multiple executions of the protocol to find the probability of catching Eve

```
1   #!/bin/bash
2
3   #=====================================================================
4   # BB84 PROTOCOL WITH EAVESDROPPING - determine chance of catching Eve
5   # USAGE: ./bb84_detections.sh <num_qubits> <num_executions>
6   #=====================================================================
7
8   [ $# -ne 2 ] && { echo "[!] USAGE:  $0 <num_qubits> <num_executions>"; exit 1; }
9
10  [ $1 -ge 10 ] 2> /dev/null && n=$1 || { echo "[!] Number of qubits should be at least 10";
    ↪  exit 1; }
11  [ $2 -ge 1 ] 2> /dev/null && s=$2 || { echo "[!] Number of executions should be at least
    ↪  1"; exit 1; }
12
13  echo -e "\nRunning $s simulation(s) with $n qubits to find out the number of undetected
    ↪  interferences..."
14
15  d=$(for i in $(seq 1 $s); do ./bb84_eavesdropping.py $n; done | grep 'abort' | wc -l)
16  p=$(echo "$d/$s" | bc -l)
17
18  printf "Eve managed to get away with her tampering in $[$s-$d] instance(s), leaving Alice
    ↪  and Bob with a %.2f chance of catching her.\n\n" "$p"
```

Listing 6: Finding the probability of detecting Eve after 100 runs for n = 40

```
$ ./bb84_detections.sh 40 100

Running 100 simulation(s) with 40 qubits to find out the number of undetected interferences...
Eve managed to get away with her tampering in 18 instance(s), leaving Alice and Bob with a 0.82 chance of catching her.
```

References

1. Hughes, R.J., et al.: Quantum cryptography. Contemporary Phys. **36**(3), 149–163 (1995). https://doi.org/10.1080/00107519508222149.eprint

2. Shor, P.W., Preskill, J.: Simple proof of security of the BB84 quantum key distribution protocol. Phys. Rev. Lett. **85**, 441–444 (2000). https://doi.org/10.1103/PhysRevLett.85.441

3. Renner, R., Gisin, N., Kraus, B.: Information-theoretic security proof for quantum-key-distribution protocols. Phys. Rev. A **72**, 012332 (2005). https://doi.org/10.1103/PhysRevA.72.012332

4. Bennett, C.H., Brassard, G.: Quantum cryptography: public key distribution and coin tossing. In: Proceedings of IEEE International Conference on Computers, Systems, and Signal Processing, pp. 175–179, December 1984

5. Bennett, C.H., Brassard, G.: Experimental quantum cryptography: the dawn of a new era for quantum cryptography: the experimental prototype is working. In: SIGACT News 20.4, pp. 78–80, November 1989. ISSN: 0163–5700. https://doi.org/10.1145/74074.74087

6. Liao, S.-K., et al.: Satellite-to-ground quantum key distribution. Nature **549**(7670), 43–47 (2017)

7. Boaron, A., et al. Secure quantum key distribution over 421 km of optical fiber. Phys. Rev. Lett. **121**, 190502 (2018). https://doi.org/10.1103/PhysRevLett.121.190502

8. Chen, J.-P., et al.: Sending-or-not-sending with independent lasers: secure twin-field quantum key distribution over 509 km. Phys. Rev. Lett. **124**, 070501 (2020). https://doi.org/10.1103/PhysRevLett.124.070501

9. Wootters, W.K., Zurek, W.H.: A single quantum cannot be cloned. Nature **299**(5886), 802–803 (1982)

10. Dieks, D.: Communication by EPR devices. Phys. Lett. A **92**(6), 271–272 (1982). ISSN: 0375–9601. https://doi.org/10.1016/0375-9601(82)90084-6, http://www.sciencedirect.com/science/article/pii/0375960182900846

11. Bennett, C.H., Bessette, F., Brassard, G., Salvail, L., Smolin, J.: Experimental quantum cryptography. J. Cryptol. **5**(1), 3–28, (1992). ISSN: 1432-1378. https://doi.org/10.1007/BF00191318

12. IBM Quantum Challenge announcement. https://www.ibm.com/blogs/research/2020/04/ibm-quantum-challenge/

13. Abraham, H., et al.: Qiskit: An Open-source Framework for Quantum Computing (2019). https://doi.org/10.5281/zenodo.2562110

14. IBM Quantum Challenge BB84 exercise. https://github.com/qiskitcommunity/may4challengeexercises/blob/master/ex03/Challenge3BB84.ipynb

15. IBM Quantum Challenge repository. https://github.com/qiskit-community/may4challengeexercises

Approach to Cryptography from Differential Geometry with Example

Tetsuya Nagano$^{(\boxtimes)}$ and Hiroaki Anada

University of Nagasaki, Nagasaki 851-2195, Japan
{hnagano,anada}@sun.ac.jp

Abstract. We propose a public-key encryption scheme that arise from a kind of differential geometry called Finsler geometry. Our approach is first to observe a map of a tangent space to another tangent space, and find asymmetricity of linear parallel displacement, which is easy to compute but hard to invert. Then we construct an example of the map over the real numbers. By quantization, we propose a public-key encryption scheme. The scheme is proved to be IND-CCA2 secure under the new assumption of the decisional linear parallel displacement problem.

Keywords: Public-key encryption · IND-CCA2 · Finsler space · Linear parallel displacement · Differential geometry

1 Introduction

Mathematical structures that provides computationally hard problems form security basis in public-key cryptography. The integer-factoring and the discrete-logarithm are the representative two of them. In addition, post-quantum mathematical structures and their hard problems, such as the lattice structure and the shortest vector problem, have been discussed in the research community of cryptography for a decade. These structures are mainly based on algebra over finite fields and combinatorics; that is, in discrete mathematics.

1.1 Our Contribution and Related Work

We propose in this paper a *geometric approach* to public-key cryptography. The feature is that we start with a kind of differential geometry called *Finsler* geometry, which is in *continuous* mathematics. Then we proceed into the discrete treatise by quantization. Our key observation is that there is asymmetricity in the space of Finsler geometry. Then, by quantization, we are able to propose a problem for *linear parallel displacement*, which we abbreviate as *LPD*. Assuming that any instance of the LPD problem is computationally hard (the LPD assumption), we can prove that our proposed public-key encryption scheme is secure. Actually we prove that our proposed public-key encryption is secure in the meaning of indistinguishability against adaptive chosen-ciphertext attacks (IND-CCA2 secure).

© Springer Nature Switzerland AG 2021
D. Maimut et al. (Eds.): SecITC 2020, LNCS 12596, pp. 110–129, 2021.
https://doi.org/10.1007/978-3-030-69255-1_8

The base idea of our public-key encryption was first stated at Computer Security Symposium 2019 (CSS2019) by T. Nagano and H. Anada [29]. Further, at 2020 Symposium on Cryptography and Information Security (SCIS2020) [28], a new problem for linear parallel displacement are proposed. They proved onewayness security of their scheme under the assumption of computational difficulty of a variant of the LPD problem. In this paper, we prove a stronger security; that is, IND-CCA2 security, under the LPD assumption. The most factor leading this work successfully is to find out asymmetricity which Finsler spaces involve and computational difficulty of a problem for linear parallel displacement (the LPD assumption). This paper is the first work which applies Differential Geometry to Cryptography in earnest.

1.2   Overview of Our Strategy

Intuitively, the asymmetricity in the space of Finsler geometry means that a linear parallel displacement of any vector in a tangent space into another tangent space can be calculated by multiplying a square matrix, but the inverse linear parallel displacement of the image vector cannot be calculated by multiplying the inverse matrix. Actually it is mathematically (and hence computationally) impossible to find the matrix of the inverse direction. Quantizing the whole treatment from the set of real numbers to a discrete set, we obtain a map that is easy to compute but hard to invert. Assuming the computational hardness of a problem that is related to the onewayness of the map, we obtain a scheme that is prove to be IND-CCA2 secure.

2   Preliminaries

2.1   Finsler Geometry

Firstly we introduce Finsler geometry and Finsler space in roughly. Finsler geometry is one field of the differential geometry [11–16, 18–20]. It is an extension of Riemannian geometry which has been already known to many mathematicians. Many objects in Riemannian geometry have the coordinate x of a point $p(x)$ on M which is the base manifold with a local coordinate system $\{U_p, (x)\}$. Finsler geometry, however, many objects have not only a position x but a direction y at a point $p(x)$. Further tensorial calculus are extended to the tangent bundle TM of M [21–26]. In the following we put the definition of (real) Finsler space.

Definition 21. *Let $\mathcal{R}$ be the set of real numbers. For an n-dimensional real base manifold M and its tangent bundle TM, when a real continuous function $F(x, y) : TM \longrightarrow \mathcal{R}$ on TM satisfying the following conditions $(1) - (4)$ is given to TM, $(M, F(x, y))$ is called an n-dimensional real Finsler space and F is called a fundamental function or Finsler metric, where $x = (x^1, \cdots, x^n) = (x^i) \in M, y = (y^1, \cdots, y^n) = (y^i) \in T_x M, (x, y) \in TM.$*

(1) *(Positive value)* $\forall (x, y) \in TM, \ F(x, y) \geq 0 \ and \ F(x, y) = 0 \Leftrightarrow y = 0$

(2) *(Positively homogeneous)* $\forall (x,y) \in TM \setminus \{0\}, \forall \lambda > 0, \quad F(x, \lambda y) = \lambda F(x,y)$

(3) *(Differentiability)* $F : TM \setminus \{0\} \longrightarrow \mathcal{R}$

(4) *(Strongly convex)*

Symmetric matrix $(g_{ij}(x,y))$ *defined by* *(metric tensor field)*

$$g_{ij}(x,y) := \frac{1}{2} \frac{\partial^2 F^2}{\partial y^i \partial y^j} \quad (i,j = 1, \cdots, n)$$

is positive definite.

Hereafter, we call $(M, F(x,y))$ *Finsler space, shortly.*

Remark 21. *All objects on Finsler space depend on a position x and a direction y. In particular, if $F(x,y) \neq F(x,-y)$ is satisfied, in general,*

(1) *Curves c on M have different length, namely, when a point p is a start point and a point q is an end point, the length from q to p along c is different from the length from p to q.*

(2) *Geodesics on M have different image, namely, the image of geodesic from p to q is different from the image of it from q to p.*

(3) *From (2), if the distance of two points p and q is defined by the arc-length of the geodesic of p and q, there are two distances.*

(4) *There are also different phases on parallel displacement. Move a tangent vector v from p to q on a curve c, and further, move back from q to p then we have a vector unlike v at p(**asymmetric property of linear parallel displacement**) [27].*

Hereafter we consider the only case that Finsler space $(M, F(x,y))$ satisfies $F(x,y) \neq F(x,-y)$.

We use the asymmetric property of linear parallel displacement of tangent vectors to construct a new public key encryption. So in the following the notion of it is shown in detail.

Necessary objects

(1) Metric tensor field $g_{ij}(x,y)$ (in (4) of Definition 21),

(2) Nonlinear connection $N_j^i(x,y)$ $(i,j = 1, 2, \cdots, n = dimM)$,

(3) Horizontal connection $F_{rj}^i(x,y)$ $(i,j,r = 1, 2, \cdots, n = dimM)$,

(4) Geodesic

(5) Linear parallel displacement Π_c

Calculation of (2) and **Calculation of (3)** (See (1) in §6 Appendix)

Calculation of (4)

Geodesic is the curve which is minimizing of the distance between two points locally. Then, a geodesic $c(t) = (c^i(t))$ satisfies the following equation

$$\frac{d^2 c^i}{dt^2} + \sum_{j,r} F_{jr}^i(c, \dot{c}) \dot{c}^j \dot{c}^r = 0 \quad (\dot{c} = (\dot{c}^i), \dot{c}^i = \frac{dc^i}{dt}), \tag{1}$$

where t is an affine parameter.

Calculation of (5)

Let $c(t) = (c^i(t))$ be a curve with a start point $p(t_0)$ and an end point $q(t_1)$. Then, for a curve $c(t) = (c^i(t))$ and a tangent vector field $v(t) = (v^i(t))$ along $c(t)$, $v(t)$ is called a **parallel vector field** along $c(t)$ if $v(t)$ satisfies the following equation

$$\frac{dv^i}{dt} + \sum_{j,r} F^i_{jr}(c,\dot{c})v^j\dot{c}^r = 0 \quad (\dot{c}^r = \frac{dc^r}{dt}), \tag{2}$$

and we call the linear map $\Pi_c : \; v(t_0) \in T_pM \;\longrightarrow\; v(t_1) \in T_qM$ a **linear parallel displacement** along c [27,30–33].

Asymmetric Property of Linear Parallel Displacement

For a curve $c(t) = (c^i(t))(t_0 \leq t \leq t_1)$, the reverse curve $c^{-1}(\tau)$ is defined by $c^{-1}(\tau) := c(t_0 + t_1 - \tau)(t_0 \leq \tau \leq t_1)$, where $p = c(t_0), q = c(t_1), q = c^{-1}(t_0), p = c^{-1}(t_1)$. If the linear parallel displacement $\Pi_c : T_pM \;\longrightarrow\; T_qM$ and the reverse displacement $\Pi_{c^{-1}} : T_qM \;\longrightarrow\; T_pM$ satisfy

$$\Pi_{c^{-1}} \circ \Pi_c = Identity \tag{3}$$

then the linear parallel displacement Π_c is called symmetric on c. **If (3) is not satisfied, namely, $\Pi_{c^{-1}} \circ \Pi_c \neq Identity$, then Π_c is called which has asymmetric property.**

Remark 22. *Our new public-key encryption depends on asymmetric property of linear parallel displacement.*

(1) *We put the following Finsler tensor field*

$$H^i_j(x,y) := \sum_r F^i_{rj}(x,y)y^r + \sum_r F^i_{rj}(x,-y)(-y^r). \tag{4}$$

Then, for a curve c, Π_c is symmetric if and only if

$$H^i_j(c,\dot{c}) = 0 \tag{5}$$

is satisfies. Therefore **we have to use the curve c satisfying $H^i_j(c,\dot{c}) \neq 0$.** (2) *We use a geodesic as a curve playing linear parallel displacement role. The following quantity $E(v)$*

$$E(v) := \sum_{i,j} g_{ij}(c,\dot{c})v^iv^j \tag{6}$$

is called **energy** *of a vector v on c. Then it is known* **energy of parallel vector field is preserved on a geodesic by linear parallel displacement** *[27,30–33].*

3   Our Proposed Public-Key Encryption

In this section, we introduce the plan of new public-key encryption applying Finsler space and asymmetric linear parallel displacement. Follow the recipe (Step1-Step13) , then we can obtain a public-key encryption. Note that, though we describe our scheme using the technical terms over $\mathcal{R}$, we assume λ-bit uniform quantization for each variable, where λ is the security parameter.

Recipe

Step1. From Finsler metric $F(x, y)$, calculate g_{ij}, N_j^i, F_{rj}^i.

Step2. Put the start point $p(t_0)$ and the end point $q(t_1)$.

Step3. From (1), get the geodesic $c(t)$ between p and q.

Step4. Check $H_j^i(c, \dot{c}) \neq 0$. If $H_j^i(c, \dot{c}) = 0$, then return to Step2.

Step5. From (2), get the linear parallel displacement Π_c.

Step6. Give a regular matrix $C(\tau)(\tau \in_R \mathcal{R})$ as a linear transformation on T_pM.

Step7. Put n-dimensional vectors $v_0 := (v_0^1, \cdots, v_0^n)(v_0^i \neq 0; i = 1.2.\cdots, n)$ and $v_1 := C(\tau)v_0$.

Step8. Put a point $r(t_2)(t_0 < t_2 < t_1)$ on c.

Step9. Move v_1 to $r(t_2)$ by Π_c and put the value by $v_2(:= \Pi_c(t_2)v_1)$.

Step10. Give $n + 1$ pieces non-zero forms $f_0, f_1 \cdots, f_n$ defined by parameters of Finsler metric $F(x, y)$, the geodesic c and t_0, t_1.

Step11. Calculate the energy $E(v_1)$ at the point r in the following splitting form $E_0 + E_1 + \cdots + E_n$

$$
\begin{aligned}
E(v_1) &= \sum_{i,j} g_{ij}(p, \dot{c})v_1^i v_1^j = {}^t v_1 G(p, \dot{c})v_1 \\
&= \sum_{i,j} g_{ij}(r, \dot{c})v_2^i v_2^j = {}^t v_2 G(r, \dot{c})v_2 = {}^t v_0 \, {}^t C(\tau) \, {}^t \Pi_c(t_2) G(r, \dot{c}) \Pi_c(t_2) C(\tau)v_0 \\
&= E_0 + E_1 + \cdots + E_n \\
&= \frac{E_0}{f_0} f_0 + \frac{E_1}{f_1 v_0^1} f_1 v_0^1 + \cdots + \frac{E_n}{f_n v_0^n} f_n v_0^n
\end{aligned}
$$

where $G(r, \dot{c}) = (g_{ij}(r, \dot{c}))$ and $E_0, \cdots, E_n$ have parameters $v_0^1, \cdots, v_0^n, t_2$ and τ.

Step12. Let consider a vector $V = (\frac{E_1}{f_1 v_0^1}, \cdots, \frac{E_n}{f_n v_0^n})$, and move V to a point $s(\tau)$ on c by $\Pi_c(\tau)$.

Step13. Put the value by $V_3 = \Pi_c(\tau)V = {}^t(V_3^1, \cdots, V_3^n)$.

Finally, we obtain "Public-key encryption" in the following

Secret key $SK = \{f_0, f_1, \cdots, f_n, \Pi_c(\tau), E(v_1)\}$

Public key $PK = \{\frac{E_0}{f_0}, V_3^1, \cdots, V_3^n\}$.

Encryption

1. Given a constant vector: $dv = (dv^1, \cdots, dv^n)$, where $dv^i > 0 (i = 1, 2, \cdots, n)$.
2. **Plaintext**: n-dimensional vector $v = (v^1, \cdots, v^n)(v^i \geq 0; i = 1, 2, \cdots, n)$.
3. Put $v_0 := v + dv$.
4. Given random values $\alpha, \beta_0, \beta_1, \cdots, \beta_n$, where $\alpha, \beta_i > 0$ and $\beta_i \neq \beta_j (i \neq j)$ $(i, j = 0, 1, \cdots, n)$.
5. (1) Set $\tau := \alpha$, $t_2 := \beta_0$ and calculate PK

$$ct_0 := \{\frac{E_0(v_0, \alpha, \beta_0)}{f_0}, V_3^1(v_0, \alpha, \beta_0), \cdots, V_3^n(v_0, \alpha, \beta_0)\}.$$

(2) Set $\tau := \alpha$, $t_2 := \beta_1$ and calculate PK

$$ct_1 := \{\frac{E_0(v_0, \alpha, \beta_1)}{f_0}, V_3^1(v_0, \alpha, \beta_1), \cdots, V_3^n(v_0, \alpha, \beta_1)\}.$$

$$\vdots \qquad\qquad \vdots \qquad\qquad \vdots$$

$(n+1)$ Set $\tau := \alpha$, $t_2 := \beta_n$ and calculate PK

$$ct_n := \{\frac{E_0(v_0, \alpha, \beta_n)}{f_0}, V_3^1(v_0, \alpha, \beta_n), \cdots, V_3^n(v_0, \alpha, \beta_n)\}.$$

Then a **ciphertext** ct of v is given by

$$ct = \{ct_0, ct_1 \cdots, ct_n\}.$$

Decryption

1. For $X^1, X^2, \cdots, X^n$, put $SKX := \{f_0, f_1 X^1, \cdots, f_n X^n\}$.
2. For a ciphertext $ct = \{ct_0, ct_1 \cdots, ct_n\}$, firstly calculate V, namely,

$$(ct_0) \quad V := \Pi_c^{-1}(\tau)V_3 = (\frac{\bar{E}_1(v_0, \alpha, \beta_0)}{f_1 v_0^1}, \cdots, \frac{\bar{E}_n(v_0, \alpha, \beta_0)}{f_n v_0^n}),$$

$$(ct_1) \quad V := \Pi_c^{-1}(\tau)V_3 = (\frac{\bar{E}_1(v_0, \alpha, \beta_1)}{f_1 v_0^1}, \cdots, \frac{\bar{E}_n(v_0, \alpha, \beta_1)}{f_n v_0^n}),$$

$$\vdots \qquad\qquad \vdots \qquad\qquad \vdots$$

$$(ct_n) \quad V := \Pi_c^{-1}(\tau)V_3 = (\frac{\bar{E}_1(v_0, \alpha, \beta_n)}{f_1 v_0^1}, \cdots, \frac{\bar{E}_n(v_0, \alpha, \beta_n)}{f_n v_0^n})$$

and construct the following $n+1$ pieces linear forms of $X^1, X^2, \cdots, X^n$

$$ct_0 \cdot SKX := \frac{E_0(v_0, \alpha, \beta_0)}{f_0} f_0 + \frac{\bar{E}_1(v_0, \alpha, \beta_0)}{f_1 v_0^1} f_1 X^1 + \cdots + \frac{\bar{E}_n(v_0, \alpha, \beta_0)}{f_n v_0^n} f_n X^n$$

$$ct_1 \cdot SKX := \frac{E_0(v_0, \alpha, \beta_1)}{f_0} f_0 + \frac{\bar{E}_1(v_0, \alpha, \beta_1)}{f_1 v_0^1} f_1 X^1 + \cdots + \frac{\bar{E}_n(v_0, \alpha, \beta_1)}{f_n v_0^n} f_n X^n$$

$$\vdots \qquad\qquad \vdots \qquad\qquad \vdots$$

$$ct_n \cdot SKX := \frac{E_0(v_0, \alpha, \beta_n)}{f_0} f_0 + \frac{\bar{E}_1(v_0, \alpha, \beta_n)}{f_1 v_0^1} f_1 X^1 + \cdots + \frac{\bar{E}_n(v_0, \alpha, \beta_n)}{f_n v_0^n} f_n X^n,$$

where each component $\bar{E}_i(v_0, \alpha, \beta_j)$ $(i, j = 1, \cdots, n)$ has unknown value τ.

3. For $X^1, X^2, \cdots, X^n$, solve the following simultaneous system of linear equations

$$
\begin{cases}
ct_1 \cdot SKX = ct_0 \cdot SKX \\
ct_2 \cdot SKX = ct_0 \cdot SKX \\
\quad \vdots \qquad \vdots \qquad \vdots \\
ct_n \cdot SKX = ct_0 \cdot SKX
\end{cases}
\tag{7}
$$

Then obtained answers X^1, X^2, $\cdots$, X^n have unknown value τ. Next, input X^1, X^2, $\cdots$, X^n to the following energy equation

$$
ct_0 \cdot SKX = E(v_1)|_{v_0^1 = X^1, v_0^2 = X^2}.
\tag{8}
$$

Then we have an algebraic equation of τ. By solving the above equation, we can obtain the value $\tau = \alpha$. Then by using the value α to the X^1, X^2, $\cdots$, X^n, we have the initial vector $v_0 = (v_0^1, \cdots, v_0^n)$ as follows

$$
v_0^1 = X^1, \ v_0^2 = X^2, \ \cdots, \ v_0^n = X^n.
$$

Finally, we get the plaintext $v = (v^1, \cdots, v^n)$ as follows

$$
v^1 = X^1 - dv^1, v^2 = X^2 - dv^2, \cdots, v^n = X^n - dv^n.
$$

Remark 31. (1) *The solution c of (1) is obtained in the continuous real number field $\mathcal{R}$.*
(2) *The solution Π_c of (2) is also obtained in the continuous real number field $\mathcal{R}$.*
(3) *The components of the matrix $C(\tau)$ depend on a real parameter τ.*
(4) *The energy $E(v_1)$ depends on only $p(t_0)$ and v_1 on c. Even if at other point $r(t_2)$ the energy is calculated, the value $E(v_1)$ is independent of t_2. We must take the form $E(v_1)$ apart by $E_0, E_1, \cdots, E_n$ involving t_2. It is very important.*
(5) *The regularity of system of linear Equations (7) is shown in a special case in Sect. 4.*

4   Example

In this section, we show an example of public-key encryption using 2-dimensional Finsler space [27]. Let (x, y) be the coordinate of the base manifold $M = \mathcal{R}^2$ and $(\dot{x}, \dot{y})$ the coordinate of $T_{(x,y)}M$, namely, $x = x^1, y = x^2, \dot{x} = y^1, \dot{y} = y^2$. The Finsler metric $F(x, y, \dot{x}, \dot{y})$ is as follows

$$
F(x, y, \dot{x}, \dot{y}) = \sqrt{a^2 \dot{x}^2 + b^2 \dot{y}^2} - h_1 x \dot{x} - h_2 y \dot{y},
\tag{9}
$$

where all a, b, h_1, h_2 are positive numbers.

According to Recipe in Sect. 3, various objects are obtained. However, in the following representation of them are on the geodesic c only.

Geodesic: straight line

$$c_m(t) = (c^1(t), c^2(t)) = \left(\frac{1}{a\sqrt{1+m^2}} t, \frac{m}{b\sqrt{1+m^2}} t \right) \tag{10}$$

$$p = c_m(t_0), \quad q = c_m(t_1), \quad r = c_m(t),$$

where the equation of the above straight line is $y = \frac{a}{b}mx$ on M.

Metric tensor field: $g_{ij}(c, \dot{c})$ (See (2) in §6 Appendix)

Nonlinear connection: $N_j^i(c, \dot{c}) = \sum_r F_{jr}^i \dot{c}^r$ (See (3) in §6 Appendix)

Linear parallel displacement: $\Pi_{c_m}(t)$ (See (4) in §6 Appendix))

$$\Pi_{c_m}(t) = \begin{pmatrix} B_1^1 & B_2^1 \\ B_1^2 & B_2^2 \end{pmatrix} \tag{11}$$

Hereafter we treat a special case which have a parameters set FNA of the Finsler metric $F(x, y, \dot{x}, \dot{y})$, the geodesic $c(t)$ and t_0, t_1 as follows:

$$\text{FNA} = \{a, \ b, \ h_1, \ h_2, m, t_0, t_1\} = \{10, \ 6, \ 4, \ 7, \frac{1}{3}, \frac{351}{499}, 13\} \tag{12}$$

and **Transformation of** $T_p M$: $C(\tau)$ and $\Pi_c(\tau)$

$$C(\tau) = \begin{pmatrix} \tau & 1 \\ \tau - 1 & 1 \end{pmatrix} \text{ and } \Pi_c(\tau) = \begin{pmatrix} \frac{3\left(5425\tau^2 + 1309392\tau - 34902900\right)}{499\tau^3} & -\frac{135\left(217\tau^2 - 5169\tau - 1396116\right)}{499\tau^3} \\ -\frac{180\left(93\tau^2 - 12124\tau + 323175\right)}{499\tau^3} & \frac{9\left(3348\tau^2 + 43075\tau + 11634300\right)}{499\tau^3} \end{pmatrix} \tag{13}$$

In Step10, we put the secret key SK, the constant vector dv and the energy $E(v_1)$:

$$SK = \{f_0, \ f_1, \ f_2\} = \{mh_1, at_0h_2, bt_1h_2^2\} = \{\frac{4}{3}, \frac{24570}{499}, \ 3822\} \tag{14}$$

$$dv = (1234, 5432) \tag{15}$$

$$E(v_1) = \frac{1}{1245005000}((15443226319 7\tau^2 - 78738768234\tau + 42104793807)(v_0^1)^2$$
$$+ 2(154432263197\tau - 39369384117)v_0^1 v_0^2 + 154432263197(v_0^2)^2) \tag{16}$$

In Remark 22, it is stated that the energy of a vector v is preserving on geodesics. Namely, if a vector field v on a geodesic c is parallel, the energy of the parallel vector v is constant value on every point on c. On the other hand, at every point of c, the values of metric tensor $g_{ij}(c, \dot{c})$ and the components v^i of the vector v are different. However the value of (6) is constant. Namely, the components $g_{ij}(c, \dot{c})$ and v^i depend on the parameter t_2, however, the form (6) is independent of t_2.

In Step11, understanding above, we must split the energy $E(v_1)$ as $E_0 + E_1 \cdots + E_n$ which each $E_i(i = 0, 1, \cdots, n)$ involves t_2. Another important point is that each $E_i(i = 0, 1, \cdots, n)$ is a rational expression with respect to all parameters. It is better than a real expression because that every plaintext is regarded as a positive integer with the finite number of digits. This is very important for encryption. The method of transport to the rational expression is different case by case. In this case, from coefficients of Π_{cm}, choose a rational number $k(> 0)$ as $a^2 b^2 + a^2 b^2 m^2 - (b^2 h_1 + a^2 h_2 m^2)t_0$ is equal to k^2, then you have a rational expression. We show an example of splitting $E(v_1) = E_0 + E_1 \cdots + E_n$ in Appendix.

Last we calculate $V_3 = \Pi_c(\tau)V = {}^t(V_3^1, V_3^2)$, where $V = {}^t(\frac{E_1}{f_1 v_0^1}, \frac{E_2}{f_2 v_0^2})$ (See Appendix).

Then we have the public key $PK = \{\dfrac{E_0}{f_0}, V_3^1, V_3^2\}$.

Next we consider about solutions of the linear system (7). It is to be desirable that the system (7) has a unique solution. It owes the regularity of the following matrix MLS because of ${}^t(\frac{E_1}{f_1 v_0^1}, \frac{E_2}{f_2 v_0^2}) = \Pi_c^{-1}(\tau)V_3$:

$$
MLS = \begin{pmatrix} \dfrac{E_1(v_0, \alpha, \beta_1) - E_1(v_0, \alpha, \beta_0)}{v_0^1} & \dfrac{E_2(v_0, \alpha, \beta_1) - E_2(v_0, \alpha, \beta_0)}{v_0^2} \\ \dfrac{E_1(v_0, \alpha, \beta_2) - E_1(v_0, \alpha, \beta_0)}{v_0^1} & \dfrac{E_2(v_0, \alpha, \beta_2) - E_2(v_0, \alpha, \beta_0)}{v_0^2} \end{pmatrix}.
$$

MLS is the main part of coefficient matrix of (7). Under considering the positivity of $v_0^1, v_0^2, \beta_0, \beta_1, \beta_2((\beta_0 - \beta_1)(\beta_1 - \beta_2)(\beta_2 - \beta_0) \neq 0)$ we calculate the determinant of MLS. For example, we have $v_0^1 = 8040, v_0^2 = 7778, \beta_0 = 1, \beta_1 = 2, \beta_2 = 3$, then the regularity of MLS is equivalent to that the following polynomial $f(\tau)$ of degree four is not zero.

$$f(\tau) = 3.60310 \times 10^{39} \tau^4 - 1.12581 \times 10^{40} \tau^3 + 6.96943 \times 10^{39} \tau^2 + 7.27339 \times 10^{39} \tau - 6.79067 \times 10^{39}$$

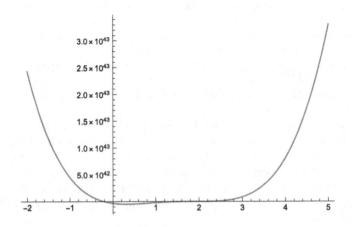

Fig. 1. $y = f(\tau)$

The number of zero points τ is four at most. If $\tau = \alpha > 3$(or $\alpha < -1$), then $f(\alpha) \neq 0$ is satisfied (cf. Fig. 1). Thus we have enough α satisfying $f(\alpha) \neq 0$. In general, for given $v_0^1, v_0^2, \beta_0, \beta_1, \beta_2$, the determinant of MLS is polynomial of degree four with respect to τ. We have enough $\tau = \alpha$ satisfying $f(\alpha) \neq 0$ at any time.

(We explain the concrete example in (7) of §6 Appendix.)

5   IND-CCA2 Security

In this section, we prove that our proposed public-key encryption is secure in the meaning of indistinguishability against adaptive chosen-ciphertext attacks (IND-CCA2 secure). On the line of recent work [28,29], we state a computational problem and assumption for linear parallel displacement in a refined forms, as follows.

Computational Problem for Linear Parallel Displacement (LPD)
Suppose that each variable is quantized with λ-bit, uniformly. Let (M, F) be a Finsler space and p, q be points on M. For a geodesic c from p to q, the problem is stated as the computational problem to find values of the parameters of linear parallel displacement along c from $T_p M$ to $T_q M$, where $T_p M, T_q M$ are tangent spaces at p, q respectively.

LPD Assumption
For a fixed Finsler space with $H_j^i \neq 0$, there exists no polynomial time algorithm to solve a random instance of LPD. As for the example in Sect. 4, the LPD assumption means that seven parameters $a, b, h_1, h_2, m, t_0, t_1$(or t_2) is not determined by any polynomial time algorithm in λ.

First of all, we state that asymmetric property of linear parallel displacement is necessary condition to keep LPD assumption.

Remark 51. *If Finsler space $(M, F(x, y))$ satisfies $H_j^i = 0$, then the linear parallel displacement is symmetric. Then, (3) is true. The geodesics of Finsler space with its metric (3) are straight lines. The inverse curve c_m^{-1} of a geodesic (10) is also geodesic as follows*

$$c_m^{-1}(t) = \left(\frac{1}{a\sqrt{1+m^2}}(t_0 + t_1 - t), \frac{m}{b\sqrt{1+m^2}}(t_0 + t_1 - t) \right).$$

Further, since the linear parallel displacement is symmetric, the inverse vector field $v^{-1}(t) = (v^1(t_0 + t_1 - t), v^2(t_0 + t_1 - t))$ of a parallel vector field $v(t)$ is also parallel along c_m^{-1}. Then we can calculate the matrix $\Pi_{c_m^{-1}}$ of the inverse linear parallel displacement by the same way as Π_{c_m}. In this time we note $\Pi_{c_m^{-1}}$ having the same parameters to Π_{c_m}. Therefore, from (3), we can recognize all parameters a, b, h_1, h_2, t_0, t_1(or t_2) are not independent. This fact show to us that the attacker already knows some informations of $\Pi_{c^{-1}}$ for Π_c. Namely, LPD assumption is broken.

According to above argument, we have

Proposition 51. *For Finsler space $(M, F(x, y))$ with the metric (9), included parameters in Π_c are independent.*

$(\because)$ *The Matrix $\Pi_{c-1} \circ \Pi_c$ has the parameter t_1 or t_2. Namely, $\Pi_{c-1} \circ \Pi_c$ is not constant.*   □

Proposition 52. *In general, there is no Riemannian space where the LPD assumption holds.*

$(\because)$ *All Riemannian spaces are symmetric.*   □

From now, we study IND-CCA2 for this public-key encryption(PKE) in Sect. 4.

For any given PPT attacker $\mathcal{A}$ on PKE, we construct a PPT solver $\mathcal{B}$ of a random instance of the LPD problem as below, where PPT is probabilistic polynomial-time.

First, it is assumed that $\mathcal{A}$ knows that each term of the inverse matrix $\Pi_c^{-1}(\tau)$ is a polynomial of degree m at most, namely, the form of the inverse matrix $\Pi_c^{-1}(\tau)$ is as follows

$$\Pi_c^{-1}(\tau) = \begin{pmatrix} a_0 + a_1\tau + \cdots + a_m\tau^m & b_0 + b_1\tau + \cdots + b_m\tau^m \\ c_0 + c_1\tau + \cdots + c_m\tau^m & d_0 + d_1\tau + \cdots + d_m\tau^m \end{pmatrix},$$

where unknown a_i, b_i, c_i, d_i $(i = 0, 1, \cdots m)$ are all rational numbers and m is unknown. Next, after $\mathcal{A}$ is given the public key PK,

(1) $\mathcal{A}$ assume $m = 1$ and by using a plaintext v_0 and parameters $\alpha_1, \alpha_2, \cdots, \alpha_j$ $(j \geq 4)$, $\mathcal{A}$ can obtain triples $(v_0, ct_1, \alpha_1), \cdots, (v_0, ct_j, \alpha_j)$, where $ct_i = \{\frac{E_0(\alpha_i)}{f_0}, V_3^1, V_3^2\}$.

From $ct_1 = \{\frac{E_0(\alpha_1)}{f_0}, V_3^1, V_3^2\}$, $\mathcal{A}$ can, formally, make the form $\bar{V} = \Pi_c^{-1}(\alpha_1)V_3$, $V_3 = (V_3^1, V_3^2)$ as follows

$$\bar{V} = \left(\bar{E}_1(\alpha_1), \bar{E}_2(\alpha_1)\right),$$

where $\bar{E}_1(\alpha_1), \bar{E}_2(\alpha_1)$ have eight unknown a_i, b_i, c_i, d_i $(i = 0, 1)$. Then using the formal $\overline{SKX} = (Y_0, v_0^1 Y_1, v_0^2 Y_2)$ $(v_0 = (v_0^1, v_0^2))$, $\mathcal{A}$ has the form

$$\frac{E_0(\alpha_1)}{f_0}Y_0 + \bar{E}_1(\alpha_1)v_0^1 Y_1 + \bar{E}_2(\alpha_1)v_0^2 Y_2.$$

From others $ct_2 = \{\frac{E_0(\alpha_2)}{f_0}, V_3^1, V_3^2\}$, $ct_3 = \{\frac{E_0(\alpha_3)}{f_0}, V_3^1, V_3^2\}$, he has the following system

$$\begin{cases} \frac{E_0(\alpha_2)}{f_0}Y_0 + \bar{E}_1(\alpha_2)v_0^1 Y_1 + \bar{E}_2(\alpha_2)v_0^2 Y_2 = \frac{E_0(\alpha_1)}{f_0}Y_0 + \bar{E}_1(\alpha_1)v_0^1 Y_1 + \bar{E}_2(\alpha_1)v_0^2 Y_2 \\ \frac{E_0(\alpha_3)}{f_0}Y_0 + \bar{E}_1(\alpha_3)v_0^1 Y_1 + \bar{E}_2(\alpha_3)v_0^2 Y_2 = \frac{E_0(\alpha_1)}{f_0}Y_0 + \bar{E}_1(\alpha_1)v_0^1 Y_1 + \bar{E}_2(\alpha_1)v_0^2 Y_2 \end{cases}$$

If $\mathcal{A}$ solve this system for (Y_1, Y_2), Y_1 and Y_2 can be expressed as forms with a_i, b_i, c_i, d_i $(i = 0, 1)$ and Y_0. From other three triples (v_0, ct_k, α_k), $(v_0, ct_{k'}, \alpha_{k'})$, $(v_0, ct_{k''}, \alpha_{k''})$ $\mathcal{A}$ also has a pair (Y_1, Y_2). Then, from the former Y_1 and the latter Y_1, $\mathcal{A}$ has one equation with respect to a_i, b_i, c_i, d_i $(i = 0, 1)$. Further, from the former Y_2 and the latter Y_2, $\mathcal{A}$ also has one more equation with respect to a_i, b_i, c_i, d_i $(i = 0, 1)$. According to the same manner, $\mathcal{A}$ can have eight independent equations for a_i, b_i, c_i, d_i $(i = 0, 1)$ from $j \gg 4$. If $\mathcal{A}$ solve them with respect to a_i, b_i, c_i, d_i $(i = 0, 1)$, then $\mathcal{A}$ can obtain the eight values of a_i, b_i, c_i, d_i $(i = 0, 1)$. Further, when $\mathcal{A}$ issues a decryption query with ciphertext ct, $\mathcal{A}$ has a pair (v, ct) of the plaintext v and a cipher ct. By using (v, ct) and $\Pi_c^{-1}(\tau)$, $\mathcal{A}$ can obtain $\tau = \alpha$. Finally, $\mathcal{A}$ tries encryption with (v, α) and if $\mathcal{A}$ can obtain the cipher ct, then $\Pi_c^{-1}(\tau)$ is correct, else (2) assume $m = 2$ and $\mathcal{A}$ does the same calculations till obtaining the correct inverse matrix $\Pi_c^{-1}(\tau)$. This trial go to the end with a polynomial time because m is finite.

Here we assume that there exists a polynomial time algorithm which can solve the ciphertext. $\mathcal{A}$ gives two plaintexts m_0, m_1 to $\mathcal{B}$ and $\mathcal{A}$ have a ciphertext ct^* from $\mathcal{B}$. If $\mathcal{B}$ adapts the determined $\Pi_c(\tau)$ to this pair $(m_b, ct^*)(b = 0$ or $1)$, $\mathcal{B}$ can obtain the value $\tau = \alpha$. What is the mean of $\alpha(= \tau)$? It is clear that α expresses the end point of the linear parallel displacement $\Pi_c(\alpha)$. This fact means that if there exists a polynomial time algorithm which can solve the ciphertext, then LPD assumption is broken through by the polynomial time algorithm. Namely, we get the PPT solver $\mathcal{B}$ of a random instance of the LPD problem.

Then we have

Theorem 51. *If the LPD assumption holds, then our public-key encryption scheme is IND-CCA2 secure.*

Remark 52. (1) *Let consider the inverse problem in the following*

Inverse Problem: *If the LPD assumption is broken, is any ciphertext solved ? The answer is "Yes".*

Because. *The attacker can obtain the linear parallel displacement Π_c by the broken LPD assumption, easily.*

(2) *We notice one more desirable situation. There is the case that a different curve giving the inverse parallel displacement exists even if Finsler space is asymmetric. That is, there is a curve $\bar{c}$ such that $\Pi_{\bar{c}} \circ \Pi_c = I$. The Finsler space with the following metric*

$$F(x, y, \dot{x}, \dot{y}) = \sqrt{\dot{x}^2 + \dot{y}^2} - y\dot{x}$$

is asymmetric and its geodesics are circles with diameter 1 [27].

(3) *Finally we notice about quantization. By transformation to rational expressions of exact solutions $\Pi_c, E_0, V_3^1, \cdots$, we succeed the quantization of this public key encryption, namely, any rational values plaintext corresponds to rational values ciphertext. If a plaintext is integer, then decrypted ciphertext is also integer. In this paper, all calculation are done by "Mathematica 11.3" and components value of a ciphertext have sixteen decimal places. In particular, all approximate values of decrypted integers have five decimal places exactly.*

6   Appendix

(1) Calculation of (2) (in p.3)

$$N_j^i(x,y) = \sum_r \gamma_{rj}^i(x,y)y^r - \sum_{p,q,r} C_{jr}^i(x,y)\gamma_{pq}^r(x,y)y^p y^q,$$

where

$$\gamma_{pq}^i(x,y) = \sum_h \frac{1}{2}g^{hi}\left(\frac{\partial g_{ph}}{\partial x^q} + \frac{\partial g_{hq}}{\partial x^p} - \frac{\partial g_{pq}}{\partial x^h}\right),$$

$$C_{jr}^i(x,y) = \sum_h \frac{1}{2}g^{hi}\frac{\partial g_{jh}}{\partial y^r}.$$

Calculation of (3) (in p.3)

$$F_{jr}^i(x,y) = \sum_h \frac{1}{2}g^{hi}\left(\frac{\delta g_{jh}}{\delta x^r} + \frac{\delta g_{hr}}{\delta x^j} - \frac{\delta g_{jr}}{\delta x^h}\right),$$

where

$$\frac{\delta}{\delta x^i} = \frac{\partial}{\partial x^i} - \sum_r N_i^r \frac{\partial}{\partial y^r}.$$

Here the indices $h, i, j, \cdots, p, q, r, \cdots$ of $\sum$ run from 1 to $n(= dim M)$.

(2) Metric tensor field: $g_{ij}(c, \dot{c})$ (in p.8.)

$$g_{11} = \frac{1}{a^2 b^2 (m^2+1)^2}(b^2 m^4 a^4 + b^2 a^4 + 2b^2 m^2 a^4 - (h_2 m^4 a^4 + 3b^2 h_1 m^2 a^2$$
$$+ 2b^2 h_1 a^2)t + (b^2 h_1^2 + b^2 h_1^2 m^2)t^2)$$

$$g_{12} = \frac{-1}{ab(m^2+1)^2}((h_2 a^2 m + b^2 h_1 m^3)t - (h_1 h_2 m^3 + h_1 h_2 m)t^2)$$

$$g_{21} = g_{12}$$

$$g_{22} = \frac{1}{a^2 b^2 (m^2+1)^2}(a^2 m^4 b^4 + a^2 b^4 + 2a^2 m^2 b^4 - (h_1 b^4 + 2a^2 h_2 m^4 b^2$$
$$+ 3a^2 h_2 m^2 b^2)t + (a^2 h_2^2 m^4 + a^2 h_2^2 m^2)t^2)$$

(3) Nonlinear Connection: $N^i_j(c, \dot{c}) = \sum_r F^i_{jr} \dot{c}^r$ (in p.8)

$$N^1_1 = \frac{1}{2\left(a^2\left(h_2 m^2 t - b^2\left(m^2+1\right)\right) + b^2 h_1 t\right)^2}\left(a^4 h_2 m^4\left(h_2 t - b^2\right) + a^2 b^2 h_1\left(3 h_2 m^2 t\right.\right.$$
$$\left.\left.- b^2\left(3m^2+2\right)\right) + 2b^4 h_1^2 t\right)$$

$$N^1_2 = \frac{1}{2\left(a^2\left(h_2 m^2 t - b^2\left(m^2+1\right)\right) + b^2 h_1 t\right)^2}\left(abm\left(b^2 h_2\left(h_1 t - a^2\left(m^2+2\right)\right)\right.\right.$$
$$\left.\left. + a^2 h_2^2 m^2 t + b^4 h_1\right)\right)$$

$$N^2_1 = \frac{1}{2\left(a^2\left(h_2 m^2 t - b^2\left(m^2+1\right)\right) + b^2 h_1 t\right)^2}\left(abm\left(a^4 h_2 m^2 + h_1 t\left(a^2 h_2 m^2 + b^2 h_1\right)\right.\right.$$
$$\left.\left. - a^2 b^2 h_1\left(2m^2+1\right)\right)\right)$$

$$N^2_2 = \frac{1}{2\left(a^2\left(h_2 m^2 t - b^2\left(m^2+1\right)\right) + b^2 h_1 t\right)^2}\left(a^4 h_2 m^2\left(2 h_2 m^2 t - b^2\left(2m^2+3\right)\right)\right.$$
$$\left. - a^2 b^2 h_1\left(b^2 - 3 h_2 m^2 t\right) + b^4 h_1^2 t\right)$$

(4) The components $B^1_1, B^2_1, B^1_2, B^2_2$ **of** $\Pi_{cm}(t)$ (in p.8)

$$B^1_1 = -\frac{1}{\left(a^2\left(b^2\left(m^2+1\right) - h_2 m^2(t+t_0)\right) - b^2 h_1(t+t_0)\right)^{3/2}}$$
$$\times\left(a^2\left(h_2 m^2(t+t_0)\sqrt{a^2\left(b^2\left(m^2+1\right) - h_2 m^2 t_0\right) - b^2 h_1 t_0}\right.\right.$$
$$\left.- b^2\left(\sqrt{a^2\left(b^2\left(m^2+1\right) - h_2 m^2(t+t_0)\right) - b^2 h_1(t+t_0)} + m^2\sqrt{a^2\left(b^2\left(m^2+1\right) - h_2 m^2 t_0\right) - b^2 h_1 t_0}\right)\right)$$
$$\left. + b^2 h_1 t_0\sqrt{a^2\left(b^2\left(m^2+1\right) - h_2 m^2(t+t_0)\right) - b^2 h_1(t+t_0)}\right)$$

$$B^1_2 = \frac{1}{\left(a^2\left(b^2\left(m^2+1\right) - h_2 m^2(t+t_0)\right) - b^2 h_1(t+t_0)\right)^{3/2}}$$
$$\times\left(abm\left(b^2\left(\sqrt{a^2\left(b^2\left(m^2+1\right) - h_2 m^2(t+t_0)\right) - b^2 h_1(t+t_0)}\right.\right.\right.$$
$$\left.\left.- \sqrt{a^2\left(b^2\left(m^2+1\right) - h_2 m^2 t_0\right) - b^2 h_1 t_0}\right) + h_2\left(t\sqrt{a^2\left(b^2\left(m^2+1\right) - h_2 m^2 t_0\right) - b^2 h_1 t_0}\right.\right.$$
$$\left.\left.\left. + t_0\sqrt{a^2\left(b^2\left(m^2+1\right) - h_2 m^2 t_0\right) - b^2 h_1 t_0} - t_0\sqrt{a^2\left(b^2\left(m^2+1\right) - h_2 m^2(t+t_0)\right) - b^2 h_1(t+t_0)}\right)\right)\right)$$

$$B^2_1 = \frac{1}{\left(a^2\left(b^2\left(m^2+1\right) - h_2 m^2(t+t_0)\right) - b^2 h_1(t+t_0)\right)^{3/2}}$$
$$\times\left(abm\left(a^2\left(\sqrt{a^2\left(b^2\left(m^2+1\right) - h_2 m^2(t+t_0)\right) - b^2 h_1(t+t_0)}\right.\right.\right.$$
$$\left.\left.- \sqrt{a^2\left(b^2\left(m^2+1\right) - h_2 m^2 t_0\right) - b^2 h_1 t_0}\right) + h_1\left(t\sqrt{a^2\left(b^2\left(m^2+1\right) - h_2 m^2 t_0\right) - b^2 h_1 t_0}\right.\right.$$
$$\left.\left.\left. + t_0\sqrt{a^2\left(b^2\left(m^2+1\right) - h_2 m^2 t_0\right) - b^2 h_1 t_0} - t_0\sqrt{a^2\left(b^2\left(m^2+1\right) - h_2 m^2(t+t_0)\right) - b^2 h_1(t+t_0)}\right)\right)\right)$$

$$B^2_2 = -\frac{1}{\left(a^2\left(b^2\left(m^2+1\right) - h_2 m^2(t+t_0)\right) - b^2 h_1(t+t_0)\right)^{3/2}}$$
$$\times\left(-a^2 b^2\left(m^2\sqrt{a^2\left(b^2\left(m^2+1\right) - h_2 m^2(t+t_0)\right) - b^2 h_1(t+t_0)}\right.\right.$$
$$\left.+ \sqrt{a^2\left(b^2\left(m^2+1\right) - h_2 m^2 t_0\right) - b^2 h_1 t_0}\right) + b^2 h_1(t+t_0)\sqrt{a^2\left(b^2\left(m^2+1\right) - h_2 m^2 t_0\right) - b^2 h_1 t_0}$$
$$\left. + a^2 h_2 m^2 t_0\sqrt{a^2\left(b^2\left(m^2+1\right) - h_2 m^2(t+t_0)\right) - b^2 h_1(t+t_0)}\right).$$

(5) The components E_0, E_1, E_2 of the energy $E(v_1)$ (in p.9)

$$E_0 = \frac{108}{19336717189061875t_2^6} \Big((v_0^1)^2 \Big[131250 \Big(549586599785242\tau^2 - 260094969234444\tau$$

$$+103758540202387 \Big) t_2^4 + 4468469250(9 - 4\tau)^2 t_2^8 + 1350830425(4\tau - 9)(14619\tau - 2495)t_2^7$$

$$+ 6(\tau(2341493221579117\tau - 578018213009874) - 199546861202523)t_2^6$$

$$- 7463338098125(4\tau - 9)(14619\tau - 2495)t_2^5 - 42247221541875000(4\tau - 9)(14619\tau - 2495)t_2^3$$

$$+2239661022345468750000(9 - 4\tau)^2 t_2^2 + 4370724277949531250000000(9 - 4\tau)^2 \Big]$$

$$+ v_0^1 v_0^2 \Big[35747754000(4\tau - 9)t_2^8 + 1350830425(116952\tau - 141551)t_2^7$$

$$+ 12(2341493221579117\tau - 289009106504937)t_2^6 - 7463338098125(116952\tau - 141551)t_2^5$$

$$+ 525000(274793299892621\tau - 65023742308611)t_2^4 - 42247221541875000(116952\tau - 141551)t_2^3$$

$$+1791728817876375000000(4\tau - 9)t_2^2 + 34965794223596250000000000(4\tau - 9) \Big]$$

$$+ 6(v_0^2)^2 \Big[11915918000t_2^8 + 13165193322050t_2^7 + 2341493221579117t_2^6 - 72737693104326250t_2^5$$

$$+ 12022206870302168750t_2^4 - 4117414211471137500000t_2^3 + 5972429392921250000000t_2^2$$

$$+11655264741198750000000000 \Big] \Big),$$

$$E_1 = \frac{63}{7734686875624751t_2^6} \Big((v_0^1)^2 \Big[2 \Big(314843868178587\tau^2 - 386844477123606\tau$$

$$+367139769800999 \Big) t_2^6 - 617118390(9 - 4\tau)^2 t_2^8 - 23157093(4\tau - 9)(59841\tau - 11345)t_2^7$$

$$+ 127942938825(4\tau - 9)(59841\tau - 11345)t_2^5 - 250(4\tau(4845528878317753\tau - 1143052319603196)$$

$$- 2680065490221693)t_2^4 + 724238083575000(4\tau - 9)(59841\tau - 11345)t_2^3$$

$$-309308608144856250000(9 - 4\tau)^2 t_2^2 - 603619310917743750000000(9 - 4\tau)^2 \Big]$$

$$+ v_0^1 v_0^2 \Big[-4936947120(4\tau - 9)t_2^8 - 23157093(478728\tau - 583949)t_2^7 + 12(104947956059529\tau$$

$$- 64474079520601)t_2^6 + 127942938825(478728\tau - 583949)t_2^5 - 2000(4845528878317753\tau$$

$$- 571526159801598)t_2^4 + 724238083575000(478728\tau - 583949)t_2^3$$

$$-2474468865158850000000(4\tau - 9)t_2^2 - 4828954487341950000000000(4\tau - 9) \Big]$$

$$- 2(v_0^2)^2 \Big[4936947120t_2^8 + 2771487204426t_2^7 - 314843868178587t_2^6 - 15312466804453650t_2^5$$

$$+ 2422764439158876500t_2^4 - 86678262318423150000t_2^3 + 2474468865158850000000t_2^2$$

$$+4828954487341950000000000 \Big] \Big),$$

$$E_2 = \frac{49}{1237549900099960t_2^6}\left((v_0^1)^2\left[639172944(9-4\tau)^2t_2^8 + 65025117144(\tau-1)(4\tau-9)t_2^7\right.\right.$$

$$+ ((483513021595098 - 144314472257429\tau)\tau - 487491840800919)t_2^6$$

$$- 359263772220600(\tau-1)(4\tau-9)t_2^5 - 1170000(4\tau(44285942747\tau - 526506550992)$$

$$+ 2819944148355)t_2^4 - 2033660538678600000(\tau-1)(4\tau-9)t_2^3 + 32036266764387000000(9-4\tau)^2t_2^2$$

$$\left. + 6251914353330900000000000(9-4\tau)^2\right]$$

$$+ 2v_0^1v_0^2\left[2556691776(4\tau-9)t_2^8 + 32512558572(8\tau-13)t_2^7 + (241756510797549\right.$$

$$- 144314472257429\tau)t_2^6 - 179631886110300(8\tau-13)t_2^5 - 4680000(44285942747\tau$$

$$- 263253275496)t_2^4 - 1016830269339300000(8\tau-13)t_2^3 + 1281450670575480000000(4\tau-9)t_2^2$$

$$\left. + 250076574133236000000000000(4\tau-9)\right]$$

$$+ (v_0^2)^2\left[10226767104t_2^8 + 260100468576t_2^7 - 144314472257429t_2^6\right.$$

$$- 1437055088882400t_2^5 - 207258212055960000t_2^4 - 8134642154714400000t_2^3$$

$$\left.\left. + 5125802682301920000000)t_2^2 + 100030629653294400000000000\right]\right).$$

(6) The components V_3^1, V_3^2 of $V_3 = \Pi_c(\tau)V = (V_3^1, V_3^2)$ (in p.9)

$$V_3^1 = -\frac{1}{401399310097422026000\tau^3 t_2^6 v_0^1 v_0^2}$$

$$\times(7984(7\tau(775\tau + 187056) - 34902900)((t_2(t_2(9t_2(t_2(548549680t_2^2$$

$$+ 307943022714t_2 - 34982652019843) - 1701385200494850) + 2422764439158876500)$$

$$- 8667826231842315000) + 2474468865158850000000)t_2^2 + 48289544873419500000000000)(v_0^2)^3$$

$$+ 1125(\tau-93)(217\tau + 15012)(v_0^1)^3(639172944(9-4\tau)^2t_2^8 + 65025117144(\tau-1)(4\tau-9)t_2^7$$

$$+ ((483513021595098 - 144314472257429\tau)\tau - 487491840800919)t_2^6$$

$$- 359263772220600(\tau-1)(4\tau-9)t_2^5 - 1170000(4\tau(44285942747\tau - 526506550992)$$

$$+ 2819944148355)t_2^4 - 2033660538678600000(\tau-1)(4\tau-9)t_2^3$$

$$+ 32036266764387000000(9-4\tau)^2t_2^2 + 6251914353330900000000000(9-4\tau)^2)$$

$$+ 2(v_0^1)^2v_0^2(360(4\tau-9)(\tau(7\tau(10606893749900\tau + 2536489416683421) - 518055054639992712)$$

$$+ 1063652655897548100)t_2^8 + 92628372(\tau(7\tau(\tau(92568042900\tau + 22116731971591)$$

$$- 650025696188556) + 10232705506079115) - 1771149754674000)t_2^7$$

$$+ (50774746594745843899778700 - \tau(\tau(21\tau(32468798645697082020 0\tau$$

$$+ 7797026815703397830 7533) - 4588296370644403786264 9034)$$

$$+ 5559377525301358569 7856061))t_2^6 - 511771755300(\tau(7\tau(\tau(92568042900\tau$$

$$+ 22116731971591) - 650025696188556) + 10232705506079115) - 1771149754674000)t_2^5$$

$$+ 1000(\tau(\tau(28\tau(18738871554674330289 25\tau + 4518423857406052881044 82)$$

$$- 34056269718370655154196 4847) + 78199341036596845695 259056)$$

$$+ 4474243028252615890920 0300)t_2^4 - 2896952334300000(\tau(7\tau(\tau(92568042900\tau$$

$$+ 22116731971591) - 650025696188556) + 10232705506079115) - 1771149754674000)t_2^3$$

$$+ 180437175000000(4\tau-9)(\tau(7\tau(10606893749900\tau + 2536489416683421)$$

$$- 518055054639992712) + 1063652655897548100)t_2^2$$

$$+ 35212522500000000 0(4\tau-9)(\tau(7\tau(10606893749900\tau$$

$+ 2536489416683421) - 518055054639992712) + 1063652655897548100))$

$+ v_0^1(v_0^2)^2(5760(\tau(7\tau(10606893749900\tau + 2536303657046571) - 518024080718609562)$

$+ 1072018526902724700)t_2^8 + 185256744(\tau(7\tau(185136085800\tau + 44459144726707)$

$- 8719341380879292) + 10168170097275900)t_2^7 - 3(\tau(7\tau(1298751945827883280800\tau$

$+ 312673919289799276888957) - 598389203717701215404111731)$

$+ 358577520624838602981657200)t_2^6 - 1023543510600(\tau(7\tau(185136085800\tau$

$+ 44459144726707) - 8719341380879292) + 10168170097275900)t_2^5$

$+ 8000(\tau(7\tau(374777431093486605785000\tau + 9041295289383133666533939)$

$- 169531468291083394182432393) + 199487153207871362548791000)t_2^4$

$- 5793904668600000(\tau(7\tau(185136085800\tau + 44459144726707) - 8719341380879292)$

$+ 10168170097275900)t_2^3 + 2886994800000000(\tau(7\tau(10606893749900\tau$

$+ 2536303657046571) - 518024080718609562) + 1072018526902724700)t_2^2$

$+ 5634003600000000000(\tau(7\tau(10606893749900\tau + 2536303657046571)$

$- 518024080718609562) + 1072018526902724700)))$

$$V_3^2 = \frac{1}{80279862019484405200\tau^3 t_2^6 v_0^1 v_0^2}$$

$\times (3(v_0^1(v_0^2)^2(11520(\tau(2545654499976\tau^2 - 337578616237966\tau + 9593038531826103)$

$- 19852194942643050)t_2^8 + 5773989600000000(\tau(2545654499976\tau^2 - 337578616237966\tau$

$+ 9593038531826103) - 19852194942643050)t_2^2 + 11268007200000000000(\tau(2545654499976\tau^2$

$- 337578616237966\tau + 9593038531826103) - 19852194942643050)$

$+ 741026976(\tau(3\tau(7405443432\tau - 974446161077) + 80734642415549) - 94149723122925)t_2^7$

$+ (\tau(36(6804350698804124018299 - 519500778331153312325\tau)\tau$

$- 664876893019668017156859) + 398419467360931781090730000)t_2^6$

$- 4094174042400(\tau(3\tau(7405443432\tau - 974446161077) + 80734642415549)$

$- 94149723122925)t_2^5 + 8000(\tau(4\tau(4497329173121839269427 - 58682851787430995788103)$

$+ 6278943270040125710460459) - 738841308177301342773300)t_2^4$

$- 23175618674400000(\tau(3\tau(7405443432\tau - 974446161077) + 80734642415549)$

$- 94149723122925)t_2^3) + 31936(\tau - 93)(93\tau - 3475)((t_2(t_2(9t_2(t_2(548549680t_2^2$

$+ 307943022714t_2 - 34982652019843) - 1701385200494850) + 2422764439158876500)$

$- 86678262318423150000) + 2474468865158850000000)t_2^2 + 48289544873419500000000000)(v_0^2)^3$

$+ 5(\tau(3348\tau + 43075) + 11634300)(v_0^1)^3(639172944(9 - 4\tau)^2 t_2^8 + 65025117144(\tau - 1)(4\tau - 9)t_2^7$

$+ ((483513021595098 - 144314472257429\tau)\tau - 487491840800919)t_2^6$

$- 359263772220600(\tau - 1)(4\tau - 9)t_2^5 - 1170000(4\tau(44285942747\tau - 526506550992)$

$+ 2819944148355)t_2^4 - 2033660538678600000(\tau - 1)(4\tau - 9)t_2^3$

$+ 320362667643870000000(9 - 4\tau)^2 t_2^2 + 625191435333090000000000(9 - 4\tau)^2)$

$+ 2(v_0^1)^2 v_0^2(1440(4\tau - 9)(\tau(\tau(1272827249988\tau - 168767016962561) + 4796806061481414)$

$- 9848635702755075)t_2^8 + 92628372(\tau(4\tau(3\tau(3702721716\tau - 491736696209) + 42138563413454)$

$- 378989092817745) + 65598139062000)t_2^7 + (\tau(\tau(108(569672047105888213721$

$- 4329173152759610936\tau)\tau - 1700202486097907530951783) + 2059028713074577248068743)$

$- 1880546170175771996288100)t_2^6 - 511771755300(\tau(4\tau(3\tau(3702721716\tau - 491736696209)$

$+ 42138563413454) - 378989092817745) + 65598139062000)t_2^5$

$+ 4000(\tau(\tau(4\tau(224866458656091963471\tau - 2936811134114141683313550)$

$+ 315317469716756821561518_3) - 724067972561081904585732) - 414281761875242212122225)t_2^4$

$- 2896952334300000(\tau(4\tau(3\tau(3702721716\tau - 491736696209) + 42138563413454)$

$- 378989092817745) + 65598139062000)t_2^3 + 721748700000000(4\tau - 9)(\tau(\tau(1272827249988\tau$

$- 168767016962561) + 4796806061481414) - 9848635702755075)t_2^2$

$+ 1408500900000000000(4\tau - 9)(\tau(\tau(1272827249988\tau - 168767016962561)$

$+ 4796806061481414) - 9848635702755075))))$

(7) We explain the concrete example as below

Let $v = (6806, 2346)$ be a plaintext.

Encryption

$v_0 = d + dv = (8040, 7778)$,

$\tau = 3, \beta_0 = 1$ then $ct_0 = \{5.58763 \times 10^{19}, 2.64606 \times 10^{18}, 1.47664 \times 10^{18}\}$,

$\tau = 3, \beta_1 = 2$ then $ct_1 = \{8.73996 \times 10^{17}, 4.13985 \times 10^{16}, 2.31025 \times 10^{16}\}$,

$\tau = 3, \beta_2 = 3$ then $ct_2 = \{7.68363 \times 10^{16}, 3.64162 \times 10^{15}, 2.03221 \times 10^{15}\}$,

then we obtain the ciphertext $= \{ct_0, ct_1, ct_2\}$.

Decryption

First, from ct_0,

$$V = \Pi_c^{-1}(\tau)V_3 = (-3.10237 \times 10^{15} - 1.14863 \times 10^{13}\tau + 3.06421 \times 10^{14}\tau^2,$$
$$- 1.72354 \times 10^{15} + 6.4659 \times 10^{13}\tau + 1.70234 \times 10^{14}\tau^2)$$

Further, from ct_1 and ct_2, we have others V. Next, from $SKX = \{\frac{4}{3}, \frac{24570}{499}X^1, 3822X^2\}$, we can construct $ct_i \cdot SKX$ as follows:

$ct_0 \cdot SKX = 7.45018 \times 10^{19} + (-1.52756 \times 10^{17} - 5.65566 \times 10^{14}\tau + 1.50877 \times 10^{16}\tau^2)X^1 + (-6.58736 \times 10^{18} + 2.47127 \times 10^{17}\tau + 6.50633 \times 10^{17}\tau^2)X^2$,

$ct_1 \cdot SKX = 1.16533 \times 10^{18} + (-2.38991 \times 10^{15} - 8.84846 \times 10^{12}\tau + 2.36052 \times 10^{14}\tau^2)X^1 + (-1.03061 \times 10^{17} + 3.86638 \times 10^{15}\tau + 1.01794 \times 10^{16}\tau^2)X^2$,

$ct_2 \cdot SKX = 1.02448 \times 10^{17} + (-2.10229 \times 10^{14} - 7.78354 \times 10^{11}\tau + 2.07643 \times 10^{13}\tau^2)X^1 + (-9.06579 \times 10^{15} + 3.40106 \times 10^{14}\tau + 8.95428 \times 10^{14}\tau^2)X^2$,

then we have the following linear system from (7)

$$\begin{cases} (1.50366 \times 10^{17} + 5.56717 \times 10^{14}\tau - 1.48516 \times 10^{16}\tau^2)X^1 \\ \quad + (6.4843 \times 10^{18} - 2.4326 \times 10^{17}\tau - 6.40454 \times 10^{17}\tau^2)X^2 \quad = \quad 7.33365 \times 10^{19} \\ (1.52546 \times 10^{17} + (5.64787 \times 10^{14}\tau - 1.50669 \times 10^{16}\tau^2)X^1 \\ \quad + (6.5783 \times 10^{18} - 2.46787 \times 10^{17}\tau - 6.49738 \times 10^{17}\tau^2)X^2 \quad = \quad 7.43993 \times 10^{19}, \end{cases}$$

and this system is solved unique and the solution (X^1, X^2) is

$$(X^1, X^2) = ((-7.49942 \times 10^7 + 2.81343 \times 10^6 \tau + 7.419 \times 10^6 \tau^2)/\tau^3,$$
$$(1.73906 \times 10^6 + 6.43871 \times 10^3 \tau - 1.72041 \times 10^5 \tau^2)/\tau^3)) \tag{17}$$

Next, input the above (X^1, X^2) to the Equations (8) and (16), then we have the equation of $E(v_1)$

$$- 1.73632 \times 10^{44} + 3.51579 \times 10^{44} \tau - 5.99366 \times 10^{44} \tau^2 - 2.21611 \times 10^{43} \tau^3$$
$$+ 1.20382 \times 10^{44} \tau^4 - 1.20558 \times 10^{42} \tau^5 - 5.9622 \times 10^{42} \tau^6 = 0.$$

If we solve this equation, finally we have the integer α as the value of τ as follows

$$\alpha = 3,$$

where $\tau = 3.00000,\ 2.98760$. By using the solution α to (17), we can obtain the value of $v_0 = (v_0^1, v_0^2)$ and the plaintext $v = (v^1, v^2)$ as follows:

$$v_0^1 = X^1 = 8039.99999 \sim 8040, \quad v_0^2 = X^2 = 7778.00000 \sim 7778,$$

$$v^1 = v_0^1 - dv^1 = 8040 - 1234 = 6806, \quad v^2 = v_0^2 - dv^2 = 7778 - 5432 = 2346. \quad \square$$

References

1. Abate, M., Patrizio, G.: Finsler Metrics—A Global Approach. LNM, vol. 1591. Springer, Heidelberg (1994). https://doi.org/10.1007/BFb0073980
2. Atanasiu, Gh: Partial Nondegenerate Finsler Spaces, pp. 35–60. Kluwer Academic Publishers, Lagrange and Finsler Geometry (1996)
3. Akhbar-Zadeh, H.: Sur les espaces de Finsler isotropes. C. R. Acad. Sci. de Paris **252**, 2061–2063 (1961)
4. Anastasiei, M.: A historical remark on the connections of Chern and Rund. Contemp. Math. Finsler Geom. **176**, 171–177 (1996)
5. Anastasiei, M., Antonelli, P.: The differential geometry of Lagrangian which generate sprays. In: vol. of Kluwer Academic Publishers FTPH, no. 76, pp. 15–34 (1996)
6. Anastasiei, M., Shimada, H.: Deformations of Finsler metrics. In: Finsler Geometries, Kluwer Academic Publishers FTPH, vol. 109, pp. 53–67 (2000)
7. Anastasiei, M., Shimada, H., Sabău, V.S.: On the nonlinear connection of a Second Order Finsler Space, Algebras, Groups and Geometries, Hadronic Press, vol. 16, no. 1, pp. 1–10, March 1999
8. Antonelli, P.L.: Finslerian Geometries. A Meeting of Minds, Kluwer Publication (FTPH), vol. 1909 (2000)
9. Antonelli, P.L., Hrimiuc, D.: Symplectic transformations of the differential geometry of T^*M. Nonlinear Anal. **36**, 529–557 (1999)
10. Antonelli, P.L., Miron, R.: Lagrange and Finsler Geometry Applications to Physics and Biology. Kluwer Academic Publishers (1996)
11. Miron, R.: A Lagrangian theory of relativity, Preprint Nr.84, Univ. Timişoara, 53 (1985)
12. Miron, R.: A Lagrangian theory of relativity, (I, II), Analele Şt. Univ. "Al. I. Cuza" Iaşi, XXXII, s.1., Math., f.2, f.3, 37–62, 7–16 (1986)

13. Miron, R.: Lagrange geometry. Math. Comput. Model. **20**(4/5), 25–40 (1994)
14. Miron, R.: General randers spaces. Lagrange and Finsler geometry, Ed. by Antonelli, P.L., Miron, R., no. 76, pp. 123–140 (1996)
15. Miron, R.: The Geometry of Higher-Order Lagrange Spaces, Applications to Mechanics and Physics, Kluwer Academic Publishers FTPH, no. 82 (1997)
16. Miron, R.: The Geometry of Higher-Order Finsler Spaces. Hadronic Press. Inc., USA (1998)
17. Miron, R.: The notion of higher order Finsler spaces. theory and applications. In: Finslerian Geometries. Kluwer Academic Publishers FTPH, vol. 109, pp. 193–200 (2000)
18. Miron, R., Anastasiei, M.: The Geometry of Lagrange Spaces: Theory and Applications. Kluwer Academic Publishers (1994)
19. Miron, R., Anastasiei, M.: Vector Bundles and Lagrange spaces with Applications to Relativity, Balkan Society of Geometers Monographs and Textbooks Nr.1, Geometry Bàlkan press (1997)
20. Munteanu, G.: Generalized complex Lagrange spaces. In: Finslerian Geometries. Kluwer Academic Publishers. FTPH, vol. 109, pp. 209–223 (2000)
21. Aikou, T., Kozma, L.: Global aspects of Finsler geometry. In: Handbook of Global Analysis, pp. 1–39, 1211. Elsevier Sci. B. V., Amsterdam (2008)
22. Bao, D., Chern, S.-S., Shen, Z.: An Introduction to Riemann-Finsler Geometry. Graduate Texts in Math. Springer-Verlag, New York (2000)
23. Chern, S.-S., Shen, Z.: Riemann-Finsler Geometry, volume 6 of Nankai Tracts in Mathematics. World Scientific Publishing Co., Pte. Ltd., Hackensack, NJ (2005)
24. Crampin, M.: Randers spaces with reversible geodesics. Publ. Math. Debrecen **67**(3–4), 401–409 (2005)
25. Matsumoto, M.: Foundations of Finsler Geometry and Special Finsler Spaces. Kaiseisha Press, Shigaken (1986)
26. Matsumoto, M.: Finsler geometry in the 20th-century. Handbook of Finsler Geometry, vol. 1, pp. 557–966. Kluwer Academic Publishers, Dordrecht (2003)
27. Nagano, T., Innami, N., Itokawa, Y., Shiohama, K.: Notes on reversibility and branching of geodesics in Finsler spaces, Iasi Ploytechic Inst. Bull.-Math. Theor. Mech. Phys. Sect. 9–18 (2019)
28. Nagano, T., Anada, H.: One-wayness of Public-Key Encryption Scheme Using Non-symmetry of Finsler Spaces (in Japanese) (Original title: Indistinguishability of Public-Key Encryption Scheme Using Non-symmetry of Finsler Spaces). In: Proceeding of SCIS2020 (2020)
29. Nagano, T., Anada, H.: Public-key encryption scheme using non-symmetry of Finsler spaces (in Japanese). Proc. CSS2019, 415–421 (2019)
30. Nagano, T.: Notes on the notion of the parallel displacement in Finsler geometry. Tensor (N.S.) **70**(3), 302–310 (2008)
31. Nagano, T.: On the parallel displacement and parallel vector fields in Finsler geometry. Acta Math. Acad. Paedagog. Nyhazi. **26**(2), 349–358 (2010)
32. Nagano, T.: A note on linear parallel displacements in Finsler geometry. J. Faculty Global Commun. Univ. Nagasaki **12**, 195–205 (2011)
33. Nagano, T.: On the quantities W. L, K derived from linear parallel displacements in Finsler geometry. J. Faculty Global Commun. Univ. Nagasaki **14**, 123–132 (2013)
34. Nagano, T.: On the existence of the curve to give the inverse linear parallel displacement (in Japanese). In: Proceeding of Annual meeting of 2018 The Mathematical Society of Japan, Geometry session, pp. 1–2 (2018)
35. Katz, J., Lindell, Y.: Introduction to Modern Cryptography, 2nd edn. CRC Press, Florida (2014)

On Using zk-SNARKs and zk-STARKs in Blockchain-Based Identity Management

Andreea-Elena Panait[1,2]([⊠]) and Ruxandra F. Olimid[1,3,4]([⊠])

[1] Department of Computer Science, University of Bucharest, Bucharest, Romania
andreea-elena.panait@drd.unibuc.ro, ruxandra.olimid@fmi.unibuc.ro
[2] certSIGN, Bucharest, Romania
[3] Department of Information Security and Communication Technology,
NTNU - Norwegian University of Science and Technology, Trondheim, Norway
[4] The Research Institute of the University of Bucharest (ICUB), Bucharest, Romania

Abstract. One possible applicability of blockchain technology is in identity management. Especially for public blockchains, the need to reduce (ideally to zero) the exposure of sensitive identification data is clear. Under these settings, zero-knowledge proofs, in particular in the advanced forms of *Zero-Knowledge Succinct Non-Interactive ARguments of Knowledge (zk-SNARK)* and *Zero-Knowledge Scalable Transparent ARguments of Knowledge (zk-STARK)*, can be used as a potential privacy-preserving technique. The current work looks at the existing libraries that implement zk-SNARKs and zk-STARKs and exemplifies and discusses the use of zk-SNARKs in blockchain-based identity management solutions.

Keywords: Identity management · Blockchain · zk-SNARK · zk-STARK

1 Introduction

There is a high demand for secure, efficient, and interoperable digital identification nowadays. This is a direct consequence of the increasing number of parties (e.g., users, devices, services) that need to access and operate in the digital environment. Identification is a prerequisite and a first-step for functionalities such as access-control, permissions, confidential communication, etc.

Blockchain technology is a candidate for enhancing identity management by introducing decentralization and other advantages (e.g., *self-sovereignty*, which enables the user to own and control his identity). Nevertheless, for public blockchains, the transaction details might contain sensitive data, and therefore it is important to minimize the exposure of such data within certain use cases. Consequently, there has been a growing interest in using privacy-enhancing

© Springer Nature Switzerland AG 2021
D. Maimut et al. (Eds.): SecITC 2020, LNCS 12596, pp. 130–145, 2021.
https://doi.org/10.1007/978-3-030-69255-1_9

techniques for this type of blockchain [50]. Despite the added complexity, zero-knowledge proofs, particularly *Zero-Knowledge Succinct Non-Interac-tive ARguments of Knowledge (zk-SNARKs)* [8] and *Zero-Knowledge Scalable Transparent ARguments of Knowledge (zk-STARKs)* [4] seem promising.

We provide a comparison between zk-SNARKs and zk-STARKs and an overview of the existent libraries that implement them. We refer to how zk-SNARKs might be used for identity management on the blockchain and present use-cases. We give practical examples of zk-SNARK programs for verification of identity attributes compliance, for which we provide measurements in terms of generation time and verification costs.

The remaining of the paper is organized as follows. Section 2 presents the related work. Section 3 gives the necessary background. Section 4 presents available zk-SNARK and zk-STARK libraries. Section 5 exemplifies the applicability of zk-SNARKs for blockchain identity management. Section 6 discusses the measurements results, security aspects, and limitations. Section 7 concludes.

2   Related Work

The concept of *zero-knowledge proof* (zk-proof) was introduced in [27] by Goldwasser et al. Later, Blum et al. showed that non-interactive zk-proofs can exist in the computational settings under the assumption of a Common Reference String (CRS) [9]. Since then, several positive and negative results have been given for zk-proofs in different models. Succinct zk-proofs were first presented in [34], and succinct non-interactive zero-knowledge (NIZK) has been discussed in [41]. SNARKs were first built in [8], together with some applicability (e.g., delegation of computation, two-party secure computation), under the assumption that extractable collision-resistant hash functions exist. In [28], Groth presents the NIZK arguments in sub-linear size and give a reduction to a constant number of group elements for a large CRS. Succinct arguments of NP-statements that are fast to construct and verify, using Quadratic Span Programs instead of Probabilistically Checkable Proofs (PCPs) were introduced in [25].

Various zero-knowledge proving systems were proposed during the years. From these, we mention the Pinocchio system [49], SNARKs for C [5], Geppetto computation [18], and NIZK for a von Neumann Architecture [7]. Scalable zero-knowledge was introduced in [6] and later used, for example, in the Coda protocol [40]. Coda uses the recursive composition of zk-SNARKs to obtain a succinct blockchain, removing the blockchain scalability issue. A pairing-based (pre-processing) SNARK for arithmetic circuit satisfiability, which is an NP-complete language, was presented in [29]. Based on this, various implementations were given [10,30,56]. *Bulletproofs*, a more recent type of constraint zk-proofs (i.e., the statement cannot be general), was introduced in [13]. zk-STARKs were proposed in [4]. Valuable overviews on SNARKs, STARKs, and bulletproofs are given in [13,50]. Recent proving systems include Sonic [39], Halo [11] and Libra [57]. Distributed zk-proof generation was proposed in [56]. We recall a special type of zk-proofs that was introduced in [24], somehow connected to our field of interest, the *zero-knowledge proof-of-identity* which proves a party's identity by demonstrating the knowledge of the private key that corresponds to the party's public key. Much subsequent work followed, which we deliberately omit here.

The usability of zk-proofs (in particular zk-SNARKs and zk-STARKs) in blockchain-based solutions has been discussed in several scenarios [50]. To exemplify, in [54], the authors presented an interoperable healthcare blockchain-based system that uses zk-proofs to authenticate the beneficiaries, Zcash uses zk-SNARKs to create shielded transactions [59], and zero-knowledge proof-of-identity has been proposed to overcome Sybil attacks [15]. A proposal of an identity management system that claims to preserve privacy in the blockchain by the usage of zk-SNARKs was described in [38]. Currently, not much literature exists on zk-SNARKs and zk-STARKs usage for identity management on the blockchain. But a considerable number of proposals exist for identity management on blockchain in general. A brief survey of current work and existing solutions can be found in [48]. However, despite the apparently large number of such solutions, their maturity remains still questionable [47].

3   Background

3.1   Blockchain-Based Identity Management

A blockchain stores data in a *decentralized* and *distributed* manner, by using nodes that agree on the stored data using a *consensus* protocol. The data is stored in *blocks*, which are collections of *transactions*. A nice overview on blockchain is given in [58]. From the various blockchain implementations, we mention *Ethereum* [22], which we will refer to in the paper because of its ability to implement *smart contracts*. Smart contracts allow execution via a function-based interface stored in the blockchain and hence might be used for identity and attributes verification of the parties. Every operation performed in the Ethereum blockchain (e.g., simple transactions, smart contract executions) requires *gas*.

A blockchain-based identity management solution uses the blockchain capabilities to implement identity management functionalities. The identities can be attested either by recognized authorities or by other entities in the blockchain (normally considered of trust and above a certain threshold number). Each entity has an *identifier* and some *attributes*, which can be stored on- or off-chain [19]. A more detailed look over the identity management on blockchain is given in [48].

3.2   Zero-Knowledge Protocols

In a zero-knowledge protocol, a *prover* assures a *verifier* about the validity of a statement, without revealing any information other than its validity. It is guaranteed that a malicious prover cannot fool the verifier to accept a false statement (*soundness*). A more relaxed notion, named *zero-knowledge arguments*, computationally bounds the capabilities of the malicious prover to polynomial strategies (*computational soundness*) [12]. Throughout the paper, we will refer to *zero-knowledge proofs-of-knowledge* for which a prover can also demonstrate that he knows a *witness* that satisfies the statement. The zero-knowledge property assures that the proof does not disclose or damage the secrecy of the witness. They exist in both *interactive* (i.e., requires interaction between the prover and the verifier) and *non-interactive* (i.e., does not require interaction between the prover and the verifier) versions, with heuristics (e.g., Fiat-Shamir [24]) that can transform the former in the latest under certain conditions or with some necessary changes. For general statements, non-interactive zero-knowledge protocols are only possible under the assumption of a Common Reference String (CRS) that needs to be known by both the prover and the verifier [13].

A type of non-interactive argument of knowledge is the zk-SNARK [8]. Besides the zero-knowledge property, the zk-SNARKs provide the property of *succintness*, meaning that the proofs are small, and the verification is cheap and does not require expensive processing [14,50,56]. Nevertheless, they come with some drawbacks: the necessity of a trusted setup (they work in the CRS model) and (still quite) a significant overhead for the setup and on the prover side [56].

Another zero-knowledge non-interactive construction is the *scalable* and *transparent* argument of knowledge, zk-STARK [3]. Here transparency means that randomness used by the verifier is publicly available, so the necessity of a trusted setup is eliminated [4]. On the drawbacks, the proof size is considerably larger than for zk-SNARKs [4]. Similar to SNARKs, STARKs can be executed with or without *zero-knowledge* and designed to be interactive or non-interactive [3].

3.3   zk-SNARK and zk-STARK Program Representation

Quadratic Arithmetic Program (QAP)-based zk-SNARKs are used for implementing practical use-cases. The predicate statement is internally codified in terms of an arithmetic circuit and based on this codification, appropriate tools can generate zk-SNARKs, by transforming the circuits into a QAP. QAPs are based on pairings over elliptic curves, used to encode the computational steps. Examples of elliptic curves include: the Barreto-Naehrig (BN) curves [2], Edwards [21], MNT [42], BLS12-381 [61]. The arithmetic circuit used in a specific zk-SNARK corresponds to the finite field that underlines the elliptic curve used, and a circuit wire corresponds to a single elliptic curve field element. After assigning values to all of the circuit's wires (the circuit represents a single computation for specific public and private set of inputs), the next step for constructing a zk-SNARK is to provide a specific set of constraints that attest that computation has been correctly performed. This set of constraints represents the Rank-1 Constraint System (R1CS) and is used for preventing a malicious prover to provide a verifier with an output that has not been created from its inputs [50]. Other representing proof systems are considered to be Bilinear Arithmetic Circuit Satisfiability (BACS), Unitary-Square Constraint Systems (USCS), and Two-input Boolean Circuit Satisfiability (TBCS) [36]. BACS internally reduces to R1CS and TBCS internally reduces to USCS, being more efficient than using R1CS [36]. The tools that allow the proof predicate (i.e., the statement) to be stated in a high-level language (so that is easier to learn and use it) are called *Domain-Specific Languages (DSL)* tools. For zk-STARKs, the predicate should be transformed in an Algebraic Intermediate Representation (AIR) or a Permuted Algebraic Intermediate Representation (PAIR) [4].

4   zk-SNARK and zk-STARK Comparison and Available Development Libraries

In this section, we compare zk-SNARKs and zk-STARKs and give an overview of the main libraries that implement them. As already mentioned in Sect. 2, other types of zk-proofs (e.g., bulletproofs) exist but are outside of the goal of this paper. Nice comparisons between more types of zk-proofs are given in [13,50].

zk-SNARKs are defined in the CRS model, so they require an initial trusted setup phase during which parties gain knowledge on a string (which can be further thought of in terms of secret keys) [50,56]. The security of the zk-SNARKs is based on the security of the trusted setup. Hence, if the trusted setup is compromised, the whole system is damaged. On the contrary, zk-STARKs make use of public randomness (they are *transparent*), thus eliminating the need for a secret pre-shared value [4]. In many scenarios, this is a clear advantage of zk-STARKs over zk-SNARKs because the setup might be a much too strong assumption and transparency is necessary for public, distributed trust [4].

The proof size of the zk-SNARKs is small (they are *succint*), and the verification of such proof is fast [14,50,56]. They gain practicality due to the constant proof size, regardless of the statement to be proved (e.g., Groth et al. give a construction for which the proof consists of three group elements [29]). In comparison, zk-STARKs generate much larger proofs (roughly 1000 times larger [4]). In terms of verification, both systems have fast verification time, with zk-SNARKs slightly outperforming zk-STARKs. zk-SNARKs are traditionally based on strong number-theoretical hardness assumptions that do not hold against a quantum adversary [13]. Recently, post-quantum resistant zk-SNARKs were introduced [16,26,45]. In comparison, zk-STARKs are normally post-quantum secure [4] due to the quantum-resistant cryptographic primitives they base on (e.g., collision-resistant hash functions, which are not known to be broken by quantum computers [3]).

4.1   Development Libraries

Several libraries that implement zk-SNARKs and zk-STARKs have been developed. Table 1 lists some of the existing zk-SNARK libraries together with the language in which they are implemented, their representing proof predicate language, the underlying elliptic curves, SNARK constructions that can be used in the library, and the available DSL tools. Table 2 looks into the zk-SNARK DSL tools and lists them with the associated language and the corresponding back-end

Table 1. zk-SNARKs and zk-STARTKs libraries [46,50]

Library	Language	Representing proof predicate language	Eliptic curves	zk-SNARK/ zk-STARKs Types	DSL Tools
libsnark [36]	C++	R1CS; BACS; USCS; TBCS	BN [2]; Edwards [21]; MNT [42]	BCTV14 [7]; Groth16 [29]; GM17 [30]	ZoKrates [62]; JSnark/xjSnark [1,35]; Snarky [37]
DIZK [52]	Java	R1CS	BN254 [2]	Groth16 [29]	–
Snarkjs [33]	Javascript	R1CS	BN254 [2]	BCTV14 [7]; Groth16 [29]	Circom[32]
Bellman [60]	Rust	R1CS	BLS12-381 [61]	Groth16 [29]	ZoKrates [62]
ZEXE [53]	Rust	R1CS	Edwards [21]; MNT [42], BN [2]	Groth16 [29], GM17 [30]	ZEXE's snark-gadgets [53]
libSTARK [3]	C++	–	–	BN18 [4]	–
genSTARK [31]	Javascript	-	-	BN18 [4]	–

Table 2. DSL tools [46,50]

DSL tool	Language	Back-end zk-SNARK Library
ZoKrates [62]	Rust; C++	libsnark [36]; Bellman [60]
JSnark/xjSnark [1,35]	Java	libsnark [36]
Circom [32]	Javascript	Snarkjs [33]
Snarky [37]	OCaml	libsnark [36]
ZEXE's snark-gadgets [53]	Rust	ZEXE [53]

libraries. Table 1 also lists the available development libraries for zk-STARKs. To the best of our knowledge, there are no DSL tools available for zk-STARKs at the moment. Notice the significantly less number of implementations for zk-STARKs, which we assume to be a natural consequence of a later definition of zk-STARKs than zk-SNARKs and a currently lower practical interest.

5   Blockchain-Based Identity Management Using zk-SNARKs

Currently, zk-SNARKs are more suitable to be used in a blockchain due to their better capabilities (e.g., small and constant proof size). In time, if zk-STARKs become more efficient, they could dominate because they do not use a trusted setup [3]. Further, we looked into the applicability of zk-SNARKs into blockchain-based identity management.

5.1   General Architecture

In [38], Lee et al. gave a blockchain-based identity management scheme that makes use of zk-SNARKs and is compatible with the ZoKrates process [20]. We do not claim their proposal is secure, nor discuss other aspects here (this is out of our scope) but only consider the general architecture depicted in Fig. 1 for further testing. Important security considerations are discussed in Sect. 6.

Step 1. A user Alice asks a Certified Authority (CA) to certify her identity and attributes. For security reasons (to prevent disclosure and changes), the certificate $cert_A$ is issued on a modified version of the data that is both *hidding* and *binding*. For simplicity, we further consider this to be a cryptographically hashed value H_A. Step 1 is executed off-chain and the method by which the authority verifies the validity of the identity attributes is out of our interest.

Step 2. The certificate $cert_A$ for H_A is uploaded in the blockchain. The scope of $cert_A$ is to certify that H_A indeed corresponds to the identity and attributes of Alice. As the certificate is publicly verified, this step can be performed either by the CA (step 2") or directly by Alice (step 2').

Step 3. A Third Party publishes on the blockchain a smart contract to verify some attributes of the users. For this, a one-time setup phase takes place, during which a zk-SNARK proving and a verification key are generated. The Third Party securely transmits the proving key to Alice. Based on the verification key, a Solidity smart contract is generated and deployed on the blockchain to further verify the given proofs against the value H_A stored in the blockchain. Note that the setup is independent of the first steps (up to the usage of a standard hash function), so the user might join the system after the smart contract is deployed.

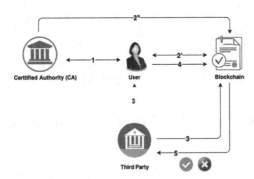

Fig. 1. General architecture of a blockchain-based identity management system that uses zk-SNARKs

Step 4. Alice now wants to prove something about herself (that derives directly from her attributes) to the Third Party without exposing anything else about her attributes. In fact, she does not want to reveal anything else except that her attributes do satisfy a statement (e.g., she is an adult). To do so, she generates a proof that will be verified by the smart contract previously deployed on the blockchain. The proof is generated based on a witness that corresponds to H_A (and to Alice's attributes) and the proving key. Alice sends the generated proof together with the publicly stored value H_A as input to the smart contract.

Step 5. The Third Party checks the result of the smart contract execution by the public address of Alice. If the proof is valid, then Alice proved that she satisfies the statement without revealing anything else about her attributes (under the assumptions of the zero-knowledge property of the proof and the one-way property of H_A). Otherwise, Alice is not able to prove that she satisfies the required statement (this can mean that her attributes do not fulfill the requirements, or that a malicious actor tried to use a fake identity). Note that H_A needs to be available in the public proof so that the validity of $cert_A$ for H_A can be publicly checked (this prevents Alice to use different attributes than the certified ones).

5.2   Use-Cases

We looked into the European Union (EU) regulation on electronic identification and trust services for electronic transactions in the European Single Market (eIDAS) [55]. The eIDAS Security Assertion Markup Language (SAML) Attribute Profile provides the list of attributes included in the eIDAS interoperability framework that supports cross-border identification and authentication processes [55]. The mandatory identity attributes required by the above-mentioned regulation are *FamilyName, FirstName, DateOfBirth, PersonIdentifier*, whereas optional attributes are the *BirthName* (either *First Names at Birth* or *Family Name at Birth*), *PlaceOfBirth, CurrentAddress*, and *Gender*. The optional attributes may be supplied if available and acceptable by an EU country's national law [55]. We will refer to a simplified example, where we are interested in letting a user prove that he/she is older than a certain age, while not exposing his/her exact age or other information about the age (up to a negligible probability). This is an example that might be useful for online shopping, access to different services, or voting, and it has been previously considered in the literature [38].

5.3   zk-SNARK Implementation

We propose two simplified real-life examples of how zk-SNARKs can be used in identity management. In Sect. 6, we provide measurements of the proposed examples, in terms of proof generation time, amount of Ethereum gas used to deploy the verifier smart contract on a blockchain testnet and the amount of Ethereum gas used for making a verification transaction to the smart contract.

Program 1. zk-SNARK for identity management

```
import "hashes/sha256/512bitPacked.zok" as sha256packed
def main(field pub_year1, field pub_year2, field check_year, field pub_id, private field
year, private field rand) -> (field):
field[2] hash_year = sha256packed([0, pub_id, year, rand])
assert(pub_year1 == hash_year[0])
assert(pub_year2 == hash_year[1])
field rez = if year < check_year then 1 else 0 fi
return rez
```

Program 2. zk-SNARK for identity management

```
import "hashes/sha256/512bitPacked.zok" as sha256packed
def main(field hash_ident1, field hash_ident2, field check_year, field pub_id, private field
year, private field id, private field rand) -> (field):
field[2] result = sha256packed([pub_id, year, id, rand])
assert(hash_ident1 == result[0])
assert(hash_ident2 == result[1])
field rez = if year < check_year then 1 else 0 fi
return rez
```

Tools and Environments. For implementing the zk-SNARK program we used the ZoKrates DSL tool [62]. ZoKrates provides a plugin for Remix IDE tool [51] and enables compiling a proof, computing a witness for the proof, performing the SNARK setup, as well as generating and offering the possibility of exporting the verifier smart contract (that further should be deployed on the blockchain public network). However, ZoKrates is also providing an API, in the *zoktares-js* Javascript library, which can be installed as a Node package [62] and used to perform the above-mentioned steps. Besides those reasons, we choose this tool also because it supports integration with the blockchain network and is easier and straightforward to implement and test such zk-proofs. The ZoKrates zk-SNARK programs were written in Rust language. The default proving scheme for the ZoKrates Remix plugin is the one from [29], and it uses the Bellman library [60] as back-end. To compute the hash value, we used the *sha256packing* function, a component of the standard ZoKrates library [62].

For conducting the tests we used an Intel(R) Core(TM) i7-3632QM CPU @ 2.20 GHz with 8 GB of RAM, Windows 8.1 64-bit Operating System, and Chrome 85 as web browser version. We note that better configurations of the machine used for calculations could improve the results, but to what extent the configuration matters, is not a subject of this research. We also note that by using the Remix IDE tool, the time required for the generation of proof might not be accurate because the calculations are made by calling methods from an interface and not by calling them thought the command line.

zk-SNARK Usage Examples. Similar to [55], we exemplify how to use a zk-SNARK to prove that the attributes committed in the blockchain (and certified by the CA) correspond to a user who satisfies a certain statement. We are interested if the user is born before a year of interest. In the first case, we assumed that each identity attribute is separately hashed and certified in the blockchain. For demonstrating purposes, in *Program 1*, we only used the *year of birth* attribute, but adding more attributes to the scheme can be done similarly. In the given example, *pub_id* is the public identifier of the user (which, for our example is just 128-bits long but can be easily expanded), *(pub_year1, pub_year2)* is the value H_A, certified and stored in the blockchain, which is further compared to the hash *hash_year* computed on the private inputs (the private random value *rand* is added to eliminate immediate brute force attacks on the year of birth, if *pub_id* is small enough). Finally, the validity of the statement is checked. In the second case, we assume that a single certificate is issued for all the user's attributes. For demonstrating purposes, we assume that the user has only two attributes: the year of birth (*year*) and a personal identification number (*id*).

One can add more attributes, such as the ones from Sect. 5.2 [55]. The ZoKrates code that acts as basics for the general proof is illustrated in *Program 2*. The difference between the code in *Program 1* and *Program 2* is that in the latter the sha256 is applied to all the attributes at once, whereas in the first example, each attribute will require the storage of a hash and a certification in the blockchain. We will discuss more about this in the next session.

Table 3 shows the measurements for the exemplified zk-SNARKs programs given before. We used Remix environments for deploying and running blockchain transactions: Javascript Ethereum Virtual Machine (VM) and Injected Web3 (with Metamask Ethereum wallet, a Google Chrome extension [17]). Remix makes a distinction between *execution* and *transaction* costs: execution costs are the costs used on the virtual machine without deployment costs or costs related to function calling, whereas transaction costs include the execution costs as well as the cost of sending contracts and data to the blockchain. When executing transactions using a testnet on Remix, the transactions can be viewed on Etherscan [23], and there are other gas-related measurement fields available, such as the *gas limit* (i.e., the maximum gas amount that can be used in a function execution) and the *gas used* (i.e., the actually used gas amount). Taking this into consideration, for organizing reasons, we choose to represent them together in the last four lines of Table 3, with the mention that the significance of the value depends on the used environment: execution or transaction cost if the environment is Javascript Ethereum VM and gas used or gas limit if the environment is Injected Web3 over Kovan public testnet network.

The setup and the proof generation time do not require Ethereum transactions. They are performed by the ZoKrates plugin and, therefore, have the same values irrespective of the Remix environments. We note that the setup generation time is indeed the highest computational step of the zk-SNARK generation process, but the time for generating a proof is quite acceptable (in the settings mentioned before, using an interface).

We deployed the verifier smart contracts on Kovan testnet, available at [43,44]. The cost of deploying the verifier depends on the environment, and not on the

Table 3. ZoKrates Remix plugin generation and verification measurements

	Program 1		Program 2	
Setup (seconds)	187		237	
Proof (seconds)	70		90	
Environment	Javascript Ethereum VM	Injected Web3 (Kovan network)	Javascript Ethereum VM	Injected Web3 (Kovan network)
Trans. Cost/Gas Limit Deploy Verifier	1299416 gas	1060320 gas	1299148 gas	1060104 gas
Exec. Cost/Gas Used Deploy Verifier	933368 gas	1060320 gas	933168 gas	1060104 gas
Trans. Cost/Gas Limit *verifyTx*	287032 gas	–	286904 gas	–
Exec. Cost/Gas Used *verifyTx*	245280 gas	–	245280 gas	–

proposed example, which is expected as the syntax for the smart contract is the same, and the internal parameters differ slightly. Also, it seems that the gas limit for deploying the smart contract into a public testnet is less than the transaction cost for deploying the verifier on the other environment.

6   Results and Discussion

The verifier smart contract provides a public function called *verifyTx* that can be executed to verify the correctness of a proof. For the Ethereum VM environment, the execution cost for calling this function is the same, irrespective of the program. For the Kovan network, at the moment of writing, we were not able to determine the gas limit and the gas used for performing such transactions, as there seemed to be a bug in the Remix IDE. For the testnet, the transaction fees (calculated as gas price multiplied by the gas used, where the gas price, for our case, equals 9 Gwei) at the exchange from October, 3rd 2020 are 0.00954288 Ether for the first program, respectively 0.009540936 Ether for the second one (2.84 EUR). For smart contract deployments, these are rather acceptable fees that can make more feasible the usage of zk-SNARKs on the blockchain.

Similar experiments were undertaken at the end of June 2020. Then we obtained a significantly larger setup and proof generation time. However, we were able to determine the cost for making *verifyTx* transactions on Kovan testnet: the gas limit for making such transactions was smaller than the transaction cost of making such transactions on the Ethereum VM environment. We noted that the price for smart contract transactions has increased since our previous experiments, therefore, the costs for using such solutions should be taken into consideration. Consequently, we remark the continuous development of the ZoKrates Remix plugin, but also its instability.

On the implementation side, the public user identifier used for the given zk-SNARK programs is of type *field* and can store a maximum of 128 bits (a ZoKrates library constraint). This limitation can cause problems, for example when using an Ethereum public address as a public identifier. However, it can be mitigated by using two parameters of type *field* (an Ethereum address has 256 bits), but one should pay attention to their concatenation.

The considered solution stores the certificates in the blockchain which might be arguable by itself, as certification is by construction publicly verifiable. Despite an overload, certification in blockchain might bring some benefits (e.g., transparency in the sense that anyone can see the certificates and their history). However, the implication of such certification regarding the overall security must be thought of. We assumed certification over a simple hashing on the data, so by using a cryptographically weak hash function the system becomes vulnerable. Brute force attacks caused by a possible small set of values for the attributes (e.g.., possible years of birth) must be mitigated.

Moreover, mechanisms against malleable proof must be considered, preventing an adversary to generate a valid proof, different than, but computed from an eavesdropped valid proof [62]. In the absence of other mechanisms (e.g., verification of correspondence between the committed value on-chain and the executor of the smart contract), the scheme is directly vulnerable to replay attacks: an adversary can fake Alice's identity by reusing a proof that Alice had previously used. Another risk, introduced by construction, resides in the number of users that need to share the proving key generated at setup and used as input together with the witness to generate a valid proof for the deployed smart contract [50].

Depending on the application, the attributes can be individually hashed and certificated or a single hash and one certificate can be used for all attributes. If a single hash is used, the prover is obliged to use all the attributes to generate the proof, regardless of the statement of interest. Adding more parameters to the proof will increase its complexity and therefore the cost of the *verifyTx* will increase. The advantage is in terms of storage space and computation of certifications (constant, regardless of the number of attributes). Choosing what to be stored on the blockchain and the exact form (e.g., the hash, or more general the commitment scheme) remains open to specific application requirements. If sensitive data are stored on-chain, the confidentiality is always at risk, being computationally secured and thus, in time, predisposed to attacks.

Considering the above-mentioned aspects, we highlight that we do not claim the general architecture in Fig. 1 is secure but only use it as an example for our experiments. The motivation or feasibility of applying zk-SNARKs in off-chain settings might be separately investigated. More in-depth implementation details and security analysis of the approach [38] we have considered for our examples, as well as finding better zk-SNARKs solutions or arguing about their utility are outside of the goal of this paper. They remain of interest for future work.

7   Conclusions

Blockchain-based identity management is a domain that might benefit from the usage of zk-SNARKs and zk-STARKs. In this paper, we looked into the practical side of using zk-SNARKs in identity management, by using the ZoKrates library [62] and proposing programs for certain use cases. Although these privacy-preserving technologies seem promising, they are not yet ready to be used in production: the open-source libraries are under development, continuously improved and tested, and still not fully analyzed in terms of security. Improvements in the efficiency of SNARKs and STARKs are also topics for further research.

Acknowledgment. This work was partially supported by a grant of Romanian Ministry of Research and Innovation project no. 17PCCDI/2018.

References

1. Kosba, A.: xJsnark (2020).https://github.com/akosba/xjsnark
2. Barreto, P.S.L.M., Naehrig, M.: Pairing-friendly elliptic curves of prime order. In: Preneel, B., Tavares, S. (eds.) SAC 2005. LNCS, vol. 3897, pp. 319–331. Springer, Heidelberg (2006). https://doi.org/10.1007/11693383_22
3. Ben-Sasson, E.: libSTARK (2020). https://github.com/elibensasson/libSTARK
4. Ben-Sasson, E., Bentov, I., Horesh, Y., Riabzev, M.: Scalable, transparent, and post-quantum secure computational integrity. IACR Cryptology ePrint Archive 2018, 46 (2018)
5. Ben-Sasson, E., Chiesa, A., Genkin, D., Tromer, E., Virza, M.: SNARKs for C: verifying program executions succinctly and in zero knowledge. In: Canetti, R., Garay, J.A. (eds.) CRYPTO 2013. LNCS, vol. 8043, pp. 90–108. Springer, Heidelberg (2013). https://doi.org/10.1007/978-3-642-40084-1_6
6. Ben-Sasson, E., Chiesa, A., Tromer, E., Virza, M.: Scalable zero knowledge via cycles of elliptic curves. In: Garay, J.A., Gennaro, R. (eds.) CRYPTO 2014. LNCS, vol. 8617, pp. 276–294. Springer, Heidelberg (2014). https://doi.org/10.1007/978-3-662-44381-1_16
7. Ben-Sasson, E., Chiesa, A., Tromer, E., Virza, M.: Succinct non-interactive zero knowledge for a von neumann architecture. In: 23rd USENIX Security Symposium (USENIX Security 2014), San Diego, CA, pp. 781–796. USENIX Association, August 2014. https://www.usenix.org/conference/usenixsecurity14/technical-sessions/presentation/ben-sasson
8. Bitansky, N., Canetti, R., Chiesa, A., Tromer, E.: From extractable collision resistance to succinct non-interactive arguments of knowledge, and back again. In: Proceedings of the 3rd Innovations in Theoretical Computer Science Conference, pp. 326–349 (2012)
9. Blum, M., Feldman, P., Micali, S.: Non-interactive zero-knowledge and its applications. In: Proceedings of the Twentieth Annual ACM Symposium on Theory of Computing, STOC 1988, New York, NY, USA, pp. 103–112. Association for Computing Machinery (1988). https://doi.org/10.1145/62212.62222
10. Bowe, S., Gabizon, A.: Making groth's zk-snark simulation extractable in the random oracle model. IACR Cryptology ePrint Archive 2018, 187 (2018). http://dblp.uni-trier.de/db/journals/iacr/iacr2018.html#BoweG18

11. Bowe, S., Grigg, J., Hopwood, D.: Recursive proof composition without a trusted setup. Technical report, Cryptology ePrint Archive, Report 2019/1021 (2019). https://eprint.iacr.org/2019/1021
12. Brassard, G., Chaum, D., Crépeau, C.: Minimum disclosure proofs of knowledge. J. Comput. Syst. Sci. **37**(2), 156–189 (1988)
13. Bünz, B., Bootle, J., Boneh, D., Poelstra, A., Wuille, P., Maxwell, G.: Bulletproofs: short proofs for confidential transactions and more. In: 2018 IEEE Symposium on Security and Privacy (SP), pp. 315–334. IEEE (2018)
14. Campanelli, M., Fiore, D., Querol, A.: LegoSNARK: modular design and composition of succinct zero-knowledge proofs. In: Proceedings of the 2019 ACM SIGSAC Conference on Computer and Communications Security, pp. 2075–2092 (2019)
15. Cerezo Sánchez, D.: Zero-knowledge proof-of-identity: Sybil-resistant, anonymous authentication on permissionless blockchains and incentive compatible, strictly dominant cryptocurrencies. Anonymous Authentication on Permissionless Blockchains and Incentive Compatible, Strictly Dominant Cryptocurrencies, 22 May 2019 (2019)
16. Chiesa, A., Manohar, P., Spooner, N.: Succinct arguments in the quantum random oracle model. In: Hofheinz, D., Rosen, A. (eds.) TCC 2019. LNCS, vol. 11892, pp. 1–29. Springer, Cham (2019). https://doi.org/10.1007/978-3-030-36033-7_1
17. Consensys: Metamask (2020). https://chrome.google.com/webstore/detail/metamask/nkbihfbeogaeaoehlefnkodbefgpgknn?hl=en
18. Costello, C., et al.: Geppetto: versatile verifiable computation. In: 2015 IEEE Symposium on Security and Privacy, pp. 253–270 (2015)
19. Dunphy, P., Petitcolas, F.A.: A first look at identity management schemes on the blockchain. IEEE Secur. Privacy **16**(4), 20–29 (2018)
20. Eberhardt, J., Tai, S.: Zokrates-scalable privacy-preserving off-chain computations. In: 2018 IEEE International Conference on Internet of Things (iThings) and IEEE Green Computing and Communications (GreenCom) and IEEE Cyber, Physical and Social Computing (CPSCom) and IEEE Smart Data (SmartData), pp. 1084–1091. IEEE (2018)
21. Edwards, H.: A normal form for elliptic curves. Bull. Am. Math. Soc. **44**(3), 393–422 (2007)
22. Ethereum (2020). https://ethereum.org/en
23. Etherscan: Ethereum Blockchain Explorer (2020). https://etherscan.io
24. Fiat, A., Shamir, A.: How To prove yourself: practical solutions to identification and signature problems. In: Odlyzko, A.M. (ed.) CRYPTO 1986. LNCS, vol. 263, pp. 186–194. Springer, Heidelberg (1987). https://doi.org/10.1007/3-540-47721-7_12
25. Gennaro, R., Gentry, C., Parno, B., Raykova, M.: Quadratic span programs and succinct NIZKs without PCPs. In: Johansson, T., Nguyen, P.Q. (eds.) EUROCRYPT 2013. LNCS, vol. 7881, pp. 626–645. Springer, Heidelberg (2013). https://doi.org/10.1007/978-3-642-38348-9_37
26. Gennaro, R., Minelli, M., Nitulescu, A., Orrù, M.: Lattice-based ZK-snarks from square span programs. In: Proceedings of the 2018 ACM SIGSAC Conference on Computer and Communications Security, pp. 556–573 (2018)
27. Goldwasser, S., Micali, S., Rackoff, C.: The knowledge complexity of interactive proof-systems. In: Proceedings of the Seventeenth Annual ACM Symposium on Theory of Computing, STOC 1985, New York, NY, USA, pp. 291–304 (1985). Association for Computing Machinery (1985). https://doi.org/10.1145/22145.22178

28. Groth, J.: Short pairing-based non-interactive zero-knowledge arguments. In: Abe, M. (ed.) ASIACRYPT 2010. LNCS, vol. 6477, pp. 321–340. Springer, Heidelberg (2010). https://doi.org/10.1007/978-3-642-17373-8_19

29. Groth, J.: On the size of pairing-based non-interactive arguments. In: Fischlin, M., Coron, J.-S. (eds.) EUROCRYPT 2016. LNCS, vol. 9666, pp. 305–326. Springer, Heidelberg (2016). https://doi.org/10.1007/978-3-662-49896-5_11

30. Groth, J., Maller, M.: Snarky signatures: minimal signatures of knowledge from simulation-extractable SNARKs. In: Katz, J., Shacham, H. (eds.) CRYPTO 2017. LNCS, vol. 10402, pp. 581–612. Springer, Cham (2017). https://doi.org/10.1007/978-3-319-63715-0_20

31. GuildOfWeavers: genSTARK (2020). https://github.com/GuildOfWeavers/genSTARK

32. iden3: Circom (2020). https://github.com/iden3/circom

33. iden3: Snarkjs (2020). https://github.com/iden3/snarkjs

34. Kilian, J.: A note on efficient zero-knowledge proofs and arguments (extended abstract). In: Proceedings of the Twenty-Fourth Annual ACM Symposium on Theory of Computing, STOC 1992, New York, NY, USA, pp. 723–732. Association for Computing Machinery (1992). https://doi.org/10.1145/129712.129782

35. Kosba, A.: jsnark (2020). https://github.com/akosba/jsnark

36. Lab, S.: libSNARK (2020). https://github.com/scipr-lab/libsnark

37. o1 labs: Snarky (2020). https://github.com/o1-labs/snarky

38. Lee, J., Hwang, J., Choi, J., Oh, H., Kim, J.: Sims: Self sovereign identity management system with preserving privacy in blockchain. IACR Cryptology ePrint Archive 2019, 1241 (2019)

39. Maller, M., Bowe, S., Kohlweiss, M., Meiklejohn, S.: Sonic: Zero-knowledge snarks from linear-size universal and updatable structured reference strings. In: Proceedings of the 2019 ACM SIGSAC Conference on Computer and Communications Security, pp. 2111–2128 (2019)

40. Meckler, I., Shapiro, E.: Coda: Decentralized cryptocurrency at scale (2018)

41. Micali, S.: Cs proofs. In: Proceedings of the 35th Annual Symposium on Foundations of Computer Science, SFCS 1994, pp. 436–453. IEEE Computer Society, USA (1994). https://doi.org/10.1109/SFCS.1994.365746

42. Miyaji, A., Nakabayashi, M., Takano, S.: New explicit conditions of elliptic curve traces for FR-reduction. IEICE Trans. Fund. Electron. Commun. Comput. Sci. **84**(5), 1234–1243 (2001)

43. Network, K.T.: Address Smart Contract Program 2 (2020). https://kovan.etherscan.io/address/0x0d0771402acb9d11c73a2df84525b030914a3c47

44. Nework, K.T.: Address Smart Contract Program 1 (2020). https://kovan.etherscan.io/address/0xd7df4c356b182057265a8b36703fb91a9e293b36

45. Nitulescu, A.: Lattice-based zero-knowledge SNARGs for arithmetic circuits. In: Schwabe, P., Thériault, N. (eds.) LATINCRYPT 2019. LNCS, vol. 11774, pp. 217–236. Springer, Cham (2019). https://doi.org/10.1007/978-3-030-30530-7_11

46. Github Pages: Zero-Knowledge Proofs (2020). https://zkp.science

47. Panait, A.-E., Olimid, R.F., Stefanescu, A.: Analysis of uPort open, an identity management blockchain-based solution. In: Gritzalis, S., Weippl, E.R., Kotsis, G., Tjoa, A.M., Khalil, I. (eds.) TrustBus 2020. LNCS, vol. 12395, pp. 3–13. Springer, Cham (2020). https://doi.org/10.1007/978-3-030-58986-8_1

48. Panait, A.E., Olimid, R.F., Stefanescu, A.: Identity management on blockchain-privacy and security aspects. Proc. Romanian Acad. Ser. A **21**(1), 45–52 (2020)

49. Parno, B., Howell, J., Gentry, C., Raykova, M.: Pinocchio: nearly practical verifiable computation. In: 2013 IEEE Symposium on Security and Privacy, pp. 238–252 (2013)
50. Pinto, A.: An Introduction to the use of ZK-SNARKs in Blockchains, pp. 233–249, January 2020. https://doi.org/10.1007/978-3-030-37110-4_16
51. Remix: Remix Ethereum-IDE Tool (2019). https://remix.ethereum.org
52. SCIPR Lab: Dizk (2020). https://github.com/scipr-lab/dizk
53. SCIPR Lab: Zexe (2020). https://github.com/scipr-lab/zexe
54. Sharma, B., Halder, R., Singh, J.: Blockchain-based interoperable healthcare using zero-knowledge proofs and proxy re-encryption. In: 2020 International Conference on COMmunication Systems NETworkS (COMSNETS), pp. 1–6 (2020)
55. eIDAS eID Technical Subgroup: eIDAS SAML Attribute Profile (2019). https://ec.europa.eu/cefdigital/wiki/download/attachments/82773108/eIDAS%20SAML%20Attribute%20Profile%20v1.2%20Final.pdf?version=2&modificationDate=1571068651772&api=v2
56. Wu, H., Zheng, W., Chiesa, A., Popa, R.A., Stoica, I.: DIZK: a distributed zero knowledge proof system. In: 27th USENIX Security Symposium (USENIX Security 2018), pp. 675–692 (2018)
57. Xie, T., Zhang, J., Zhang, Y., Papamanthou, C., Song, D.: Libra: succinct zero-knowledge proofs with optimal prover computation. In: Boldyreva, A., Micciancio, D. (eds.) CRYPTO 2019. LNCS, vol. 11694, pp. 733–764. Springer, Cham (2019). https://doi.org/10.1007/978-3-030-26954-8_24
58. Yaga, D., Mell, P., Roby, N., Scarfone, K.: Blockchain technology overview. https://nvlpubs.nist.gov/nistpubs/ir/2018/NIST.IR.8202.pdf
59. Zcash: What are zk-SNARKs? (2018). https://z.cash/technology/zksnarks
60. zkcrypto: Bellman (2020). https://github.com/zkcrypto/bellman
61. zkcrypto: Bls12-381 (2020). https://github.com/zkcrypto/bls12_381
62. ZoKrates: Zokrates tutorial (2020). https://zokrates.github.io (All links were last accessed October)

Manager Asks: Which Vulnerability Must be Eliminated First?

David Pecl[2], Yehor Safonov[1], Zdenek Martinasek[1](✉)(iD), Matej Kacic[2], Lubomir Almer[2], and Lukas Malina[1](iD)

[1] Department of Telecommunications, Brno University of Technology, Technicka 12, 616 00 Brno, Czech Republic
{xsafon00,martinasek,malina}@feec.vutbr.cz
[2] AEC, Veveri 102, 616 00 Brno, Czech Republic
{david.pecl,matej.kacic,lubomir.almer}@aec.cz

Abstract. Nowadays, the number of discovered vulnerabilities increases rapidly. In 2018, the $17,308$ vulnerabilities were discovered and during the 2019 even more, so up to $20,362$. The serious problem is that a substantial part of them is rated as critical or at least labeled as high according the CVSS (Common Vulnerability Scoring System). This fact causes a problem, the designers and/or developers do not know which vulnerability should be eliminated at the first place. Time for removal of the vulnerability is crucial from the practical point of cyber security. The main contribution of the article is a proposal of a new method that is used for prioritizing vulnerabilities. The aim of the proposed method is to eliminate the disadvantages of approaches commonly used today. Our method improves the prioritization of vulnerabilities utilizing the parameters: the possibility of exploitation, availability of information about them and knowledge obtained by Threat Intelligence. These three parameters are highly important, especially for newly discovered vulnerabilities, where a priority can differ from day to day. We evaluate the functionality of the proposed method utilizing the production environment of a medium-sized company and we copare results with CVSS method (30 servers, 200 end-stations).

Keywords: CVSS · Priority · Security · Vulnerability assessment

1 Introduction

Every year a significant number of vulnerabilities is discovered worldwide. According to the information published by the Imperva organization 14 086 vulnerabilities were discovered in 2017. In 2018 the number has risen to $17,308$ and during 2019 even more, so up to $20,362$ [3]. When we take a more detailed look at the vulnerability it may be observed that a substantial part of them is

Research described in this paper was financed by the Technology Agency of the Czech Republic (TACR), project no. TJ04000456.

D. Maimut et al. (Eds.): SecITC 2020, LNCS 12596, pp. 146–164, 2021.
https://doi.org/10.1007/978-3-030-69255-1_10

rated as critical or at least as high. In 2018, almost 59 % of them got more than 7 points according to the Common Vulnerability Scoring System (CVSS) and 15 % obtained a score of more than 9 points [5] on a 10-point scale.

Because of more than a tenth of all newly discovered vulnerabilities are currently assessed as critical, it is important to consider whether the currently widely used CVSS vulnerability assessment methodology is still appropriate and whether its prioritization function is sufficient for the rapidly growing number of new vulnerabilities. It is important to define key terms and discuss their meaning in the context of the study. These terms include *prioritization* [5], *vulnerability* [14], *vulnerability evaluation* [8], *vulnerability assessment* [6] and *risk* [9].

1.1 State of the Art

Common Vulnerability Scoring System [1,13] is the most widely used methodology for vulnerability assessment. The CVSS methodology evaluates vulnerabilities on a scale from zero (the least severe) to ten points (the most severe). In addition to the numerical assessment each vulnerability has a CVSS vector, which reflects the values of the individual metrics used to calculate the final assessment. The CVSS methodology is based on three areas of vulnerability severity assessment - Base Score, Temporal Score and Environmental Score. Furthermore, each of these areas is evaluated based on several metrics depending on the version of the CVSS.[1]

On the one hand the main advantage of the CVSS methodology is its complexity, on the other hand it brings significant disadvantages. If the latest Environmental Score is used to prioritize vulnerabilities, the resulting value accurately reflects the severity for the environment. Unfortunately, a great amount of information is needed to determine such score, which in most cases cannot be processed automatically [11]. If we take a detailed look at the Temporal Score, it is also designed well for its purpose. Unfortunately, its real usage is negligible. Most of the vulnerability detection tools or the "vulnerability finders" do not take it into consideration. Another disadvantage of the CVSS is the most tools used for vulnerability detection and risk assessment use only the Base Score metric. They do so precisely because it is almost impossible to calculate the Environmental Score automatically without providing a large amount of information. The task of prioritization is therefore left up to the user's tool. To properly prioritize vulnerabilities, it is necessary to know which vulnerable system is being analyzed. The CVSS base score does not take into consideration the information about the importance of a system, whether it is a production server in DMZ (*DeMilitarized Zone*) or a server in a closed testing environment.

Another methodology that is often used to assess the severity of vulnerabilities is the OWASP Risk Rating Methodology [18]. The basic idea of this assessment is the connection between risk, the probability of exploitation and the impact while it is exploited. The whole methodology is based on the fact

---

[1] The currently used version of the CVSS is 3.1. This and elder versions are described in detail in the methodology's documentation on https://www.first.org/cvss/v3-1/.

that the risk score is directly proportional to the probability of exploitation and its impact. The first area for determining the final risk of analyzed vulnerability is the probability of exploitation of such vulnerability. There are eight different factors in this area which are evaluated. All mentioned factors are divided into two groups - Threat Agent Factors and Vulnerability Factors. The second area for determining the final risk is the impact of exploiting the vulnerability. As well as in the previous area there are eight different factors being evaluated and they are divided into two groups - Technical Impact Factors and Business Impact Factors. The main advantage of this methodology is its simplicity, which is ensured as a result of a smaller number of factors (parameters/metrics) than in the CVSS methodology and also due to a simple principle of evaluation of the overall level of risk. The second big advantage is the preference of business factors over technical ones. For each system in different organizations, the same vulnerability may reflect a different level of risk, so it is appropriate to assess it differently. Furthermore, the OWASP methodology reflects parameters that CVSS either does not have at all or does not take them into assessment of the baseline score. These are exploitation factors and vulnerability information included in the temporary CVSS score.

Simplicity of the OWASP methodology is from another point of view also its the disadvantage. Areas which are assessed in the CVSS score using four parameters (attack vector, attack complexity, authorization level, user interaction) are in the OWASP approach evaluated only by two, which are a factor of difficulty of vulnerability exploitation and the factor of the threat carrier group. Therefore, it is impossible to specify all parameters in depth for vulnerability assessment, while the CVSS methodology allow this in all its assessments.

Nowadays, while running security tests, most vulnerability databases work with the assessment of vulnerabilities by CVSS or OWASP (in case of web applications). However, there are other methods that are mostly proprietary and which are used by security organizations in their vulnerability scanning tools (e.g. Nessus [12,15], Netsparker [2,4] or Rapid7 [10,16]). However, some of them often do not publish in detail their core working principles and the resulting prioritization of vulnerabilities. From a modern perspective it is clear that the CVSS methodology, to some extent, is outdated and its algorithm for assessing the severity of vulnerabilities does not reflect some important parameters of them.

There are several CVSS enhancements that have already been proposed or several new methodologies that have already been developed, which for example take into the final assessment the availability of exploits or the context of a vulnerable asset.

Ruyi Wang *et al.* [17] describe a method that removes the subjective and obscure factors that have a place in the CVSS method. However, this method does not pay enough attention to the priority of the asset, or to the requirements for security of the CIA (Confidentiality Integrity Availability) triad, which may be perceived as its disadvantage.

Christian Frühwirth and Tomi Männistö deal with the improvement of the traditional CVSS method [7]. The authors use a distribution model used to estimate the complexity of exploitation and the availability of the appropriate patch. Nonetheless, even this improvement lacks the context of the asset's vulnerability.

Further, Feutrill *et al.* [6] describe the dependence of the CVSS evaluation on the amount of time it takes to create a functional exploit. The authors do not suggest any improvements to the CVSS methodology but analyze the assessment of vulnerability and the difficulty of their exploitation.

Lastly, Marjan Keramati [8] focuses on the complexity of vulnerability's exploitation. In addition, it improves the CVSS evaluation with the aim to reflect the availability and quality of exploits more accurately. However, from the assessment point of view, this provides only a partial improvement and does not operate with the information about the vulnerable asset sufficiently.

1.2 Our Contribution

The main contribution of this work is a proposal of a new method which is used for prioritizing vulnerabilities and eliminates the disadvantages of the methods described above. The proposed method improves the prioritization of vulnerabilities considering the parameters of the possibility of exploitation, availability of information about them and knowledge obtained by Threat Intelligence. These three parameters are highly important, especially for newly discovered vulnerabilities, where priority can differ from day to day. Using the proposed method of the assessing a newly discovered vulnerability is going to have a lower final priority in case there is not any exploit publicly available, any technical information about it and the vulnerability is not being actively exploited. In contradiction, the final score of the vulnerability will be higher even if it has the same CVSS score, but is actively exploited by attackers and its working principle is well described and documented[2].

In addition to the technical parameters, the method also operates with the priority of the asset, or with the requirement to provide elements of the CIA triad. From a vulnerable asset point of view, this context helps to prioritize vulnerabilities which are important from a business point of view or exist in critical and production systems. Another important property of the proposed method takes the implemented countermeasures as a part of the assessment evaluation, which may reduce the risk of exploiting a vulnerability or the final impact on the protected system or data in case the exploitation has already occurred.

---

[2] For example there is an available exploit in Metasploit DB.

2   New Method Proposal

The suggested method for prioritizing vulnerabilities is based on the principle that the evaluation process does not contain only the vulnerability itself, but includes the information about the vulnerable system and implemented countermeasures (protections) which help ensure the confidentiality, integrity and availability of the system. As a result, all these factors may reduce or increase the priority of a vulnerability. The basis of proposed assessment method includes three parts - vulnerability assessment, vulnerable system and countermeasures.

2.1   Basic Principle of Method

The following text describes the basic principle of the proposed method and discuss the operations of individual blocks.

The first area used for prioritizing is **Vulnerability evaluation**, which consists of nine different parameters. Each parameter has from two to six different word descriptions, which are additionally converted to a number ranged from 0 to 1. The verbal description is used for determining the value of a parameter, because it is almost impossible for a human to exactly choose the value from 0 to 1, for example, the difficulty of a vulnerability's abuse. With the motivation to avoid the mentioned problem the verbal description is used, which gives examples for individual values and it can help handle this determination process much more accurately. All parameters in this area are divided into two groups - permanent parameters and alterable parameters. The permanent parameters, as the name implies, are left unchanged over time in terms of prioritization. They are: impact on the CIA triad, difficulty of abuse, user interaction and required permissions. Mentioned permanent parameters are similar to the ones CVSS methodology uses.

On the contrary, the alterable parameters may change over time and thus significantly affect the priority of assessed vulnerabilities. They are: availability of information, possibility of exploitation and information about current vulnerability's exploitation from Threat Intelligence services. The first alterable parameter is availability of information. It describes whether technical information about the vulnerability is available, whether there exists a description of the vulnerability's exploitation principles etc. The second alterable parameter is exploitation. For example, it includes the possibilities of automation, the quality of the exploit etc. The last alterable parameter is obtained from Threat Intelligence services. Such data contains information which describes the relation between analyzed vulnerability and exploitation count.

Asset evaluation (vulnerable system's asset evaluation) is determined depending on the basis of three parameters - the requirement for confidentiality, integrity and availability of the system or its data. A questionnaire was chosen as a form for the suggested method of asset evaluation. There are several questions in the evaluation process, which help to analyze a chosen asset from the CIA triad's point of view and help asset's owner to determine the importance of the data stored in a given system. The requirement for one of the three parameters of the CIA triad is used to prioritize the vulnerability, and the resulting vulnerability priority is assessed both in terms of this requirement and in terms of the impact of vulnerability exploitation.

In order to properly assess the impact on the CIA triad, it is also advisable to take into calculation the **Countermeasure evaluation**, which may affect these values. As an example, it is possible to discuss a vulnerability that has a high impact on system availability. In case we had the system in a high availability mode, where backups are created regularly, the impact on its availability would not be as high as if it were a normal server that would not be backed up and did not have its redundant copy in operation. Countermeasures are evaluated in the same way as the asset evaluation, it means using a sort of questionnaire. The asset owner or infrastructure manager can determine which countermeasures are used for a particular system.

2.2   Calculation of Vulnerability Priority

The following text sequentially introduces the definitions of parameters that are leading to the final result of the vulnerability priority parameter.

The numerical evaluation of vulnerability parameters, except for the impact on the CIA triad, is written in the set D.

Definition 1. *The set of all parameters that describes a vulnerability is denoted as D. This set has exactly 6 elements (excluding the impact on confidentiality, integrity and availability) and the number of parameters is exactly given.*

$$D = \{d_1, d_2, \ldots, d_6\} \tag{1}$$

Each parameter has its own weight to take into consideration their respective importance. Each of them is defined on a set of real numbers in the range of 0 to 1. The weight of individual elements is given in the Table 1.

Definition 2. *The set of weight values corresponding to the elements of the set of parameters D is known as D_W.*

$$D_W = \{d_{W1}, d_{W2}, \ldots, d_{W6}\} \tag{2}$$

When evaluating parameters describing the vulnerability, there are predefined options in order to determine mentioned parameters easier and more precisely. Each parameter has a precisely defined word description. Followingly every definition is converted to a numerical value ranged from 0 to 1. Numerical value just like the word description is strictly defined and is unchangeable.

In addition to the mentioned parameters, it is important to determine the final impact on the confidentiality, integrity and availability of a vulnerable system. In a similar way possible values of parameters are predetermined. The method was made this way for easier choosing, because the description of each vulnerability is chosen by the person, not by the algorithm. Additionally, it is advisable to define these three parameters for calculations.

Definition 3. *Confidentiality Impact* C *is the possible impact on the confidentiality of a system in case of its exploitation. The parameter is defined by an element from the set of values, Eq. 3. A higher numerical rating means a higher impact on confidentiality (see Table 6 for word definition).*

$$C \in \{0,22;\ 0,67;\ 0,78;\ 1\} \tag{3}$$

Definition 4. *Integrity Impact* I *is a numerical expression of the possible impact on the integrity of a vulnerable system in case of its exploitation. It is defined by an element from the set of values, Eq. 4. A higher numerical rating means a higher impact on integrity (see Table 6 for word definition).*

$$I \in \{0,11;\ 0,33;\ 0,56;\ 0,78;\ 1\} \tag{4}$$

Definition 5. *Availability Impact* A *is a numerical expression of the possible impact on the availability of a vulnerable system in case of its exploitation. It is defined by an element from the set of values, Eq. 5. A higher numerical rating means a higher impact on availability (see Table 6 for word definition).*

$$A \in \{0,11;\ 0,56;\ 0,78;\ 1\} \tag{5}$$

Once all required parameters describing the vulnerability are defined, it is necessary to characterize the requirements for confidentiality, integrity and availability. These requirements are based on the replies to the suggested questionnaire. It is advisable to define these requirements for following calculations.

Definition 6. *Confidentiality Requirement* C_R *is a numerical expression of the required confidentiality measurement of the investigated asset. It is defined on the interval* $\langle 0,1 \rangle$ *above the set of real numbers (see Eq. 6). A higher numerical rating means a higher confidentiality requirement.*

$$C_R = \langle 0,1 \rangle \subset \mathbb{R} \tag{6}$$

Definition 7. *Integrity Requirement* I_R *is a numerical expression of the required integrity measurement of the investigated asset. It is defined on the interval* $\langle 0,1 \rangle$ *above the set of real numbers (see Eq. 7). A higher numerical rating means a higher integrity requirement.*

$$I_R = \langle 0,1 \rangle \subset \mathbb{R} \tag{7}$$

Definition 8. *Availability Requirement* A_R *is a numerical expression of the required availability measurement of the investigated asset. It is defined on the interval $\langle 0, 1 \rangle$ above the set of real numbers (see Eq. 8). A higher numerical rating means a higher availability requirement.*

$$A_R = \langle 0, 1 \rangle \subset \mathbb{R} \qquad (8)$$

As was mentioned in the previous chapter, the questionnaire is divided into four sections. Parts dealing with confidentiality, integrity and availability have a maximum number of points which equals 15. The general part of questions has a maximum number of points which equals 4. Each question has two or more possible word answers, which correspond to a predetermined numerical evaluation. It is defined on the interval $\langle 0, 1 \rangle$ above the set of real numbers. The final score is calculated as the sum of the numerical evaluations of the individual answers included in related area. The evaluation of all three requirements is calculated as the ratio of the sum of the score given from a relevant area and from general questions. The maximum number of points is 19.

$$C_R = \frac{Confidentiality\,Questions\,Score + General\,Questions\,Score}{19}$$

$$I_R = \frac{Integrity\,Questions\,Score + General\,Questions\,Score}{19}$$

$$A_R = \frac{Availability\,Questions\,Score + General\,Questions\,Score}{19} \qquad (9)$$

However, there is one exception in case the obtained question score equals 0. In this situation mentioned requirement is equal to 0 as well.

$$\text{if } (Confidentiality\,Questions\,Score == 0) \text{ then } C_R = 0$$
$$\text{if } (Integrity\,Questions\,Score == 0) \text{ then } I_R = 0$$
$$\text{if } (Availability\,Questions\,Score == 0) \text{ then } A_R = 0 \qquad (10)$$

The last task before final calculations of the vulnerability priority are made is to determine the numerical evaluation of the countermeasures. It affects the CIA triad or more precisely a modified version of the impact on the CIA triad, which is also included into assessing the requirement to ensure all three parameters. As a result, countermeasures are linked to both the vulnerability itself and the asset containing a vulnerability. Firstly, it is important to define these three values for the following calculations.

Definition 9. *Confidentiality Protection* C_P *is the protection of the asset's confidentiality using defined countermeasures. This value is defined on the interval $\langle 0, 1 \rangle$ in real numbers. A higher numerical rating means less influence of confidentiality protection, i.e. a higher priority of vulnerability.*

$$C_P = \langle 0, 1 \rangle \subset \mathbb{R} \qquad (11)$$

Definition 10. *Integrity Protection* I_P *is a numerical expression of the asset's integrity protection using defined countermeasures. This value is defined on the interval $\langle 0, 1 \rangle$ above the set of real numbers. A higher numerical rating means less integrity protection and as a result a higher priority of vulnerability.*

$$I_P = \langle 0, 1 \rangle \subset \mathbb{R} \tag{12}$$

Definition 11. *Availability Protection* A_P *is a numerical expression of the protection of asset's availability using defined countermeasures. This value is defined on the interval $\langle 0, 1 \rangle$ above the set of real numbers. A higher numerical rating means less impact on accessibility protection and as a result a higher priority of vulnerability.*

$$A_P = \langle 0, 1 \rangle \subset \mathbb{R} \tag{13}$$

The questionnaire for the evaluation of countermeasures includes 13 items divided into groups according to the parameter of the CIA triad. The evaluation of confidentiality, integrity and availability of protection is calculated as the product of all numerical values of individual items in a given group.

For example, a confidentiality assessment includes five items: encryption, access control, firewall, microsegmentation and antivirus system. Next, it is necessary to calculate a product from given parameters and the result identifies a degree of asset's confidentiality protection.

If the numerical value of the countermeasure from the confidentiality group is denoted as $P_C i$, where i is an iterator across all items in the group. Analogously it is possible to express the value of the countermeasure from the integrity group using $P_I i$ and the value of the countermeasure from the availability group using a $P_A i$ notation. Then in order to calculate a protection score of individual elements of the CIA triad, the following statements are used.

$$\begin{aligned} C_P &= P_C 1 \cdot P_C 2 \cdot P_C 3 \cdot P_C 4 \cdot P_C 5 \\ I_P &= P_I 1 \cdot P_I 2 \cdot P_I 3 \cdot P_I 4 \cdot P_I 5 \\ A_P &= P_A 1 \cdot P_A 2 \cdot P_A 3 \cdot P_A 4 \cdot P_A 5 \end{aligned} \tag{14}$$

Once the set of parameters describing the vulnerability and the requirements for ensuring the CIA triad of the vulnerable system is described. It is possible to pay attention to the final calculation of the priority. First, a vulnerability score is calculated. The score does not include the impact on the CIA triad and is calculated as the sum of all parameters multiplied by their weight.

Definition 12. *Vulnerability Score* S *is a numerical expression of the vulnerability parameters that affect its priority. It is defined as the product of the elements of the set D and the corresponding weights from the set D_W, see the Definitions 1 and 2.*

$$S = \sum_{i=1}^{6} D_i D_W i \tag{15}$$

Once the vulnerability score is calculated, the modified impact on the individual parameters of the CIA triad should be counted up. This means correlating values representing the requirements of confidentiality, integrity and availability with the impact coefficient and with the protection coefficient. The impact coefficient is determined during vulnerability assessment. The protection coefficient is defined by implemented measures. The modified impact is calculated as the product of the impact, the parameter's requirement and the degree of protection.

Definition 13. Modified Confidentiality Impact C_M *expresses the possible impact on vulnerable system's confidentiality in case of a vulnerability exploitation, which already includes the confidentiality requirement* C_R *and the confidentiality protection* C_P. C_M *is defined as a real number on the interval* $\langle 0,1 \rangle$. *A higher numerical rating means a higher impact on confidentiality.*

$$C_M = \langle 0,1 \rangle \subset \mathbb{R}$$
$$C_M = C \cdot C_R \cdot C_P \tag{16}$$

Definition 14. Modified Integrity Impact I_M *is a numerical expression of the possible impact on vulnerable system's integrity in case of a vulnerability exploitation, which already includes the integrity requirement* I_R *and integrity protection* I_P. I_M *is defined on the interval* $\langle 0,1 \rangle$ *above the set of real numbers. A higher numerical rating means a higher impact on integrity.*

$$I_M = \langle 0,1 \rangle \subset \mathbb{R}$$
$$I_M = I \cdot I_R \cdot I_P \tag{17}$$

Definition 15. Modified Availability Impact A_M *is a numerical expression of the possible impact on vulnerable system's availability in case of a vulnerability exploitation, which already includes the availability requirement* A_R *and availability protection* A_P. A_M *is defined on the interval* $\langle 0,1 \rangle$ *above the set of real numbers. A higher numerical rating means a higher impact on availability.*

$$A_M = \langle 0,1 \rangle \subset \mathbb{R}$$
$$A_M = A \cdot A_R \cdot A_P \tag{18}$$

Next, the modified vulnerability score should be calculated. The score already covers the modified impacts on the elements of the CIA triad.

Definition 16. Modified Vulnerability Score S_M *is a numerical expression of the vulnerability parameters that affect its priority. Instead of the parameters of confidentiality, integrity and availability, their modified forms are taken into calculation. Modified parameters take into account the information about asset priority, the level of protection provided by the implemented countermeasures etc. Modified score is defined as the product of the vulnerability score and the sum of all modified parameters of the CIA triad.*

$$S_M = S \cdot (C_M + I_M + A_M) \tag{19}$$

Definition 17. *Vulnerability Priority* P *is the severity of a vulnerability in terms of necessity of its remediation. It is defined as an integer number on the interval $\langle 0, 1000 \rangle$. A higher numerical rating means a higher priority.*

$$P = \langle 0, 1000 \rangle \subset \mathbb{R} \tag{20}$$

Vulnerability priority is calculated as the ratio of the modified vulnerability score to the maximum possible score. The maximum score equals 12.3 in this methodology. The result is multiplied by 1000 for better prioritization without decimal numbers. Finally, the result is rounded to an integer.

$$P = \frac{S_M}{12.3} \cdot 1000 \tag{21}$$

For better understanding of the final priority of vulnerability and its calculations, the raw statement is given below 22.

$$P = \frac{\sum_{i=1}^{6} D_i D_W i \cdot (C \cdot C_R \cdot C_P + I \cdot I_R \cdot I_P + A \cdot A_R \cdot A_P)}{12.3} \cdot 1000 \tag{22}$$

3   Evaluation of the Method Suitability

In order to evaluate the functionality of the suggested approach, the proposed method was applied on the environment of a medium-sized company, whose basic infrastructure includes approximately 30 servers and 200 endpoints.

Firstly, identified vulnerabilities were evaluated based on the CVSS score, next using our method. In order to analyze the appropriateness of the method, several vulnerabilities were selected on different company assets (in order to make it more readable the comparison results). All end-stations in the company were similar (installed applications, application version, operating system), therefore only a representative sample of vulnerabilities end stations was included in the comparison. Not all vulnerabilities of 30 servers were included in the comparison, but a representative sample of different types of servers with different purposes (database, web server and application server). Based on the above written facts, a total of 56 vulnerabilities were selected for comparison, however this selection is sufficient to present the strengths of the proposed method[3].

The obtained vulnerability score are summarized in Table 3. Moreover, the graphical representation of the comparison is depicted in Fig. 1. The x-axis in the graph (Fig. 1) corresponds to the numerical label in the Table 3, for example, the number 1 corresponds to vulnerability CVE-2014-3566. The values related to the asset's priority and countermeasures were determined using suggested questionnaires and were filled in by the owners of the monitored assets. It is evident, many vulnerabilities are classified with the same CVSS score, which equals 5.5 or 5.6 points. For example vulnerabilities labeled with number 11 to 20 or 31 to 35.

---

[3] Together 200 vulnerabilities were not selected for the comparisons, there were recurrent or not relevant for comparison due to low severity, no prioritization is required.

Eight vulnerabilities were critical (CVSS score higher that 8.8, marked with blue and orange color in the Table 3). All vulnerabilities were classified with CVSS score 5.5 or higher, it means almost all take place in the upper half of the graph. There was only one exception, CVE-2014-3566 with score 3.4 with wrong prioritisation. It means CVSS method does not reflect parameters such implemented countermeasures, asset importance or current technical parameters.

On closer inspection (Table 3), we observe vulnerabilities that are repeated on more company assets. In terms of the CVSS method, all occurrences of these vulnerabilities have the same rating, for example vulnerabilities with number 11 to 13, 14 to 16 or 17 to 19. However, in terms of the priority based on the proposed method, the score is different for each occurrence. This result is based on the different priority of the asset, the implemented countermeasures and the related complexity of exploitation. From this point of view, the proposed method can prioritize differently the identical types of vulnerabilities, that occur on different company assets. This eliminates the often criticized deficiency of CVSS score.

The proposed method takes advantage of the priority of the asset and the implemented countermeasures during the calculation. Therefore, a lot of vulnerabilities are located at the bottom part of the graph (the priority of the implementation of the measure is not critical). Furthermore, our method prioritizes more effectively the critical ones that have high security requirements for CIA's triad. On the other side, the method suppresses critical vulnerabilities on non-priority assets. Based on the obtained results, it is clear that prioritizing of vulnerabilities is more effectively and the results correspond to real requirements.

The selected specific examples of vulnerabilities are shown in the Table 2, 3, 4 and 5 in order to inspect the functionality of the method in more detailed. Vulnerabilities in Table 3 marked with the dark blue color are examined in detail in Table 2, vulnerabilities marked with light blue color are examined in Table 3, vulnerabilities marked with yellow color are examined in Table 4 and red vulnerabilities from Table 5. These tables provide examples of the vulnerabilities with height CVSS score. Even though, the CVSS score is equal, the final score based on the method proposed using our method is diametrically opposed.

A good example of method functionality is the prioritization of vulnerability CVE-2020-1350 listed in Table 2. This vulnerability was found on two different servers. The first one was placed in a test environment, so the requirements for ensuring the CIA triad are naturally low. The second one was part of the production environment which is critical for business processes of the company. For this reason, the second server has high requirements to ensure the CIA triad. This crucial difference that asset priority is not reflected with the CVSS score. Moreover, CVSS score does not reflect the countermeasures, which was paradoxically more sophisticated on the test server, because the production server was still under construction. Purposed method can take all these crucial parameters into account and only the vulnerability on the production server is prioritized.

4   Conclusion and Future Work

A motivation for proposing a new method for vulnerability assessment was the occurrence of the large number of critical vulnerabilities in common networks. Currently used methods (e.g. CVSS) fail while being applied on prioritization problem. As a result, it complicates the implementation of countermeasures. Our proposed method includes not only the technical parameters of the vulnerability, but also takes into account asset's level of implemented countermeasures. The obtained results show the suitability of our method for real assessing of assets and. The formal calculation of the final priority is based on basic mathematical operations. It means that our method is computationally effective. Furthermore, the obtained priority of vulnerability is very precise.

In the future, we focus on following practical improvement of the method. It is necessary to test the method on a larger set of assets and vulnerabilities in order to evaluate whether the weights of individual parameters are appropriate for practical usage. For easier method's integration into existing company infrastructures, which already have own asset management, a mechanism will be necessary to create that imports asset priorities from existing evaluation databases. Finally, permanent parameters describing vulnerabilities with information about patches and their availability should be added in a similar way as in the temporary CVSS score.

5   Attachments

Table 1. Weight of individual parameters describing the vulnerability.

Parameter	Weight
Threat intelligence	1
Exploitation	0,8
Information availability	0,4
User interaction	0,7
Privileges required	0,7
Difficulty of exploitation	0,5

Table 2. Comparison of vulnerabilities with CVSSv3 10.0 according to the evaluation of the new method.

Vulnerability CVE	CVE-2020-1350	CVE-2020-1350
Asset CIA Requirements	0.24; 0.56; 0.24	1; 0.91; 0.96
Countermeasures	0.47; 0.47; 0.58	0.47; 0.9; 1
Threat Intelligence	1	1
Exploitation	0.33	0.33
Information Availability	1	1
User Interaction	1	1
Privileges Required	1	1
Difficulty of Exploitation	1	1
Confidentiality Impact	1	1
Integrity Impact	1	1
Availability Impact	1	1
CVSSv3	**10**	**10**
Method proposed	**149**	**652**

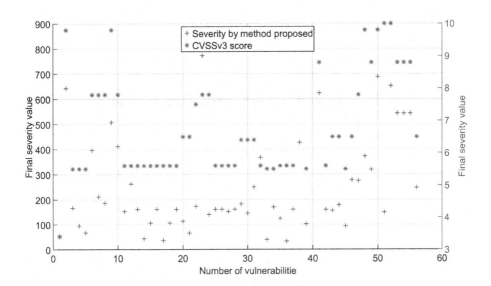

Fig. 1. Comparison of CVSSv3 and our method.

Table 3. Labeled vulnerabilities depicted in Fig. 1 including the final score.

		Counterme			Asset			Vulnerability										
Label	CVE	Cp	Ip	Ap	Cr	Ir	Ar	Threat Intelligence	Exploitation	Information Availability	User Interaction	Privileges Required	Dificulty of Exploitation	C	I	A	CVSSv3.x	Own method
1	CVE-2014-3566	0,5	0,8	1	0,7	0,5	0,5	0,25	0,11	1	0,4	1	0,78	0,67	0,11	0,11	3,4	56
2	CVE-2016-0132	0,9	0,9	0,9	1	0,9	1	0,5	0,33	1	1	1	1	1	1	1	9,8	643
3	CVE-2016-3209	0,9	0,9	0,9	1	0,9	1	0,25	0,11	0,44	0,4	1	0,78	1	0,11	0,11	5,5	166
4	CVE-2016-3262	0,7	0,8	0,8	0,8	0,6	0,4	0,25	0,11	0,44	0,4	1	0,78	1	0,11	0,11	5,5	95
5	CVE-2016-3263	0,5	0,8	1	0,7	0,5	0,5	0,25	0,11	0,44	0,4	1	0,78	1	0,11	0,11	5,5	67
6	CVE-2016-3270	0,9	0,9	0,9	1	0,9	1	0,25	0,11	0,44	0,4	1	0,78	1	1	1	7,8	396
7	CVE-2016-3393	0,7	0,8	0,8	0,8	0,6	0,4	0,25	0,11	0,44	0,4	1	0,78	1	1	1	7,8	211
8	CVE-2016-3396	0,5	0,8	1	0,7	0,5	0,5	0,25	0,11	0,44	0,4	1	0,78	1	1	1	7,8	186
9	CVE-2016-7182	0,9	0,9	0,9	1	0,9	1	0,25	0,11	0,44	1	1	1	1	1	1	9,8	507
10	CVE-2017-0160	0,9	0,9	0,9	1	0,9	1	0	0,33	0,11	1	0,8	0,78	1	1	1	7,8	411
11	CVE-2017-5715	0,7	0,7	1	0,8	0,5	0,5	1	0,11	1	1	0,8	0,44	1	0,11	0,11	5,6	152
12	CVE-2017-5715	0,9	0,9	0,9	1	0,9	1	1	0,11	1	1	0,8	0,44	1	0,11	0,11	5,6	262
13	CVE-2017-5715	0,5	0,9	1	1	0,9	1	1	0,11	1	1	0,8	0,44	1	0,11	0,11	5,6	161
14	CVE-2017-5753	0,5	0,5	0,6	0,2	0,6	0,2	1	0,56	1	1	0,8	0,78	1	0,11	0,11	5,6	44
15	CVE-2017-5753	0,5	0,8	1	0,7	0,5	0,5	1	0,11	1	1	0,8	0,44	1	0,11	0,11	5,6	106
16	CVE-2017-5753	0,5	0,9	1	1	0,9	1	1	0,11	1	1	0,8	0,44	1	0,11	0,11	5,6	161
17	CVE-2017-5754	0,5	0,5	0,6	0,2	0,6	0,2	0,75	0,11	1	1	0,8	0,78	1	0,11	0,11	5,6	37
18	CVE-2017-5754	0,5	0,8	1	0,7	0,5	0,5	1	0,11	1	1	0,8	0,44	1	0,11	0,11	5,6	106
19	CVE-2017-5754	0,5	0,9	1	1	0,9	1	1	0,11	1	1	0,8	0,44	1	0,11	0,11	5,6	161
20	CVE-2017-8529	0,7	0,7	1	0,8	0,5	0,5	0,25	0,11	1	0,4	1	1	1	0,11	0,11	6,5	113
21	CVE-2017-8529	0,5	0,8	1	0,7	0,5	0,5	0,25	0,11	0,11	0,4	1	1	1	0,11	0,11	6,5	66
22	CVE-2017-8547	0,5	0,8	1	0,7	0,5	0,5	0,25	0,11	0,11	0,4	1	0,78	1	1	1	7,5	173
23	CVE-2017-8759	0,9	0,9	0,9	1	0,9	1	1	1	1	0,4	1	1	1	1	1	7,8	773
24	CVE-2018-1039	0,7	0,8	0,8	0,8	0,6	0,4	0	0,11	0,11	1	0,8	0,78	0,22	1	1	7,8	140
25	CVE-2018-12126	0,5	0,9	1	1	0,9	1	1	0,11	1	1	0,8	0,44	1	0,11	0,11	5,6	161
26	CVE-2018-12127	0,5	0,9	1	1	0,9	1	1	0,11	1	1	0,8	0,44	1	0,11	0,11	5,6	161
27	CVE-2018-12130	0,7	0,7	1	0,8	0,5	0,5	1	0,11	1	1	0,8	0,44	1	0,11	0,11	5,6	152
28	CVE-2018-12130	0,5	0,9	1	1	0,9	1	1	0,11	1	1	0,8	0,44	1	0,11	0,11	5,6	161
29	CVE-2018-3615	0,7	0,7	1	0,8	0,5	0,5	1	0,11	1	1	0,8	0,44	1	0,56	0,11	6,4	183
30	CVE-2018-3615	0,5	0,8	1	0,7	0,5	0,5	1	0,11	1	1	0,8	0,44	1	0,56	0,11	6,4	145
31	CVE-2018-3615	0,5	0,9	1	1	0,9	1	1	0,11	1	1	0,8	0,44	1	0,56	0,11	6,4	250
32	CVE-2018-3620	0,5	0,9	1	1	0,9	1	1	0,11	1	1	0,8	0,44	1	0,11	0,11	5,6	36?
33	CVE-2018-3639	0,5	0,5	0,6	0,2	0,6	0,2	1	0,11	1	1	0,8	0,78	1	0,11	0,11	5,5	40
34	CVE-2018-3639	0,5	0,9	1	1	0,9	1	1	0,11	1	1	0,8	0,78	1	0,11	0,11	5,5	170
35	CVE-2018-3640	0,7	0,7	1	0,8	0,5	0,5	0,5	0,33	0,44	1	0,8	0,44	1	0,11	0,11	5,6	124
36	CVE-2018-3646	0,5	0,5	0,6	0,2	0,6	0,2	0,5	0,11	1	1	0,8	0,78	1	0,11	0,11	5,6	34
37	CVE-2018-3646	0,5	0,9	1	1	0,9	1	1	0,11	1	1	0,8	0,44	1	0,11	0,11	5,6	161
38	CVE-2018-8421	0,9	0,9	0,9	1	0,9	1	0	0,11	0,11	1	1	1	1	1	1	9,8	427
39	CVE-2019-0663	0,7	0,8	0,8	0,8	0,6	0,4	0,25	0,11	0,11	1	0,8	0,78	1	0,11	0,11	5,5	102
40	CVE-2019-0708	0,9	0,9	0,9	1	0,9	1	1	1	1	1	1	1	1	1	1	9,8	861
41	CVE-2019-1113	0,9	0,9	0,9	1	0,9	1	1	0,11	1	0,4	1	1	1	1	1	8,8	623
42	CVE-2019-11135	0,7	0,7	1	0,8	0,5	0,5	1	0,11	1	1	0,8	0,78	1	0,11	0,11	5,6	160
43	CVE-2019-11135	0,7	0,8	0,8	0,8	0,6	0,4	0,25	1	1	1	0,8	0,78	1	0,11	0,11	6,5	156
44	CVE-2019-11135	0,5	0,9	1	1	0,9	1	1	0,33	1	1	0,8	0,78	1	0,11	0,11	6,5	179
45	CVE-2019-1142	0,5	0,8	0,8	0,8	0,6	0,4	0	0,11	0,11	1	0,8	0,78	0,22	1	0,11	5,5	94
46	CVE-2019-20503	0,5	0,9	1	1	0,9	1	1	0,11	1	0,4	1	1	0,22	0,11	1	6,5	278
47	CVE-2019-9854	0,5	0,9	1	1	0,9	1	0	0,11	0,11	0,4	1	0,78	1	1	1	7,8	275
48	CVE-2019-9855	0,5	0,9	1	1	0,9	1	0	0,11	0,11							9,8	372
49	CVE-2020-0605	0,9	0,9	0,9	1	0,9	1	1	0,56	0,44	0,4						8,8	319
50	CVE-2020-0646	0,9	0,9	0,9	1	0,9	1	0,75	0,56	0,44	0,4						9,8	688
51	CVE-2020-1350	0,5	0,5	0,6	0,2	0,6	0,2	1	0,33	1	1	1	1	1	1	1	10	493
52	CVE-2020-1350	0,5	0,9	1	1	0,9	1	1	0,33	1	1	1	1	1	1	1	10	652
53	CVE-2020-6805	0,5	0,9	1	1	0,9	1	1	0,11	1	0,4	1	1	1	1	1	8,8	543
54	CVE-2020-6806	0,5	0,9	1	1	0,9	1	1	0,11	1	0,4						8,8	
55	CVE-2020-6807	0,5	0,9	1	1	0,9	1	1	0,11	1	0,4	1	1	1	1	1	8,8	543
56	CVE-2020-6808	0,5	0,9	1	1	0,9	1	1	0,11	1	0,4	1	1	0,22	1	0,11	6,5	248

Table 4. Comparison of vulnerabilities with CVSSv3 8.8 according to the evaluation of the new method.

Vulnerability CVE	CVE-2019-1113	CVE-2020-0605	CVE-2020-6806
Asset CIA Requirements	1; 0.91; 0.96	0.81; 0.62; 0.44	1; 0.91; 0.96
Countermeasures	0.9; 0.9; 0.9	0.65; 0.8; 0.8	0.47; 0.9; 1
Threat Intelligence	1	0.75	1
Exploitation	0.11	0.56	0.11
Information Availability	1	0.44	1
User Interaction	0.4	0.4	0.4

(*continued*)

Table 4. (*continued*)

Vulnerability CVE	CVE-2019-1113	CVE-2020-0605	CVE-2020-6806
Privileges Required	1	1	1
Dificulty of Exploitation	1	1	1
Confidentiality Impact	1	1	1
Integrity Impact	1	1	1
Availability Impact	1	1	1
CVSSv3	**8.8**	**8.8**	**8.8**
Method proposed	**623**	**319**	**543**

Table 5. Comparison of vulnerabilities with CVSSv3 5.6 according to the evaluation of the new method.

Vulnerability CVE	CVE-2018-12126	CVE-2018-3620	CVE-2018-3646
Asset CIA Requirements	1; 0.91; 0.96	1; 0.91; 0.96	0.24; 0.56; 0.24
Countermeasures	0.47; 0.9; 1	0.47; 0.9; 1	0.47; 0.47; 0.58
Threat Intelligence	1	1	0.5
Exploitation	0.11	0.11	0.11
Information Availability	1	1	1
User Interaction	1	1	1
Privileges Required	0.8	0.8	0.8
Dificulty of Exploitation	0.44	0.44	0.78
Confidentiality Impact	1	1	1
Integrity Impact	0.11	0.11	0.11
Availability Impact	0.11	1	0.11
CVSSv3	**5.6**	**5.6**	**5.6**
Method proposed	**161**	**367**	**34**

Table 6. Parameters used in the purposed method for calculations

Possible values of the Impact on Confidentiality	
Verbal evaluation	*Numerical evaluation*
Minimum amount of stolen insensitive data	0.22
Minimum amount of stolen critical data	0.67
Extensive amount of stolen insensitive data	0.67
Extensive amount of stolen critical data	0.78
Theft of all data	1
Possible values of the Impact on Integrity	
Verbal evaluation	*Numerical evaluation*
Minimum amount of slightly corrupted data	0.11
Minimum amount of severely corrupted data	0.33
Extensive amount of slightly corrupted data	0.56
Extensive amount of seriously corrupted data	0.78
Complete corruption of all data	1
Possible values of Difficulty of Exploitation	
Verbal evaluation	*Numerical evaluation*
Very High	0.00
High	0.44
Low	0.78
Very Low	1
Possible values of the Exploitation	
Verbal evaluation	*Numerical evaluation*
Not defined	0.50
Theoretical	0.11
Proof-of-Concept	0.33
Simple	0.56
Using automated tools	1
Possible values of Privileges Required	
Verbal evaluation	*Numerical evaluation*
None	1
Low	0.80
High	0.40
Possible values of User Interaction	
Verbal evaluation	*Numerical evaluation*
None	1
Required	0.40
Possible values of the Threat Intelligence	
Verbal evaluation	*Numerical evaluation*
Not defined	0.50
None	0.00
Low	0.25
Medium	0.50
High	0.75
Very High	1

(continued)

Table 6. (*continued*)

Possible values of the Impact on Confidentiality	
Possible values of the Information Availability	
Verbal evaluation	*Numerical evaluation*
Not defined	0.50
Unknown	0.11
Secret	0.44
Known	0.67
Publicly known	1
Possible values of the Impact on Availability	
Verbal evaluation	*Numerical evaluation*
Minimal unavailability of secondary service	0.11
Minimum unavailability of primary service	0.56
Extensive unavailability of secondary service	0.56
Extensive unavailability of primary service	0.78
Complete unavailability of all services	1

References

1. Common vulnerability scoring system v3.1: Specification document (2019). https://www.first.org/cvss/v3-1/cvss-v31-specification_r1.pdf
2. Albeniz, Z.: Cvss: characterizing and scoring vulnerabilities (2019). https://www.netsparker.com/blog/web-security/cvss-characterizing-and-scoring-vulnerabilities/
3. Bekerman, D., Yerushalmi, S.: The state of vulnerabilities in 2019 (2020). https://www.imperva.com/blog/the-state-of-vulnerabilities-in-2019/
4. Bhatt, N., Anand, A., Yadavalli, V.S.S., Kumar, V.: Modeling and characterizing software vulnerabilities (2017)
5. Davis, P., et al.: Vulnerability intelligence report (2018). https://static.tenable.com/translations/en/Vulnerability_Intelligence_Report-ENG.pdf
6. Feutrill, A., Ranathunga, D., Yarom, Y., Roughan, M.: The effect of common vulnerability scoring system metrics on vulnerability exploit delay. In: Sixth International Symposium on Computing and Networking (CANDAR), pp. 1–10 (2018). https://doi.org/10.1109/CANDAR.2018.00009, https://ieeexplore.ieee.org/document/8594738/
7. Fruhwirth, C., Mannisto, T.: Improving cvss-based vulnerability prioritization and response with context information. In: 3rd International Symposium on Empirical Software Engineering and Measurement, pp. 535–544 (2009). https://doi.org/10.1109/ESEM.2009.5314230, http://ieeexplore.ieee.org/document/5314230/
8. Keramati, M.: New vulnerability scoring system for dynamic security evaluation. In: 8th International Symposium on Telecommunications (IST), pp. 746–751 (2016). https://doi.org/10.1109/ISTEL.2016.7881922, http://ieeexplore.ieee.org/document/7881922/
9. Nist, S.: 800–53, revision 4. Security and Privacy Controls for Federal Information Systems and Organizations (2013)
10. Palanov, N.: Vulnerability categories and severity levels: "informational" vulnerabilities vs. true vulnerabilities (2016). https://blog.rapid7.com/2016/12/15/vulnerability-categories-and-severity-levels-informational-vulnerabilities-vs-true-vulnerabilities/

11. Scarfone, K., Mell, P.: An analysis of cvss version 2 vulnerability scoring. In: 3rd International Symposium on Empirical Software Engineering and Measurement, pp. 516–525 (2009)
12. Sibal, Ritu., Sharma, Ruchi, Sabharwal, Sangeeta: Prioritizing software vulnerability types using multi-criteria decision-making techniques. Life Cycle Reliab. Saf. Eng. **6**(1), 57–67 (2017). https://doi.org/10.1007/s41872-017-0006-8
13. Spring, J., Hatleback, A., Manion, A., Shic, D.: Towards improving CVSS. Software Engineering Institute, Carnegie Mellon University, Tech. Rep (2018)
14. for Standardization, I.O.: ISO/IEC 27001: 2013: Information Technology-Security Techniques-Information Security Management Systems-Requirements. International Organization for Standardization (2013)
15. Tai, W.: What is vpr and how is it different from cvss? (2020). https://www.tenable.com/blog/what-is-vpr-and-how-is-it-different-from-cvss
16. Tripathi, A., Singh, U.K.: On prioritization of vulnerability categories based on cvss scores. In: 6th International Conference on Computer Sciences and Convergence Information Technology (ICCIT), pp. 692–697. IEEE (2011)
17. Wang, R., Gao, L., Sun, Q., Sun, D.: An improved cvss-based vulnerability scoring mechanism. In: Third International Conference on Multimedia Information Networking and Security, pp. 352–355 (2011). https://doi.org/10.1109/MINES.2011.27, http://ieeexplore.ieee.org/document/6103789/
18. Williams, J.: Owasp risk rating methodology (2020). https://owasp.org/www-community/OWASP_Risk_Rating_Methodology

An IND-CCA2 Attack Against the 1st- and 2nd-Round Versions of NTS-KEM

Tung Chou[✉]

Academia Sinica, 128 Academia Road, Sect. 2, Nankang, Taipei 11529, Taiwan
blueprint@crypto.tw

Abstract. This paper presents an IND-CCA2 attack against the 1st-and 2nd-round versions of NTS-KEM, i.e., the versions before the update in December 2019. Our attack works against the 1st- and 2nd-round specifications, with a number of decapsulation queries upper-bounded by $n - k$ and an advantage lower-bounded by roughly $0.5(n - k)t/n^2$, where n, k, and t stand for the code length, code dimension, and the designed decoding capacity, for all the three parameter sets of NTS-KEM. We found that the non-reference implementations are also vulnerable to our attack, even though there are bugs. There are also bugs in the reference implementations, but in a way invulnerable to our attack.

Keywords: NIST PQC standardization · Post-quantum cryptogrphy · Code-based cryptography · IND-CCA2

1 Introduction

NTS-KEM [1] is a key encapsulation mechanism submitted to the NIST Post-Quantum Cryptography Standardization Process. NTS-KEM is one of the 25 submissions that entered the second round of the process. On 3 December, 2019, during the second round of the process, Paterson, one of the principal submitters of NTS-KEM, wrote the message in Appendix A (without the emphasis added) in an email to NIST's pqc-forum mailing list, to announce an update in their specification.

We call this new version the *updated* 2nd-round version of NTS-KEM, of which the specification can be found in [3], while the 2nd-round version of NTS-KEM refers to the version submitted in March 2019 [2]. NTS-KEM did not advance to the 3rd round as NTS-KEM and Classic McEliece [5] have merged. The merged submission is called Classic McEliece and equals the 2nd-round version of Classic McEliece.

Maram's recent paper [13] discusses more about this "subtle issue" caused by omission of re-encryption. In particular, [13, Section 3.1] argues that it might be possible for an IND-CCA2 adversary against the 1st- and 2nd-round NTS-KEM to modify the last $n - k$ bits of the challenge ciphertext (where n and k stand for

This work was supported by Taiwan Ministry of Science and Technology (MOST) Grant 109-2222-E-001-001-MY3. Permanent ID of this document: eb8cb246e2f1ea188ad29d 70680e73f8. Date: 2020.12.8.

the code length and code dimension), such that the decapsulation oracle returns the encapsulated session key. If this happens with a sufficiently high probability, clearly IND-CCA2 security of the 1st- and 2nd-round version of NTS-KEM is broken. However, Maram did not present any concrete IND-CCA2 attack in the paper.

1.1   Our Contribution

In this paper, we present a simple IND-CCA2 attack against the 1st- and 2nd-round versions of NTS-KEM [1,2]. The attack takes only a few decapsulation queries and bit flips, and it succeeds with a high probability. Our attack follows Maram's strategy: the adversary recovers the encapsulated session key by modifying the last $n - k$ bits of the challenge ciphertext. Our attack does exploit NTS-KEM's Berlekamp-Massey algorithm, but in a way without forcing the algorithm to "operate beyond its natural decoding capacity": what we did is to force the algorithm to operate *below* the designed decoding capacity t.

To be more precise, our attack works against the 1st- and 2nd-round specifications. The attack takes at most $n - k$ decapsulation queries and at most $n - k$ bit flips, and has an advantage lower-bounded by roughly $0.5(n - k)t/n^2$, for all the three parameter sets of NTS-KEM. We found that the non-reference implementations are also vulnerable to our attack, even though there are bugs. There are also bugs in the reference implementations, but in a way invulnerable to our attack.

One might argue that since the NTS-KEM team has updated their specification, it is not meaningful to study the security of the old specifications. However, we think it is meaningful to study the security of the 1st- and 2nd-round versions of NTS-KEM for the following reasons.

- In April 2018, Cheng from PQ Solutions Limited wrote the following message in an email to the pqc-forum mailing list.

  "We are particularly excited that one entity is already going to perform a substantial test on the performance and resilience of NTS-KEM in the not too distant future."

  On the 22 May, 2019, Cho from ADVA gave a talk [7] in the 7th Code-Based Cryptography Workshop. Cho presented experimental results of using code-based KEMs, including NTS-KEM, for secure optical communication. This shows that the source code of the 1st- and 2nd- round versions of NTS-KEM has been used by some people, and clearly they need to be warned about the attack.
- Maram wrote the following in [13, Section 3.1].

  "At the same time, we stress that the above described attack is just a possibility and is not a concrete attack. Because it is quite possible that, by analyzing the decoding algorithm used in NTS-KEM decapsulation, one might show such invalid ciphertexts are computationally hard to generate adversarially."

The sentences and Paterson's message suggest that the 1st- and 2nd-round versions of NTS-KEM are not nessarily insecure. Indeed, a scheme can be IND-CCA2 secure even if people do not know how to prove that. However, we show that there is a concrete IND-CCA2 attack against the 1st- and 2nd-round versions of NTS-KEM.

To demonstrate that our attack works against the 1st- and 2nd-round specifications and non-reference implementations, we have modified the files nts_kem.c, ntskem_test.c, and berlekamp_massey.c in the submission packages. The contents of the modified ntskem_test.c and berlekamp_massey.c are available at Appendix E and F. More details about these modified files and how to use them to demonstrate our attack are shown in Appedix D.

1.2 Related Works

We note that re-encryption is not a new countermeasure against attacks. For example, re-encryption is required in the well-known Fujisaki-Okamoto transform [10,11], which converts weakly secure public-key encryption schemes into CCA-secure ones. Dent [9] also makes use of re-encryption to construct CCA-secure key encapsulation mechanisms from weakly secure public-key encryption schemes. For comparison, a re-encryption step is included in the decapsulation algorithm of the 1st- and 2nd-round versions of Classic McEliece [5].

1.3 Organization

Section 2 gives some basic knowledge about key encapsulation mechanisms and code-based cryptography. Section 3 introduces the 1st- and 2nd-round NTS-KEM. Section 4 presents our attack and how it works against the 1st- and 2nd-round specifications and non-reference implementations. For completeness, Appendix C explains why our attack does not work against the reference implementations.

2 Preliminaries

This section presents some basic knowledge on key encapsulation mechanisms and code-based cryptography.

2.1 Key Encapsulation Mechanisms (KEMs)

The concept of KEM was first introduced by Shoup [18]. A KEM KEM consists of the following three algorithms.

- The key generation algorithm KEM.KeyGen is a probabilistic, polynomial-time algorithm that outputs a key pair (PK, SK), where PK is the *public key* and SK is the *secret key*.

- The encapsulation algorithm KEM.Enc is a probabilistic polynomial-time algorithm that on input a public key PK, outputs (K, ψ), where $K \in \{0,1\}^\ell$ is the *session key* and ψ is the *ciphertext* encapsulating K.
- The decapsulation algorithm KEM.Dec is a deterministic polynomial-time algorithm that on input a secret key SK and a ciphertext ψ, outputs either a session key K or the special symbol $\perp$.

A KEM is required to be *sound*. For the purpose of this paper, one may simply assume that this means that the decapsulation algorithm always outputs the encapsulated session key as long as the input ciphertext is valid.

2.2   IND-CCA2 Security of KEMs

In order to define IND-CCA2 security of a KEM KEM, we consider a game consisting of the following steps played by an *adversary* and a *challenger*.

1. The challenger generates a key pair (PK, SK) by running KEM.KeyGen and sends PK to the adversary.
2. The adversary runs until it is ready to move to the next step. During this step, the adversary may make a sequence of queries to a *decapsulation oracle*. In each of the queries, the adversary submits a ciphertext ψ, and the oracle responds with KEM.Dec(SK, ψ).
3. The challenger prepares a pair (K^*, ψ^*) by carrying out the following steps and sends the pair to the adversary.

$$(K_0, \psi^*) \leftarrow \text{KEM.Enc(PK)};$$
$$K_1 \xleftarrow{\$} \{0,1\}^\ell;$$
$$\tau \xleftarrow{\$} \{0,1\};$$
$$K^* \leftarrow K_\tau;$$

4. The adversary runs until it is ready to move to the next step. During this step, the adversary may make a sequence of queries to the decapsulation oracle, under the condition that any ciphertext submitted by the adversary must be different from ψ^*.
5. The adversary outputs $\tau' \in \{0,1\}$.

The *advantage* of an adversary is defined as $|\Pr[\tau = \tau'] - 1/2|$. Traditionally, a KEM is said to be IND-CCA2 secure if for all probablistic, polynomial-time adversary, the advantage grows negligible in the security parameter λ. However, this definition requires that the KEM is defined as a family of systems. For KEMs with specific parameter sets, such as NTS-KEM, we evaluate the efficiency of an adversary by its actually running time and advantage.

2.3   Linear Codes

A *linear code* of *length* n and *dimension* k over a field $\mathbb{F}_q$ is a dimension-k linear subspace of $\mathbb{F}_q^n$. The elements in a code are called *codewords*. A linear code C can thus be represented by the row space of a matrix, in which case we call such a matrix a *generator matrix*. A linear code can also be represented by the right kernel space of a matrix, in which case we call such a matrix a *parity-check matrix*. Note that a generator matrix has at least k rows, and a parity-check matrix has at least $n - k$ rows.

Given a generator matrix $G \in \mathbb{F}_q^{k \times n}$ for a linear code, it is easy to compute a parity-check matrix H of the code using simple linear algebra techniques. In particular, if G has *systematic form*, which means $G = (I_k | Q)$ where Q is a $k \times (n - k)$ matrix, then $H = (-Q^T | I_{n-k})$ is a parity-check matrix for the same code, and vice versa. The *syndrome* of $v \in \mathbb{F}_q^n$ with respect to a parity-check matrix H is defined as vH^T.

The *Hamming weight* of a vector in $\mathbb{F}_q^n$ is the number of non-zero coordinates in it. We denote the Hamming weight of a vector v as $|v|$. The *minimum distance* of a nonzero linear code is the smallest Hamming weight of any nonzero codeword in C.

For a linear code C, a *decoding algorithm* takes $r \in \mathbb{F}_q^n$ and a positive integer w as inputs and outputs $e \in \mathbb{F}_q^n$ such that $|e| \leq w$ and $r - e \in C$, if such e exists. When the minimum distance is at least $2w + 1$, for any r, the vector e such that $|e| \leq w$ and $r - e \in C$ must be unique if it exists; In this case, we say that C can correct w errors.

2.4   Binary Goppa Codes

Given a field $\mathbb{F}_{2^m}$, a sequence $\alpha_1, \ldots, \alpha_n$ (called the *support*) of n distinct elements from $\mathbb{F}_{2^m}$, and a degree-t polynomial $g \in \mathbb{F}_{2^m}[x]$ (called the *Goppa polynomial*) such that $g(\alpha_1) \cdots g(\alpha_n) \neq 0$, the Goppa code $\Gamma_2(\alpha_1, \ldots, \alpha_n, g)$ is defined as the set of vectors $c = (c_1, \ldots, c_n) \in \mathbb{F}_2^n$ such that

$$\sum_{i=1}^{n} \frac{c_i}{x - \alpha_i} \equiv 0 \mod g(x).$$

The dimension k of the code is at least $n - mt$. When g is square-free, the minimum distance of $\Gamma_2(\alpha_1, \ldots, \alpha_n, g)$ is known to be at least $2t + 1$, and

$$\Gamma_2(\alpha_1, \ldots, \alpha_n, g) = \Gamma_2(\alpha_1, \ldots, \alpha_n, g^2).$$

A specific parity-check matrix of $\Gamma_2(\alpha_1, \ldots, \alpha_n, g)$, which we denote as $\mathcal{H}(\alpha_1, \ldots, \alpha_n, g)$, is given as follows.

$$\begin{pmatrix} 1/g(\alpha_1) & 1/g(\alpha_2) & \cdots & 1/g(\alpha_n) \\ \alpha_1/g(\alpha_1) & \alpha_2/g(\alpha_2) & \cdots & \alpha_n/g(\alpha_n) \\ \vdots & \vdots & \ddots & \vdots \\ \alpha_1^{\mathrm{Deg}(g)-1}/g(\alpha_1) & \alpha_2^{\mathrm{Deg}(g)-1}/g(\alpha_2) & \cdots & \alpha_n^{\mathrm{Deg}(g)-1}/g(\alpha_n) \end{pmatrix},$$

where each of the tn entries is actually a column vector in $\mathbb{F}_2^m$, formed by the coordinates with respect to a chosen $\mathbb{F}_2$-basis of $\mathbb{F}_{2^m}$.

2.5   The McEliece Cryptosystem

The McEliece cryptosystem [15] is a public-key encryption system: it allows a sender to encrypt his/her messages as a ciphertext using the receiver's public key, such that the messages can only be decrypted from the ciphertexts using the receiver's secret key.

To generate the public key and secret key, the receiver first generates a code C over $\mathbb{F}_q$ of length n and dimension k with a decoder which is able to correct t errors. The receiver then computes a generator matrix G of C and generates a uniform random permutation matrix $P \in \mathbb{F}_q^{n \times n}$ and a uniform random invertible matrix $S \in \mathbb{F}_q^{k \times k}$. The receiver then publishes $\hat{G} = SGP$ as its public key and keeps (G, P, S) as its secret key.

To perform encryption, the sender computes the ciphertext $y = m\hat{G} + e$ where $m \in \mathbb{F}_q^k$ is the message and $e \in \mathbb{F}_q^n$ is a uniform random vector of weight t. To perform decryption, the receiver computes $yP^{-1} = mSG + eP^{-1}$ and applies a decoding algorithm to find mSG. From mSG the receiver then computes mS and m using linear algebra.

3   The 1st- and 2nd-Round Versions of NTS-KEM

This section presents the specifications of the 1st- and 2nd-round versions of NTS-KEM. The difference between the two versions is small: the 1st-round NTS-KEM uses *explicit rejection* in the decapsulation algorithm, meaning that the decapsulation algorithm returns $\perp$ when the ciphertext is considered invalid. The 2nd-round NTS-KEM uses *implicit rejection* in the decapsulation algorithm, meaning that it returns an ℓ-bit string when the ciphertext is considered invalid.

The reader might find that the key generation algorithm and the decoding algorithm presented in this section look simpler than the ones shown in the 1st- and 2nd-round specifications. We emphasize that this is because we decided to omit irrelevant details in the specifications to simplify our discussions. It is easy to see that the algorithms presented in this section are in fact equivalent to the ones shown in the specifications.

3.1   Public Parameters and Parameter Sets

The public parameters of an instance of NTS-KEM are as follows.

- $n = 2^m$, the length of the binary Goppa code.
- t, the number of errors that the code is designed to correct.
- $f(x) \in \mathbb{F}_2[x]$, an irreducible polynomial of degree m, which is used to construct $\mathbb{F}_{2^m} \cong \mathbb{F}_2[x]/f(x)$.
- $\ell = 256$, which denotes the length of session keys.

Table 1. The three parameter sets of NTS-KEM.

Parameter set	m	n	t
ntskem1264	12	4096	64
ntskem1380	13	8192	80
ntskem13136	13	8192	136

NTS-KEM also makes use of a pseudorandom bit generator, denoted as $H_\ell(\cdot)$, which outputs ℓ-bit strings. The three parameter sets of NTS-KEM are listed in Table 1.

3.2 Key Generation

To generate a secret key, the user starts with generating a uniform random square-free Goppa polynomial $g(x) \in \mathbb{F}_{2^m}[x]$ of degree t, and a uniform random support $\alpha_1, \ldots, \alpha_n$. Note that the support contains all elements of $\mathbb{F}_{2^m}$. The support and the Goppa polynomial then define the binary Goppa code $\Gamma_2(\alpha_1, \ldots, \alpha_n, g)$.

To compute the public key, the user first computes a "parity-check matrix"

$$H = \begin{pmatrix} 1/g^2(\alpha_1) & 1/g^2(\alpha_2) & \cdots & 1/g^2(\alpha_n) \\ \alpha_1/g^2(\alpha_1) & \alpha_2/g^2(\alpha_2) & \cdots & \alpha_n/g^2(\alpha_n) \\ \vdots & \vdots & \ddots & \vdots \\ \alpha_1^{t-1}/g^2(\alpha_1) & \alpha_2^{t-1}/g^2(\alpha_2) & \cdots & \alpha_n^{t-1}/g^2(\alpha_n) \end{pmatrix}$$

where each of the tn entries is again a column vector in $\mathbb{F}_2^m$ and then computes its "reduced row echelon form". Let $k = n - mt$. Once the reduced row echelon form is obtained, the user "reorders its columns if necessary" to get a parity-check matrix of the form $(Q^T | I_{n-k})$ and the corresponding generator matrix $(I_k | Q)$. Note that elements in the support need to be reordered in the same way as the columns. The public key is then (Q, t, ℓ).

It is not clear why H is used instead of $\mathcal{H}(\alpha_1, \ldots, \alpha_n, g)$. In fact, we have not found any existing literature showing that H is guaranteed to be a parity-check matrix of the binary Goppa code. Any H that has full rank are guaranteed to be a parity-check matrix, though. Indeed, as $\Gamma_2(\alpha_1, \ldots, \alpha_n, g) = \Gamma_2(\alpha_1, \ldots, \alpha_n, g^2)$, $\mathcal{H}(\alpha_1, \ldots, \alpha_n, g^2)$ is a parity-check matrix of the code; Observe that H consists of the first mt rows of $\mathcal{H}(\alpha_1, \ldots, \alpha_n, g^2)$, and the dimension of the code is at least $n - mt$; Therefore, if H has rank mt, it must have the same row space and right kernel as $\mathcal{H}(\alpha_1, \ldots, \alpha_n, g^2)$.

A secret key of the 1st-round version of NTS-KEM consists of three pieces of data which can be easily derived from $(\alpha_1, \ldots, \alpha_n, g)$. A secret key of the 2nd-round version of NTS-KEM consists of four pieces of data where the first three are the same as those in the 1st-round NTS-KEM, and the last one is simply a uniform random bit string $z \in \mathbb{F}_2^\ell$. To simplify our discussion, we consider that the secret key is simply $(\alpha_1, \ldots, \alpha_n, g)$ or $(\alpha_1, \ldots, \alpha_n, g, z)$.

The key generation algorithm above is *not* well-defined for the following reasons.

- It is possible that H is not full-rank, in which case it will be impossible to bring H to the form $(Q^T|I_{n-k})$, it is not written in the specifications how to deal with this case.
- It is not written in the specifications what "reduced row echelon form" means and how the columns should be re-ordered exactly. Even if one assumes the most common definition of reduced row echelon form, there are still multiple deterministic and non-deterministic ways to reorder the columns.

The implementations of NTS-KEM, however, show that H is reduced to a matrix that satisfies the following criteria.

- There is a sequence $c_{n-k-r+1} < c_{n-k-r+2} < \cdots < c_{n-k}$ such that for each $i \in \{n-k-r+1, \ldots, n-k\}$, row i ends with a 1 in column c_i, which is the only non-zero entry in column c_i.
- All rows before row $n - k - r + 1$ are zero rows.

Existence of zero rows means H is not full-rank. The implementations simply fail to generate a key pair when H is not full-rank, which seems extremely unlikely to happen for NTS-KEM's parameter sets. After reducing H, the implementations then swap column c_{n-k} with column $n - k$, swap column c_{n-k-1} with column $n - k - 1$, and so on to produce $(Q^T|I_{n-k})$.

As the key generation algorithm is not well-defined in the specifications, we simply assume that the implemented key generation algorithm is what the NTS-KEM team intended to specify, and we consider the implemented key generation algorithm for our discussion.

3.3   Encapsulation

Given an NTS-KEM public key (Q, t, ℓ), the encapsulation algorithm computes a session key and a ciphertext encapsulating it by carrying out the following steps.

- Generate a uniform random error vector $e \in \mathbb{F}_2^n$ with $|e| = t$.
- Partition e into $(e_a \mid e_b \mid e_c)$, where $e_a \in \mathbb{F}_2^{k-\ell}$, $e_b \in \mathbb{F}_2^\ell$, and $e_c \in \mathbb{F}_2^{n-k}$.
- Compute $k_e = H_\ell(e) \in \mathbb{F}_2^\ell$. Let $m = (e_a \mid k_e) \in \mathbb{F}_2^k$.
- Following McEliece encryption, compute $c \in \mathbb{F}_2^n$ as follows.

$$
\begin{aligned}
c &= m \cdot (I \mid Q) + e \\
&= (m \mid m \cdot Q) + e \\
&= (e_a \mid k_e \mid (e_a \mid k_e) \cdot Q) + (e_a \mid e_b \mid e_c) \\
&= (0_a \mid k_e + e_b \mid (e_a \mid k_e) \cdot Q + e_c) \\
&= (0_a \mid c_b \mid c_c),
\end{aligned}
$$

where 0_a is the zero vector of length $k - \ell$. Let the ciphertext be $(c_b \mid c_c)$.
- Compute the session key $k_r = H_\ell(k_e \mid e) \in \mathbb{F}_2^\ell$.
- Return $(k_r, (c_b \mid c_c))$.

3.4 Decapsulation

Given a ciphertext $(c_b \mid c_c)$, the decapsulation works as follows.

- Taking the vector $(0_a \mid c_b \mid c_c) \in \mathbb{F}_2^n$ and the secret key as inputs, compute $e \in \mathbb{F}_2^n$ using the decoding algorithm (see Sect. 3.5).
- Partition e into $(e_a \mid e_b \mid e_c)$, where $e_a \in \mathbb{F}_2^{k-\ell}$, $e_b \in \mathbb{F}_2^\ell$, and $e_c \in \mathbb{F}_2^{n-k}$, and compute $k_e = c_b - e_b$.
- Check if $H_\ell(e) = k_e$ and $|e| = t$. If both are true, return $k_r = H_\ell(k_e \mid e) \in \mathbb{F}_2^\ell$; Otherwise return $\perp$ for the 1st-round NTS-KEM or $H_\ell(z \mid 1_a \mid c_b \mid c_c)$ for the 2nd-round NTS-KEM.

3.5 The Decoding Algorithm

A strategy for decoding is to consider $\Gamma_2(\alpha_1, \ldots, \alpha_n, g)$ as an alternant code and use an alternant decoder to decode. A well-known alternant decoder is the Berlekamp decoder. To find the error positions, the Berlekamp decoder makes use of the Berlekamp-Massey algorithm ([4,14]) to compute an *error locator*, of which the roots are $\{\alpha_i^{-1} \mid e_i = 1, \alpha_i \neq 0\}$. In other words, by finding the roots of the error locator, we can find the error positions $\{i \mid e_i = 1, \alpha_i \neq 0\}$. Some more operations are required to figure out whether $e_i = 0$ or not.

NTS-KEM's decoding algorithm uses the strategy above but introduces some modifications. NTS-KEM's decoding algorithm makes use of NTSKEM_BM, which is a modified Berlekamp-Massey algorithm. In NTSKEM_BM, the error locator is computed and converted into a polynomial σ^*, of which the roots are simply $\{\alpha_i \mid e_i = 1, \alpha_i \neq 0\}$. NTSKEM_BM also computes a value $\xi \in \{0,1\}$, to indicate whether $e_{\text{pos}(0)} = 1$. Given an input vector $r \in \mathbb{F}_2^n$, NTS-KEM's decoding algorithm works as follows.

- Compute the syndrome $s = r \cdot \mathcal{H}(\alpha_1, \ldots, \alpha_n, g^2)^T \in \mathbb{F}_{2^m}^{2t}$.
- Compute $(\sigma^*(x), \xi) \leftarrow \text{NTSKEM\_BM}(s)$, where $\sigma^*(x) \in \mathbb{F}_{2^m}[x]$ and $\xi \in \{0, 1\}$.
- Set $e = 0 \in \mathbb{F}_2^n$.
- Set $e_i = 1$ for all i such that $\sigma^*(\alpha_i) = 0$.
- Set $e_{\text{pos}(0)} = 1$ if $\xi = 1$.
- Return e.

3.6 NTS-KEM's Berlekamp-Massey Algorithm

The Berlekamp-Massey algorithm in NTS-KEM's specifications is shown in Algorithm 1 (we put it in Appendix B due to the page limit). The algorithm is the same as Algorithm 3 in the 1st- and 2nd-round supporting documentations, except that we use t to indicate the designed decoding capacity. Without the lines involving R, ξ, or σ^*, the algorithm is the same as Xu's inversion-free Berlekamp-Massey algorithm [20]. The following section presents an attack against NTS-KEM. The attack makes use of the lines involving R, ξ, or σ^*, in particular line 16 to line 20, and the following theorem.

Theorem 1. *If the input to Algorithm 1 is in*

$$(c + e) \cdot \mathcal{H}(\alpha_1, \dots, \alpha_n, g^2)^T,$$

where $g(x) \in \mathbb{F}_{2^m}[x]$ *is square-free and of degree-t,* $c \in \Gamma_2(\alpha_1, \dots, \alpha_n, g)$, $e \in \mathbb{F}_2^n, |e| \leq t$, *then at the end of the algorithm we have*

$$\sigma(x) = \sigma_0 \prod_{e_i=1} (1 - \alpha_i x),$$

where $\sigma_0 \in \mathbb{F}_{2^m} \setminus \{0\}$.

Proof. As discussed in Sect. 3.2, $\mathcal{H}(\alpha_1, \dots, \alpha_n, g^2)^T$ is a parity-check matrix of $\Gamma_2(\alpha_1, \dots, \alpha_n, g)$. Following the discussion in [12], the original Berlekamp-Massey algorithm ([4,14]) then computes $A(x) = \prod_{e_i=1}(1 - \alpha_i x)$ on input $(c + e) \cdot \mathcal{H}(\alpha_1, \dots, \alpha_n, g^2)^T$. It is shown in [20] that the inversion-free version computes a similar polynomial $\sigma(x) = \sigma_0 \cdot A(x)$ with $\sigma_0 \neq 0$.

4   Our Attack

This section presents our IND-CCA2 attack and explains why it can be used to attack the specifications and non-reference implementations. The reason why it does not work for the reference implementations is shown in Appendix C.

4.1   The Adversary

We consider an adversary who does nothing before receiving (K^*, ψ^*) from the challenger. After receiving (K^*, ψ^*) from the challenger, the adversary partitions ψ^* into (c_b, c_c) as in regular decapsulation and performs the following two simple steps for each of the $n - k$ bits of c_c:

- Flip the bit of c_c to obtain (c_b, c_c').
- Send (c_b, c_c') to the decapsulation oracle.
- If the decapsulation oracle returns K^*, return $\tau' = 0$.

If the decapsulation oracle does not return K^* in any of the $n - k$ iterations, the adversary returns $\tau' = 1$.

Clearly, the adversary takes at most $n - k$ queries, and it takes only one bit flip for each query. The following discussion shows that $\Pr[\tau' = \tau]$ is lower-bounded by roughly $0.5(n - k)t/n^2 + 0.5$, so the advantage of the adversary is lower-bounded by roughly $0.5(n - k)t/n^2$.

4.2 Attacking the Specifications

To understand the success probability of our attack against the 1st- and 2nd-round specifications, assume that in one of the $n - k$ iterations, the adversary sends (c_b, c'_c) to the decapsulation oracle, such that

$$(0_a, c_b, c'_c) \in e' + \Gamma_2(\alpha_1, \ldots, \alpha_n, g),$$

where $|e'| = t - 1$ and $e'_{\mathrm{pos}(0)} = 0$. Let $e \in \mathbb{F}_2^n$ be the unique vector such that $|e + e'| = 1$ and $e_{\mathrm{pos}(0)} = 1$. According to Theorem 1, on input $(0_a, c_b, c'_c)$, Algorithm 1 computes

$$\sigma(x) = \sigma_0 \prod_{e'_i = 1} (1 - \alpha_i x),$$

which is of degree $t - 1$. There are two cases for the return value of Algorithm 1, one for $\xi = 0$ and one for $\xi = 1$. If $\xi = 0$, Algorithm 1 returns

$$(x^t \sigma(x^{-1}), 0) = (\sigma_0 x \prod_{e'_i = 1} (x - \alpha_i), 0),$$

and therefore the decoding algorithm will return e instead of e'. If $\xi = 1$, Algorithm 1 returns

$$(x^{t-1} \sigma(x^{-1}), 1) = (\sigma_0 \prod_{e'_i = 1} (x - \alpha_i), 1),$$

and therefore the decoding algorithm will again return e instead of e'. In other words, no matter what the value of ξ is, the decoding algorithm will return e.

Now consider the case when $\mathrm{pos}(0) > k$ and $e_{\mathrm{pos}(0)} = 1$, where e is the error vector used to generate ψ^*. In this case, in one of the $n - k$ iterations carried out by the adversary, the adversary will send to the decapsulation oracle (c_b, c'_c) of the form discussed in the previous paragraph. Therefore, in the iteration, the error vector e will be returned by the decoding algorithm. As $H_\ell(e) = k_e = c_b - e_b$ and $|e| = t$, the session key encapsulated by (c_b, c_c) will be returned by the decapsulation oracle.

To compute $\Pr[\tau = \tau']$, it suffices to compute $\Pr[\tau = 0 \text{ and } \tau = \tau']$ and $\Pr[\tau = 1 \text{ and } \tau = \tau']$. Assuming $\tau = 0$, there is a probability at least

$$\Pr[e_{\mathrm{pos}(0)} = 1] \cdot \Pr[\mathrm{pos}(0) > k]$$

Table 2. The number of decapsulation queries and advantage of our IND-CCA2 attack.

	n	k	#queries	Advantage
ntskem1264	4096	3328	≤ 768	≥ 0.00146
ntskem1380	8192	7152	≤ 1040	≥ 0.00061
ntskem13136	8192	6424	≤ 1768	≥ 0.00179

that our attack will recover the session key and thus return $\tau' = 0$. In other words, we have

$$\Pr[\tau = 0 \text{ and } \tau = \tau'] \geq 0.5 \cdot \Pr[e_{\text{pos}(0)} = 1] \cdot \Pr[\text{pos}(0) > k]$$
$$= 0.5 \cdot t/n \cdot \Pr[\text{pos}(0) > k].$$

Assuming $\tau = 1$, the probability that one of $n - k$ decapsulation queries returns K^* is upper bounded by $(n - k)/2^\ell$ as K^* is a random string. Therefore,

$$\Pr[\tau = 1 \text{ and } \tau = \tau'] \geq 0.5 \cdot (2^\ell - (n - k))/2^\ell.$$

What is the actual value of $\Pr[\text{pos}(0) > k]$? Intuitively, $\Pr[\text{pos}(0) > k]$ should be $(n - k)/n$, and this seems to be true according to our experiments. Therefore, under the assumption that $\Pr[\text{pos}(0) > k] = (n - k)/n$, we may conclude that

$$\Pr[\tau = \tau'] \geq 0.5 \cdot (n - k)t/n^2 + 0.5 \cdot (2^\ell - (n - k))/2^\ell.$$

For real parameters, the term $0.5 \cdot (2^\ell - (n - k))/2^\ell$ is usually extremely close to 0.5, so one may also simply consider that the advantage is lower bounded by roughly $0.5(n - k)t/n^2$. Based on the discussion above, it is easy to compute the number of queries and advantage of our attack against the 3 parameter sets of NTS-KEM; The numbers are shown in Table 2.

We note that if the challenger generates a key pair with $\text{pos}(0) \leq k$, the advantage of our attack will be close to 0. If the challenger generates a key pair with $\text{pos}(0) > k$, the advantage of our attack will be lower-bounded by roughly $0.5 \cdot t/n$.

4.3   Attacking the Non-reference Implementations

In addition to the reference implementations, some other implementations are also included in the 1st- and 2nd-round submission packages. These are the implementations under the directories `Additional_Implementation` and `Optimized_Implementation`. We found the following bugs in the code for Algorithm 1 in these implementations.

- In the last of the 2t iterations, R is not updated.
- In the first $2t - 1$ of the 2t iterations, R is updated as follows.

```
if d == 0 OR i < 2L then
    if d == 0 then
        R ← R + 1
    end if
else
    R ← 0
end if
```

These bugs can make R smaller and thus can change the value of ξ. However, as discussed in Sect. 4.2, our attack is independent of the actual value of ξ, so the numbers in Table 2 still apply.

Acknowledgements. The author would like thank Daniel J. Bernstein and Tanja Lange for all their suggestions.

A   Paterson's Message

"We have added a re-encapsulation step during decapsulation, in order to fix a subtle issue in the ROM security proof for NTS-KEM. This issue was identified by Varun Maram from ETH Zurich. This change necessitates the inclusion of the public key as part of the private key and increases the running time of decapsulation. Fortuitously, this change facilitates a QROM proof for NTS-KEM which we plan to make public soon.
[In more detail: our proof did not fully address the possibility that certain adversarially generated ciphertexts not output by encapsulation might decapsulate correctly. This is due to possible behaviour of the decoder, including the Berlekamp-Massey algorithm, when operating beyond its natural decoding capacity. Adding the re-encapsulation step ensures that only correctly generated ciphertexts lead to valid decapsulations; other ciphertexts are implicitly rejected. Our new security proof still tightly relates breaking IND-CCA security of (the new version of) NTS-KEM to breaking one-wayness of the McEliece scheme with the same parameters. We also stress that we are not aware of any concrete attack arising from the issue identified in our proof. Since re-encapsulation makes use of the public key, we now include the public key as part of the private key; an alternative whose cost can be amortised over many invocations of decapsulation is to regenerate the public key from the private key when needed.]"

B   NTS-KEM's Berlekamp-Massey Algorithm

Algorithm 1. NTS-KEM's Berlekamp-Massey Algorithm

1: **function** BERLEKAMPMASSEY(s)
Require: $s = (s_0, s_1, \ldots, s_{2t-1})$
Require: $\sigma(x) = \sum \sigma_i x^i = 1$
Require: $\beta(x) = \sum \beta_i x^i = x$
Require: $\delta = 1$
Require: $L = R = \xi = 0$
2:     **for** $i = 0$ to $2t - 1$ step 1 **do**
3:         $d \leftarrow \sum_{j=0}^{\min\{i,t\}} \sigma_j s_{i-j}$
4:         $\psi(x) \leftarrow \delta\sigma(x) - d\beta(x)$
5:         **if** $d == 0$ OR $i < 2L$ **then**
6:             $R \leftarrow R + 1$
7:             $\beta(x) \leftarrow x\beta(x)$
8:         **else**
9:             $R \leftarrow 0$
10:             $\beta(x) \leftarrow x\sigma(x)$
11:             $L \leftarrow i - L + 1$
12:             $\delta \leftarrow d$
13:         **end if**
14:         $\sigma(x) \leftarrow \psi(x)$
15:     **end for**
16:     **if** Degree of $\sigma(x) < t - \frac{R}{2}$ **then**
17:         $\xi \leftarrow 1$
18:     **end if**
19:     $\sigma^*(x) \leftarrow x^{t-\xi}\sigma(x^{-1})$
20:     **return** $(\sigma^*(x), \xi)$
21: **end function**

C   Attacking the Reference Implementations

We found the following bugs in the code for Algorithm 1 in the reference implementations.

- In each of the $2t$ iterations, R is updated in the same way as the pseudocode in Sect. 4.3.
- $\sigma^*(x)$ is computed as $x^{\mathrm{Deg}(\sigma(x))}\sigma(x^{-1})$.

We also found that after obtaining $(\sigma^*(x), \xi)$, the reference implementations compute the error vector e as follows.

- Set $e = 0 \in \mathbb{F}_2^n$.
- Set $e_i = 1$ for all i such that $\sigma^*(\alpha_i) = 0$ and $\alpha_i \neq 0$.
- Set $e_{\mathrm{pos}(0)} = 1$ if $\xi = 1$.

Note that this is different from what is described in Sect. 3.5.

Our attack relies on forcing the decoding algorithm to take an input vector which is the sum of a codeword and an error vector e' with $|e'| = t - 1$ and $e'_{pos(0)} = 0$. In this case, according to Theorem 1, Algorithm 1 computes

$$\sigma(x) = \sigma_0 \prod_{e'_i=1} (1 - \alpha_i x),$$

so the reference implementations compute

$$\sigma^*(x) = \sigma_0 \prod_{e'_i=1} (x - \alpha_i).$$

How about the value of ξ? It turns out that Algorithm 1 computes $\sigma(x)$ in the first $2t - 2$ iteration; See [14] for discussions on the number of iterations required to compute the linear feedback shift register. This forces d to be 0 in the last 2 iterations, so we have $R \geq 2$. As $\mathrm{Deg}(\sigma) = t - 1 \geq t - R/2$, the reference implementations computes $\xi = 0$. Therefore, the decoding algorithm returns the weight-$(t-1)$ vector e', and the decapsulation oracle returns $\perp$ or $H_\ell(z, 1_a, c_b, c'_c)$ instead of the session key.

D Implementations

To demonstrate that our attack works against the non-reference implementations, We modified `ntskem_test.c` in the non-reference implementations included in the 1st-round and 2nd-round submission packages. The content of the modified file is available in Appendix F. The modified `testkem_nts` function keeps generating ciphertext-session-key pairs. For each ciphertext, it is checked whether flipping any of the last $n - k$ bits will result in a ciphertext that decapsulates to the same session key. If this happens, a message

`Original session key returned!`

will be printed. One can replace the original `ntskem_test.c` by the modified one and compile each non-reference implementation using `make`. Then by running the executables `ntskem-*-test`, the user can see that the message usually shows after trying a several hundreds of ciphertext-session-key pairs.

To demonstrate that our attack works against the specifications, we fixed the bugs in `berlekamp_massey.c` and `nts_kem.c` in the reference implementations included in the 1st-round and 2nd-round submission packages. The content of the modified `berlekamp_massey.c` is available in Appendix E. The modified `berlekamp_massey` function updates R and computes σ^* in the correct way. For `nts_kem.c`, we only change the code segment

```
memset(e_prime, 0, sizeof(e_prime));
for (i=1; i<NTS_KEM_PARAM_N; i++) {
    e_prime[i>>3] |= (CT_is_equal_zero(evals[i]) << (i & 7));
}
e_prime[0] |= ((uint8_t)extended_error);
```

in the `nts_kem_decapsulate` function into the following.

```
memset(e_prime, 0, sizeof(e_prime));
for (i=0; i<NTS_KEM_PARAM_N; i++) {
    e_prime[i>>3] |= (CT_is_equal_zero(evals[i]) << (i & 7));
}
e_prime[0] |= ((uint8_t)extended_error);
```

The modification changes the way the error vector e is computed from σ^* and ξ to the way specified in Sect. 3.5 (which is equivalent to what is specified in NTS-KEM's specifications). The user can replace `ntskem_test.c` by the modified one replace `berlekamp_massey.c` by the modified one, apply the same change to `nts_kem.c`, do `make` and execute `ntskem-*-test`. Then the user will again see that the message usually shows after trying a several hundreds of ciphertext-session-key pairs.

E   The modified `berlekamp_massey.c`

```
#include <stdint.h>
#include <stdlib.h>
#include <string.h>
#include "berlekamp_massey.h"
#include "bits.h"

poly *berlekamp_massey(const FF2m *ff2m,
                       const ff_unit *S,
                       int slen,
                       int *extended_error)
{
    poly *ex = NULL;
    ff_unit *sigma = NULL, *beta = NULL, *varphi = NULL;
    ff_unit *src0_ptr = NULL, *src1_ptr = NULL, *dst_ptr = NULL;
    ff_unit d, delta = 1;
    ff_unit inv = 0;
    uint32_t control, d_eq_0;
    int32_t i, j, v, t, L = 0, R = 0;

    t = slen >> 1;
    sigma  = (ff_unit *)calloc(t+1, sizeof(ff_unit));
    beta   = (ff_unit *)calloc(t+1, sizeof(ff_unit));
    varphi = (ff_unit *)calloc(t+1, sizeof(ff_unit));
    if (!sigma || !beta || !varphi) {
        goto BMA_fail;
    }
    sigma[0] = 1;    /* sigma(x) = 1 */
    beta[1] = 1;     /* beta(x) = x */
    *extended_error = 0;

    /* Loop until we process all 2t syndromes */
    for (i=0; i<slen; i++) {
        /**
         * d = \sum_{i}^{\min{i, t}} sigma_j * S_{i-j}
         **/
        v = CT_min(i, t);
        for (d=0,j=0; j<=v; j++) {
            d = ff2m->ff_add(ff2m, d,
                        ff2m->ff_mul(ff2m, sigma[j], S[i-j]));
        }
        /**
         * varphi(x) = delta.sigma(x) - d.beta(x)
```

```
        **/
        for (j=0; j<=t; j++) {
            varphi[j] = ff2m->ff_add(ff2m,
                                     ff2m->ff_mul(ff2m, delta, sigma[j]),
                                     ff2m->ff_mul(ff2m, d, beta[j]));
        }

        d_eq_0 = CT_is_equal_zero((uint32_t)d);   /* d == 0? */
        control = d_eq_0 || CT_is_less_than(i, (L << 1)); /* (d == 0) OR (i < 2L) */

        /**
         * if control is 1 -> beta(x) = x.beta(x)
         * otherwise        -> beta(x) = x.sigma(x)
         **/
        v = t;
        src0_ptr = (ff_unit *)&sigma[t-1];
        src1_ptr = (ff_unit *)&beta[t-1];
        dst_ptr = (ff_unit *)&beta[t];
        while (v-- > 0) {
            *dst_ptr = CT_mux(control, *src1_ptr, *src0_ptr);
            --dst_ptr;
            --src1_ptr;
            --src0_ptr;
        }
        beta[0] = 0x00;

        /**
         * if control is 1 ->
         *     R = R + 1 if d == 0
         * otherwise       ->
         *     R = 0
         *     L = i - L + 1
         *     delta = d
         **/
        L = (int32_t)CT_mux(control, L, i-L+1);
        R = (int32_t)CT_mux(control, R + 1, 0);
        delta = (ff_unit)CT_mux(control, delta, d);

        memcpy(sigma, varphi, (t+1)*sizeof(ff_unit));
    }

    ex = init_poly(t+1);
    if (!ex) {
        goto BMA_fail;
    }
    ex->degree = t;
    while (ex->degree > 0 && !sigma[ex->degree]) --ex->degree;
    inv = ff2m->ff_inv(ff2m, sigma[0]);

    *extended_error = CT_is_less_than(ex->degree, t - (R>>1));

    for (i=0; i <= t-*extended_error ; i++) {
        if (t-*extended_error-i <= ex->degree)
            ex->coeff[i] = ff2m->ff_mul(ff2m, sigma[t-*extended_error-i], inv);
    }

    ex->degree = t - *extended_error;

BMA_fail:
    if (varphi) {
        memset(varphi, 0, (t+1)*sizeof(ff_unit));
        free(varphi);
    }
    if (beta) {
        memset(beta, 0, (t+1)*sizeof(ff_unit));
        free(beta);
    }
    if (sigma) {
```

```
        memset(sigma, 0, (t+1)*sizeof(ff_unit));
        free(sigma);
    }

    return ex;
}
```

F   The modified ntskem_test.c

```c
#include <stdio.h>
#include <stdlib.h>
#include <string.h>
#include "api.h"
#include "ntskem_test.h"
#include "nts_kem_params.h"
#include "random.h"

int testkem_nts(int iterations)
{
    int i, it = 0;
    uint8_t *pk, *sk;
    uint8_t *encap_key, *decap_key, *ciphertext, *flipped;
    FILE *fp = NULL;
    unsigned char entropy_input[] = {
        0xaa, 0xe7, 0xd7, 0x4e, 0x3c, 0x3a, 0x52, 0xdd,
        0x87, 0xc7, 0x2a, 0xa4, 0x38, 0x54, 0x7e, 0x37,
        0x1e, 0x97, 0x29, 0x78, 0x22, 0xa2, 0xcd, 0x83,
        0x43, 0x64, 0x84, 0xcf, 0x77, 0x6b, 0x9e, 0xa5,
        0x53, 0xf3, 0x50, 0xc5, 0xc7, 0x8d, 0x46, 0xb3,
        0xa5, 0xf2, 0xe3, 0x99, 0x63, 0x10, 0x1d, 0x10
    };
    unsigned char nonce[48];

    fprintf(stdout, "NTS-KEM(%d, %d) Test\n", NTSKEM_M, NTSKEM_T);

    do {
        if ((fp = fopen("/dev/urandom", "r"))) {
            if ((sizeof(entropy_input) !=
                fread(entropy_input, 1, sizeof(entropy_input), fp)) ||
                (sizeof(nonce) != fread(nonce, 1, sizeof(nonce), fp))) {
                break;
            }
        }
        fclose(fp);

        memcpy(&entropy_input[48-sizeof(it)], &it, sizeof(it));

        fprintf(stdout, "Iteration: %d, Seed: ", it);
        for (i=0; i<sizeof(entropy_input); i++)
          fprintf(stdout, "%02x", entropy_input[i]);
        fprintf(stdout, "\n"); fflush(stdout);

        randombytes_init(entropy_input, nonce, 256);

        pk = (uint8_t *)calloc(CRYPTO_PUBLICKEYBYTES, sizeof(uint8_t));
        sk = (uint8_t *)calloc(CRYPTO_SECRETKEYBYTES, sizeof(uint8_t));
        crypto_kem_keypair(pk, sk);

        ciphertext = (uint8_t *)calloc(CRYPTO_CIPHERTEXTBYTES, sizeof(uint8_t));
        flipped = (uint8_t *)calloc(CRYPTO_CIPHERTEXTBYTES, sizeof(uint8_t));
        encap_key = (uint8_t *)calloc(CRYPTO_BYTES, sizeof(uint8_t));
        decap_key = (uint8_t *)calloc(CRYPTO_BYTES, sizeof(uint8_t));

        crypto_kem_enc(ciphertext, encap_key, pk);

        for (i = 0; i < NTS_KEM_PARAM_M*NTS_KEM_PARAM_T; i++)
```

```
    {
        memcpy(flipped, ciphertext, CRYPTO_CIPHERTEXTBYTES);

        flipped[CRYPTO_CIPHERTEXTBYTES-1 - i/8] ^= 1 << (i%8);

        crypto_kem_dec(decap_key, flipped, sk);

        if (0 == memcmp(encap_key, decap_key, CRYPTO_BYTES))
        {
            fprintf(stderr, "Original session key returned!\n");
            getchar();
        }
    }

    free(decap_key);
    free(encap_key);
    free(ciphertext);
    free(flipped);
    free(sk);
    free(pk);
}
while (++it < iterations || 1);

return 0;
}
```

References

1. Albrecht, M., Cid, C., Paterson, K.G., Tjhai, C.J., Tomlinson, M.: NTS-KEM, first round submission (2017). https://csrc.nist.gov/CSRC/media/Projects/Post-Quantum-Cryptography/documents/round-1/submissions/NTS_KEM.zip. Citations in this document: §1

2. Albrecht, M., Cid, C., Paterson, K.G., Tjhai, C.J., Tomlinson, M.: NTS-KEM, second round submission (2019). https://csrc.nist.gov/CSRC/media/Projects/Post-Quantum-Cryptography/documents/round-2/submissions/NTS-KEM-Round2.zip. Citations in this document: §1

3. Albrecht, M., Cid, C., Paterson, K.G., Tjhai, C.J., Tomlinson, M.: NTS-KEM, updated second round submission (2019). https://nts-kem.io/. Citations in this document: §1

4. Berlekamp, E.R.: Algebraic coding theory, McGraw-Hill. MR 38 #6873. Citations in this document: §3.5, §3.6 (1968)

5. Albrecht, M., etal.: Classic McEliece (2020). https://classic.mceliece.org/. Citations in this document: §1, §1.2

6. Bertoni, G., Coron, J.-S. (eds.): CHES 2013. LNCS, vol. 8086. Springer, Heidelberg (2013). https://doi.org/10.1007/978-3-642-40349-1

7. Cho, J.Y.: Implementation of code-based KEMs submitted to NIST on optical communication systems (2019). https://cbc2019.dii.univpm.it/program. Citations in this document: §1.1

8. Cramer, R., Shoup, V.: Design and analysis of practical public-key encryption schemes secure against adaptive chosen ciphertext attack (2001). https://eprint.iacr.org/2001/108

9. Dent, A.W.: A designer's guide to KEMs. In: Paterson, K.G. (ed.) Cryptography and Coding 2003. LNCS, vol. 2898, pp. 133–151. Springer, Heidelberg (2003). https://doi.org/10.1007/978-3-540-40974-8_12

10. Fujisaki, E., Okamoto, T.: Secure integration of asymmetric and symmetric encryption schemes. In: Wiener, M. (ed.) CRYPTO 1999. LNCS, vol. 1666, pp. 537–554. Springer, Heidelberg (1999). https://doi.org/10.1007/3-540-48405-1_34

11. Fujisaki, E., Okamoto, T.: Secure integration of asymmetric and symmetric encryption schemes. J. Cryptol. **26**, 80–101 (2013)
12. Helgert, H.: Decoding of alternant codes (Corresp.). IEEE Trans. Inf. Theory **23**(4), 513-514 (1977) Citations in this document: §3.6
13. Maram, V.: On the security of NTS-KEM in the quantum random oracle model. In PQCRYPTO 2020 (to appear), p. 150 (2017). https://eprint.iacr.org/2020/150.pdf. Citations in this document: §1, §1, §1.1
14. Massey, J.: Shift-register synthesis and BCH decoding. IEEE Trans. Inf. Theory **15**, 122–127 (1969) Citations in this document: §3.5, §3.6, § C
15. McEliece, R.J: A public-key cryptosystem based on algebraic. Coding Thv, **4244**, 114-116 (1978). http://ipnpr.jpl.nasa.gov/progress_report2/42-44/44N.PDF. Citations in this document: §2.5
16. Paterson, K.G. (ed.): Cryptography and Coding 2003. LNCS, vol. 2898. Springer, Heidelberg (2003). https://doi.org/10.1007/b93924
17. Preneel, B. (ed.): EUROCRYPT 2000. LNCS, vol. 1807. Springer, Heidelberg (2000). https://doi.org/10.1007/3-540-45539-6
18. Shoup, V.: A composition theorem for universal one-way hash functions. In: Preneel, B. (ed.) EUROCRYPT 2000. LNCS, vol. 1807, pp. 445–452. Springer, Heidelberg (2000). https://doi.org/10.1007/3-540-45539-6_32
19. Wiener, M. (ed.): CRYPTO 1999. LNCS, vol. 1666. Springer, Heidelberg (1999). https://doi.org/10.1007/3-540-48405-1
20. Youzhi, X.: Implementation of Berlekamp-Massey algorithm without inversion. IEE Proc. I - Commun. Speech Vis. **138**, 138–140 (1991) Citations in this document: §3.6, §3.6

Behaviour-Based Biometrics for Continuous User Authentication to Industrial Collaborative Robots

Shurook S. Almohamade[1](✉), John A. Clark[1], and James Law[1,2,3]

[1] Department of Computer Science, The University of Sheffield, Sheffield, UK
{ssalmohamade1,john.clark,j.law}@Sheffield.ac.uk
[2] Sheffield Robotics, The University of Sheffield, Sheffield, UK
[3] The Advanced Manufacturing Research Centre, Sheffield, UK

Abstract. Collaborative robots (cobots) work in close proximity with human co-workers to accomplish tasks. The proximity of working arrangements and the power required of some cobots for particular tasks means that there is significant potential for cobots to cause damage to their surroundings and people nearby. Working with cobots requires appropriate training and skill. We must ensure that co-workers access appropriate levels of service and functionality from a cobot. We would wish to stop intruders engaging with cobots but also to protect against inappropriate informal working arrangements by colleagues. In this paper, we consider the potential for users' behaviours to be used as a biometric approach to *continuous user authentication*. More specifically, we consider how data from a cobot's internal sensors can be used to characterise a user's physical interaction with it and serve as a reference template for authentication of that user. We seek to continuously authenticate current user behaviours against these stored characteristic templates while the cobot is being manipulated (as part of a collaborative task). Our approach, based on machine learning and a recognised trust model, can provide a sensible, practical solution to authenticate users continuously as they physically interact with a cobot. Furthermore, it makes use of data that are *already maintained by the cobot* as part of its general operation. Our work is the first to exploit such data.

Keywords: Behavioural biometrics · Continuous authentication · Collaborative robots · User authentication

1 Introduction

The use of robots in manufacturing processes is rising, with around 1.7 million industrial robots expected to be employed in industries worldwide in 2020 [7]. Traditionally, such robots have been segregated from humans by walls, fences and other barriers to ensure safety, but recent advances in collaborative robotics promise opportunities for robots to share spaces with human workers.

Collaborative robots (or *cobots*) [14] are designed with more sophisticated sensing and control mechanisms than traditional industrial robots and, in the

© Springer Nature Switzerland AG 2021
D. Maimut et al. (Eds.): SecITC 2020, LNCS 12596, pp. 185–197, 2021.
https://doi.org/10.1007/978-3-030-69255-1_12

main, they are designed to handle lighter payloads. They promise to combine the benefits of automation (speed, precision, accuracy and repeatability) with those of human workers (dexterity, perception, flexibility and cognitive ability). Alongside advances in digital technologies, such as the Internet of things (IoT), augmented reality and digital twins, cobots will enable more flexible, bespoke processes. This makes them attractive to many manufacturers who have not been able to benefit from large-scale automation. (The number of cobots is forecast to increase from 8,950 in 2016 to 434,404 by 2025 [12], with the largest market share being in Europe [6].)

However, reductions in physical safety barriers and increases in technical complexity give rise to a number of challenging safety and security issues which must be resolved before the benefits of human-robot collaboration can be fully realised. One such issue is that of user authentication [10]. As cobot use becomes more widespread, there will be an increased need to authenticate users to ensure they have the appropriate skills, training and authorisation to access, re-program, update and control different elements of cobotic systems. At present, discrete authentication methods, such as passwords and identity cards, are used to lock-out functionality, but they can easily be bypassed or abused by workers, leaving safety and security risks unresolved.

Cobotic tasks in manufacturing often involve direct interaction between the user and the cobot, e.g. when the user physically moves a manipulator or takes part in some handover of items. Some users are more forceful or quicker in their interactions, or they may otherwise exhibit an interactive modus operandi that is distinguishably theirs. Consequently, a cobot able to sense how it is manipulated can use that information to distinguish users. As cobots are compliant, we propose to use this feature (combined with robots' internal positions and force sensors) to measure the actions of human operators (or co-workers) and form a biometric for their continuous authentication.

We believe that this is the first *continuous authentication* approach to be developed in the context of cobots. This is important since cobots will engage with their co-workers on a continual basis, and this may severely compromise the utility of traditional one-off password schemes. In practice, we envisage both will be used: for example, one-off schemes for initial authentication and continuous authentication for the duration of a work session. We believe that this is also the first example of biometric authentication in the context of cobots (and indeed robots).

A major benefit of our approach is that user-to-cobot authentication can be implemented with **no additional sensing**. The source data are sensed and used as part of the operational control system of the cobot. Also, if better performing classification algorithms become available, they can be directly incorporated through minor software changes.

2   Related Work

There has not been much research in the field of robotics security. As far as we know, no previous research has studied or implemented behaviour-based biometrics authentication for robots in general, let alone for cobots. However, several studies have used continuous authentication to secure computer systems and smartphones. One such approach verifies users of computer systems based on their continuing interactions with them [5]. Users' behaviours in that study were represented by patterns of both keystrokes and mouse usage. The authors collected behaviour data from 30 users in an unconstrained environment via a website. Classification was provided by support vector machines (SVMs), Bayes classifiers and ensemble classifiers. They reported a false reject rate (FRR) of 0% and an Equal Error Rate (EER) of 2.04% with authentication times ranging from 10 s to 60 s.

In [3], a continuous authentication mechanism was presented to authenticate smartphone users based on the phones' micro-movements in addition to users' finger movements on the touchscreens. Four classification methods were used: BayesNET, K-nearest neighbour (KNN), multilayer perceptron (MLP) and random forest (RF). The researchers obtained a true accept rate (TAR) of 95% with a 3.1% false accept rate (FAR) on a dataset of 30 users. In [4], to authenticate smartphone users, the authors designed an interaction-based continuous authentication system. This system considered users' motion patterns during interaction with smartphones. In real-world scenarios, the approach achieved an EER as low as 2.2% by using a deep-learning autoencoder. [8] introduced a continuous authentication approach for mobile devices based on users' typing behaviours. They collected the typing fingerprints of 300 participants. To identify authorised users, they used SVMs as machine-learning classifiers, achieving a True Positive Rate (TPR) of 92% at a False positive Rate (FPR) of 1%. However, some users could not be reliably distinguished.

3   Proposed User to Cobot Authentication

We propose to apply continuous biometric authentication to the use of an industrial cobot (see Fig. 1). Most cobots have integrated sensors, including joint position encoders, force and torque sensors, and even cameras. Thus, we consider it valuable to employ those sensors to capture co-workers' behaviours to implement continuous biometric authentication **without the need for additional, potentially intrusive hardware**. We conducted two experiments where we asked the subjects to guide a robot arm around a maze (see Fig. 2).

1. *whole-task-authentication*: Here, authentication occurs once at the end of the task (one navigation of the maze). Each user performed 15 maze-navigation tasks with a trust value calculated after each one. This value determined whether the user was authorised to continue to the next task.
2. *multiple-segment-authentication*: Here, we authenticated each user three times during each task as the user passed specific points in the maze. If users were authenticated, they were allowed to continue performing the task.

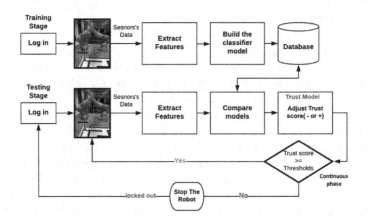

Fig. 1. Continuous biometric authentication block diagram of our system.

We divided each experiment into three phases: a training phase, a testing phase and a continuous phase, as shown in Fig. 1. In the *training phase*, we obtained readings from the robot's sensors and extracted potential features for user authentication. Features from force and torque sensors were the most informative and were used to create the users' profile templates. In the *testing phase*, these templates were used for user authentication. Each time the robot's co-worker started interacting with the robot, our authentication system compared that user's profile template against all profile templates in the database to obtain a probability value for each user in the database, with the highest probability value taken to identify indicate the user. However, only the probability value of the authorised user was used to update the current user's trust value. In the *continuous phase*, the trust value was used to determine whether the user was allowed to continue to work with the robot or be locked out of the system, reverting to the main authentication 'log-in' as shown in Fig.1.

3.1   Trust Model

We use the trust model first proposed by Bours [1] for continuous, behaviour-based biometric authentication. It adjusts the trust score of the current user by matching their dynamic profile template with the expected user's template [1]. As a default, the user starts with 100 as a trust score, and it is updated (increased or decreased) according to the probability of the genuineness (classification probability score) of the user with Eq. (1). If the behaviours of the authorised and current users are similar, the system's trust in the current user increases. Otherwise, if the behaviour is sufficiently different from the authorised user, the trust score decreases.

$$C = \begin{cases} \min\left(C + \frac{Z}{2}, 100\right) & \text{if} \quad P \geq 0.5 \\ \max\left(C - \frac{Z}{2}, 0\right) & \text{if} \quad 0.3 \leq P < 0.5 \\ \max(C - (2Z), 0) & \text{if} \quad P < 0.3 \end{cases} \tag{1}$$

where C is the trust score of the user, P is the probability score of the current user against the legitimate user's template, and Z is a constant governing the rate of increase or decrease in the trust score. (In our experiments, $Z = 15$ in whole-task authentication and 7.5 in multiple-segment authentication). The trust score can never exceed 100 or be less than 0. Equation (2) presents the decision-making process after calculating the trust value.

$$Decision = \begin{cases} \text{if} & C \geq T \text{ Trusted user - continue to next task} \\ \text{if} & C < T \text{ Not trusted user - lock out} \end{cases} \quad (2)$$

where T represents the threshold between the trusted user and the untrusted user. (In our experiments the value $T = 80$ was used.)

4   Methodology

4.1   Experimental Design

The experiment involved participants interacting with an industrial robot arm to solve a maze. A two-dimensional maze was attached to the work surface within the robot's operating envelope. Start and end points were indicated by red and green circles, and an additional authentication point was marked as a yellow circle, as shown in Fig. 2. A handle and pointer were attached to the robot's end-effector to provide an intuitive mechanism for manipulating the robot through the maze.

4.2   Selected Collaborative Robot

We used a KUKA iiwa R800 lightweight industrial robotic arm (see Fig. 2). The KUKA iiwa R800 has seven joints, each of which has force, torque and position sensing. Data from these sensors were logged during the experiment to capture co-workers' behaviours while manipulating the robot, although in this paper we used only the end-effector data for classification purposes.

4.3   Subjects and Data Collection

The experiment took place in the Sheffield Robotics Lab on the Sheffield University campus. We obtained 30 volunteers (16 males and 14 females) from students and faculty members at the University of Sheffield. Users were asked to guide the robot's attached pointer around the maze to trace a trajectory from the start point (red circle) to the endpoint (green circle). They were asked to repeat the same task 15 times. Participants were given a brief introduction to the purpose of the study and then they performed three practice runs for which data was not recorded. Our data collection controller was based on the ROS-integrated application programming interface for the KUKA iiwa [11]. The robot was placed in compliant mode, with each user instructed to trace a path from the start point

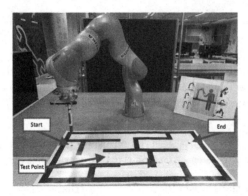

Fig. 2. Experimental design. (Color figure online)

to the end point of the maze. Force and torque data at the end-effector were continually logged (every 0.1 s) as each user traced this path. (We also recorded position data.) When the user released the end-effector on completion of the task, the robot autonomously returned to the start point to begin the next run. In addition, we also calculated the magnitudes of the force and torque.

4.4 Feature Extraction

After recording data, the next step was to extract relevant features from the stream sensor data. We sampled the components of the force and torque applied to the end-effector along the X, Y and Z axes together with their overall magnitudes. (Magnitudes can, of course, be derived from the components.) Figure 3 shows how these vary across example runs by four users. We used the first four statistical moment features: mean, standard deviation (SD), skewness and kurtosis. Table 1 shows the equations for calculating these statistical features. N represents the number of samples so far in a run. The feature-extraction process yielded a total of $32 = 2(force\_or\_torque) \times 4(component\_measurements) \times 4(moment\_measures)$ features. To this we added a task number and time (the time period to complete the task). This increased the number of features to 34.

4.5 Feature Selection

We selected the most suitable features to reduce the training time and increase the performance of the machine-learning algorithm. We used the recursive feature elimination (RFE) [9] selection method to analyse and evaluate our feature set. We applied RFE with 10-fold cross-validation using a random forest (RF)

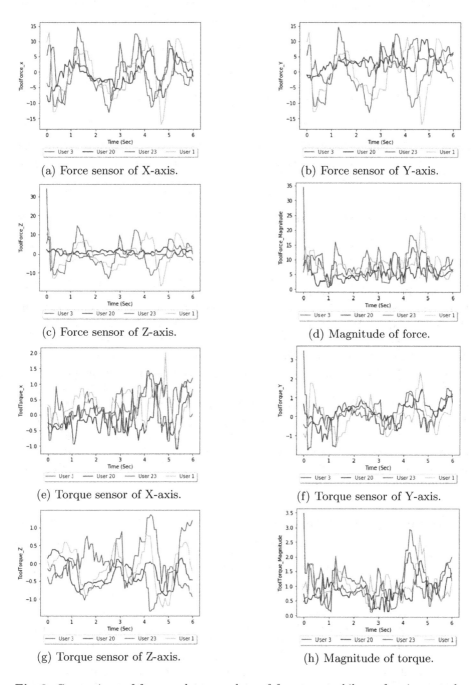

(a) Force sensor of X-axis.

(b) Force sensor of Y-axis.

(c) Force sensor of Z-axis.

(d) Magnitude of force.

(e) Torque sensor of X-axis.

(f) Torque sensor of Y-axis.

(g) Torque sensor of Z-axis.

(h) Magnitude of torque.

Fig. 3. Comparison of force and torque data of four users while performing a task. Task duration has been normalised to 6 s.

Table 1. The equations of the statistical moments used as features where X_i is the sample of a data-stream and N is the total number of samples.

Features	Equation	Features	Equation
Mean	$\mu = \frac{\sum_{i=1}^{N} X_i}{N}$	SD	$\sigma = \sqrt{\frac{\sum_{i=1}^{N}(X_i-\mu)^2}{N}}$
Skewness	$S = \frac{\frac{1}{N}\sum_{i=1}^{N}(X_i-\mu)^3}{\sigma^3}$	Kurtosis	$K = \frac{\frac{1}{N}\sum_{i=1}^{N}(X_i-\mu)^4}{\sigma^4}$

classifier. The feature selection was performed only with the training set to prevent over-fitting. In our experiment, we used the top 19 features (all features with an importance score more than 0.02) out of the total set of 34 features.

4.6 Considered Classifiers

Our approach uses the multi-class classification approach. Each user is profiled as the 'authorised user' and the remaining users as 'unauthorised users' for validation objectives. We implemented RF, SVMs, KNN and decision tree (DT) classifiers.We trained these classifiers on the full set of extracted features with three train-test splits (75%–25%, 70%–30% and 65%–35% of the dataset) from the 'split' method. We also used a 60%–40% split with the first nine tasks as the training set and the remaining six tasks as the test set. The basic performance metrics were used to compare classifiers (i.e. precision, recall and f1-score). Precision indicates the number of true positive results divided by the number of all positive results returned by the classifier. Recall denotes the number of true positive results returned divided by the total number of actual positive instances. The f1-score represents the weighted average of precision and recall. Table 2 presents a summary of the classifier results for each training regime. Based on the results in Table 2, we found that RF gave the highest f1-score. Consequently, we chose RF as the classifier for our subsequent experiments. The scikit-learn Python package [13] was used for training and evaluation.

5   Results and Discussion

In the whole-task experiments each of the 30 users performed 15 task runs, giving rise to $450 = 30 \times 15$ profiles. In the multiple-segment authentication experiment, each task had 3 segments and so gave rise to $1350 = 30 \times 15 \times 3$ profiles.

5.1   Performance Evaluation of Single-Use Biometric Authentication System

We first evaluated whether the user of a single witnessed task (or sub-task) could be identified. We had multiple task templates from each user and could use them to train a classifier. We could then see how additional templates from the set (not used in training) are classified. The results are reported on the basis of

Table 2. Result of different classifiers with different training–test splits

Classifier	Metric	Test set 25%	Test set 30%	Test set 35%	Test set 6 tasks
RF	Precision	91%	91%	89%	96%
	Recall	89%	88%	85%	94%
	f1-score	89%	88%	85%	94%
SVMs	Precision	88%	86%	82%	62%
	Recall	82%	79%	74%	60 %
	f1-score	82%	79%	75%	57%
KNN	Precision	81%	80%	75%	45%
	Recall	75%	71%	68%	44%
	f1-score	74%	70%	67%	41%
DT	Precision	76%	70%	71%	69%
	Recall	70%	65%	66%	68%
	f1-score	72%	65%	65%	68%

Table 3. Evaluation of RF classifier on full sets of features and a subset of features over each experiment, training–test split of (9–6 tasks).

Experiment	No. Features	(FAR)	(TAR)	(EER)	f1-score
Whole-task	34	0.2%	94%	2.9%	94%
authentication	19	0.1%	96%	2.6%	96%
Multiple-segment	34	0.5%	87%	6.8%	86%
authentication	19	0.4%	87%	6.5%	87%

FAR, TAR, EER and f1-score. EER is the percentage at which FAR and FRR are equal.

Table 3 shows the performance of the RF classifier on RFE-based feature subsets over two experiments. According to Table 3, RF gave the best f1-score of 96% in the experiment on whole-task authentication on the subset of 19 features obtained by the RFE feature-selection method. The corresponding confusion matrix for all 30 subjects is shown as a heat map in Fig. 4. The heat map shows how tasks from the test set are classified. The corresponding RF was developed with a 9–6 tasks train–test split, so the heat map shows the results for classifying $180 = 30 \times 6$ test task templates.

5.2 Performance Evaluation of the Continuous Biometric Authentication (CBA) System

Measuring the performance of the Continuous Biometric Authentication (CBA) system [2] requires a more nuanced means of evaluation. Minimising the number of tasks imposters can perform before being identified is critical. As with any authentication process, it is also crucial that the system does not reject genuine

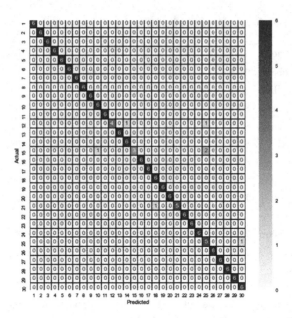

Fig. 4. Confusion matrix for all 30 subjects in a whole-task authentication experiment, training–test split of (9–6 tasks)

users. Hence, the number of tasks genuine users can perform before they are rejected is important. For CBA, we used the average number of genuine actions (ANGA) and the average number of imposter actions (ANIA) [1], with high values of ANGA and low values of ANIA representing the best results. Equation 3 shows how to calculate the ANIA of imposter j [2].

$$\text{ANIA}_g^j = \frac{1}{k} \cdot \sum_{j=1}^{k} T_k \tag{3}$$

where k is the number of times imposter j was locked out if they were classified as a user other than the genuine user g after $T_1, T_2...T_k$ tasks. If we assume that N represents all participants, the ANIA of overall imposters $(N-1)$ against one genuine user can be calculated by (4) [2].

$$\text{ANIA} = \frac{1}{N-1} \cdot \sum_{j=1}^{N-1} \text{ANIA}_g^j \tag{4}$$

We used the trust model described in Sect. 3.1. Figure 5(b) and 6(b) show how the trust value changes when test data for a genuine user and 29 imposters are examined. For example, over 6 tasks, it can be seen that the genuine users were never locked out because the trust scores of the legitimate users were higher than the selected threshold (80%) for every task. In contrast, the imposters

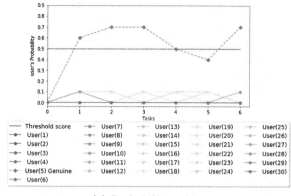

(a) Probability value.

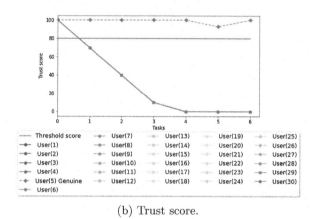

(b) Trust score.

Fig. 5. Results of whole-task authentication with one example of a genuine user and 29 imposters. Results identical for all imposters attempts.

were locked out after the first task, as their trust score fell below the required threshold.

In the whole-task authentication experiment, we tested 30 users (each user is profiled as 'genuine' and the remaining users as 'imposters'). This yields an ANIA of 1, meaning that all the imposters managed only one task out of 6 before being identified. We also obtained an ANGA score of 5 when we tested 30 genuine users for 6 tasks. However, we obtained an ANIA of 2 in the multiple-segment authentication experiments, meaning that all the imposters managed only two sub-tasks out of 18 before being identified. The ANGA score for the multiple-segment authentication experiment was 12 when we tested 30 genuine users on 18 sub-tasks.

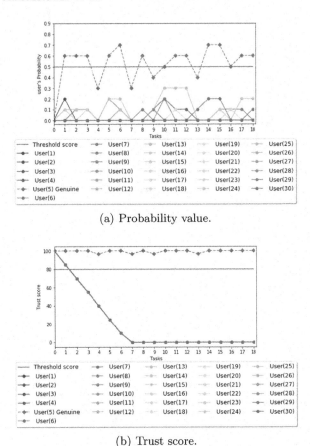

(a) Probability value.

(b) Trust score.

Fig. 6. Results of multi-segment authentication with one example of a genuine user and 29 imposters. Results identical for all imposters attempts.

6   Conclusions and Future Work

We have proposed a novel continuous, behavioural-biometric authentication system for a cobot, using internal cobot sensor data to authenticate users who engage physically with a cobot. This method increases security over existing systems while avoiding additional worker processes and potentially intrusive monitoring. In the future, we will examine the implementation of behavioural, biometric-based continuous authentication using wearable sensor devices for manufacturing situations in which co-workers are not directly manipulating robots, e.g. where a user completes some dexterous task before placing a worked artefact down to be subsequently picked up by a cobot for its (typically more dangerous) work contribution (e.g. spot welding). Our current work focuses on masquerading of one user by another, without the latter observing the former. We will also investigate the mimicking of a user actually observed by another.

References

1. Bours, P.: Continuous keystroke dynamics: a different perspective towards biometric evaluation. Inf. Secur. Tech. Rep. **17**(1–2), 36–43 (2012)
2. Bours, P., Mondal, S.: Performance evaluation of continuous authentication systems. IET Biometrics **4**(4), 220–226 (2015)
3. Buriro, A., Crispo, B., Delfrari, F., Wrona, K.: Hold and sign: a novel behavioral biometrics for smartphone user authentication. In: 2016 IEEE Security and Privacy Workshops (SPW), pp. 276–285. IEEE (2016)
4. Centeno, M.P., van Moorsel, A., Castruccio, S.: Smartphone continuous authentication using deep learning auto encoders. In: 2017 15th Annual Conference on Privacy, Security and Trust (PST), pp. 147–1478. IEEE (2017)
5. Chen, L., Zhong, Y., Ai, W., Zhang, D.: Continuous authentication based on user interaction behavior. In: 2019 7th International Symposium on Digital Forensics and Security (ISDFS), pp. 1–6. IEEE (2019)
6. Collaborative robots market by payload capacity (up to 5 kg, up to 10 kg, above 10 kg), industry (automotive, electronics, metals & machining, plastics & polymer, food & agriculture, healthcare), application, and geography - global forecast to 2023. https://www.marketsandmarkets.com/Market-Reports/collaborative-robot-market-194541294.html
7. IFR forecast 1.7 million new robots to transform the world's factories by 2020, https://ifr.org/ifr-press-releases/news/ifr-forecast-1.7-million-new-robots-to-transform-the-worlds-factories-by-20. Accessed 29 June (2020)
8. Gascon, H., Uellenbeck, S., Wolf, C., Rieck, K.: Continuous authentication on mobile devices by analysis of typing motion behavior. Sicherheit 2014-Sicherheit, Schutz und Zuverlässigkeit (2014)
9. Granitto, P.M., Furlanello, C., Biasioli, F., Gasperi, F.: Recursive feature elimination with random forest for ptr-ms analysis of agroindustrial products. Chemom. Intell. Lab. Syst. **83**(2), 83–90 (2006)
10. Maggi, F., Quarta, D., Pogliani, M., Polino, M., Zanchettin, A.M., Zanero, S.: Rogue robots: Testing the limits of an industrial robot's security. Tech. Rep, Trend Micro, Politecnico di Milano (2017)
11. IFAC-PapersOnLine A ROS-integrated API for the KUKA LBR IIWA collaborative robot. **50**(1), 15859–15864 (2017)
12. Murphy, A.: Intro: Robotics outlook 2025 (2017). https://loupventures.com/intro-robotics-outlook-2025/. Accessed 29 June 2020
13. Pedregosa, F., et al.: Scikit-learn: machine learning in Python. J. Mach. Learn. Res. **12**, 2825–2830 (2011)
14. Teresko, J.: Here come the cobots. https://www.industryweek.com/technology-and-iiot/automation/article/21938640/here-come-the-cobots. Accessed 29 June 2020

Secure Speaker Recognition System Using Homomorphic Encryption

Mihai-Cristian Chindriş⬡, Mihai Togan⬡, and Ştefan-Ciprian Arseni$^{(\boxtimes)}$⬡

"Ferdinand I" Military Technical Academy, 39-49 George Coşbuc Blvd.,
Bucharest, Romania
{cristian.chindris,mihai.togan,stefan.arseni}@mta.ro

Abstract. The ability to store and operate on cloud data provides flexibility and reduced hardware needs, but it has the disadvantage of a possible loss of data privacy. Homomorphic encryption solves this problem allowing operations on encrypted data to be performed, while maintaining its confidentiality. In this paper we focus on the introduction of homomorphic cryptosystems within neural networks. The main contribution is an implementation of a speaker recognition system whose security is based on the principles of homomorphic encryption. The application uses a convolutional neural network to classify encrypted spectral samples and it achieves an accuracy of over 99.5%. Moreover, we test different approximations for transfer functions analyzing time and memory consumption along accuracy.

Keywords: Homomorphic encryption · Speaker recognition · Machine learning · Convolutional neural networks.

1 Introduction

Outsourcing data processing in the cloud provides most entities with services that cost a lot of personal deployment. Even if these services introduce flexibility and reduced hardware needs, they may have privacy losses. Homomorphic encryption can help address this problem by computing on encrypted data while maintaining its privacy.

The current application focuses on identifying speakers based on their encrypted spectral samples. We consider that this way of using convolutional neural networks, whose security is based on homomorphic cryptography, introduces new possibilities in the field of artificial intelligence, especially in the field of Machine Learning as a Service.

In order to successfully introduce fully homomorphic encryption into the Computer Vision through different Deep Learning architectures, certain customizations must be made, either to the networks we want to use or to the communication protocols. At the level of the networks used, the transfer functions must be changed, the non-linear functions must be approximated or changed in their entirety with polynomial functions, thus making it possible to evaluate

© Springer Nature Switzerland AG 2021
D. Maimut et al. (Eds.): SecITC 2020, LNCS 12596, pp. 198–211, 2021.
https://doi.org/10.1007/978-3-030-69255-1_13

them. Also at this level, the max pooling layers must be replaced by average pooling layers. Interest in this research area began to increase rapidly with the achievement of very high accuracy in tasks such as image classification [1] or speech recognition [2].

Given the current context, speaker recognition systems based on MFCC feature vectors are the most common, with uses in the encrypted domain, or are based on GMMs [3], while maintaining speaker privacy. In [4] authors use the Paillier cryptosystem to protect biometric data taken using identity vectors, whilst in [5] they use vector quantization to extract features and create the model that is encrypted using an LHE scheme and evaluated later. In [6] authors describe a system implemented over TFHE [7] in which they use a VGGVox neural network [8] for time-efficient classification.

The main contribution of this paper is the introduction of a speaker recognition system that uses, for identification, a convolutional neural network, whose input data is represented by homomorphically encrypted spectrograms, having a fixed length over the speakers audio samples. Our starting point were some ideas from [9] and [10], which we later adapted for the current needs of the system.

This paper is organized as follows. Section 2 presents an overview of homomorphic encryption and the speaker recognition domains. Section 3 contains the general architecture and the proposed methods for approximating transfer functions, whilst Sect. 4 briefly describes the obtained results. The paper closes with a set of conclusions grouped in Sect. 5.

2   Related Work

2.1   Homomorphic Encryption

The field of homomorphic cryptography is not a recent concept and has been proposed shortly after the publication of the asymmetric RSA algorithm [11], which is, in fact, also homomorphic [12]. The idea from which they started is the following: the problem with systems that use data encryption for maintaining confidentiality of sensitive information is that they can only store or retrieve data from the user, while any other operation require, first of all, the decryption of that data, thus loosing its confidentiality.

The first 30 years after the emergence of the concept failed to produce the essence expected by the researchers, namely the possibility of performing any number of operations on encrypted data. It was not until 2009 that such a scheme could be possible with the publication of Craig Gentry's doctoral thesis [13]. The first generation of fully homomorphic schemes [14–16] that began with Gentry's doctoral thesis followed a similar, rather complicated methodology, which often was based on very strong computational assumptions. A second generation of schemes began with the work presented in [17], where authors obtained FHE in a less complicated way, based on the LWE (Learning With Errors) hypothesis. The security of these schemes is based on the weight, even in the quantum field, to approximate the problem of small vectors in the worst case scenario in lattices. Their scheme was subsequently improved by [18].

The security of most practical FHE schemes is based on the problem of Ring-Learning With Errors (RLWE), which is considered to be a difficult mathematical problem in the area of large-scale lattices. Nowadays, attempts are being made to standardize the field of homomorphic cryptography for a wide range of reasons: more and more companies and individuals are moving to the cloud storage and operation area, current deployments are not easy enough for beginners in the field, and the security properties of RLWE-based schemas can be difficult to understand.

The system we propose in this paper is implemented using the CKKS encryption scheme [19]. This scheme supports the addition and multiplication of encrypted messages, along with a new scaling procedure for managing the magnitude of messages in the plain space.

2.2 Speaker Recognition

Traditionally, the task of identifying a speaker has been addressed using Gaussian mixtures models (GMMs) on characteristic vectors containing Mel Frequency Cepstral coefficients (MFCCs) [20]. Recently, frameworks have emerged that use identity vectors and probabilistic linear discriminating analysis [21] to form compact, fixed-length representations of a speech sample. Although this technique is a standardised and functional approach in the industry, the use of MFCCs feature vectors does not exploit features other than the gross spectral envelope of short windows in an audio sample. In other words, the discriminatory characteristics of a speaker are not sought or processed: a person's characteristic manner of speaking, accent, rhythm, intonation, pronunciation model [22].

There are 2 types of systems for speaker identification: text dependent and text independent. In this work we will focus on the text independent one.

2.3 Convolutional Neural Networks

A convolutional neural network is a Deep Learning algorithm, which takes an image at the entrance, assigns importance (variable parameters during learning) to certain aspects, or parts of the image to be able to differentiate them from each other. The preprocessing used in CNN is much reduced compared to other classification algorithms. While primitive filter-based methods are created manually, CNNs have the ability to learn those filters automatically if they have enough data for training. Another interesting feature is that CNN architecture is analogous to the connectivity patterns of neurons within the human brain, inspired by the Visual Cortex organization [23]. Such a network can successfully capture the spatial-temporal dependencies of an image by applying the relevant filters. These networks emerged as the development of 3 important concepts in the Machine Learning, namely: reduced interaction, parameter sharing and covariant representation [24].

3   Speaker Recognition System

The proposed system is built using nGraph-HE [25] as a bridge for connecting the homomorphic cryptography to neural networks.

As seen in Fig. 1, the system is built from 3 main components:

- *HE – Speaker Identifier Client* - the component responsible for taking audio samples of speakers, extracting spectrograms, processing the result received from components dealing with the cryptographic part and returning a specific result to the user;
- *pyHE Client* - the cryptographic component at the client application level is the module that handles the homomorphic encryption of the data, their transmission using the TCP communication protocol and decryption of the results obtained from the server;
- *HE – Speaker Identifier Server* - the component performing homomorphic evaluations of the speaker's characteristic data by going through a homomorphic circuit, which consists of the trained convolutional neural network.

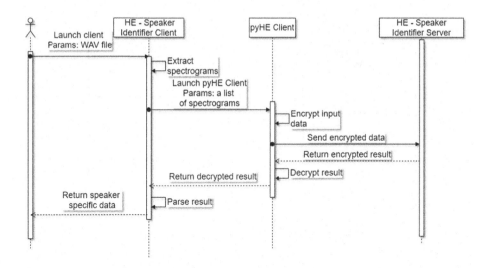

Fig. 1. Sequence diagram for the speaker recognition system.

3.1   HE - Speaker Identifier Client

As mentioned earlier, this component is intended to extract spectrograms from an audio sample, process them in a characteristic way so that they can be evaluated by the server application, and return a specific result to the user.

The process of generating spectrograms involves 2 steps: removing quiet portions from the audio signal and creating spectrograms for each window in the signal. The first step is achieved by removing frames whose energy does not exceed a certain barrier over a short period of time, and then all new frames obtained are concatenated. Step two generates the Mel-scale spectrogram, the scale of which is transformed into the whole 8-bit (0–255) range and reversed so that the low frequencies are at the bottom of the image obtained. Subsequently, a color inversion is made so that black represents higher levels of energy. The image obtained is saved according to the parameters sent earlier, in case additional checks need to be carried out. Parameters used for generating the spectrograms are as follows: 128 Mel filters, 16 kHz sampling rate, 1024 length points and 160 points for interframe length. The extraction of spectrograms from audio samples is done in *Python*, using the *Librosa library*.

3.2   pyHE Client

This component, inspired from [26], deals with the homomorphic encryption of the values received from the previous component, their transmission to the server, and the decryption of the results received from the server. Encryption and decryption operations are performed using the Microsoft SEAL library [27], the CKKS scheme.

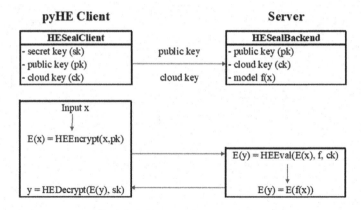

Fig. 2. Architectural design used for pyHE Client and its connection to the Server.

3.3   HE - Speaker Identifier Server

This component, had also a starting point in [26] and was modified accordingly to the needs of the speaker recognition system. It is the module dealing with the actual recognition of speakers through a neural network that classifies the input data. In order to reach this goal, we developed a neural network for classifying a number of speakers based on voice samples.

Figure 3 shows the structure of the neural network used to identify speakers. It contains 4 convolutional layers for a smooth and accurate choice of voice characteristics extracted from the spectrograms sent for identification, 2 average pooling layers and 2 fully connected layers.

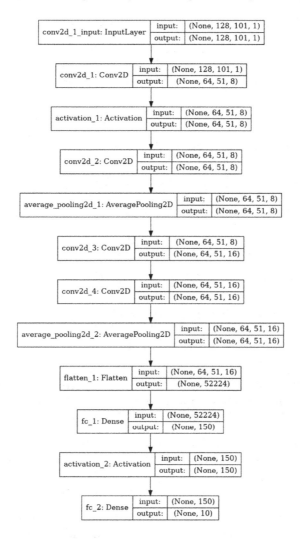

Fig. 3. Network architecture used to identify speakers.

This model was too complex to be homomorphically evaluated, so we chose to narrow it and we obtained the model depicted in Fig. 4.

The network training was carried out on a database containing 13 speakers. The processing of the spectrograms that are sent for network training is carried out by loading all the speakers samples together with the associated labels, whilst 25% of this data was used for testing. The network is trained with the following characteristics:

– the *Categorical Cross-entropy* algorithm is used to calculate losses;
– the *RMSProp* method is used for optimizing the metric;
– the metric is based on the calculation of accuracy.

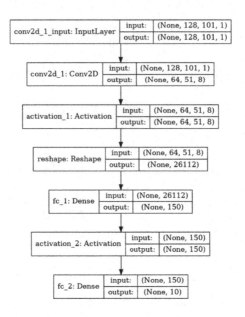

Fig. 4. The restricted model used in the speaker identification system.

Based on the network presented in Fig. 3, it can be observed that the layers conv2d_2, average_pooling2d_1, conv2d_3, conv2d_4, average_pooling2d_2, flatten_1 and fc_1 can be reduced to a single layer. This reduction consists in the generation of 2 matrices that correspond to the operations that are performed in those 7 layers:

- one for the coefficients corresponding to each transition from one neuron to another;
- one for the values added to the above mentioned coefficients.

Once these matrices are obtained, the new model can be generated. To do so and obtain the model presented in Fig. 4, we began with 2 convolutional layers, an average pooling layer and 2 fully connected layers for classification, as also proposed in [28]. But, for our case, given the limited number of training data, the results were not good enough for the current state of speaker recognition systems. Therefore, after a series of successive changes to the model, we were able to reach its final form, for which we achieved 99.6% accuracy, with an average evaluation duration of 340 s.

As mentioned in Sect. 1, securing the use of a neural network with homomorphic encryption means that we have to either create a special communication protocol between client and server, or approximate the transfer functions with different polynomials. Our approach tried to find a suitable approximation for the non-linear transfer functions ReLU and Sigmoid.

4   Experimental Results

In order to find a good approximation for the 2 transfer function mentioned earlier, we tried 3 different methods: numerical analysis, Taylor expansion and Bernstein polynomial approximation. An important thing to note is that the polynomial used as a transfer function must be of a low degree so that the evaluation of the entire network does not exceed critical memory thresholds or very high execution times. Taking this into consideration, we limited our tries to approximate polynomials with a maximum degree of 5.

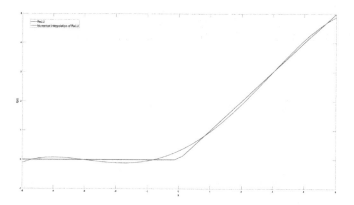

Fig. 5. ReLU and its numerical approximation with a degree of 5.

The first step to approximate the two functions consisted of a numerical analysis of their values and an interpolation of these data sets. The results obtained were of very poor quality, the degree of polynomials obtained by interpolation far exceeding 5, for a valid approximation over a reduced input area.

From the graphs depicted in Fig. 6 and Fig. 7, we can see the difference obtained for classical interpolation and the functions themselves. These approximations were not used further in the code. The second step consisted in approximating the 2 functions using Taylor expansion.

$$taylor(ReLU) = -\frac{x^4}{192} + \frac{x^2}{8} + \frac{x}{2} + ln2 \tag{1}$$

$$taylor(Sigmoid) = \frac{x^5}{480} - \frac{x^3}{48} + \frac{x}{4} + \frac{1}{2} \tag{2}$$

Both approximations are valid over a range between $[-3, 3]$. Since the approximation obtained for ReLU in Eq. 1, contains a polynomial whose degree is lower, we have carried out a series of tests using this polynomial as a transfer function.

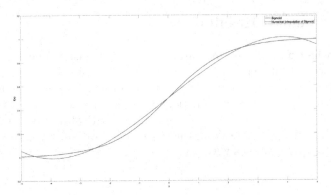

Fig. 6. Sigmoid and its numerical approximation with a degree of 5.

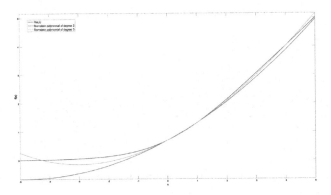

Fig. 7. Bernstein polynomials for ReLU.

Table 1 present the results obtained using this approximation for ReLU. We observed that, for the first 2 models, the obtained accuracy is not as we have expected, thus, we only carried further experiments on the third model.

Table 1. Results obtained using Taylor expansion for ReLU.

Model	Accuracy	Evaluation time	Memory consumption
2 convolutional + 1 pooling + 2 activation	48.7%	290 s	65 GB
3 convolutional + 2 pooling + 2 activation	82.7%	420 s	95 GB
4 convolutional + 2 pooling + 2 activation	99.2%	–	–

Since by using this approximation we could not obtain results in encrypted domain, we further tried to use Bernstein polynomials. We conducted a series of tests using a fifth, third and second-degree polynomials for the ReLU transfer function and polynomials of degree 3 and 2 for Sigmoid.

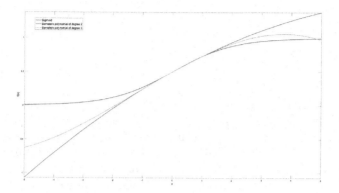

Fig. 8. Bernstein polynomials for Sigmoid.

Although the fifth-degree polynomial for ReLU, or the third-degree polynomial for Sigmoid, is a close approximation, we chose to check the third model to maintain the high level of accuracy, using as transfer function the polynomials in the Eq. 3, ReLU and respectively 4, Sigmoid. This decision was based on the fact that there is a relatively small difference between the results obtained by approximation using the big degree polynomial or a second-degree polynomial for both functions.

$$(x - 1)^2 ln2 + x^2 ln(e + 1) - 2x(x - 1)ln(e^{\frac{1}{2}} + 1) \tag{3}$$

$$\frac{(x - 1)^2}{2} + \frac{x^2}{e^{-1} + 1} - \frac{2x(x - 1)}{e^{-\frac{1}{2}} + 1} \tag{4}$$

During the research undertaken and in the view of obtained experimental results, the choice of the x^2 polynomial as a transfer function came through articles [28,29], where the usefulness of this polynomial was demonstrated.

Table 2 shows the results obtained on the complex model in Fig. 4 using as transfer functions the polynomial x^2, the polynomial in the Eq. 3 and the polynomial in the Eq. 4. Approximations of the ReLU and Sigmoid transfer functions achieve slightly higher accuracy for data training than that obtained by using the x^2 polynomial. On the other hand, given the very high memory consumption and the evaluation time of the model using the 2 approximations for the transfer functions, the difference for the accuracy metric can be neglected, so, in our view, the optimal choice of transfer function would be the polynomial x^2. Due to insufficient resources we were unable to complete the evaluation of the model using one of the 2 polynomials in the Eqs. 3 and 4. As a result, we checked the differences between the results of the functions in plain and the results obtained using the CKKS cryptosystem and their polynomial approximations.

Table 2. Results obtained on the complex model for different polynomials as transfer functions.

Transfer function	Accuracy	Evaluation time	Memory consumption
x^2	99.62%	340 s	73 GB
Polynomial from Eq. 3	99.69%	–	–
Polynomial from Eq. 4	99.69%	–	–

Table 3 shows the differences, obtained by applying to a set of points in the range $[-3,3)$, between the RELU function and the evaluation of its polynomial approximation and the differences between the Sigmoid function and the assessment of its approximation using the CKKS on 2-level scheme. The evaluation time on encrypted data is approximately 29 times longer, and the errors obtained are significant, 0.1372 for the Sigmoid function and its approximation, respectively 0.2124 for the RELU function and its approximation.

Table 3. Results for ReLU, Sigmoid and their Bernstein polynomials of degree 2.

Function	Data	Evaluation time (seconds)	RMSE
ReLU	Range [-3,3) sampled in 48 points	0.004	0.2124
Polynomial from Eq. 3		0.118	
Sigmoid		0.004	0.1372
Polynomial from Eq. 4		0.114	

Because we are in the homomorphic domain, each multiplication brings with it the question of the number of levels for the homomorphic scheme considered, in this case, CKKS. As a network with fewer layers produces a result with lower accuracy, the number of levels can be considered as a function given by the polynomial degree used for the transfer function. For the model in Fig. 4, a 7-level configuration is used, using the x^2 polynomial as a transfer function. For various changes to this polynomial, the configuration must be adapted consequently.

All the evaluations mentioned above were carried on a system having 100 GB of RAM, 20 cores and Ubuntu 18.04 LTS operating system. The database consisted in 5242 spectral samples taken from 13 speakers. All approximations, computations and graphs were created with MATLAB R2018b.

During evaluations conducted in the encrypted domain, the application has an accuracy of 99.99%, following more than 30 evaluations with 1391 spectral samples, different from one evaluation to another, the neural network miscalculated a maximum of 2 samples per evaluation. Using the client-server system, we checked with samples that did not appear in the original database for some of the speakers, and the results were correct for all the tests performed.

5 Conclusions

In our view, looking at the rise and optimizations of FHE encryption schemes, from Gentry's 2009 schema [13] to the present day, the field is a continuous research area. In the near future, schemes created and their implementations will be able to provide full and easy access to the development of the cloud computing, thus data security, alongside the speed and accuracy of results, will be increased. In relation to the applications developed in this paper, in particular the speaker recognition system, it can easily be observed that, at the moment, although the results obtained do not indicate excellent performance of the system, one must take account of the existing and recognized complexity of operations in homomorphic cryptography, as well as of the infrastructure used, which is more than 5 times less than those often used in the literature. The performance achieved in terms of speaker recognition also indicates that the method is a good one, with a good projection of use in the future.

Another problem that arises on the use of neural networks in the homomorphic field is given by the transfer function, as it can be observed from the experiments performed, that the usual transfer functions (Sigmoid, Hyperbolic Tangent, ReLU) cannot be used directly in this context. Based on the experiments carried out, we can say that the approximations made using Bernstein polynomials achieve better results compared to the other methods. A direct consequence involves altering the number of layers used within the model, or using larger parameters for the encryption scheme. Therefore, homomorphic cryptography has its limits in certain applications, but the applicability of these schemes proves to be useful and good results can be achieved in most areas.

A possible disadvantage of the method used in the speaker identification system is the need to retrain the network used for classification. At the same time, from the point of view of the tests carried out by the method described in the paper, it is possible that the number of users for whom the detection process is carried out may also be necessary to modify the parameters of the neural network. This change will be made by adding a larger number of layers, depending on the granularity index required to uniquely identify each user. In this respect, a research direction will be to identify an empirical method of assessing the ratio between the number of parameters and the number of speakers, by conducting tests using the current system on a large number of users (the increase in the number of users will be carried out gradually, on the basis of fixed intervals) or by modifying the parameters of spectral samples taken from the users' voice samples. A second direction of research will be the comparative analysis of the performance between the classical methods of voice signal analysis and the method proposed in this paper, also taking into account the degree of influence that the number of end-users can have on such a system.

References

1. Krizhevsky, A., Sutskever, I., Hinton, G.E.: Image classification with deep convolutional neural networks. Commun. ACM **25**(2), 84–90 (2017). https://doi.org/10.1145/3065386
2. Dahl, G.E., Yu, D., Deng, L., Acero, A.: Context-dependent pre-trained deep neural networks for large-vocabulary speech recognition. IEEE Trans. Audio Speech Lang. Process. **20**(1), 30–42 (2012). https://doi.org/10.1109/TASL.2011.2134090
3. Pathak, M.A., Raj, B.: Privacy-preserving speaker verification and identification using Gaussian mixture models. IEEE Trans. Audio Speech Lang. Process. **21**(2), 397–406 (2013). https://doi.org/10.1109/TASL.2012.2215602
4. Nautsch, A., Isadskiy, S., Kolberg, J., Gomez-Barrero, M., Busch, C.: Homomorphic Encryption for speaker recognition: protection of biometric templates and vendor model parameters. In: Proceedings of Odyssey 2018 The Speaker and Language Recognition Workshop, pp. 16–23 (2018). https://doi.org/10.21437/Odyssey
5. Ene, A., Togan, M., Toma, S.-A.: Privacy preserving vector quantization based speaker recognition system. Proc. Rom. Acad. Seri. A **18**, 371–380 (2017)
6. Zuber, M., Carpov, S., Sirdey, R.: Towards real-time hidden speaker recognition by means of fully homomorphic encryption. In: Meng, W., Gollmann, D., Jensen, C.D., Zhou, J. (eds.) ICICS 2020. LNCS, vol. 12282, pp. 403–421. Springer, Cham (2020). https://doi.org/10.1007/978-3-030-61078-4_23
7. Chillotti, I., Gama, N., Georgieva, M., Izabachène, M.: Faster fully homomorphic encryption: bootstrapping in less than 0.1 seconds. In: Cheon, J.H., Takagi, T. (eds.) ASIACRYPT 2016. LNCS, vol. 10031, pp. 3–33. Springer, Heidelberg (2016). https://doi.org/10.1007/978-3-662-53887-6_1
8. Chung, J.S., Nagrani, A., Zisserman, A.: VoxCeleb2: Deep speaker recognition. In: Proceedings of Interspeech, pp. 1086–1090 (2018). https://doi.org/10.21437/Interspeech.2018-1929
9. Lukic, Y., Vogt, C., Durr, O., Stadelmann, T.: Speaker identification and clustering using convolutional neural networks. In: 2016 IEEE 26th International Workshop on Machine Learning for Signal Processing (MLSP), Vietri sul Mare, pp. 1–6 (2016). https://doi.org/10.1109/MLSP.2016.7738816
10. Bunrit ,S., Inkian, T., Kerdprasop, N., Kerdprasop, K.: Text-independent speaker identification using deep learning model of convolution neural network. Int. J. Mach. Learn. Comput. **9**(2), 143–148 (2019). https://doi.org/10.18178/ijmlc.2019.9.2.778
11. Rivest, R., Shamir, A., Adleman, L.: A method for obtaining digital signatures and public-key criptosystems. Commun. ACM **21**(2), 126–126 (1978). https://doi.org/10.1145/359340.359342
12. Rivest, R., Adleman, L., Dertouzos, M.: On data banks and privacy homomorphisms. Found. Secure Comput. **4**(11), 169–179 (1978)
13. Gentry, C.: A Fully Homomorphic Encryption Scheme. Ph.D. Dissertation. Stanford University, Stanford, CA, USA. Advisor(s) Dan Boneh (2009)
14. Gentry, C.: Fully homomorphic encryption using ideal lattices. In: Proceedings of the forty-first annual ACM symposium on Theory of computing (STOC 2009). Association for Computing Machinery, New York, NY, USA, pp. 169–178 (2009). https://doi.org/10.1145/1536414.1536440
15. van Dijk, M., Gentry, C., Halevi, S., Vaikuntanathan, V.: Fully homomorphic encryption over the integers. In: Gilbert, H. (ed.) EUROCRYPT 2010. LNCS, vol. 6110, pp. 24–43. Springer, Heidelberg (2010). https://doi.org/10.1007/978-3-642-13190-5_2

16. Brakerski, Z.: Fully homomorphic encryption without modulus switching from classical GapSVP. In: Safavi-Naini, R., Canetti, R. (eds.) CRYPTO 2012. LNCS, vol. 7417, pp. 868–886. Springer, Heidelberg (2012). https://doi.org/10.1007/978-3-642-32009-5_50

17. Brakerski, Z., Gentry, C., Vaikuntanathan, V.: (Leveled) Fully homomorphic encryption without bootstrapping. In: Proceedings of the 3rd Innovations in Theoretical Computer Science Conference (ITCS 2012). Association for Computing Machinery, New York, NY, USA, pp. 309–325 (2012). https://doi.org/10.1145/2090236.2090262

18. Brakerski, Z., Vaikuntanathan, V.: Efficient fully homomorphic encryption from (standard) LWE. In: 2011 IEEE 52nd Annual Symposium on Foundations of Computer Science, Palm Springs, CA, pp. 97–106 (2011). https://doi.org/10.1109/FOCS.2011.12

19. Cheon, J.H., Kim, A., Kim, M., Song, Y.: Homomorphic encryption for arithmetic of approximate numbers. In: Takagi, T., Peyrin, T. (eds.) ASIACRYPT 2017. LNCS, vol. 10624, pp. 409–437. Springer, Cham (2017). https://doi.org/10.1007/978-3-319-70694-8_15

20. Reynolds, D.A., Quatieri, T.F., Dunn, R.B.: Speaker verification using adapted Gaussian mixture models. Digital Sig. Process. 10(1–3), 19–41 (2000). https://doi.org/10.1006/dspr.1999.0361

21. Lee, H.S., Tsao, Y., Wang, H.M., Jeng, S.K.: Clustering-based i-vector formulation for speaker recognition. In: Proceedings of the Annual Conference of the International Speech Communication Association, INTERSPEECH, Singapore, pp. 1101–1105 (2014)

22. Kinnunen, T., Li, H.: An overview of text-independent speaker recognition: from features to supervectors. Speech Commun. 52(1), 12–40 (2010). https://doi.org/10.1016/j.specom.2009.08.009

23. Towards Data Science. https://towardsdatascience.com/a-comprehensive-guide-to-convolutional-neural-networks-the-eli5-way-3bd2b1164a53. Accessed 15 May 2020

24. Goodfellow, I., Bengio, Y., Courville, A.: Deep Learning. MIT Press, Cambridge (2016)

25. Boemer, F., Cammarota, R., Costache, A., Wierzynski, C.: nGraph-HE2: a high-throughput framework for neural network inference on encrypted data. In: Proceedings of the 7th ACM Workshop on Encrypted Computing & Applied Homomorphic Cryptography (WAHC 2019). Association for Computing Machinery, New York, NY, USA, pp. 45–56 (2019). https://doi.org/10.1145/3338469.3358944

26. nGraph-HE: Deep learning with Homomorphic Encryption (HE) through Intel nGraph. https://github.com/IntelAI/he-transformer. Accessed 4 June 2020

27. Microsoft SEAL. https://github.com/Microsoft/SEAL. Accessed 24 Apr 2020

28. Dowlin, N., Gilad-Bachrach, R., Laine, K., Lauter, K., Naehrig, M., Wernsing, J.: CryptoNets: applying neural networks to encrypted data with high throughput and accuracy. In: Proceedings of the 33rd International Conference on Machine Learning 48, JMLR.org, New York, NY, USA, pp. 201–210 (2016)

29. Livni, R., Shalev-Shwartz, S., Shamir, O.: On the Computation Efficiency of Training Neural Networks. In: Proceedings of the 27th International Conference on Neural Information Processing Systems 1. MIT Press, Cambridge, MA, USA, pp. 855–863 (2014)

Reliable RFID Offline Privacy

Cristian Hristea[1,2(✉)]

[1] Simion Stoilow Institute of Mathematics of the Romanian Academy,
Bucharest, Romania
cristi.hristea@gmail.com
[2] Advanced Technologies Institute, Bucharest, Romania

Abstract. The paper discusses a privacy definition for offline RFID schemes, called *privacy+*. We analyse this notion and we describe an attack that proves that it can not be achieved by the accompanying protocol. In order to achieve offline privacy we develop a novel approach based on using PUFs on the reader together with encrypting the reader database. Our approach contradicts the standard assumption that privacy must be lost when a reader is compromised and that privacy restoring mechanisms must be developed. We design a protocol that implements this idea and prove it to be secure, destructive-private and immune to reader corruption in a slightly modified version of Vaudenay's model.

1 Introduction

The potential of RFID technology has become evident as more and more applications have employed the benefits of contactless communication. Domains such as asset tracking, animal or object identification, public transportation or access control have come to rely on this technology [1]. Typically, RFID involves two main entities: a small device, called *tag*, that gets attached to an object that it identifies and a powerful device, called *reader* or interrogator, that communicates wirelessly with the tag. Besides the above components one may also introduce a backend *server* that stores a database with relevant information and communicates through a secure channel with the reader.

The widespread adoption of RFID comes, however, with a potential for security and privacy violations. The wireless nature of the communication between reader and tag allows malicious scanning of tags and traffic interception. Tracking a person through her RFID possessions (access card, bus ticket) becomes a reality. The lack of physical protection of the tag gives rise to another serious threat: corruption. An attacker can gain access to a tag and extract its secrets, allowing him to permanently violate the user's privacy. The research community has addressed these concerns by designing authentication protocols for RFID [2–5] and formal privacy models [2,6–8] for analysing these protocols.

The connection type of the reader with the server (permanent or not) gives rise to RFID schemes that are online or offline. In the first scenario, the reader is considered to always be connected to the backend server through a secure connection. Furthermore, the reader cannot function offline as it does not hold any

© Springer Nature Switzerland AG 2021
D. Maimut et al. (Eds.): SecITC 2020, LNCS 12596, pp. 212–226, 2021.
https://doi.org/10.1007/978-3-030-69255-1_14

database information. This approach is the most common one and has received more attention from the research community in terms of security and privacy [2,4,6,7].

In contrast, offline RFID schemes assume that the reader is only sporadically connected to the central database. Since most or all of the reader's activity must be conducted without access to the server, the reader must accommodate a partial (or full) database with tag information. Applications that fit this descriptions are access control systems where many individual rooms are equipped with electronic locks [1], sporting events or public transportation [9]. For example, bus readers connect to the central database only at the end of the day. Thus, it is natural to consider the privacy implications of the attacker compromising a reader. The common approach to this threat is to assume that privacy is inherently lost after an adversary corrupts a reader [5,9–11]. Therefore, privacy-restoring mechanisms have to be defined in order to regain the privacy of the scheme after such an event. In order to implement this view, special privacy experiments, such as the one from [10] or *privacy+* from [5], need to be created.

Contribution. First of all, in this paper we discuss the notion of *privacy+* from [5], that was proposed as a modification of Vaudenay's privacy experiment [2,6] for offline schemes with privacy-restoring mechanims. We show that *privacy+* is not adequately described and does not provide the intended privacy level. We present an attack against the scheme from [5] that breaks *privacy+*. Secondly, we suggest a general approach to construct RFID authentication protocols that do not lose privacy when the reader is compromised. As far as we know, this is the first proposal of its kind. Our idea is employing Physically Unclonable Function (PUF) [12] technology on the reader (secure key storage) and a symmetric encryption scheme for protecting sensitive information stored in the reader's local database. PUFs are lightweight constructions that have been proposed as a solution against corruption on tags [4] and have become a frequently used building block for RFID protocols [3–5,13,14]. We propose a protocol that follows this idea and does not lose privacy when the reader is compromised. The protocol is analysed in a slightly modified version of Vaudenay's model. Proof sketc.hes are provided for the protocol's security and privacy properties.

Paper Structure. The paper is divided in six sections. The first section corresponds to the introduction. In the second section we fix some notations and present useful definitions. Section 3 represents a presentation of Vaudenay's RFID privacy model and the needed modifications for offline schemes. In Sect. 4 we present a state of the art of offline privacy and discuss the notion of privacy+. Section 5 represents the proposed protocol description and the security and privacy proofs.

2 Notations, Definitions and Concepts

In this section we recall a few concepts from cryptography. For details, the reader is referred to [15].

We use *probabilistic polynomial time* (PPT) algorithms as defined in [16] that can consult *oracles*. An oracle is a black box that can perform a particular computation. When considering an oracle, we do not consider its implementation or the way it works. Whenever a PPT algorithm $\mathcal{A}$ sends a value x to some oracle $\mathcal{O}$, the oracle returns to $\mathcal{A}$ a given value in $O(1)$ time.

For a set A, $a \leftarrow A$ means that a is uniformly at random chosen from A. If $\mathcal{A}$ is a probabilistic algorithm, then $a \leftarrow \mathcal{A}$ means that a is an output of $\mathcal{A}$ for some given input.

The asymptotic approach to security makes use of security parameters, denoted by λ in our paper.

Definition 1. *A positive function $f(\lambda)$ is called* negligible *if for any positive polynomial $poly(\lambda)$ there exists n_0 such that $f(\lambda) < 1/poly(\lambda)$, for any $\lambda \geq n_0$. $f(\lambda)$ is called* overwhelming *if $1 - f(\lambda)$ is negligible.*

We say that a function F is computationally indistinguishable from a random function g if no PPT algorithm can decide with more than a negligible probability whether a given value is an output of F or g.

Physically Unclonable Functions (PUFs) [12] are hardware constructions that use variations in the manufacturing process of integrated circuits (ICs) to produce IC-specific outputs. The typical analogy for PUFs is that they can provide device identification similar to human fingerprints. Thus, PUFs have a specific challenge-response behaviour, *i.e.* when queried with a challenge they produce a response that depends not just on the challenge but also on the IC on which the PUF is implemented. Common requirements for PUFs are that they are *physically unclonable* (it is infeasible to produce two PUFs that cannot be distinguished based on their challenge/response behavior), *unpredictable* (it is infeasible to predict the response to an unknown challenge), and *tamper-evident* (any attempt to physically access the PUF irreversible changes the challenge/response behaviour).

When considering PUFs for cryptographic usage one must alleviate the unstable nature of PUFs. This can be performed by using techniques such as Helper Data Algorithms [17] or with PUF constructions that offer zero bit error rate [18].

Since provable security requires ideal primitives, we adopt the concept of *ideal PUF*, that was used in several papers [3,4,14]. This concept treats PUFs from a theoretical perspective and considers them to be tamper-evident constructions that provide consistent responses (no noise) with good entropy. Our definition is the same as the one from [3].

Definition 2. *An* ideal PUF *is a physical object with a challenge/response behaviour that implements a function $P : \{0,1\}^p \rightarrow \{0,1\}^k$, where p and k are of polynomial size in λ, such that (1) P is computationally indistinguishable from a random function and (2) any attempt to physically tamper with the object implementing P results in destruction of P (P cannot be evaluated any more).*

A *pseudo-random function* (PRF) is a family of functions with the property that if we randomly choose a function from this family then its input-output behaviour is computationally indistinguishable from that of a random function.

Definition 3. *Let $F : \{0,1\}^\lambda \times \{0,1\}^{\ell_1(\lambda)} \to \{0,1\}^{\ell_2(\lambda)}$ be an efficiently computable, keyed function, where $\ell_1(\lambda), \ell_2(\lambda)$ are two polynomials in λ. F is called a pseudo-random function if F_K is computationally indistinguishable from a random function g, where $K \leftarrow \{0,1\}^\lambda$ is chosen uniformly at random.*

To prove that F is a PRF, we usually use a *bit guessing game* between a *challenger C* and an adversary $\mathcal{A}$ (with a security parameter λ) where, based on a random bit b, the challenger provides $\mathcal{A}$ with oracle access to either F ($b = 1$) or a random function ($b = 0$). At the end, $\mathcal{A}$ outputs a guess b'. The probability that $\mathcal{A}$ wins the game is denoted $P(b' = b)$. We can say that F is a PRF if it is efficiently computable and $Adv_{\mathcal{A},F}^{prf}(\lambda) = |P(b = b') - 1/2|$ is negligible.

Definition 4. *A symmetric-key encryption (SKE) scheme is a triple of PPT algorithms $\mathcal{S} = (\mathcal{G}, \mathcal{E}, \mathcal{D})$, where $\mathcal{G}$ outputs a secret key K and takes as input a security parameter λ, $\mathcal{E}$ outputs a ciphertext y and takes as input a key K and a plaintext x, and $\mathcal{D}$ is deterministic and outputs a plaintext and takes as input a key K and a ciphertext, such that $x = \mathcal{D}(K, y)$, for any $y \leftarrow \mathcal{E}(K, x)$.*

$\mathcal{S}$ is called *IND-CPA secure* if no PPT algorithm $\mathcal{A}$ that is allowed to query the encryption algorithm $\mathcal{E}$ of $\mathcal{S}$ has a non-negligible advantage to distinguish between two plaintexts of equal length, given a ciphertext of one of them.

3   RFID Systems

3.1   RFID Schemes

Let $\mathcal{R}$ be a *reader identifier* and $\mathcal{T}$ be a set of *tag identifiers* whose cardinal is polynomial in some security parameter λ.

An *RFID scheme over* $(\mathcal{R}, \mathcal{T})$ [2,6] is a triple $\mathcal{S} = (SetupR, SetupT, Ident)$ of PPT algorithms, where *SetupR* initialises the reader and its database *DB*, *SetupT* initialises a tag and stores a corresponding entry in *DB* and *Ident* is an interactive protocol between the reader identified by $\mathcal{R}$ (with database *DB*) and a tag identified by *ID* (with state *S*). At the end of *Ident* the reader outputs either an *ID* or $\perp$, while the tag outputs *OK* or $\perp$ (*mutual authentication*).

For mutual authentication RFID schemes, *correctness* means that, regardless of how the system is set up, after each complete execution of the interactive protocol between the reader and a legitimate tag, the reader outputs the tag's identity and the tag outputs *OK* with overwhelming probability.

3.2   Adversarial Model

There have been several proposals for an adversarial model [2,6–8,19] for RFID schemes. In this paper we follow *Vaudenay's model* [2,6].

In Vaudenay's model, a tag can be either *drawn* or *free* based on adversarial access to the tag (proximity). An adversary can access a drawn tag only through a temporary unique identifier *vtag*.

Within this model, the adversary is given access to the following oracles:

1. $CreateTag^b(ID)$: Creates a free tag $\mathcal{T}_{ID}$ with the identifier ID by calling the algorithm $SetupT(pk, ID)$ to generate a pair (K, S). If $b = 1$, $(ID, f(S), K)$ is added to DB and the tag is considered *legitimate*; otherwise $(b = 0)$, the tag is considered *illegitimate*;
2. $DrawTag(\delta)$: This oracle chooses a number of free tags according to the distribution δ, let us say n, and draws them. That is, n temporary identities $vtag_1, \ldots, vtag_n$ are generated and then the oracle outputs $(vtag_i, b_i)$, where b_i specifies whether the tag $vtag_i$ is legitimate or not;
3. $Free(vtag)$: The tag identified by $vtag$ becomes free and the identifier $vtag$ will no longer be used. It is assumed that the temporary state of the tag is erased when the tag is freed. This is a natural assumption that corresponds to the fact that the tag is no longer powered by the reader;
4. $Launch()$: Launches a new protocol instance and assigns a unique identifier to it. The oracle outputs the identifier;
5. $SendReader(m, \pi)$: Outputs the reader's answer when the message m is sent to it as part of the protocol instance π. When m is the empty message, abusively but suggestively denoted by $\emptyset$, this oracle outputs the first message of the protocol instance π, assuming that the reader does the first step in the protocol;
6. $SendTag(m, vtag)$: outputs the tag's answer when the message m is sent to the tag referred to by $vtag$. When m is the empty message, this oracle outputs the first message of the protocol instance π, assuming that the tag does the first step in the protocol;
7. $Result(\pi)$: Outputs $\perp$ if in session π the reader has not yet made a decision on tag authentication (this also includes the case when the session π does not exist), 1 if in session π the reader authenticated the tag, and 0 otherwise (this oracle is both for unilateral and mutual authentication);
8. $Corrupt(vtag)$: Outputs the current permanent (internal) state of the tag referred to by $vtag$, when the tag is not involved in any computation of any protocol step (that is, the permanent state before or after a protocol step).

There has been consistent debate on whether the *Corrupt* oracle returns only the permanent state or the volatile state of a tag as well [3,20]. As stated in the oracle description, we consider that *Corrupt* returns only the permanent state. Based on access to the *Corrupt* oracle, adversaries are classified into: *weak* (no access to *Corrupt*), *forward* (no other oracles can be used after *Corrupt*), *destructive* (after corrupting a tag it is considered destroyed) and *strong* (no restrictions).

Another class of adversaries called *narrow* is created when the adversary is denied access to the *Result* oracle. This class can be combined with the previous categories and we obtain another four classes of adversaries, *narrow weak*, *narrow forward*, *narrow destructive*, and *narrow strong*.

3.3 Security

Security for RFID schemes is composed of two complementary notions: *tag authentication* and *reader authentication*.

The tag authentication property is defined by means of an experiment denoted $RFID_{\mathcal{A},\mathcal{S}}^{t\text{-}auth}(\lambda)$ where a challenger sets up for a strong adversary $\mathcal{A}$ an RFID scheme $\mathcal{S}$ in which $\mathcal{A}$ must impersonate a legitimate uncorrupted tag to the reader. The adversary is compelled to compute at least one of the messages exchanged in the protocol. In the end $\mathcal{A}$ outputs a bit b. The advantage of $\mathcal{A}$ in the experiment $RFID_{\mathcal{A},\mathcal{S}}^{t\text{-}auth}(\lambda)$ is defined as the probability that the adversary outputs 1. We say that $\mathcal{S}$ achieves *tag authentication* if $Adv_{\mathcal{A},\mathcal{S}}^{t\text{-}auth}$ is negligible, for any strong adversary $\mathcal{A}$.

The experiment $RFID_{\mathcal{A},\mathcal{S}}^{r\text{-}auth}(\lambda)$ for reader authentication is identical to the $RFID_{\mathcal{A},\mathcal{S}}^{t\text{-}auth}(\lambda)$ except that $\mathcal{A}$ has to impersonate the reader to a legitimate uncorrupted tag. An RFID scheme $\mathcal{S}$ achieves *reader authentication* if the adversarial advantage in this experiment, $Adv_{\mathcal{A},\mathcal{S}}^{r\text{-}auth}$, is negligible, for any strong adversary $\mathcal{A}$.

3.4 Privacy

The *privacy* notion that was defined in Vaundenay's model basically means that the communication between the reader and the tags does not leak any information to an eavesdropping adversary. This is modelled through the use of a blinder.

A *blinder* for an adversary $\mathcal{A}$ that belongs to some class V of adversaries is a PPT algorithm $\mathcal{B}$ that: (1) simulates the *Launch, SendReader, SendTag*, and *Result* oracles for $\mathcal{A}$, without having access to the corresponding secrets and (2) passively looks at the communication between $\mathcal{A}$ and the other oracles allowed to it by the class V. When the adversary $\mathcal{A}$ interacts with the RFID scheme by means of a blinder $\mathcal{B}$, we say that $\mathcal{A}$ is *blinded by* $\mathcal{B}$ and denote this by $\mathcal{A}^{\mathcal{B}}$. We emphasize that $\mathcal{A}^{\mathcal{B}}$ is allowed to query the oracles *Launch, SendReader, SendTag*, and *Result* only by means of $\mathcal{B}$; all the other oracles are queried as a standard adversary.

Given an adversary $\mathcal{A}$ and a blinder $\mathcal{B}$ for it, let us define two experiments (privacy games) $RFID_{\mathcal{A},\mathcal{S}}^{prv\text{-}0}(\lambda)$ and $RFID_{\mathcal{A},\mathcal{S},\mathcal{B}}^{prv\text{-}1}(\lambda)$ where the adversary interacts, according to its class, with the real RFID scheme and, respectively, with the blinded scheme. After an interaction phase, the adversary receives the hidden table of the *DrawTag* oracle, enters an analysis phase and outputs a bit b.

The *advantage* of $\mathcal{A}$ blinded by $\mathcal{B}$, denoted $Adv_{\mathcal{A},\mathcal{S},\mathcal{B}}^{prv}(\lambda)$, is

$$Adv_{\mathcal{A},\mathcal{S},\mathcal{B}}^{prv}(\lambda) = \mid P(RFID_{\mathcal{A},\mathcal{S}}^{prv\text{-}0}(\lambda) = 1) - P(RFID_{\mathcal{A},\mathcal{S},\mathcal{B}}^{prv\text{-}1}(\lambda) = 1) \mid$$

An RFID scheme achieves privacy for a class V of adversaries if for any adversary $\mathcal{A} \in V$ there exists a blinder $\mathcal{B}$ such that $Adv_{\mathcal{A},\mathcal{S},\mathcal{B}}^{prv}(\lambda)$ is negligible.

3.5 Vaudenay's Model for Offline Schemes

Vaudenay's model has been constructed for analysing online RFID schemes. Modifications for the offline setting have been proposed in [5]. In this paper we propose similar modifications, inspired from [5] and [8].

In an offline RFID scheme, the reader and the server are distinct entities. To accommodate this, the reader from Sect. 3.1 becomes the *server* of the offline one. Thus, a new PPT algorithm *SetupReader* has to be incorporated in the offline RFID scheme definition. *SetupReader* is responsible for creating a reader with an identifier ID_R, a state s and a database DB_{ID_R}. The reader database DB_{ID_R} is constructed from the system database DB.

Two additional oracles have to be incorporated in the adversarial model:

- *CreateReader*(ID_R) - creates the reader ID_R and calls *SetupReader*;
- *CorruptReader*(ID_R) - returns the internal state s of the reader ID_R as well as the reader database. The reader is considered destroyed and cannot be used anymore.

Furthermore, the *SendReader* oracle needs to take into account the reader identity besides the session identifier and the message.

After a legitimate tag is created and added in the server database, we require all reader databases to be updated with needed information regarding the created tag. For *tag authentication, reader authentication* and *privacy* we use the same security experiments as we do not allow the adversary to query the *CorruptReader* oracle. This is consistent with the model from [8] and with the modifications from [5].

We define a new privacy notion, *offline privacy* for which we use the same privacy experiment as in Sect. 3.4, with the modification that the adversary is given access to the *CorruptReader* oracle. The definition for the adversary's advantage remains unchanged.

We say that an RFID scheme achieves *offline privacy* if an adversary has negligible advantage in distinguishing the real RFID scheme from the blinded version, even in the presence of the *CorruptReader* oracle.

4 Offline Privacy in RFID Protocols

4.1 Related Work

Symmetric Encryption Protocol. In [9] an offline RFID protocol based on symmetric encryption is proposed. Each tag stores a unique secret key K_T, an identifier ID_T and a counter C_T. The readers store an identifier ID_R and for each tag ID_T a specific tag-reader secret K_{TR} and a counter C_R. The protocol debuts with the reader sending ID_R, C_R and a nonce n_R. The tag computes the tag-reader key as $K_{TR} = E_{K_T}(ID_R, C_R)$, generates a nonce n_T and sends to the reader $E_{K_{TR}}(n_R, n_T)$. The reader then searches in its database for a key K_{TR} that decrypts the message (n'_R, n'_T) such that $n'_R = n_R$. If so, the tag is authenticated and the reader sends n'_T. If the equality $n_T = n'_T$ holds then the tag authenticates the reader and decides if it updates its counter. The counters C_T, C_R are used to restore privacy. After a reader is compromised, the backend server updates the scheme counter C_B and all other readers are updated with new keys based on the new counter. Thus, the C_B counter becomes C_R. The scheme privacy is restored after all tags have replaced their C_T with the new C_R.

Indistinguishability and Hash Protocol. The subject of achieving offline privacy using symmetric cryptography was also tackled in [10]. The paper describes two versions of a protocol (simple and enhanced) that restore privacy after an adversary has corrupted a reader. The proposed protocol is a variant of the OSK protocol [21] and uses a hash function H as the cryptographic primitive. The tag is required to store a system constant C_0 and two keys K, K' (the first being a shared secret with the reader and the latter being a shared secret with the backend). The readers store for each tag the last known key K_T which is used to trigger the update procedure (that restores privacy), a communication key $\tilde{K}$ and a MAC computed as $H(K', C_0)$. Note that the reader does not posses key K'. In the protocol, the tag answers to a reader's challenge n with $c = H(K, n)$ and updates $K = H(K)$. For every entry in its database, the reader will iterate a number of times (N) for K_T and $\tilde{K}$ in order to identify the tag, that is find $0 < i < N$ such that $c = H(H^i(K_T))$ or $c = H(H^i(\tilde{K}))$. If any of the two conditions is met then the reader identifies and authenticates the tag. However, if the first condition is met the reader will trigger an update of the tag's secrets, which happens during a privacy restore phase. The proposed protocol offers only tag authentication and not mutual authentication. The paper also describes a privacy model used for the offline setting. The model is a combination between the models from [2] and [7]. The online privacy experiment is based on indistinguishability: the adversary is required to distinguish between two uncorrupted tags. In an initial step the adversary interacts with the system and outputs two uncorrupted tags T_0, T_1. The challenger then chooses a bit $b \leftarrow \{0, 1\}$ and gives the adversary access to T_b. After a second session of interacting with the system the adversary outputs a bit b'. The adversary wins if $b = b'$. For the offline case, the authors modify this experiment by adding a system synchronisation and successful protocol runs with T_0, T_1 after the challenger chooses b.

Hash and PUF Protocol. The first attempt at achieving offline privacy in Vaudenay's model has been performed in [5], where a PUF-based RFID scheme and an offline privacy experiment $(privacy+)$ are proposed. We will present this scheme with some simplification: the double PUF protection method, proposed by the authors in order to thwart the *cold boot attack*, will be omitted.

The scheme is based on a hash function H and requires each tag to be equipped with a PUF P and to store a seed G, a counter C_T and an identifier ID. The secret key of the tag S is protected by the PUF. The reader needs an identifier ID_R, a counter C_R and a database DB_R that contains entries (ID_i, K_i) for each tag, where the key K_i is computed from the tag's secret key and from the reader identifier and counter by means of H. After receiving ID_R, C_R and a nonce r_1 from the reader, the tag also generates a nonce r_2. The tag then checks if the reader is up to date $(C_R \geqslant C_T)$ and evaluates the PUF to obtain its key $S = P(G)$. Next, the reader specific key is obtained by $K = H(S, ID_R, C_R)$ and the tag computes $v_1, v_2 = H(K, r_1, r_2)$. v_1, r_2 will be sent to the reader, while v_2 will be kept to perform the reader authentication. The reader searches its database for an entry (ID_i, K_i) such that for $v'_1, v'_2 = H(K_i, r_1, r_2)$ the equality $v_1 = v'_1$ holds. If it finds such a tag then the reader authenticates the tag and sends v_2' to the tag (otherwise a random number will be sent). If $v_2 = v_2'$ then the tag will authenticate the reader and perform an update if necessary (a reader was compromised and counters were increased). The protocol is depicted in Appendix A.

4.2 Privacy+ Discussion

In [5] *privacy+* is introduced as an adaptation of the privacy from Sect. 3.4 for offline schemes with privacy-restoring mechanisms, where the adversary is allowed to query the *CorruptReader* oracle. The definition for *privacy+* (definition 3.6 from [5]) states that an RFID scheme achieves this level of privacy if it is still private after (1) an adversary has corrupted some of the readers, (2) the remaining readers are updated with new information and (3) all existing tags run at least one successful protocol instance with an updated reader. This falls in line with the offline privacy experiment defined in [10] for the indistinguishability-based privacy model.

Unfortunately the details for the *privacy+* experiment are not adequately adapted for Vaudenay's model which uses a blinder-based approach. If we consider the original privacy experiment from [2] and add the conditions from above (i.e after a *CorruptReader* query, the system updates the readers and the tags) then the result of Theorem 5.7 from [5], claiming *destructive privacy+* (for the proposed protocol) becomes invalid. Since in Vaudenay's model the goal of the privacy adversary is to distinguish with non-negligible probability between the real RFID scheme and the blinded version, the adversary may simply perform a complete session between a reader and a tag, corrupt the reader and obtain the tag's key (K_i). With this key the adversary may check if the messages from the protocol run were exchanged correctly (the protocol is assumed to be correct). Clearly, in the real RFID case the verification will be successful while in the blinded version the result will be unsuccessful since the blinder simulates the messages without knowing the key K_i. This gives the adversary a non-negligible advantage of distinguishing between the two RFID schemes. The details of this attack are presented below.

1. $CreateTag^1(ID)$ ($\mathcal{A}$ creates a legitimate tag);
2. $CreateReader(ID_R)$ ($\mathcal{A}$ creates a reader ID_R);
3. $vtag \leftarrow DrawTag(P(ID) = 1)$ ($\mathcal{A}$ draws ID);
4. $\pi \leftarrow Launch()$;
5. $(ID_R, c_1, r_1) \leftarrow SendReader(ID_R, \bot, \pi)$;
6. $(r_2, v_1) \leftarrow SendTag(vtag, (ID_R, c_1, r_1))$;
7. $v_2 \leftarrow SendReader(ID_R, (r_2, v_1), \pi)$;
8. $b = Result(\pi)$;
9. $DB_{ID_R} \leftarrow CorruptReader(ID_R)$;
10. The system gets updated as definition 3.6 requires;
11. Find (ID, K) in DB_{ID_R};
12. if $(v1, v2) == H(K, r_1, r_2)$ *and* $b == 1$
    then output 0 ($\mathcal{A}$ interacts with the real system)
    else output 1 ($\mathcal{A}$ interacts with the blinder)

We point out that the system wide update, of both readers and tags, is useless against this attack as the adversary uses the secrets from the reader to verify protocol runs that occurred before the *CorruptReader* query and not after.

Given the above, we consider that a different approach must be taken when designing a blinder-based privacy experiment for offline schemes with privacy-restoring mechanisms. We consider *privacy+* to be more in line with the *extended soundness* notion from [8], that defines tag and reader authentication when the adversary is allowed access to the *CorruptReader* oracle.

5   Proposed Protocol

In this section we build upon the efforts of [3,5,10] and we propose an RFID scheme that offers offline privacy, mutual authentication and destructive privacy. For our scheme we use symmetric cryptography (a PRF $F = (F_K)_{K \in \{0,1\}^k}, F_K : \{0,1\}^{2\alpha+1} \rightarrow \{0,1\}^k$ and an $IND - CPA$ symmetric encryption scheme $S = (\mathcal{E}, \mathcal{D}, \mathcal{G})$ with key length k and block length k) and endow both tags and readers with PUFs ($P : \{0,1\}^p \rightarrow \{0,1\}^k$) in order to make them resilient to invasive adversaries. The parameters k, α, p are all polynomial in a security parameter λ.

5.1   Protocol Description

In the proposed scheme each tag is associated a unique secret key K. This key is only known to the tag and the backend server. Each reader will communicate with a tag based on a common key K_{TR} derived with the tag's secret key from the reader's identifier. Note that the reader does not need to know K because the backend server will supply the reader with K_{TR} when the reader is created, or when a tag is added. In order to prevent the attack from Sect. 4.2, we require the reader to store $\tilde{K}_{TR}$, which is the encrypted form of K_{TR} so as to prevent the adversary from breaching privacy. We will achieve this by means of a symmetric encryption scheme that is *IND-CPA* secure. The reader will encrypt or decrypt using a reader specific key K_R which in turn will be protected from corruption by means of a PUF $K_R = P(S_R)$.

Now let us describe the protocol. The reader starts by generating a random number x and sending ID_R, x to the tag. In turn, the tag will also generate a nonce y and then prepare the reader's answer. After extracting the tag key from the PUF $K = P(S)$, the tag will compute its shared key with the reader $K_{TR} = F_K(0, 0^\alpha, ID_R)$ and then $z = F_{K_{TR}}(0, x, y)$. The tuple y, z will be sent to the reader. Using its PUF, the reader will extract its key $K_R = P(S_R)$ and assign to w a random value. For each entry in the database $(ID, \tilde{K}_{TR})$, the reader will decrypt the tag key $K_{TR} = \mathcal{D}(K_R, \tilde{K}_{TR})$ and check if the tag answer is valid $z = F_{K_{TR}}(0, x, y)$. If such an entry is found then the tag is authenticated and w becomes the reader's answer $w = F_{K_{TR}}(1, x, y)$. The tag will verify w and decide if it outputs OK (reader is authenticated) or $\bot$.

Reader $(ID_R, S_R, DB = [(ID, \tilde{K}_{TR})])$		Tag (ID, S)
1	$x \leftarrow \{0,1\}^\alpha$ $\xrightarrow{ID_R, x}$	
2	$\xleftarrow{y,\ z}$	$y \leftarrow \{0,1\}^\alpha$ $K = P(S)$ $K_{TR} = F_K(0, 0^\alpha, ID_R)$ $z = F_{K_{TR}}(0, x, y)$
3	$K_R = P(S_R)$ $w \leftarrow \{0,1\}^{2\alpha+1}$ For $(ID, \tilde{K}_{TR}) \in DB$ $\quad K_{TR} = \mathcal{D}(K_R, \tilde{K}_{TR})$ $\quad$ If $z = F_{K_{TR}}(0, x, y)$ $\quad\quad$ then output ID (T. auth.) $\quad\quad\quad w = F_{K_{TR}}(1, x, y)$ $\quad$ else output $\perp$ $\xrightarrow{w}$	
4		If $w = F_{K_{TR}(1,x,y)}$ then output OK (R. auth.) else output $\perp$

Fig. 1. Proposed RFID scheme

5.2 Security and Privacy Analysis

We will now perform a security and privacy analysis of our protocol in Vaudenay's model. Due to lack of space we will only give the main idea of the proofs. For detailed security and privacy proofs the reader is referred to [3].

Theorem 1. *The RFID scheme in Fig. 1 achieves tag authentication, provided that F is a PRF and the tags are endowed with ideal PUFs.*

Proof. Let us assume that there exists an adversary A_{t-auth} that breaks this property with non-negligible probability. Then we will use A_{t-auth} to construct a PPT algorithm A_{PRF} that wins the PRF experiment against F with non-negligible probability. For simplicity we will assume there is only one reader R in the RFID system. A_{PRF} will engage in the PRF security game against a challenger $\mathcal{C}$, which will provide it with oracle access to $F_{K_{TR}}$ for some randomly chosen K_{TR} (or a random function). A_{PRF} will simulate the RFID scheme and play the role of challenger for A_{t-auth} in the tag authentication experiment. A_{PRF} will guess which tag ID will be impersonated by A_{t-auth} (this probability is polynomial) and associate this tag with the oracle from the PRF challenger (*i.e.* all queries from A_{t-auth} related to ID will be answered with the help of the oracle). Eventually A_{t-auth} will output a message (y, z). A_{PRF} will then submit $(0, x, y)$ to the PRF oracle and decide whether it is playing with F or a random function based on the equality between z and the PRF oracle output (z should be the output of F for some key chosen by C, $z = F_{K_{TR}}(0, x, y)$). The probability that A_{PRF} wins is the probability that A_{t-auth} wins the tag authentication game multiplied by the probability that A_{PRF} guesses the impersonated tag. This clearly contradicts the fact that F is a PRF.

Theorem 2. *The RFID scheme in Fig. 1 achieves reader authentication, provided that F is a PRF and the tags are endowed with ideal PUFs.*

Proof. The proof is similar to the one presented above. We can construct an adversary A_{PRF} that breaks the pseudo-randomness of F by using A_{r-auth}. This contradicts the hypothesis.

Theorem 3. *The RFID scheme in Fig. 1 achieves destructive privacy, provided that F is a PRF and the tags are endowed with ideal PUFs.*

Proof. We will use the sequences of games approach [22] to prove that for any destructive-private adversary A there exists a blinder B such that A's advantage of distinguishing between the real RFID scheme and the blinder is negligible. For simplicity we assume that there is a single reader in the RFID system. We define a series of games $G_0, ..., G_7$ where G_0 is the real RFID scheme and G_7 is the blinded version. In each game a probability distribution (the output of the PUF and the blinder simulated oracles *Launch, SendReader, SendTag, Result*) is replaced by another distribution indistinguishable from the replaced one. Since the adversary has a negligible advantage in distinguishing between the transition of two consecutive games, we conclude that A has a negligible advantage of distinguishing between the real RFID scheme G_0 and the blinded version G_7, *i.e.* the scheme achieve destructive privacy.

Theorem 4. *The RFID scheme in Fig. 1 achieves offline privacy, provided that S is $IND - CPA$ secure and the readers are endowed with ideal PUFs.*

Proof. We will use the sequences of games approach, same as above. We will define two additional games G_8, G_9 and show that the advantage of the adversary of distinguishing between the real RFID scheme and the blinder does not change when the adversary is allowed access to *CorruptReader*. We replace in G_8 the output distribution of the PUF from the reader and in G_9 the distribution of the ciphertexts of the reader encryption scheme with indistinguishable probability distributions. Since the PUFs are ideal and the encryption scheme is $IND-CPA$ secure we conclude that the scheme offers destructive privacy and offline privacy.

6   Conclusions

In this paper we have analysed the *privacy+* security notion and have proven that it is not an adequate modification of Vaudenay's privacy experiment. Therefore, RFID schemes relying on privacy-restoring mechanisms cannot use it. An attack on the accompanying protocol has been provided in this sense. Designing a blinder-based privacy experiment that allows privacy-restoring mechanisms remains an open problem.

This paper has also presented a novel approach for providing privacy in offline RFID schemes without losing privacy when a reader is compromised. This technique is based on using PUFs on the reader together with encrypting the reader database. Following this idea, we have designed a protocol that provides destructive privacy and is immune to reader corruption attacks. To the best of our knowledge, this is the first protocol to achieve this. The protocol is proven secure and private in a slightly modified version of Vaudenay's model.

A   Hash and PUF-Based RFID Scheme

Reader $(ID_R, c_R, DB = [(ID_i, K_i)])$		Tag (ID, G, c_T)
1	$r_1 \leftarrow \{0,1\}^\alpha$	$\xrightarrow{\quad ID_R, r_1, c_R \quad}$	
2		$\xleftarrow{\quad r_2,\ v_1 \quad}$	$r_2 \leftarrow \{0,1\}^\alpha$ If $c_R \geqslant c_T$ then $\quad S = P(G)$ $\quad K = H(S, ID_R, c_R)$ $\quad v_1, v_2 = H(K, r_1, r_2)$ else $v_1 \leftarrow \{0,1\}^\gamma$
3	If $\exists (ID_i, K_i) \in DB$ s.t. $v'_1, v'_2 = H(K_i, r_1, r_2)$ $v'_1 = v_1$ then $\quad$ output ID (T. auth.) $\quad$ else output $\perp$ $\quad v'_2 \leftarrow \{0,1\}^\gamma$	$\xrightarrow{\quad v'_2 \quad}$	
4			If $v_2 = v'_2$ && $c_R > c_T$ $\quad$ then output OK (R. auth.) $\quad c_T = c_R$ $\quad$ else output $\perp$

Fig. 2. RFID scheme from [5]

References

1. Finkenzeller, K.: RFID Handbook: Fundamentals and Applications in Contactless Smart Cards and Identification, 3rd ed. Wiley Publishing (2010)
2. Vaudenay, S.: On privacy models for RFID. In: Proceedings of the Advances in Cryptology 13th International Conference on Theory and Application of Cryptology and Information Security, service. ASIACRYPT 2007, pp. 68–87. Springer-Verlag (2007)
3. Hristea, C., Tiplea, F.L.: Destructive privacy and mutual authentication in Vaudenay's RFID model. IACR Cryptol. ePrint Arch., 2019, 73 (2019). https://eprint.iacr.org/2019/073
4. Sadeghi, A.-R., Visconti, I., Wachsmann, C.: PUF-enhanced RFID security and privacy. In: Workshop on Secure Component and System Identification (SECSI), vol. 110 (2010)
5. Kardaş, S., Çelik, S., Yildiz, M., Levi, A.: PUF-enhanced offline RFID security and privacy. J. Netw. Comput. Appl. **35**(6), 2059–2067 (2012)
6. Paise, R.-I., Vaudenay, S.: Mutual authentication in RFID: Security and privacy. In: Proceedings of the 2008 ACM Symposium on Information, Computer and Communications Security, ser. ASIACCS 2008, pp. 292–299. ACM, New York (2008)
7. Juels, A., Weis, S.A.: Defining strong privacy for RFID. ACM Trans. Inf. Syst. Secur. **13**(1), 1–23 (2009)
8. Hermans, J., Peeters, R., Preneel, B.: Proper RFID privacy: model and protocols. IEEE Trans. Mob. Comput. **13**(12), 2888–2902 (2014)
9. Avoine, G., Lauradoux, C., Martin, T.: When compromised readers meet RFID. In: Youm, H.Y., Yung, M. (eds.) WISA 2009. LNCS, vol. 5932, pp. 36–50. Springer, Heidelberg (2009). https://doi.org/10.1007/978-3-642-10838-9_4
10. Garcia, F.D., van Rossum, P.: Modeling privacy for off-line RFID systems. In: Gollmann, D., Lanet, J.-L., Iguchi-Cartigny, J. (eds.) CARDIS 2010. LNCS, vol. 6035, pp. 194–208. Springer, Heidelberg (2010). https://doi.org/10.1007/978-3-642-12510-2_14
11. Avoine, G., Coisel, I., Martin, T.: A privacy-restoring mechanism for offline RFID systems. In: Proceedings of the fifth ACM Conference on Security and Privacy in Wireless and Mobile Networks, pp. 63-74 (2012)
12. Maes, R.: Physically Unclonable Functions: Constructions. Springer Verlag, Properties and Applications (2013)
13. Devadas, S., Suh, E., Paral, S., Sowell, R., Ziola, T., Khandelwal, V.: Design and implementation of PUF-based "unclonable" RFID ICs for anti-counterfeiting and security applications. In: 2008 IEEE International Conference on RFID, pp. 58-64. IEEE (2008)
14. Tuyls, P., Batina, L.: RFID-tags for anti-counterfeiting. In: Pointcheval, D. (ed.) CT-RSA 2006. LNCS, vol. 3860, pp. 115–131. Springer, Heidelberg (2006). https://doi.org/10.1007/11605805_8
15. Katz, J., Lindell, Y.: Introduction to Modern Cryptography. CRC press, United States (2020)
16. Sipser, M.: Introduction to the Theory of Computation. Cengage Learning (2012)
17. Delvaux, J., Gu, D., Schellekens, D., Verbauwhede, I.: Helper data algorithms for puf-based key generation: overview and analysis. IEEE Trans. Comput. Aided Des. Integr. Circuits Syst. **34**(6), 889–902 (2014)

18. Chuang, K.-H., Bury, E., Degraeve, R., Kaczer, B., Linien, D., Verbauwhede, I.: A physically unclonable function with 0% ber using soft oxide breakdown in 40nm cmos. In: IEEE Asian Solid-State Circuits Conference (A-SSCC), pp. 157–160. IEEE (2018)

19. Hermans, J., Pashalidis, A., Vercauteren, F., Preneel, B.: A new RFID privacy model. In: Atluri, V., Diaz, C. (eds.) ESORICS 2011. LNCS, vol. 6879, pp. 568–587. Springer, Heidelberg (2011). https://doi.org/10.1007/978-3-642-23822-2_31

20. Tiplea, F.L., Hristea, C.: Privacy and reader-first authentication in Vaudenay's RFID model with temporary state disclosure. In: IACR Cryptol. ePrint Arch., p. 113 (2019)

21. Ohkubo, M., Suzuki, K. and Kinoshita, S.: Cryptographic approach to privacy-friendly tags. In: RFID Privacy Workshop. vol. 82 (2003)

22. Shoup, V.: Sequences of games: a tool for taming complexity in security proofs (2004)

Virtualization and Automation for Cybersecurity Training and Experimentation

Ion Bica[✉], Roxana Larisa Unc, and Ştefan Ţurcanu

Faculty of Information Systems and Cybersecurity,
"Ferdinand I" Military Technical Academy, 050141 Bucharest, Romania
{ion.bica,roxana.unc,stefan.turcanu}@mta.ro

Abstract. In response to the increasing number and complexity of cyber threats, universities, industry, and government agencies are widely employing network emulation environments for cybersecurity training and experimentation. These environments, known as "cyber ranges", can model enterprise networks and sophisticated attacks, providing a realistic experience for the users. Building and deploying such environments is currently very time consuming, especially for complex scenarios and a high number of participants to the training exercises. This paper presents how virtualization and automation tools can be used to address this issue, starting from the formal specification of the emulated network environment to the automated deployment and replication of virtual machines. Our approach is based on widely used technologies and allows building tailored environments that fulfill organization needs for specific training, exercise, research, and development.

Keywords: Cybersecurity · Cyber range · Automation

1 Introduction

The number and the complexity of cyber-attacks have increased considerably over the last years, with attackers targeting all kinds of sectors and organizations. Cybersecurity has become a hot topic, which requires a lot of effort in terms of acquiring the necessary knowledge and developing adequate protection mechanisms to cope with these attacks. In this context, more and more organizations are employing network emulation environments for developing advanced cyber-security technologies, as well as for hands-on training using state-of-the-art methodologies and techniques. These environments, known as "cyber ranges", are isolated environments used to model enterprise networks and sophisticated attacks. The use cases of cyber ranges vary from security testing, security research, competence building, and security education to the development of cyber capabilities, the development of cyber resilience, and improving the organization's digital dexterity [1].

Cyber ranges mainly make use of virtualization technologies and automation tools. Virtualization technologies enable running virtual machines and emulating complex networks on one or more physical servers. Conversely, automation tools are used for

© Springer Nature Switzerland AG 2021
D. Maimut et al. (Eds.): SecITC 2020, LNCS 12596, pp. 227–241, 2021.
https://doi.org/10.1007/978-3-030-69255-1_15

the creation, configuration, modification, and deletion of virtual machines and networks. In addition to these technologies, when more realistic scenarios are required, advanced tools for internet services, attack and user activity simulation are employed.

Building and deploying cyber ranges is currently very time-consuming, especially for complex scenarios and a large number of participants to the training exercises. Usually, cyber exercises last several hours or days but the preparation phase takes several months due to the effort required to define the scenario, to install the virtual machines and to replicate them for each participant [2]. To address this issue, new kinds of specification languages and tools are being developed that automate the definition and deployment of cyber ranges [3].

This paper presents a novel approach for automating the tasks required to build cyber ranges. The approach is based on widely used technologies and enables creating tailored environments that fulfill organization needs for specific training, exercise, research and development. It uses YAML language to describe the target infrastructure and a deployment system, consisting of Ansible playbooks and Python scripts, that instantiate the target infrastructure, starting from a pool of virtual machine templates. The advantages of the proposed approach are: flexibility, scalability, reproducibility, and portability.

The paper is organized into six sections. Section 2 provides an overview of existing approaches and solutions. Section 3 presents the main technologies used to build cyber ranges. Section 4 describes the architecture and the workflows of the proposed solution. Section 5 presents the use cases and the advantages of our solution. Finally, Sect. 6 concludes the paper and outlines future work.

2   Related Work

Various approaches and solutions have been proposed by researchers to build cyber range infrastructures. In this section we review the most notable ones to identify the underlying technologies, advantages and limitations.

CyRIS is the core component of the training support framework called CyTRONE, which was developed by JAIST (Japan Advanced Institute of Science and Technology) [4]. This project is implemented in Python and uses a description file, written under YAML, which represents the cyber range training scenario. CyRIS is a dedicated solution for deploying virtual cyber range environments using the KVM virtualization platform and facilitates cybersecurity training by preparation, content installation and cloning of the training environment. Our solution is different from CyRIS in the following ways: we provide support for different types of guest operating systems (CyRIS supports ContOS and Ubuntu only), the capability to deallocate resources at the end of the exercise, the parse functions, and the folder structure which has a very important role in resource management.

KYPO cyber range is a modular, distributed system, based on cloud platform OpenStack and supports multiple use cases: research, education, and training [5]. It provides an environment for performing complex cyber-attacks against simulated cyber environments. Security scenarios are defined as structured JSON files, with predefined templates based on attack types. The architecture of this platform is based on five main components: infrastructure management driver, sandbox management, sandbox datastore, monitoring management, and the platform management portal. For the deployment of a scenario, a sandbox is created by orchestrating the environment via an infrastructure management driver. OpenNebula is used to provide and create virtual machines and configure networking. All related details about the deployed sandbox are provided by the sandbox data store component. For accessing a specific scenario, which is equivalent to a sandbox, users and admins use a Web based application called platform management portal. The main disadvantages of this solution are the lack of automation tools for the preparation and execution of different training and exercises scenarios.

EduRange is a cloud-based framework with a web frontend based on Ruby and infrastructure (virtual machines and network) hosted on Amazon Elastic Compute Cloud [6]. This open-source project, sponsored by the National Science Foundation, consists of a collection of cybersecurity exercises. The solution is easily scalable and very flexible, using Chef as an automation tool for installing software in the virtual environment. The disadvantage of EduRange is that it requires the installation of Chef agents on the managed virtual machines. Also, according to the specifications, automation tools are used for different purposes: to install software on existing environments and to keep track of the process by which a student solves a cybersecurity problem.

ADLES is an open-source project, consisting of a specification language and an associated deployment system, developed with the purpose of offering formal declarative specifications for educational exercises [7]. The virtual environment can be built semi-automatically, by using ADLES specifications and the ADLES tool-set. This solution currently supports only VMware vSphere as a virtualization platform by using a custom-built wrapper over the pyVmomi library, which is the standard Python SDK for the VMware vSphere API. For the deployment of a scenario, ADLES requires pre-configured templates for the virtual machines and the configuration of multiple files that should comply with the ADLES specification language. Further changes to the scenario after deployment require manual interaction with the systems or using automation tools like Ansible, Chef, Puppet, etc. Compared to ADLES, our solution is based on a Python script orchestrator that uses multithreading, performs validation of configurations, and supports additional changes to the deployed infrastructure by leveraging Ansible playbooks. Additionally, for the deployment of multiple instances of the same environment, the script automatically calculates the required parameters (for example, the next valid subnet).

Clusus is a cyber range developed by students from the Delft University of Technology, used to provide a safe isolated environment for learning [8]. This project has a design consisting of three main components: a main server that handles the communications between the learning management system and the virtual environment, a Docker container exercise which consists of all virtual machines required for the scenario and a tracking program for monitoring the progress, in addition to another program that deploys these containers. The configuration files are written in YAML and the Moodle platform is used as a learning instantiation system. The solution requires nested virtualization support, which means that only Microsoft Azure and Google Cloud can be used as cloud providers.

AIT Cyber Range is a solution with a flexible and scalable architecture used for cybersecurity exercise, training, or research [9]. AIT uses OpenStack as a cloud computing platform, Terraform as an infrastructure provisioning solution, Ansible for software provisioning and in-house software to define and execute injects inside a scenario. AIT Cyber Range was developed in parallel with our solution and tries to overcome many of the limitations of previous solutions.

3 Underlying Technologies

The diagram below illustrates the main technical components of a cyber range. Depending on the requirements, additional components may be added on top of this foundation (for example, Learning Management Systems (LMS), Competency Management System, etc.) [10] (Fig. 1).

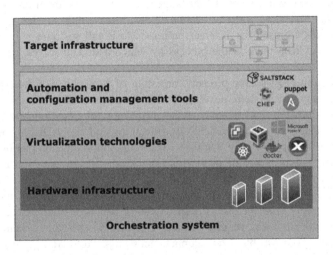

Fig. 1. Cyber range components

3.1 Hardware Infrastructure

The environments used for cybersecurity training and experimentation are on top of the hardware infrastructure. The underlying hardware resources can be divided into two types: traditional infrastructure and hyper-converged infrastructure.

In the traditional infrastructure, the compute, storage and networking components have to be configured and managed separately. While this infrastructure provides the greatest flexibility, it also requires more effort to ensure that all the components work together.

The hyper-converged infrastructure puts the compute, storage and networking components together. This architecture enables local storage from multiple nodes to be used as shared storage. All the resources are controlled by software and no component can be managed separately, thus reducing the complexity of resource-management and deployment time.

Both types of infrastructures can be used a cyber range, the choice being made according to the particularities presented above. For complex scenarios or a large number of users, the number of CPUs, RAM, and the use of SSD drives have a great impact on the performance of the environment.

3.2 Virtualization Technologies

Virtualization is an ideal solution for creating cyber ranges. It offers the advantage of isolating the guest system (virtual machine) from the host system, the flexibility to define the characteristics of the system (CPU, RAM, etc.) and the ability to restore the system to an initial state. Compared to a non-virtualized environment, a virtualized one offers lower costs, reduced downtime, efficient use of a physical server that can host multiple virtual machines with different operating systems in which run different applications.

To emphasize how virtualization is used in the cyber range context, two comparisons are presented, as follows:

- **Client-side virtualization vs server-side virtualization.** Using client-side virtualization, the users run one or several virtual machines on a host, using a virtualization platform like VMware Workstation or VirtualBox. In the context of a cyber range, depending on the complexity of implemented scenarios, the participant`s machine may not have sufficient resources, which makes it impossible to solve the scenario. Also, when using client-side virtualization, centralized control and monitoring are difficult to implement. The solution to these problems is server-side virtualization, which consists of a hypervisor that offers virtual machines access to hardware resources. The main benefits of this approach are centralized control and scalability. Although it involves much larger initial investments (purchasing the hardware components), it is the optimal option when it comes to organizing a cyber exercise because the organizers are responsible for managing the virtual machines, instead of the participants, as it is the case for client-side virtualization. VMware vSphere, XenServer, Microsoft Hyper-V are server-side virtualization platforms, providing automated monitoring, security, business continuity, simplicity in the virtual environment's configuration and migration.
- **Virtualization vs Containerization.** For infrastructure development, two approaches may be taken into consideration: virtualization and containerization. Through virtualization, the whole system can be emulated, including the hardware components. A virtual machine is completely isolated from another one, each having virtual hardware components and their own operating system. This offers a major advantage for cyber exercises by providing high security. Notable examples of virtualization solutions are: VMware vSphere, XenServer, Microsoft Hyper-V. By using containers, the user profile can be emulated from the operating system level, so one container is completely separated from another container in terms of processes, memory, but they share the same operating system and hardware. The main advantage of containers is the efficiency of the use of resources. However, from the perspective of implementing a cyber-exercise, it is much more difficult to reach a high level of isolation. Docker, Kubernetes and OpenShift are examples of container technologies.

For our solution we selected VMware vSphere 6.7, having ESXi as hypervisor and vCSA for centralized management of virtual infrastructure. VMware is currently the industry-leading compute virtualization platform and is ubiquitous in today's data-centers. VMware vSphere stands out for its compatibility with a wide variety of guest operating systems, high scalability, stability, and last but not least, for the technical support offered by the company.

3.3   Automation and Configuration Management Tools

The use of a modular system is a very effective way to create a virtual environment in which cyber exercises can be implemented. A modular system consists of the deployment of several components which can be combined to generate different scenarios. Thus, general templates (mail server, AD server, DNS server, workstations with various operating systems, etc.) are built and employed to deploy the virtual machines used in the implementation of the scenario. The process of deploying the virtual environment can be automated by using automation and configuration management tools. These considerably optimize the entire process of creating the exercise, both in terms of time required for implementation and in terms of resources used. The main automation and configuration management tools that can be used in the implementation of a cyber range are described below.

Ansible is one of the most popular automation solutions that can be used for cloud provisioning, configuration management, application development, etc. Ansible connects to nodes using SSH, loads Ansible modules (playbooks) on these nodes and then runs loaded playbooks.

Puppet is an automation tool used for infrastructure management. This tool has a master server called Puppet Server that manages the agents. Puppet Agents are installed on the managed virtual machines.

Chef is an infrastructure management tool. This solution has three main components: Chef Clients (managed machines that periodically download cookbooks from the Chef-Server and then run these cookbooks), Chef Server (the central node used to store data like cookbooks, policies, and data about clients) and Chef Workstations (station used to create cookbooks).

Saltstack is a solution that offers a distributed system used to execute commands and perform queries on remote nodes. Salt architecture can be associated with the hub-and-spoke model. Usually, Salt architecture consists of a single master component and several slave components organized hierarchically that communicate with each other.

When selecting the automation and configuration management solution for cyber range implementation, the following trade-offs and choices need to be made in terms of having: mutable or immutable infrastructure, agent or agentless, procedural or declarative style of coding and the complexity of implementation. Table 1 provides a comparison of the above tools.

Ansible, Puppet, Chef, and SaltStack usually provide mutable infrastructure. This means that changes can be done directly to the existing infrastructure without deploying new servers.

Puppet, Chef, and SaltStack require installing agent software on managed servers. They also have support for agentless implementation but this limits the feature set of these tools. Ansible is agentless which makes it more suitable for the implementation of the scenarios considering both the security and the complexity of the implementation.

By using a procedural style of coding, the user can specify in the code, step by step, how to achieve the desired state. A declarative style means that the user writes code that specifies the desired end state, and other tools are responsible to achieve that state. Ansible and Chef use procedural style, while Puppet and SaltStack use declarative style of coding.

Table 1. Comparison of automation and configuration management tools

	Language	Architecture	Communication	Easy of setup
Ansible	YAML	Client only	SSH	Easy
Puppet	PuppetDSL	Client/Server	SSL	Not very easy
Chef	Ruby	Client/Server	SSL	Not very easy
SaltStack	YAML	Client/Server	SSH	Easy

For our solution, we decided to use Ansible, which is simple to install and use and does not require any agents on the managed systems. It creates a mutable infrastructure and uses a portable language with simple syntax. In addition, Ansible is integrated with the virtualization platform used in our implementation, providing various modules to manage VMware infrastructure, which includes datacenter, cluster, host system and virtual machine.

3.4   Target Infrastructure

The target infrastructure represents the virtual environment used for training and experimentation. It can vary from a simple lab exercise to entire domains, the limit being the hardware resources and the imagination of the architect designing the scenario.

Its purpose is to offer a realistic environment for the users. Moreover, by using a variety of available tools and systems such as networking devices, firewalls, simulated Internet, simulated attacks, etc., it can be an important asset in teaching how to interact with common applications and systems, and also in helping to explain the principles of the underlying protocols.

3.5   Orchestration System

The orchestration system controls the entire flow when the required components have to be deployed to create the training or experimentation environment according to a scenario. The most important role of this layer is to supervise the automation and the configuration tools which manage the components used to implement the scenario.

To properly understand the role of this layer, we make a comparison between the automation and configuration tools and the orchestration system: the automation tools are designed to manage the deployment and the configuration process for the environment components, while the orchestration layer leverages these tools in order to create the environment's layout and structure.

4   Architecture and Workflows

This section presents the architecture and implementation details of the proposed solution. The solution is designed to easily enable the specification of different scenarios for training and experimentation and to rapidly deploy the associated virtual machines and networks in a multithreaded way. It has a simple and modular design, using dedicated hardware with VMware virtualization software on top of it. An Ansible server is used for the automation process and a Python script for orchestrating the entire workflow, as illustrated in Fig. 2.

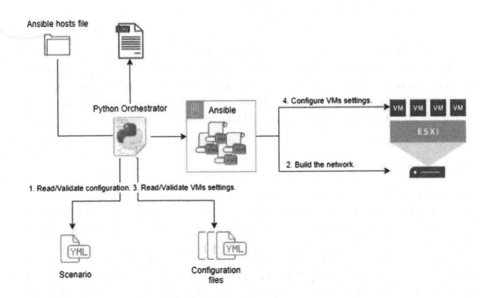

Fig. 2. The orchestration process

First, the orchestration process starts by validating the scenario and configuring the components, which are used to build the required infrastructure. Then, it uses an Ansible playbook to start deploying virtual machines based on predefined templates. An example of such a template is presented in see Fig. 3. The next step involves reading and configuring the settings for each virtual machine, while at the same time configuring the network devices, to obtain a routable environment. The entire deployment and configuration process is being run by using multiple threads, which increases the speed and makes it efficient when deploying large networks. Besides this, every step done by the orchestration script is being logged for debugging purposes and multiple Ansible hosts files are generated, which can be used for additional configurations in the deployed environment.

```
---
- name: "Manage a Host VM from a template"
  hosts: vcenter
  connection: local
  gather_facts: no
  tasks:
  - name: Clone the template
    vmware_guest:
      hostname: "{{ vcenter_hostname }}"
      username: "{{ vcenter_username }}"
      password: "{{ vcenter_password }}"
      validate_certs: False
      name: "{{ vm_name }}"
      template: "{{ vm_template }}"
      datacenter: "{{ vcenter_datacenter }}"
      folder: "{{ vm_folder }}"
      state: "{{ state }}"
      networks:
        - name: "{{ network_name }}"
          ip: "{{ ip_address }}"
          netmask: "{{ netmask }}"
          gateway: "{{ gateway }}"
          dns_servers:
            - "{{ dns_server }}"
      wait_for_customization: yes
```

Fig. 3. Ansible playbook for deploying a virtual machine

The entire virtual environment is implemented in a datacenter that uses the vSphere virtualization platform with a pool of templates used to configure different services for web servers, mail servers, DNS servers, Linux/Windows workstations, etc., for different types of scenarios. Ansible is installed on a virtual machine in the datacenter and its role is to deploy all the components needed when a scenario is created.

Each scenario has associated a main.yml file that defines all of the assets that the exercise contain, such as:

- Metadata - contains data about the exercise, including the name, description, and the relative path to other .yml files.
- Groups - defines which entities (student, team, etc.) are in the exercise, including the number of instances and an associated configuration file for each entity.
- Services - contains a list of virtual machines, with the associated template, and Ansible configuration files to be run after deployment.

- Networks - the list of subnets and the name of virtual switches related to each network which is used in the virtual environment.

```
metadata:
  name: "Demo" # REQUIRED
  description: "Pentesting Lab" # OPTIONAL
  prefix: "Pentest" # REQUIRED
  folder: "scenarios/pentest" # REQUIRED
groups:
  lab-group:
    instances: 3 # OPTIONAL (DEFAULT: 1)
    conf-file: "pentest-lab.yml" # REQUIRED
services:
  kali-vm:
    conf-file: ["kali-vm-conf.yml"] # REQUIRED
    template: "kali_template" # REQUIRED
  domain-controller:
    conf-file: ["win-vm-conf.yml", "domain-controller-conf.yml"]
    template: "winsrv_template"
  firewall-pfSense:
    conf-file: ["pfSense-conf.yml"]
    template: "pfsense_template"
  vyos-router:
    conf-file: ["vyos-conf.yml"]
    template: "vyos_template"
networks:
  rt-nt:
    description: "Routing network" # OPTIONAL
    subnets: ["10.12.0.0/24"] # REQUIRED
    vswitch: "ROUTING" # REQUIRED
  lan-nt:
    description: "LAN network"
    subnets: ["172.16.0.0/24"]
    vswitch: "LAN"
  wan-nt:
    description: "Internet network"
    subnets: ["172.19.1.0/24"]
    vswitch: "WAN"
    unique: yes # OPTIONAL (Default: no)
```

Fig. 4. Configuration file defining the scenario's assets

For example, as described in Fig. 4, we define three instances of a group with the associated configuration file (Fig. 5), where we list the required services for our scenario: a Kali machine, a Domain Controller, a firewall and a router as the default gateway. We also configured several networks, which are used to define the network segments for these virtual machines.

```
metadata:
  description: "Demo Lab"
  prefix: "demo"
services:
  default-gateway: # REQUIRED
    description: "Default user:pass -> vyos:vyos"
    service: vyos-router # REQUIRED
    type: gateway # REQUIRED
    inside: # REQUIRED
      networks: ["rt-nt"] # REQUIRED
      suffix: 1 # OPTIONAL
    outside:  # REQUIRED
      networks: ["wan-nt"] # REQUIRED
      suffix: 13 # OPTIONAL
  firewall:
    description: "Default user:pass -> admin:pfsense"
    type: gateway
    service: firewall-pfSense
    inside:
      networks: ["lan-nt"]
      suffix: 1
    outside:
      networks: ["rt-nt"]
      suffix: 3
    gateway: default-gateway
  dc:
    instances: 1 # OPTIONAL (Default: 1)
    description: "Domain controller." # OPTIONAL
    service: win-hosts # REQUIRED
    networks: ["lan-nt"] # REQUIRED

    suffix: 10 # OPTIONAL
    gateway: firewall # OPTIONAL
  kali:
    description: "Kali machine for pentesting the network."
    service: kali-vm
    networks: ["lan-nt"]
    gateway: firewall
```

Fig. 5. Configuration file defining group's assets

After creating the main file, the next step is to create a configuration file for each group, which defines the assets related to it. These files contain additional information, such as:

- Metadata - some additional data about each group, used to create the folder structure.
- Services - these are virtual machines associated with the group, which are related and linked to the services and networks from the main.yml file.

One can think of this file structure as a shop, where first all of the assets are listed and then each client can select only the products they desire to add to the cart.

In Fig. 5 we provide a simple demo, where the group has been assigned a Domain Controller and a Kali machine in a LAN network, separated by a firewall with two network controllers. One is in the same network as the host machines and can be used to filter the traffic for a more realistic approach, while the another one can be used for communications with the default gateway, which provides access to the Internet. Each service contains some additional information, like the gateway, type, or suffix for static addressing. Based on the configuration examples, the virtual environment will look similar to Fig. 6.

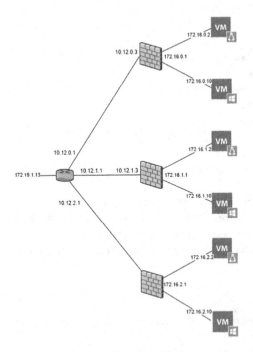

Fig. 6. Example of deployed infrastructure

The Python script parses the defined configuration files and encapsulates all the information in predefined classes used for process management, where each group has the defined list of assets. Each virtual machine has been associated with an IP address and other information required for deployment and integration. The orchestrator starts by creating the folder structure and the network environment (virtual switches, port groups, etc.), and then begins the deployment of the virtual machines, which are of two types: network devices (have predefined dynamic playbooks to be able to create a routable environment despite the configuration you had to implement) and host devices (servers and client virtual machines). Finally, the script runs the defined playbooks that are required for the configuration of the virtual machines based on their role in the virtual environment. For multiple instances of the same group, it automatically calculates the next valid subnets.

Moving forward, when a participant wants to attend the exercise, the scenario is automatically deployed and he can access the related virtual machines in an isolated environment, using a secure VPN connection (see Fig. 7).

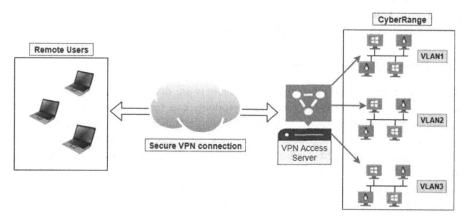

Fig. 7. Secure remote access using VPN

At the end of the exercise, all resources are deallocated by deleting the virtual machines and all of the associated network configurations.

5   Use Cases

This section presents the main use cases of cyber ranges and emphasizes the advantages of our solution in implementing the associated infrastructures.

5.1   Education and Awareness

Taking into consideration the evolution of technology and the increasing number and complexity of cyber attacks, there is a continuous need for regular courses to enhance the education and awareness of employees and decision-makers. Our solution allows organizations to combine traditional learning modules with hands-on training to improve the skills and competencies of personnel. It can be used to quickly create different lab environments that emulate networks and resources needed for training purposes, offering a significant instructional advantage in delivering a cost effective and flexible hands on learning experience.

5.2 Cyber Exercises

Cyber exercises allow participants to apply theoretical knowledge and practical skill in real life scenarios. Also, cyber exercises can help organizations to evaluate the capability to detect, investigate and respond to cyber attacks. Our solution can be used to create a virtual environment in which attack scenarios, similar to those in a real environment, can be implemented. The simulation of a cyber attack is performed in three stages: the stage preceding the occurrence of the security incident, in which the isolated environment is created and the scenario is implemented; the stage corresponding to the actual attack when the groups with the role of attack or defense act accordingly, being followed by the final stage. This last stage is designed for data analysis, resource deallocation, and reports generation.

5.3 Experimentation and Research

To mitigate the evolving cyber threats, researchers are developing new cyber defense technologies and products. Before these products can be deployed in organization networks, they must be tested and validated. Cyber ranges allow creating the environments needed to test the products in complex situations, to measure performance or to check the interoperability with the existing applications and systems. By using our solution, testbeds can be created to validate, evaluate, and compare the capabilities of different cyber defense products. Also, the solution can be used by researchers to study new attack techniques or malware in safe and isolated environments.

6 Conclusions

Cyber ranges are evolving as efficient platforms for training and experimentation. They allow users to learn practical skills by simulating complex scenarios that address emerging cyber threats. They also provide a realistic environment to test and validate new cyber defense techniques and technologies.

Virtualization and automation tools help create and operate the cyber range. Virtualization technologies can emulate computational nodes and enterprise networks. Automation tools allow the rapid instantiation of the cyber range according to the required scenario.

The main advantage of our approach is that it provides a rich automation platform and a centralized environment, which are very useful for the organizers of cyber competitions. Moreover, the solution offers flexibility because new templates can be created and playbooks can be parametrized. This solution can be used for several use cases, deployment of custom laboratories for learning, or specific cyber exercises for training.

The solution has been built with a modular approach, thus, an exercise can be created by combining predefined templates and Ansible modules that can generate different configurations. By using this approach, the solution provides flexibility; the virtual environment can simply be reconfigured by using Ansible scripts, the resources at the datacenter level being used efficiently, with no need to start the entire deployment process from the beginning. Besides this, the Ansible playbooks and the templates used to build the virtual environment can be reused between the organisations, which save time and allow to create different scenarios in a straightforward and effortless way.

Our future work includes the following directions: improve the performance of the current solution, add support for more complex scenarios and simulate users' activity and Internet services to create more realistic environments. Another objective is to integrate the solution with an eLearning platform like Moodle, to control training, monitor learning objectives and assess users' performance.

Acknowledgements. This work was supported by a grant of the Romanian Ministry of Research and Innovation, CCCDI – UEFISCDI, project number PN-III-P1-1.2-PCCDI-2017-0272/ Avant-garde Technology Hub for Advanced Security (ATLAS), within PNCDI III.

References

1. European Cyber Security Organisation, Understanding Cyber Ranges: From Hype to Reality. https://ecs-org.eu/press-releases/understanding-cyber-ranges-from-hype-to-reality. Accessed 09 Jan 2020
2. Vykopal, J., Vizváry, M., Oslejsek, R., Celeda, P., Tovarnak, D.: Lessons learned from complex hands-on defence exercises in a cyber range. In: 2017 IEEE Frontiers in Education Conference (FIE) (2017)
3. Russo, E., Costa, G., Armando, A.: Building next generation cyber ranges with CRACK. Comput. Secur. **95**, 101837 (2020)
4. Pham, C., Tang, D., Chinen, K. I., Beuran, R.: CyRIS: a cyber range instantiation system for facilitating security training. In: Proceedings of the Seventh Symposium on Information and Communication Technology (2016)
5. Vykopal, J., Oslejsek, R., Celeda, P., Vizvary, M., Tovarnak, D.: KYPO cyber range: design and use cases. In: Proceedings of the 12th International Conference on Software Technologies (2017)
6. Weiss, R., Turbak, F., Mache, J., Locasto, M.E.: Cybersecurity education and assessment in EDURange. IEEE Secur. Priv. **15**(3), 90–95 (2017)
7. Conte de Leon, D., Goes, C.E., Haney, M.A., Krings, A.W.: ADLES: specifying, deploying, and sharing hands-on cyber-exercises. Comput. Secur. **74**, 12–40 (2018)
8. Hildebrand, E., Flinterman, R., Mulder, J., Smit, A.: Clusus: a cyber range for network attack simulations, TU Delft Repositories (2019)
9. Leitner, M., et al.: AIT cyber range: flexible cyber security environment for exercises, training and research. In: European Interdisciplinary Cybersecurity Conference (EICC) (2020)
10. National Institute of Standards and Technology, The Cyber Range: A Guide. https://www.nist.gov/document/cyber-range-guide. Accessed 09 Oct 2020

Long-Term Secure Deniable Group Key Establishment

Kashi Neupane[⊠]

Department of Mathematics, University of North Georgia, Oakwood, GA, USA
kashi.neupane@ung.edu

Abstract. In this paper we present a long-term secure deniable group key establishment protocol. Long-term security provides resistance against an adversary, even if some underlying hardness assumptions become invalid later, after completion of the protocol. Deniability feature of a group key establishment protocol allows each participant to join a protocol session and authenticate a message for the other group members, but the receiver(s) cannot convince a third party that such involvement of the group members in the process ever took place.

The protocol presented here is a long-term secure deniable group key establishment protocol in the random oracle model which remains secure if either a Computational Bilinear Diffie Hellman problem is hard or a server, who shares a symmetric key with each user, is uncorrupted. The technical tools used for the protocol are ring signature, multiparty key encapsulation, and message authentication code.

Keywords: Long-term security · Group key establishment · Deniability

1 Introduction

The task of key establishment is one of the most important parts of a security system. It is a common practice to construct key establishment protocols based on asymmetric building blocks. These protocols are secure as long as the underlying hardness assumptions are valid. However the protocols collapse, whenever the underlying hardness assumptions break. To address such security concerns, Bohli et al. [BMQR07] formalized a new concept, long-term security of key establishment protocols. This approach integrates symmetric building block as a fallback technique and provides security of the protocols whenever the underlying asymmetric building blocks fail to provide the security. Moreover, Müller-Quade and Unruh [MQU07] suggested an extension of the notion of long-term security in Universally Composable framework. Based on Bohli et al. [BMQR07], Neupane and Steinwandt [NS10] presented a server-assisted long-term secure three-party key establishment protocol based on real-or-random indistinguishability and Bilinear Decisional Diffie-Hellman (BDDH) assumption. Later, Unruh [Unr13] proposed a variant of the Universal Composability framework, everlasting quantum-UC, and demonstrated that the concept of long-term security can

© Springer Nature Switzerland AG 2021
D. Maimut et al. (Eds.): SecITC 2020, LNCS 12596, pp. 242–256, 2021.
https://doi.org/10.1007/978-3-030-69255-1_16

be implemented on secure communication and general multi-party computation using signature cards as trusted setup. Neupane [Neu16] presented a long-term secure protocol using multilinear mappings along with a trusted server.

Deniability is one of the important key features of group key establishment protocols and is becoming increasingly relevant. In a deniable group key establishment protocol, the transcript of the protocol can not be used later to prove the involvement of the participant in the protocol session. Mao and Paterson [MP] offered definitions of deniability in various degrees, and also presented some deniable key establishment protocols using identity-based techniques. Bohli and Steinwandt [BS06] formalized the notion of deniability based on the security model introduced by Bresson et al. [BCPQ01]. Moreover, they presented a four-round group key exchange protocol achieving deniability in the random oracle model with the use of computational Diffie- Hellman Assumption and Schnorr's Signature.

Furthermore, Zhang et al. [ZWL10] extended the definition of deniable group key establishment suggested by Bohli and Steinwandt, and proposed a deniable group key establishment protocol in the standard model with the use of a variant of Schnorr's zero-knowledge identification scheme. Later, Neupane et al. [NSC12] presented a compiler which adds authentication and deniablitlity, still maintains the round complexity of the original protocol. As an application of their compiler, they suggested a construction of a three-round group key exchange protocol. Chen et al. [CHZL16] presented a two-round group key exchange protocol with the use of zero-knowledge identification scheme which achieves authenticity with the use of forking lemma and deniability with the construction of a simulator.

In this research, we propose a two-round long-term secure deniable group key establishment protocol in the random oracle model. To establish a key agreement, we will use local embeddings of Joux's 3-party key agreement protocol, a technique proposed by Dmeemdt and Lange [DL08] and used by Neupane and Steinwandt [NS11]. In order to make it long-term secure by integrating symmetric cryptosystem with asymmetric cryptosystem, we use the techniques introduced by Bohli et al. [BMQR07]. Deniability of the protocol is achieved by applying the techniques suggested by Bohli and Steinwandt [BS06] and used by Neupane et al. [NSC12] for a compiler . The other technical tools we will use are ring signature, multiparty key encapsulation, and message authentication code. Our main contribution compared with the existing protocols is that the proposed protocol requires only two rounds with additional security features, and is constructed with more widely acceptable cryptographic tools.

2   Preliminaries

In this section, we review mathematical and cryptographic tools which are used in the protocol. Following the formalization of Boneh and Franklin [BF03], we quickly review the concept of Bilinear Computational Diffie-Hellman assumption.—for more details we refer to [BF03]. We also briefly review the standard definitions of ring signature, multiparty key encapsulation, message authentication code, symmetric encryption, and then the main idea of real-or-random indistinguishability as discussed by Bellare et al. [BDJR00].

2.1 Bilinear Maps and the Bilinear Diffie Hellman Assumption

Let $(G_1, +)$, $(G_2, \cdot)$ be two groups of prime order q, such that $q > 2^k$ with the security parameter being k. We denote by $\hat{e} : G_1 \longrightarrow G_2$ an *admissible bilinear map*, i. e., $\hat{e}$ has all of the following properties:

Bilinear: For all $P, Q \in G_1$ and all $a, b \in \mathbb{Z}$ we have $\hat{e}(aP, bQ) = \hat{e}(P, Q)^{ab}$.

Non-degenerate: For a generator P of G_1, we have $\hat{e}(P, P)$ is a generator of G_2.

Efficiently computable: There is a polynomial time algorithm which computes $\hat{e}(Q, R)$ for all $Q, R \in G_1$.

We use a probabilistic polynomial time (ppt) algorithm $\mathcal{G}$ to specify the Bilinear Computational Diffie-Hellman (BCDH) problem. This *BCDH parameter generator* $\mathcal{G}$ takes the security parameter as its input, and returns q and a description of G_1, G_2, and $\hat{e}$. We denote this by $\langle q, G_1, G_2, \hat{e} \rangle \leftarrow \mathcal{G}(1^k)$.

Next, for a ppt algorithm $\mathcal{A}$ we consider the following experiment:

1. The BCDH parameter generator is run which yields BCDH parameters

$$\langle q, G_1, G_2, \hat{e} \rangle.$$

2. $\mathcal{A}$ obtains the output of $\mathcal{G}$ with the input uniformly at random chosen values $a, b, c \leftarrow \{0, \ldots, q-1\}$, and aP, bP and cP.
3. Now $\mathcal{A}$ outputs a value $g \in G_2$, and is successful whenever $g = \hat{e}(P, P)^{abc}$.

To measure the *advantage of $\mathcal{A}$ in solving the BCDH problem* we use the function $\mathrm{Adv}_{\mathcal{A}}^{\mathrm{bcdh}} = \mathrm{Adv}_{\mathcal{G}, \mathcal{A}}^{\mathrm{bcdh}}(k) :=$

$$\Pr \left[\mathcal{A}(q, G_1, G_2, \hat{e}, P, aP, bP, cP) = \hat{e}(P, P)^{abc} \left| \begin{array}{l} \langle q, G_1, G_2, \hat{e} \rangle \leftarrow \mathcal{G}(1^k), \\ P \leftarrow G_1 \\ a, b, c \leftarrow \{0, \ldots, q-1\} \end{array} \right. \right]$$

Definition 1 (BCDH Assumption). *A BCDH instance generator $\mathcal{G}$ satisfies the BCDH assumption if for all ppt algorithms $\mathcal{A}$, the advantage $\mathrm{Adv}_{\mathcal{A}}^{\mathrm{bcdh}}$ is negligible (in k). In this case, we say that BCDH is hard in groups generated by $\mathcal{G}$.*

2.2 Multi Key Encapsulation and Symmetric Encryption

The notion of *key encapsulation mechanism (KEM)* was introduced by Shoup [Sho00] and formalized by Cramer and Shoup [CS03]. The KEM enables sender and receiver to agree on a common random session key. Later, Smart [Sma05] introduced *multi key encapsulation mechanism (mKEM)* generalizing the notion of key encapsulation to a setting of multiple recipients. We quickly review the notion following [GBNM10].

Definition 2 (Multi Key Encapsulation Mechanism). *A* multi key encapsulation mechanism (mKEM) *is a triple of polynomial time algorithms* (mKeyGen, mEncaps, mDecaps) *as follows:*

- *A probabilistic key generation algorithm* mKeyGen *which takes the parameters* $\mathbb{D}$ *as its input, and generates a pair of public and secret keys* (pk, dk).
- *A probabilistic key encapsulation algorithm* mEncaps *which takes a (polynomial size) set* $\{pk_1, \ldots, pk_n\}$ *of public keys, and generates a pair* (K, C) *where* $K \in \{0,1\}^k$ *is a session key and* C *is an encapsulation of this session key under the public keys* $\{pk_1, \ldots, pk_n\}$.
- *A deterministic key decapsulation algorithm* mDecaps *which takes a secret key* dk *and an encapsulation* C, *and returns the session key* K *or a special error symbol* $\bot$.

For all key pairs (pk_i, dk_i) *generated by* mKeyGen, *we require the implication* $(K, C) = \text{mEncaps}(\{pk_1, \ldots, pk_n\}) \implies \text{mDecaps}_{dk_i}(C) = K$ *holds* $(i = 1, \ldots, n)$.

The protocol we propose in the next section assumes that the mKEM we employ is IND-CCA secure, i. e. no probabilistic polynomial time adversary with access to a decapsulation oracle, can distinguish with more than negligible probability which of two keys is encapsulated in the challenge for a set of public keys of his choice.

2.3 Message Authentication Codes and Ring Signatures

We use a message authentication code as well as a suitable ring signature to solve the problem of authentication without jeopardizing deniability.

Definition 3 (Message Authentication Code). *A* message authentication code (MAC) *is a tuple* (MKeyGen, Tag, Verify) *of polynomial time algorithms as follows:*

- *A probabilistic key generation algorithm* MKeyGen *which takes the domain parameters* $\mathbb{D}$ *as its input, and returns a secret key* K.
- *A probabilistic tag generation algorithm* Tag *which takes a message* $m \in \{0,1\}^*$ *and a secret key* K *as its input, and returns a message tag* $\theta := \text{Tag}_K(m) \in \{0,1\}^*$ *on* m.
- *A deterministic verification algorithm* Verify *which takes a message* m, *a secret key* K *and a candidate tag* θ *as its input, and returns* 1 *if* θ *is a valid tag for the message* m *and* 0 *otherwise.*

We consider a MAC as strongly unforgeable under adaptive chosen message attacks (SUF-CMA) if no probabilistic polynomial time adversary with access to tagging and verifying oracles for key K can produce a valid (message, tag)-pair with more than negligible probability—we refer to [BN00] for the formal definition.

Definition 4 (Ring Signature Scheme). *A ring signature scheme is a tuple of polynomial time algorithms* (RKeyGen, RSign, RVerify) *as follows:*

- *A probabilistic key generation algorithm* RKeyGen *which takes the security parameter k as its input, and returns a pair of keys* (vk, sk), *where vk is a public verification key and sk is its corresponding secret signing key.*
- *A probabilistic ring signature algorithm* RSign *which takes a message m, a polynomial size set (a* ring*) of public verification keys* $\mathcal{R} = \{vk_1, \ldots, vk_n\}$ *and a secret key sk_s such that $vk_s \in \mathcal{R}$, and produces a signature σ.*
- *A deterministic ring signature verification algorithm* RVerify *which takes a message m, a signature σ and a ring of public keys $\mathcal{R}$, and returns 1 if σ is a valid signature for the message m with respect to the ring $\mathcal{R}$, and 0 otherwise.*

We require that for any ring $\mathcal{R}$ comprised of public verification keys produced by RKeyGen *and for any message m, with the secret key sk and the corresponding public key $vk \in \mathcal{R}$ the following relation holds:*
$$\text{RVerify}(m, \text{RSign}_{sk}(m, \mathcal{R}), \mathcal{R}) = 1.$$

We consider a signature scheme as strongly unforgeable under adaptive chosen message attacks (SUF-CMA) if no probabilistic polynomial time adversary with access to signing and verifying oracles can produce a valid (message, signature)-pair with more than negligible probability. For a ring signature, it is usually expected that the adversary cannot know which user in the ring was the actual signer of a message. A strong form of this design goal is known as *anonymity against full key exposure*—we refer to [BKM06] for the formal definition.

2.4   Real-or-Random Indistinguishability

We recall the security notion of real-or-random indistinguishability, and refer Bellare et al. [BDJR00] for a more detailed discussion. Real-or-random security measures the indistinguishability of the encryption of a plaintext with the encryption of a randomized plaintext with access to decryption oracle except for the challenged ciphertext. Let $\mathcal{E}_K(\mathcal{RR}(\cdot, b))$ represents an oracle that takes $b \in \{0, 1\}$ and a plaintext $M \in \{0, 1\}^*$ as its input and returns an encryption $C \leftarrow \text{Enc}_K(M)$ of M, if $b = 1$, and an encryption $C \leftarrow \text{Enc}_K(r)$ of a uniformly at random chosen bitstring $r \leftarrow \{0, 1\}^{|M|}$ of length M if $b = 0$. We define advantage of $\mathcal{A}$ against real-or-random indistinguishability under chosen ciphertext attack (ROR-CCA) as

$$\text{Adv}_{\mathcal{A}}^{\text{ror-cca}} := \Pr\left[1 \leftarrow \mathcal{A}^{\mathcal{E}_K}(\mathcal{RR}(\cdot, 1))\right] - \Pr\left[1 \leftarrow \mathcal{A}^{\mathcal{E}_K}(\mathcal{RR}(\cdot, 0))\right]$$

Definition 5 (Real-or-Random Indistinguishability). *A symmetric encryption scheme is* secure in the sense of real-or-random indistinguishability (ROR-CCA), *if for all ppt algorithms $\mathcal{A}$, the advantage* $\text{Adv}_{\mathcal{A}}^{\text{ror-cca}}$ *is negligible (in k).*

3 Security Model

The security model used for security analysis of our protocol is based on the model used by Bohli et al. [BVS07, BS06], which in turn builds on work by Katz and Yung [KY03] and Bresson et al. [BCP01, BCPQ01]. In this section, we quickly revisit the relevant terminology and definitions from the literature.

Protocol Participants. The model assumes a polynomial size set of *users* $\mathcal{U} = \{U_0, ..., U_{n-1}\}$ modeled as ppt algorithms. Each user $U_i \in \mathcal{U}$ is considered as a probabilistic polynomial time turing machine, which can execute a polynomial number of protocol instances $\Pi_{U_i}^{s_i}$ concurrently ($s_i \in \mathbb{N}$). Each such instance is associated with the following variables:

$\mathsf{acc}_i^{s_i}$ indicates if a session key has been accepted.

$\mathsf{pid}_i^{s_i}$ stores the identities of all participants that this instance tries to establish a session key with. This includes U_i itself.

$\mathsf{sid}_i^{s_i}$ stores the session identifier for this protocol execution. This value is not considered secret and can be published.

$\mathsf{sk}_i^{s_i}$ initially stores a special symbol NULL. Once a session key is accepted, it is stored here.

Initialization. A trusted initialization phase *without adversarial interference* is allowed before actual protocol executions take place. In this phase, each user U_i generates a (public key, secret key)-pair (pk_{U_i}, dk_{U_i}) for a multi key encapsulation scheme, a set of (verification key, signing key)-pair (vk_{U_i}, sk_{U_i}) for a ring signature scheme. The public keys and the verification keys are made available to all users including the adversary. Furthermore, a secret key $K_{U_i} \leftarrow \mathsf{Gen}(1^k)$ for the underlying symmetric encryption scheme is generated for each user U_i and is given to U_i and the server S. Thus, the server shares a symmetric key K_{U_i} with each user U_i after this initialization phase.

Adversarial Capabilities and Communication Network. We assume that the network is fully asynchronous, non-private, and allows arbitrary point-to-point connections among users. The adversary $\mathcal{A}$ is modeled as ppt algorithm with full control over the communication network. More specifically, We provide the following oracles to $\mathcal{A}$ to formalize the described capabilities:

$\mathsf{Send}(U_i, s_i, M)$: Such a query sends a message M to instance $\Pi_{U_i}^{s_i}$ of user U and returns the protocol transcript. This query also enables a user to initialize a protocol run.

$\mathsf{Reveal}(U_i, s_i)$: Such a query reveals the session key $\mathsf{sk}_i^{s_i}$.

$\mathsf{Corrupt}(U_i)$: Such a query reveals either long-term secrets sk_{U_i} for ring signature or dk_{U_i} for key encapsulation of U_i or both.

$\mathsf{Test}(U_i, s_i)$: If the session key $\mathsf{sk}_i^{s_i}$ exists, then $\mathcal{A}$ can make this one-time query at any time. The Test oracle chooses a random bit $b \in \{0, 1\}$ uniformly at random, and returns a session key if $b = 0$ and returns a uniformly at random chosen element from the session key space if $b = 1$.

We define an instance as *fresh* if the adversary does not know the session key.

Definition 6 (Freshness). *An instance $\prod_{U_i}^{s_i}$ is said to be* fresh *if the adversary queried neither* Corrupt(U_j) *for some $U_j \in$ pid$_{U_i}^{s_i}$ before a query of the form* Send($U_k, s_k, *$) *with $U_k \in$ pid$_{U_i}^{s_i}$ has taken place, nor* Reveal(U_j, s_j) *for an instance $\prod_{U_j}^{s_j}$ that is partnered with $\prod_{U_i}^{s_i}$.*

We write Succ$_\mathcal{A}$ for the event when $\mathcal{A}$ queries a fresh instance and guesses correctly the bit output by the Test oracle. We define the *advantage* of $\mathcal{A}$ by

$$\mathrm{Adv}_\mathcal{A}^{\mathsf{ke}} = \mathrm{Adv}_\mathcal{A}^{\mathsf{ke}}(k) := \left| \Pr[\mathrm{Succ}] - \frac{1}{2} \right|.$$

Definition 7 (Semantic Security). *A key establishment protocol is said to be* (semantically) secure, *if* $\mathrm{Adv}_\mathcal{A}^{\mathsf{ke}} = \mathrm{Adv}_\mathcal{A}^{\mathsf{ke}}(k)$ *is negligible for all ppt algorithms $\mathcal{A}$.*

In addition to our major security goal, semantic security, the protocol also provides the other two security features which are *integrity* and *strong entity authentication*:

Definition 8 (Integrity). *A key establishment protocol fulfills integrity if with overwhelming probability for all instances $\prod_{U_i}^{s_i}$, $\prod_{U_j}^{s_j}$ of uncorrupted users the following holds: if* acc$_{U_i}^{s_i}$ = acc$_{U_j}^{s_j}$ =TRUE *and* sid$_{U_i}^{s_i}$ = sid$_{U_j}^{s_j}$, *then* sk$_{U_i}^{s_i}$ = sk$_{U_j}^{s_j}$ *and* pid$_{U_i}^{s_i}$ = pid$_{U_j}^{s_j}$.

Definition 9 (Strong entity authentication). *We say that* strong entity authentication *for an instance $\Pi_{U_i}^{s_i}$ is provided if* acc$_{U_i}^{s_i}$ =TRUE *implies that for all uncorrupted $U_j \in$ pid$_{U_i}^{s_i}$ there exists with overwhelming probability an instance $\Pi_{U_j}^{s_j}$ with* sid$_{U_j}^{s_j}$ = sid$_{U_i}^{s_i}$ *and $U_i \in$ pid$_{U_j}^{s_j}$.*

4   Deniability

Deniability is a privacy goal, the protocol achieves, in addition to semantic security and authentication. We consider the notion of deniability used by Neupane et al. [NSC12] which in turn builds on the work by Bohli and Steinwandt [BS06]. Now we quickly revisit the notion of deniability from [NSC12] and [BS06].

Let $\mathcal{A}_d$ denotes a probabilistic polynomial time algorithm which takes security parameter 1^k and public information p from the initialization phase as its input. In the first phase $\mathcal{A}_d$ is allowed to access only the Corrupt-oracle. In this phase, $\mathcal{A}_d$ (adaptively) corrupts an arbitrary subset of the users (including the case of no user or all users being corrupted). In the second phase, $\mathcal{A}_d$ is allowed to access the Reveal- and Send-oracle, but not Corrupt and Test. Once all the interactions in the second phase are done, $\mathcal{A}_d$ outputs a bitstring $T_{\mathcal{A}_d} = T_{\mathcal{A}_d}(k, p)$ as an evidence of involvement of a particular user in the group key establishment. Let $T_{\mathcal{A}_d} = T_{\mathcal{A}_d}(k)$ be the random variable describing $T_{\mathcal{A}_d}(k, p)$ with the randomness for $\mathcal{A}_d$, for all protocol instances, and in the initialization phase being chosen uniformly at random.

On the other hand, the probabilistic polynomial time simulator $\mathcal{S}_d$ obtains the same input as $\mathcal{A}_d$, but is allowed to access only the Corrupt oracle, but not the Reveal, Send, or Test. The output of $\mathcal{S}_d$ is a bitstring $T_{\mathcal{S}_d}(k, p)$, and analogously as for $\mathcal{A}_d$ we define a random variable $T_{\mathcal{S}_d}(k)$ based on uniformly at random chosen randomness. Now, we consider the following experiment for a probabilistic polynomial time distinguisher $\mathcal{X}$ outputting 0 or 1: the challenger flips a random coin $b \in \{0,1\}$ uniformly at random. If $b = 1$, the transcript $T_{\mathcal{A}_d}(k)$ is handed to $\mathcal{X}$, whereas for $b = 0$ the transcript $T_{\mathcal{S}_d}(k)$ is handed to $\mathcal{X}$. The distinguisher $\mathcal{X}$ wins whenever the guess b' it outputs for b is correct; the advantage of $\mathcal{X}$ is denoted by $\mathrm{Adv}_{\mathcal{X}}^{\mathrm{den}} := \left| \Pr[b = b'] - \frac{1}{2} \right|$.

Definition 10 (Deniability Neupane et al.). *A group key establishment protocol is* deniable *if for every polynomial time adversary $\mathcal{A}_d$ as specified above there exists a probabilistic polynomial time simulator $\mathcal{S}_d$ such that the following holds:*

- *With overwhelming probability, the number of Corrupt-queries of $\mathcal{S}_d$ is less than or equal to the number of Corrupt-queries of $\mathcal{A}_d$.*
- *For each probabilistic polynomial time distinguisher $\mathcal{X}$, the advantage $\mathrm{Adv}_{\mathcal{X}}^{\mathrm{den}}$ in the above experiment is negligible.*

5   The Proposed Group Key Establishment Protocol

The proposed protocol completes in two rounds with the help of a trusted server, and makes use of a message authentication code, a ring signature, a multi key encapsulation scheme, and a random oracle $H : \{0,1\}^* \to \{0,1\}^k$. We use the notation from Sect. 2.1 with P being a generator of the additive group G_1 of prime order q, as used in the BCDH assumption. We denote an unforgeable ring signature scheme by σ and ROR-CCA secure symmetric encryption algorithm by Enc. We denote protocol participants who want to establish a common session key by $U_0, \ldots, U_{n-1}$. We assume the number n of these participants to be even and at least four—if not even, then U_{n-1} can simulate an additional (virtual) user U_n. We assume that the participants $U_0, \ldots, U_{n-1}$ are arranged in a circle such that the participant $U_{(i+j) \bmod n}$ is j position away from U_i in clockwise direction while the participant $U_{(i-j) \bmod n}$ is j positions away from U_i in counter-clockwise direction. The proposed protocol establishes a long-term secure deniable common group session key among the participants, with the help of a trusted server.

Round 1
Computation: The initiator U_0 creates a key $K_0 \leftarrow \mathtt{MKeyGen}(\mathbb{D})$ for a message authentication code, produces a ring signature $\sigma := \mathtt{RSig}_{sk_0}(K_0, \mathsf{pid}_0)$, and computes $(K, C) \leftarrow \mathtt{mEncaps}(\mathsf{pid}_0)$. Then the initiator produces a ciphertext $E := \mathtt{Enc}_K(K_0 \| \mathsf{pid}_0 \| \sigma)$ and computes a tag $\mathsf{tag}_0 = \mathtt{Tag}_{K_0}(C, E)$. Additionally, each U_i chooses $u_i \in \{0, \ldots, q-1\}$ uniformly at random and computes $u_i P$.
Broadcast: The initiator broadcasts $u_0 P \| (C, E) \| \mathsf{tag}_0$ and the other users broadcast $u_i P$.

Round 2

Computation: First, each user recovers $K := \mathtt{mDecaps}_{dk_i}(C)$ and decrypts the ciphertext E. Second, each user verifies the ring signature for the ring pid_i and the tag tag_0; if the verification fails or if $\mathsf{pid}_0 \neq \mathsf{pid}_i$, the protocol is aborted. Third, each U_i sets $e(P, P) = g$ and computes

$$
\begin{cases}
t_i^L := H(g^{u_{i-2}u_{i-1}u_i}) \text{ and} \\
t_i^R := H(g^{u_i u_{i+1} u_{i+2}}) & , \text{ if } i \text{ is odd} \\
t_i^M := H(g^{u_{i-1} u_i u_{i+1}}) & , \text{ if } i \text{ is even}
\end{cases} .
$$

Moreover, each user sets $m_i := (\mathsf{pid}_i \| u_0 P \| u_1 P \| \dots \| u_{n-1} P)$. If i is odd then the user U_i computes $T_i := t_i^L \oplus t_i^R$, and then computes a tag $\mathsf{tag}_i = \mathsf{Tag}_{K_0}(m_i \| T_i)$. If i is even then the user U_i computes a tag $\mathsf{tag}_i = \mathsf{Tag}_{K_0}(m_i)$. The server S selects $k^{\mathsf{srv}} \leftarrow \{0,1\}^k$ uniformly at random and for $i = 0, \dots, n-1$ computes $c_i := \mathsf{Enc}_{k_{U_i}}(\mathsf{pid}_0, k^{\mathsf{srv}})$.

Broadcast: A user U_i broadcasts $m_i \| T_i \| \mathsf{tag}_i$ if i is odd and $m_i \| \mathsf{tag}_i$ if i is even while the server broadcasts $(\mathsf{pid}_0, c_0, \dots, c_{n-1})$.

Check: Each U_i verifies the tags and pid_i, and checks if $T_1 \oplus T_3 \oplus T_5 \oplus \dots \oplus T_{n-1} = 0$ holds. If any of these checks fails, U_i aborts.

Key Derivation: Each user decrypts c_i and recovers k^{srv}. Also, each U_i recovers the values t_j^R for $j = 1, 3, \dots, n-1$ as follows:

- U_i with $2 \nmid i$ finds $t_j^R = t_i^L \oplus \bigoplus_{\substack{s=2 \\ 2|s}}^{(i-j-2) \bmod n} T_{(j+s) \bmod n}$

- U_i with $2 \mid i$ finds $t_j^R = t_i^M \oplus \bigoplus_{\substack{s=2 \\ 2|s}}^{(i-j-1) \bmod n} T_{(j+s) \bmod n}$

Each U_i computes the master key $K := (k^{\mathsf{srv}}, t_1^R, t_3^R, \dots, t_{n-1}^R, \mathsf{pid}_i)$, sets session key $\mathsf{sk}_{U_i} := H(K \| 0)$ and session id $\mathsf{sid}_{U_i} := H(K \| 1)$.

5.1 Security Analysis

The security of the protocol can be ensured "long-term" provided that the underlying cryptographic tools are secure. More specifically, we have the following.

Proposition 1. *Suppose the message authentication code and the signature scheme used in the protocol are secure in the sense of* SUF-CMA, *the multi key encapsulation scheme is secure in the sense of* IND-CCA, *and the symmetric encryption scheme is secure in the sense of* ROR-CCA. *Then the protocol is semantically secure, fulfills integrity, and strong entity authentication holds to all involved instances provided that at least one of the following conditions holds:*

- *The BCDH assumption for the underlying BCDH instance generator holds.*
- *The server S is uncorrupted.*

Proof. We prove the proposition in two steps. First, we discuss the case where the BCDH assumption holds and thereafter we discuss the situation of having an uncorrupted server.

Security if BCDH Assumption for the Underlying BCDH Instance Generator Holds. We prove the security of the protocol in this case by "game hopping", letting the adversary $\mathcal{A}$ interact with a simulator $\mathcal{S}$. The advantage of $\mathcal{A}$ in Game i will be denoted by $\mathrm{Adv}_{\mathcal{A}}^{\mathrm{Game}\,i}$.

Game 0: This game is identical to the original attack game for the adversary, with all oracles of the adversary being simulated faithfully. Consequently,

$$\mathrm{Adv}_{\mathcal{A}} = \mathrm{Adv}_{\mathcal{A}}^{\mathrm{Game}\,0}.$$

Game 1: This game is identical to the Game 0 except that at the beginning the adversary randomly guesses which instance $\Pi_{i_0}^{s_{i_0}}$ will be queried to the Test oracle as well as two instances of $\Pi_{i_0}^{s_{i_0}}$ with which $\Pi_{i_0}^{s_{i_0}}$ will establish a 3-party key $t_{i_0}^R$ in Round 1. We abort the simulation and consider the adversary to be at loss whenever at least one of these guesses turns out to be wrong. Otherwise the game is identical with the previous game. Consequently,

$$\frac{1}{q_{\mathrm{send}}^3} \cdot \mathrm{Adv}_{\mathcal{A}}^{\mathrm{Game}\,0} \leq \mathrm{Adv}_{\mathcal{A}}^{\mathrm{Game}\,1},$$

and as q_{send} is polynomial in k it will suffice to recognize $\mathrm{Adv}_{\mathcal{A}}^{\mathrm{Game}\,1}$ as negligible.

Game 2: Let ForgeRS be the event that, $\mathcal{A}$ is successful in forging a new ring signature for the initiator U_0 in Round 1 before querying Corrupt(U_i) for some $U_i \in \mathrm{pid}_0$. We abort the simulation and consider $\mathcal{A}$ as successful whenever the event ForgeRS occurs. Otherwise, Game 2 is identical to Game 1. Consequently $|\mathrm{Adv}_{\mathcal{A}}^{\mathrm{Game}\,2} - \mathrm{Adv}_{\mathcal{A}}^{\mathrm{Game}\,1}| \leq \mathrm{Adv}_{\mathcal{A}_{\mathrm{rsig}}}^{\mathrm{rsig\text{-}uf}}$.

Game 3: We modify the previous game in such a way that the simulator $\mathcal{S}$ produces the ciphertext E under an encryption of a freshly generated key $K' \leftarrow \mathrm{KeyGen}(1^k)$ instead of using the real key K. We abort the protocol and consider $\mathcal{A}$ as successful whenever the adversary notices the difference. Consequently $|\mathrm{Adv}_{\mathcal{A}}^{\mathrm{Game}\,3} - \mathrm{Adv}_{\mathcal{A}}^{\mathrm{Game}\,2}| \leq \mathrm{Adv}_{\mathcal{A}_{\mathrm{mkem}}}^{\mathrm{IND\text{-}CCA}}$.

Game 4: This game is identical to the previous game except in Round 1 of the protocol the simulator replaces the ciphertext E with an encryption of a uniformly chosen random bitstring of the appropriate length. To bound $|\mathrm{Adv}_{\mathcal{A}}^{\mathrm{Game}\,4} - \mathrm{Adv}_{\mathcal{A}}^{\mathrm{Game}\,3}|$ we can derive the challenger $\mathcal{C}$ to attack the ROR-CCA security of the underlying symmetric encryption scheme: whenever the protocol requires to encrypt or decrypt a message using the symmetric key K, $\mathcal{C}$ queries its encryption or decryption oracle, respectively, simulating Corrupt, Reveal, Send and Test in the obvious way. Consequently, we obtain

$$|\mathrm{Adv}_{\mathcal{A}}^{\mathrm{Game}\,4} - \mathrm{Adv}_{\mathcal{A}}^{\mathrm{Game}\,3}| \leq |\mathrm{Adv}_{\mathcal{C}}^{\mathrm{ror\text{-}cca}}|.$$

Game 5: We modify the game in simulator's response in Round 2. The simulator replaces $t_{i_0}^R$ respectively $t_{i_0}^M$ with a uniformly at random chosen element in G_2 instead of computing $t_{i_0}^R$ resp. $t_{i_0}^M$ as specified in previous game. An adversary notices the difference only if she can compute $t_{i_0}^R$ or $t_{i_0}^M$. However, success on computing one of these yields immediately a successful adversary $\mathcal{B}$ against BCDH assumption. Consequently,

$$\left|\Pr[\mathsf{Adv}_{\mathcal{A}}^{\text{Game 5}}] - \Pr[\mathsf{Adv}_{\mathcal{A}}^{\text{Game 4}}]\right| \leq \mathsf{Adv}_{\mathcal{B}}^{\text{bcdh}}.$$

Game 6: Let ForgeMAC denotes the event that $\mathcal{A}$ succeeds in forging a new valid (message, tag)-pair for a user U_i before querying $\mathsf{Corrupt}(U_j)$ for user some $U_j \in \mathrm{pid}_j$. Whenever the event ForgeMAC occurs in either round 1 or round 2, we abort the simulation and consider $\mathcal{A}$ as successful . As an occurrence of this event yields immediately an adversary $\mathcal{A}_{\text{mac}}$ against the message authentication code, $|\mathsf{Adv}_{\mathcal{A}}^{\text{Game 6}} - \mathsf{Adv}_{\mathcal{A}}^{\text{Game 5}}| \leq \mathsf{Adv}_{\mathcal{A}_{\text{mac}}}^{\text{suf-cma}}$.

Game 7: At this point we modify the previous game by replacing the session key sk_{U_i} (as well as sk_{U_j} for all the instances $\Pi_{U_j}^{s_j}$ which are partnered with the instance $\Pi_{i_0}^{s_{i_0}}$) with a uniformly at random chosen bitstring in $\{0,1\}^k$. This game is identical to the previous game as long as the adversary cannot query the random oracle H with a bitstring of the form $* \parallel t_{i_0}^R \parallel *$. With no information about $t_{i_0}^R \in \{0,1\}^k$ other than $H(K\|0)$ and $H(K\|1)$ being available to $\mathcal{A}$, we obtain

$$\left|\mathsf{Adv}_{\mathcal{A}}^{\text{Game 7}} - \mathsf{Adv}_{\mathcal{A}}^{\text{Game 6}}\right| \leq \frac{q_{\text{ro}}}{2^k}.$$

By construction $\mathsf{Adv}_{\mathcal{A}}^{\text{Game 7}} = 0$, and we recognize the protocol as a secure one, provided that the BCDH assumption holds

Security if the Server is Uncorrupted. As we assume the uncorrupted server, the adversary $\mathcal{A}$ must not query $\mathsf{Corrupt}(S)$. To prove the security in this case, we use sequence of games to as in the previous case.

Game 0: This game is identical to the original attack game for the adversary, with all oracles being simulated faithfully:

$$\mathsf{Adv}_{\mathcal{A}} = \mathsf{Adv}_{\mathcal{A}}^{\text{Game 0}}$$

Game 1: In this game we modify the adversary in such a way that at the beginning she guesses (randomly) which instance $\Pi_{i_0}^{s_{i_0}}$ will be queried to the Test oracle as well as $(n-1)$ instances of $\Pi_{i_0}^{s_{i_0}}$ with which $\Pi_{i_0}^{s_{i_0}}$ will in Round 2 establish a session key. Whenever at least one of these guesses turns out to be wrong, we abort the simulation and consider the adversary to be at loss. Otherwise the game is identical with Game 0. Consequently,

$$\frac{1}{q_{\text{send}}^n} \cdot \mathsf{Adv}_{\mathcal{A}}^{\text{Game 0}} \leq \mathsf{Adv}_{\mathcal{A}}^{\text{Game 1}},$$

and as q_{send} is polynomial in k it will suffice to recognize $\mathsf{Adv}_{\mathcal{A}}^{\text{Game 1}}$ as negligible.

Game 2: This game is identical to the previous game except the simulator in Round 2 of the protocol replaces the server's message c_i directed to $\Pi_{i_0}^{s_{i_0}}$ with an encryption of a uniformly chosen random bitstring of the appropriate length. To bound $|\mathrm{Adv}_{\mathcal{A}}^{\mathrm{Game\ 2}} - \mathrm{Adv}_{\mathcal{A}}^{\mathrm{Game\ 1}}|$ we can derive the challenger $\mathcal{C}$ to attack the ROR-CCA security of the underlying symmetric encryption scheme: whenever the protocol requires to encrypt or decrypt a message using the symmetric key K, $\mathcal{C}$ queries its encryption or decryption oracle, respectively, simulating Corrupt, Reveal, Send and Test in the obvious way. Consequently, we obtain

$$|\mathrm{Adv}_{\mathcal{A}}^{\mathrm{Game\ 2}} - \mathrm{Adv}_{\mathcal{A}}^{\mathrm{Game\ 1}}| \leq |\mathrm{Adv}_{\mathcal{C}}^{\mathrm{ror-cca}}|.$$

Game 3: Furthermore, the simulator replaces the server's messages c_j's directed to all the instances $\Pi_{U_j}^{s_j}$ which are partnered with the instance $\Pi_{i_0}^{s_{i_0}}$ with encryption of uniformly chosen random bitstrings of the appropriate length. With the same argument for each replacement at a time as above, we recognize $\left|\mathrm{Adv}_{\mathcal{A}}^{\mathrm{Game\ 3}} - \mathrm{Adv}_{\mathcal{A}}^{\mathrm{Game\ 2}}\right|$ as negligible.

Game 4: Lastly, we modify the previous game by replacing the session key sk_{U_i} (as well as sk_{U_j} for all the instances $\Pi_{U_j}^{s_j}$ which are partnered with the instance $\Pi_{i_0}^{s_{i_0}}$) with a uniformly at random chosen bitstring in $\{0,1\}^k$. For an adversary, Game 4 and Game 3 are identical unless the adversary queries the random oracle H with a bitstring of the form $k^{\mathsf{srv}} \parallel *$. However, with no information about $k^{\mathsf{srv}} \in \{0,1\}^k$ other than $H(K \parallel 0)$ and $H(K \parallel 1)$ being available to $\mathcal{A}$, we obtain

$$\left|\mathrm{Adv}_{\mathcal{A}}^{\mathrm{Game\ 3}} - \mathrm{Adv}_{\mathcal{A}}^{\mathrm{Game\ 4}}\right| \leq \frac{q_{\mathsf{ro}}}{2^k}.$$

By construction $\mathrm{Adv}_{\mathcal{A}}^{\mathrm{Game\ 4}} = 0$, and we recognize the protocol is secure provided that the server S is uncorrupted.

Integrity. At the end of a fresh session, all the honest users obtain the same "master key" K along with the same partner identifier. Consequently, all the instances of honest users agree on a common session identifier $H(K \parallel 1)$ and a common session key $H(K \parallel 0)$ unless the event Collision occurs. We see that equality of session identifiers with overwhelming probability ensures identical session keys.

Entity authentication. Since each user verifies all the tags on the second round messages, the protocol ensures the existence of a user instance for each intended communication partner and identical m_i-values for each partnered instance. The latter implies equality of both the pid_i- and the sid_i-values. $\qquad\square$

Proposition 2. *The proposed protocol is deniable in the sense of Definition 10.*

Proof. We prove the deniability of the protocol by using sequence of games. We assume the simulator $\mathcal{S}_d$ and the adversary $\mathcal{A}_d$ interact with the challenger $\mathcal{C}$. We denote the advantage of the distinguisher $\mathcal{X}$ in Game i by $\mathrm{Adv}_{\mathcal{X}}^{\mathrm{Game}\ i}$.

Game 0: This game is identical to the original deniability game, with all oracles of the adversary and simulator being simulated faithfully by $\mathcal{C}$. Consequently, $\text{Adv}_{\mathcal{X}}^{\text{den}} = \text{Adv}_{\mathcal{X}}^{\text{Game 0}}$.

Game 1: This game is identical to Game 0 except the challenger $\mathcal{C}$ produces the Round 1 ciphertext E in simulation for U_0 by encrypting a randomly chosen bitstring of the appropriate length if no participant $U_i \in \text{pid}_0$ has been corrupted. We can argue that the advantage of the distinguisher $\mathcal{X}$ in Game 0 and Game 1 differs only negligibly by considering an adversary $\mathcal{D}$ against the real-or-random indistinguishability of the symmetric encryption scheme and derive $\left|\text{Adv}_{\mathcal{X}}^{\text{Game 0}} - \text{Adv}_{\mathcal{X}}^{\text{Game 1}}\right| \leq \left|\text{Adv}^{\text{ror}-\text{cca}}(k)\right|$, which is negligible.

Game 2: We modify the previous game that $\mathcal{C}$ changes the simulation of the Send-oracle for Round 1 messages for the initiator U_0 if some participant $U_j \in \text{pid}_0$ has been corrupted. In this case, the adversary has a secret key pair (sk_j, dk_j) (if he has more than one secret key pair, he selects one at random). The challenger faithfully simulates all computations of U_0 using sk_j to compute the required ring signature. If the distinguisher $\mathcal{X}$ notices the difference between this simulation and the one in Game 1, he could be used as blackbox to attack the anonymity of the ring signature. i.e.
$\left|\text{Adv}_{\mathcal{X}}^{\text{Game 1}} - \text{Adv}_{\mathcal{X}}^{\text{Game 2}}\right| \leq 2 \cdot \text{Adv}_{\mathcal{F}}^{\text{rsig}-\text{ano}}(k)$, which is negligible. Notice that the simulation provided now to $\mathcal{A}_d$ by the challenger $\mathcal{C}$ is the same $\mathcal{S}_d$ would provide, thus the distinguisher's advantage in this case is 0.

Collecting all advantages,
we get: $\text{Adv}_{\mathcal{X}}^{\text{den}} \leq \left|\text{Adv}_{\mathcal{D}}^{\text{ror}-\text{cca}}(k)\right| + 2 \cdot \text{Adv}_{\mathcal{F}}^{\text{rsig}-\text{ano}}(k)$, which is negligible.   □
The keys for symmetric encryption are generated by the server. Since each user shares a key with the server, both the server and the users can generate the same ciphertext. Consequently, any user cannot convince the third party that the messages was created by the sender, not by the server.   □

6   Conclusion

Long-term secure deniable group key establishment protocol we presented can be seen as an improvement of the previous protocols in terms of required number of rounds and additional security features. The fundamental building block used in the protocol is Computational Bilinear Computational Diffie-Hellman key exchange with the use of Joux's 3-party protocol. The security features established in the protocol along with the denibality property are strong. The protocol uses widely acceptable cryptographic tools such as ring signature, message authentication code, and multiparty key encapsulation.

References

[BCP01] Bresson, E., Chevassut, O., Pointcheval, D.: Provably authenticated group diffie-hellman key exchange—the dynamic case. In: Boyd, C. (ed.) ASIACRYPT 2001. LNCS, vol. 2248, pp. 290–309. Springer, Heidelberg (2001). https://doi.org/10.1007/3-540-45682-1_18

[BCPQ01] Bresson, E., Chevassut, O., Pointcheval, D., Quisquater, J.-J.: Provably authenticated group diffie-hellman key exchange. In: Proceedings of the 8th ACM conference on Computer and Communications Security CCS 2001, pp. 255–264. ACM (2001)

[BDJR00] Bellare, M., Desai, A., Jokipii, E., Rogaway, P.: A concrete security treatment of symmetric encryption, September 2000. http://cseweb.ucsd.edu/~mihir/papers/sym-enc.html

[BF03] Boneh, D., Franklin, M.: Identity-based encryption from the weil pairing. SIAM J. Comput. **32**(3), 586–615 (2003)

[BKM06] Bender, A., Katz, J., Morselli, R.: Ring signatures: stronger definitions, and constructions without random Oracles. In: Halevi, S., Rabin, T. (eds.) TCC 2006. LNCS, vol. 3876, pp. 60–79. Springer, Heidelberg (2006). https://doi.org/10.1007/11681878_4

[BMQR07] Bohli, J.-M., Müller-Quade, J., Röhrich, S.: Long-term and dynamical aspects of information security: emerging trends in information and communication security, chapter long-term secure key establishment, pages 87–95. Nova Science Publishers (2007)

[BN00] Bellare, M., Namprempre, C.: Authenticated encryption: relations among notions and analysis of the generic composition paradigm. In: Okamoto, T. (ed.) ASIACRYPT 2000. LNCS, vol. 1976, pp. 531–545. Springer, Heidelberg (2000). https://doi.org/10.1007/3-540-44448-3_41

[BS06] Bohli, J.-M., Steinwandt, R.: Deniable group key agreement. In: Nguyen, P.Q. (ed.) VIETCRYPT 2006. LNCS, vol. 4341, pp. 298–311. Springer, Heidelberg (2006). https://doi.org/10.1007/11958239_20

[BVS07] Bohli, J.-M., González Vasco, M.I., Steinwandt, R.: Secure group key establishment revisited. Int. J. Inf. Secur. **6**(4), 243–254 (2007)

[CHZL16] Chen, Y., He, M., Zeng, S., Li, X.: Two-round deniable group key agreement protocol. J. Cryptologic Res. **3**(2), 137–146 (2016)

[CS03] Cramer, R., Shoup, V.: Design and analysis of practical public-key encryption schemes secure against adaptive chosen ciphertext attack. SIAM J. Comput. **33**(1), 167–226 (2003)

[DL08] Desmedt, Y., Lange, T.: Revisiting pairing based group key exchange. In: Tsudik, G. (ed.) FC 2008. LNCS, vol. 5143, pp. 53–68. Springer, Heidelberg (2008). https://doi.org/10.1007/978-3-540-85230-8_5

[GBNM10] Gorantla, M.C., Boyd, C., González Nieto, J.M., Manulis, M.: Generic one round group key exchange in the standard model. In: Lee, D., Hong, S. (eds.) ICISC 2009. LNCS, vol. 5984, pp. 1–15. Springer, Heidelberg (2010). https://doi.org/10.1007/978-3-642-14423-3_1

[KY03] Katz, J., Yung, M.: Scalable protocols for authenticated group key exchange. In: Boneh, D. (ed.) CRYPTO 2003. LNCS, vol. 2729, pp. 110–125. Springer, Heidelberg (2003). https://doi.org/10.1007/978-3-540-45146-4_7

[MP] Mao, W., Paterson, K.: On the plausible deniability feature of Internet protocols. http://citeseer.ist.psu.edu/678290.html

[MQU07] Müller-Quade, J., Unruh, D.: Long-term security and universal composability. In: Vadhan, S.P. (ed.) TCC 2007. LNCS, vol. 4392, pp. 41–60. Springer, Heidelberg (2007). https://doi.org/10.1007/978-3-540-70936-7_3

[Neu16] Neupane, K.: Long-term secure one-round group key establishment from multilinear mappings. In: Bica, I., Reyhanitabar, R. (eds.) SECITC 2016. LNCS, vol. 10006, pp. 81–91. Springer, Cham (2016). https://doi.org/10.1007/978-3-319-47238-6_5

[NS10]   K. Neupane and R. Steinwandt. Server-assisted long-term secure 3-party key establishment. In: SECRYPT 2010 - Proceedings of the International Conference on Security and Cryptography, Athens, Greece, 26–28 July 2010, SECRYPT is part of ICETE - The International Joint Conference on e-Business and Telecommunications, pp. 372–378. SciTePress (2010)

[NS11]   Neupane, K., Steinwandt, R.: Communication-efficient 2-round group key establishment from pairings. In: Topics in Cryptology - CT-RSA 2011 - The Cryptographers' Track at the RSA Conference 2011, San Francisco, CA, USA, February 14–18, 2011. Proceedings, volume 6558 of Lecture Notes in Computer Science, pages 65–76. Springer, 2011

[NSC12] Neupane, K., Steinwandt, R., Suárez Corona, A.: Scalable deniable group key establishment. In: Garcia-Alfaro, J., Cuppens, F., Cuppens-Boulahia, N., Miri, A., Tawbi, N. (eds.) FPS 2012. LNCS, vol. 7743, pp. 365–373. Springer, Heidelberg (2013). https://doi.org/10.1007/978-3-642-37119-6_24

[Sho00] Shoup, V.: Using hash functions as a hedge against chosen ciphertext attack. In: Preneel, B. (ed.) EUROCRYPT 2000. LNCS, vol. 1807, pp. 275–288. Springer, Heidelberg (2000). https://doi.org/10.1007/3-540-45539-6_19

[Sma05] Smart, N.P.: Efficient key encapsulation to multiple parties. In: Blundo, C., Cimato, S. (eds.) SCN 2004. LNCS, vol. 3352, pp. 208–219. Springer, Heidelberg (2005). https://doi.org/10.1007/978-3-540-30598-9_15

[Unr13] Unruh, D.: Everlasting multi-party computation. In: Canetti, R., Garay, J.A. (eds.) CRYPTO 2013. LNCS, vol. 8043, pp. 380–397. Springer, Heidelberg (2013). https://doi.org/10.1007/978-3-642-40084-1_22

[ZWL10] Zhang, Y., Wang, K., Li, B.: A deniable group key establishment protocol in the standard model. In: Kwak, J., Deng, R.H., Won, Y., Wang, G. (eds.) ISPEC 2010. LNCS, vol. 6047, pp. 308–323. Springer, Heidelberg (2010). https://doi.org/10.1007/978-3-642-12827-1_23

Card-Based Covert Lottery

Yuto Shinoda[1] , Daiki Miyahara[1,4]($\boxtimes$) , Kazumasa Shinagawa[2,4] ,
Takaaki Mizuki[3] , and Hideaki Sone[3]

[1] Graduate School of Information Sciences, Tohoku University, Sendai, Japan
{yuto.shinoda.q7,daiki.miyahara.q4}@dc.tohoku.ac.jp
[2] The University of Electro-Communications, Tokyo, Japan
shinagawakazumasa@uec.ac.jp
[3] Cyberscience Center, Tohoku University, Sendai, Japan
mizuki+lncs@tohoku.ac.jp
[4] National Institute of Advanced Industrial Science and Technology, Tokyo, Japan

Abstract. Before starting to play a two-player board game such as
Chess and Shogi (namely, Japanese chess), we have to determine who
makes the first move. Players' strategies of Chess and Shogi often rely
on whether they will move first or not, and most players have their own
preferences. Therefore, it would be nice if we can take their individual
requests into account when determining who goes first. To this end, if
the two players simply tell their preferable moves to each other, they
will notice the other's strategy. Thus, we want the players to determine
the first move according to their requests while hiding any information
about them. Note that this problem cannot be solved by a typical way
done in Chess, namely, a coin-flipping. In this paper, we formalize this
problem in a cryptographic perspective and propose a secure protocol
that solves this problem using a deck of physical cards. Moreover, we
extend this problem to the multi-player setting: Assume that there is a
single prize in a lottery drawing among more than two players, each of
who has an individual secret feeling 'Yes' or 'No' that indicates whether
he/she really wants to get the prize or not. If one or more players have
'Yes,' we want to randomly and covertly choose a winner among those
having 'Yes.' If all of them have 'No,' we want to randomly pick a winner
among all the players. We solve this extended problem, which we call the
"covert lottery" problem, by proposing a simple card-based protocol.

Keywords: Secure multiparty computations · Physical cryptography ·
Card-based protocols · Real-life hands-on cryptography · Deck of cards

1 Introduction

Consider a situation where two players are about to play Chess or Shogi (namely,
Japanese chess); then, they have to determine who makes the first move. In this
case, one typical way is to flip a coin, i.e., to randomly choose a player who

© Springer Nature Switzerland AG 2021
D. Maimut et al. (Eds.): SecITC 2020, LNCS 12596, pp. 257–270, 2021.
https://doi.org/10.1007/978-3-030-69255-1_17

goes first. Another way is to use Rock paper scissors to choose a player who has a right to determine whether he/she makes the first move or not as he/she likes. On the other hand, in Chess or Shogi, there are many players' strategies depending on whether they make the first move or the second move. Therefore, they want to take their favorite turn, which implies that coin flipping is not an ideal method (because their preferable choices are not taken into account at all). In addition, since individual players tend to have their own preferences about such first-move-oriented or second-move-oriented strategies, they do not want to give out the information of the move they want to take, which implies that Rock paper scissors is not an ideal method as well (because the choice of the winner of Rock paper scissors results in possibly giving out his/her strategy to the opponent). Thus, we need a more intellectual way to determine who goes first while keeping their preferences secret and taking them into account as much as possible.

More specifically, we want to have a protocol to perform the following: If two players' preferences are different, i.e., one wants to make the first move while the other wants to make the second move, then the protocol is supposed to tell the players that the former should go first; if their preferences coincide, then the protocol randomly chooses one of the two players and tells the result. In this paper, we will construct such a protocol to solve the "Chess player's dilemma" mentioned thus far.

1.1 Defining the Functionality for Two Players

Now we formally define the functionality that we wish to achieve.

Suppose that two players P_1 and P_2 have secret input bits $x_1, x_2 \in \{0, 1\}$ that represent their preferences, respectively. That is, for each player P_i, $x_i = 1$ means that he/she wants to play the first move and $x_i = 0$ means that he/she wants to play the second move. For an input (x_1, x_2), the functionality $\mathcal{F}$ outputs a single bit $y \in \{0, 1\}$. The output bit y is determined as follows. If $x_1 \neq x_2$, i.e., they have different preferences, then y is equal to x_1 which means that P_1 (and also P_2) gets his/her preferred move. On the other hand, if $x_1 = x_2$, i.e., they have the same preference, then y is chosen uniformly randomly. Thus, $\mathcal{F} = 1$ means that P_1 is going to make the first move, and $\mathcal{F} = 0$ means that P_2 is going to make the first move.

The functionality $\mathcal{F}$ is also expressed as follows:

$$\mathcal{F}(x_1, x_2) := \begin{cases} x_1 & \text{if } x_1 \neq x_2, \\ i \xleftarrow{\$} \{0, 1\} & \text{if } x_1 = x_2. \end{cases} \tag{1}$$

Here, $\xleftarrow{\$}$ represents that the left element is randomly chosen from the right set.

We note that a player who fails to take the desired move will know that it is the case of $x_1 = x_2$. For example, when both players wish to take the first move but P_1 fails to take the first move (by the outcome of the random choice of $\mathcal{F}$), P_1

will know that P_2 also wishes to take the first move while P_2 cannot distinguish whether $x_1 = x_2$ or not. At a first glance, it seems unfair. However, we believe that this is unavoidable since when both players have the same preference, the best way is to play a coin tossing.

1.2 Defining the Functionality for Multiple Players

We moreover consider the case where the number of players is further extended to a general number of n (≥ 2). Specifically, consider the case where only one person is drawn from n players. For example, assume that there is a single prize in a lottery drawing among n players, each of who has an individual secret feeling 'Yes' or 'No' that indicates whether he/she really wants to get the prize or not. If one or more players have 'Yes,' we want to randomly and covertly choose a winner among those having 'Yes.' If all of them have 'No,' we want to randomly pick a winner among all the players. We call this extended problem the "covert lottery" problem.

Considering n players, each player P_i, $1 \leq i \leq n$, has a secret input bit $x_i \in \{0, 1\}$ that represents a wish. That is, $x_i = 0$ means that P_i does not want to be the winner, and $x_i = 1$ means that he/she wants to be the winner. First, the function $\mathsf{True} : \{0,1\}^n \to 2^{\{1,2,\dots,n\}}$ is defined as:

$$\mathsf{True}(x_1, x_2, \dots, x_n) := \{i \mid x_i = 1, 1 \leq i \leq n\}, \tag{2}$$

where $2^{\{1,2,\dots,n\}}$ is the power set of $\{1, 2, \dots, n\}$. The functionality $\mathcal{G}_n$ for the covert lottery protocol is defined as follows:

$$\mathcal{G}_n(x_1, \dots, x_n) := \begin{cases} i \xleftarrow{\$} \mathsf{True}(x_1, \dots, x_n) & \text{if } \mathsf{True}(x_1, \dots, x_n) \neq \emptyset, \\ i \xleftarrow{\$} \{1, 2, \dots, n\} & \text{otherwise.} \end{cases} \tag{3}$$

Recall that, basically, we want to draw a lottery among players P_i with $x_i = 1$, and if there is no such a player, a winner is randomly chosen from all players.

This functionality leaks to a player P_i who has $x_i = 1$ and $\mathcal{G}_n \neq i$ the fact that $x_{\mathcal{G}_n} = 1$. Also, if $x_i = 0$ and $\mathcal{G}_n = i$, this problem will leak to P_i the fact that all players P_j with $j \neq i$ also have $x_j = 0$. However, this property is inherently owned by $\mathcal{G}_n$, as well.

Let us show that $\mathcal{G}_n$ is a natural extension of $\mathcal{F}$ defined in Eq. (1). Consider the case where $n = 2$ for $\mathcal{G}_n$. In this case, it is obvious that $\mathcal{G}_2(0,0) \xleftarrow{\$} \{1, 2\}$, $\mathcal{G}_2(1,1) \xleftarrow{\$} \mathsf{True}(1,1) = \{1, 2\}$, $\mathcal{G}_2(1,0) = 1$, and $\mathcal{G}_2(0,1) = 2$. Thus, $\mathcal{G}_2$ and $\mathcal{F}$ are essentially the same, although the formats of output are different. Therefore, $\mathcal{G}_n$ is a generalization of $\mathcal{F}$.

1.3 Contribution

In this paper, we propose a card-based protocol for realizing the above-mentioned functionality $\mathcal{F}$. In particular, we construct a secure protocol for deciding the first move using a deck of physical cards. Our protocol uses only four cards and one shuffle, and its procedure is very simple.

We moreover construct a covert lottery protocol to realize the functionality $\mathcal{G}_n$ by applying the six-card AND protocol [21]. As will be explained in more details later, the proposed protocol makes use of the extra card sequence that is not used as output in the six-card AND protocol [21].

1.4 Related Work

Card-based cryptography provides ways for secure multi-party computations using a deck of physical cards, and various protocols and their computation models have been proposed (e.g., [10–12,19,20,27,28,35]) since the seminal work of Den Boer [2] in 1989. Some specific applications are three-input majority voting protocols [23,25,38,39], which output a majority vote for or against three participants while keeping their input secret, millionaire protocols [14,24,26], which secretly compare who has the largest amount of money, ranking protocols [33,34], which output the rich list without revealing each amount of money, a secret grouping protocol [8], which classifies players into groups, and zero-knowledge proof protocols (e.g., [3,5,7,13,15,16,29–31]), which prove the existence of a solution to a puzzle instance without revealing the solution itself.

In addition to using a deck of cards, cryptographic protocols based on various kinds of physical tools have been proposed (e.g., [1,4,6,18,22]).

2   Preliminary

In this section, we introduce basic primitives used in our protocols. In Sect. 2.1, we define a deck of cards. In Sects. 2.2 and 2.3, we present two shuffles, the random bisection cut and the pile-scramble shuffle. In Sect. 2.4, we introduce the existing six-card AND protocol.

2.1   Deck of Cards

We assume that the face of cards is either ♣ or ♡ and that their back sides are the same ?. All cards having the same face are assumed to be indistinguishable. We call those cards of two suits *binary cards*. A deck of binary cards is used in our protocol presented in Sect. 3.

Using two cards ♣ and ♡, a single bit of information is encoded as follows:

$$♣\,♡ = 0, \qquad ♡\,♣ = 1.$$

A pair of face-down cards ? ? is called a *commitment* to $x \in \{0,1\}$ if it encodes the value x according to the above encoding rule. It is denoted by

$$\underbrace{?\ ?}_{x}.$$

We also use another type of cards called *number cards*. The face of each number card has a positive integer like $\boxed{1}\,\boxed{2}\cdots\boxed{m}$ and their back sides are the same $\boxed{?}$ as binary cards. A deck having both binary cards and number cards is used in our protocol presented in Sect. 4.

2.2 Random Bisection Cut

A random bisection cut [21] is a shuffle operation, which is applicable to a sequence having an even number of cards. A random bisection cut for $2m$ cards proceeds as follows. First, it bisects the sequence into the left m cards and the right m cards. Then, it randomly swaps the left and right piles. As a result, a sequence of $2m$ cards (indistinguishable to the original sequence) is obtained.

The following is an example of applying a random bisection cut to two commitments $a, b \in \{0, 1\}$. First, it bisects a sequence of cards into two piles of cards having the same number of cards. In this example, a sequence of four cards is divided into commitments to a and b:

$$\underbrace{\boxed{?}\,\boxed{?}}_{a}\,\underbrace{\boxed{?}\,\boxed{?}}_{b}.$$

Next, the left and right piles are swapped randomly. This results in two commitments to (a, b) or (b, a) with a probability of $1/2$. Hereinafter, we denote a random bisection cut by $[\,\cdot\,|\,\cdot\,]$ as follows:

$$\left[\,\boxed{?}\,\boxed{?}\,\middle|\,\boxed{?}\,\boxed{?}\,\right] \rightarrow \boxed{?}\,\boxed{?}\,\boxed{?}\,\boxed{?}.$$

Ueda et al. [36,37] showed how to securely implement a random bisection cut. According to their experiments, a random bisection cut can be implemented so that nobody knows whether two piles are swapped or not.

2.3 Pile-Scramble Shuffle

A pile-scramble shuffle [9] is a shuffle operation, which is applicable to a sequence of mk cards for some positive integers m and k. A pile-scramble shuffle for m piles proceeds as follows. First, it splits a sequence of mk cards into m piles $(\mathsf{pile}_1, \mathsf{pile}_2, \ldots, \mathsf{pile}_m)$ each having k cards. Then it randomly permutes the m piles. As a result, a sequence of m piles $(\mathsf{pile}_{\pi^{-1}(1)}, \mathsf{pile}_{\pi^{-1}(2)}, \ldots, \mathsf{pile}_{\pi^{-1}(m)})$ is obtained where π is a random permutation. A pile-scramble shuffle can be securely implemented by the use of everyday objects such as envelopes.

2.4 Six-Card AND Protocol

Mizuki and Sone [21] designed a six-card AND protocol. It takes two commitments to $a, b \in \{0, 1\}$ along with two additional helping cards $\boxed{\clubsuit}\,\boxed{\heartsuit}$ and outputs a commitment to $a \wedge b$ as follows:

The protocol proceeds as follows.

1. Place two commitments to $a, b \in \{0, 1\}$ and two binary cards ♣ ♡ as:

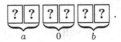

2. Rearrange the sequence as:

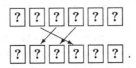

3. Apply a random bisection cut to the sequence as:

$$\left[\boxed{?}\boxed{?}\boxed{?} \middle| \boxed{?}\boxed{?}\boxed{?} \right] \rightarrow \boxed{?}\boxed{?}\boxed{?}\boxed{?}\boxed{?}\boxed{?} .$$

4. Rearrange the sequence as:

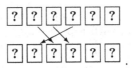

5. Turn over the leftmost two cards. If they are ♣ ♡, the middle pair is a commitment to $a \wedge b$. Otherwise, the right pair is a commitment to $a \wedge b$. The other pair is a commitment to $\overline{a} \wedge b$ in both cases.

(i) ♣ ♡ $\underbrace{\boxed{?}\boxed{?}}_{a \wedge b} \underbrace{\boxed{?}\boxed{?}}_{\overline{a} \wedge b}$ (ii) ♡ ♣ $\underbrace{\boxed{?}\boxed{?}}_{\overline{a} \wedge b} \underbrace{\boxed{?}\boxed{?}}_{a \wedge b}$.

3   A Secure Protocol for Deciding the First Turn

In this section, we design a secure protocol for deciding the first turn. That is, our protocol should realize the functionality $\mathcal{F}$ defined in Eq. (1) in Sect. 1.1. The protocol takes input commitments to $x_1, x_2 \in \{0, 1\}$, and outputs a commitment to $\mathcal{F}(x_1, x_2)$ which designates whether the first player P_1 takes the first move or not, as follows:

$$\underbrace{\boxed{?}\boxed{?}}_{x_1} \underbrace{\boxed{?}\boxed{?}}_{x_2} \rightarrow \underbrace{\boxed{?}\boxed{?}}_{\mathcal{F}(x_1, x_2)} .$$

In Sect. 3.1, we explain the idea behind constructing our protocol. In Sect. 3.2, we give the protocol construction.

3.1 Idea

First, note that when $x_1 \neq x_2$, we have $x_1 = \overline{x_2}$; when $x_1 = x_2$, we have $\{x_1, \overline{x_2}\} = \{0, 1\}$. Then, using $\overline{x_2}$, Eq. (1) is rewritten as

$$\mathcal{F}(x_1, x_2) = \begin{cases} x_1 = \overline{x_2} & \text{if } x_1 \neq x_2, \\ i \xleftarrow{\$} \{x_1, \overline{x_2}\} & \text{if } x_1 = x_2. \end{cases} \tag{4}$$

If $x_1 = \overline{x_2}$, $r \xleftarrow{\$} \{x_1, \overline{x_2}\}$ always satisfies $r = x_1 = \overline{x_2}$. Therefore, instead of Eq. (4), we can simply write

$$\mathcal{F}(x_1, x_2) = r \xleftarrow{\$} \{x_1, \overline{x_2}\}. \tag{5}$$

Therefore, if we have the following two commitments, it suffices to randomly choose one of them without knowing which is which:

$$\underbrace{\boxed{?}\,\boxed{?}}_{x_1}\,\underbrace{\boxed{?}\,\boxed{?}}_{\overline{x_2}}.$$

This can be done with a random bisection cut, as seen in the next subsection.

3.2 Description

Our protocol for performing the functionality $\mathcal{F}$ proceeds as follows.

1. Place two commitments to $x_1, x_2 \in \{0, 1\}$ where x_i is P_i's preference:

$$\underbrace{\boxed{?}\,\boxed{?}}_{x_1}\,\underbrace{\boxed{?}\,\boxed{?}}_{x_2}.$$

2. Apply the NOT computation to the commitment to x_2 by swapping the two cards:

$$\underbrace{\boxed{?}\,\boxed{?}}_{x_1}\,\underbrace{\boxed{?}\,\boxed{?}}_{x_2} \rightarrow \underbrace{\boxed{?}\,\boxed{?}}_{x_1}\,\boxed{?}\,\overset{\rightleftharpoons}{\boxed{?}} \rightarrow \underbrace{\boxed{?}\,\boxed{?}}_{x_1}\,\underbrace{\boxed{?}\,\boxed{?}}_{\overline{x_2}}.$$

3. Apply a random bisection cut:

$$\underbrace{\boxed{?}\,\boxed{?}}_{x_1}\,\underbrace{\boxed{?}\,\boxed{?}}_{\overline{x_2}} \rightarrow \left[\,\boxed{?}\,\boxed{?}\,\middle|\,\boxed{?}\,\boxed{?}\,\right] \rightarrow \underbrace{\boxed{?}\,\boxed{?}}_{x_1}\,\underbrace{\boxed{?}\,\boxed{?}}_{\overline{x_2}} \text{ or } \underbrace{\boxed{?}\,\boxed{?}}_{\overline{x_2}}\,\underbrace{\boxed{?}\,\boxed{?}}_{x_1}.$$

4. The left commitment is a commitment to $\mathcal{F}$:

$$\underbrace{\boxed{?}\,\boxed{?}}_{\mathcal{F}}\,\boxed{?}\,\boxed{?}.$$

Thus, our protocol surely follows Eq. (5), implying that it realizes $\mathcal{F}$. Our protocol uses only four cards and one random bisection cut, and is very simple.

Instead of applying a random bisection cut to the four cards in Step 3, we may apply it to the first and third cards; in this case, the result will be obtained based on the encoding $\boxed{\clubsuit} = 0$ and $\boxed{\heartsuit} = 1$.

4   Covert Lottery Protocol

In this section, we extend our protocol shown in the previous section: We propose a card-based covert lottery protocol that realizes $\mathcal{G}_n$. We first present the idea behind this protocol and then show its description. Our proposed protocol takes as input n commitments to $x_1, x_2, \ldots, x_n$ (each of which represents player's preference) along with four binary cards and n number cards, and outputs a single number card that represents a winner $w = \mathcal{G}_n(x_1, x_2, \ldots, x_n)$:

$$\boxed{?}\boxed{?}\;\boxed{?}\boxed{?}\;\cdots\;\boxed{?}\boxed{?}\;\boxed{\clubsuit}\boxed{\clubsuit}\boxed{\heartsuit}\boxed{\heartsuit}\boxed{1}\boxed{2}\cdots\boxed{n} \rightarrow \boxed{w}.$$
$$\underbrace{}_{x_1}\;\underbrace{}_{x_2}\;\;\underbrace{}_{x_n}$$

In Sect. 4.1, we explain the idea behind this protocol. In Sect. 4.2, we show the protocol construction completely.

4.1   Idea

Let us look back at Eq. (3). To realize $\mathcal{G}_n$, it suffices to randomly choose a single player from the set $\mathsf{True}(x_1, x_2, \ldots, x_n)$ if there are players who are positive to get the prize; otherwise, it suffices to randomly choose a single player from the set of all players $\{1, 2, \ldots, n\}$. To accomplish this, we first apply a pile-scramble shuffle to the n input commitments $x_1, x_2, \ldots, x_n$ to make the order of the inputs random. To keep track of correspondence between inputs and players, a number card $\boxed{i}$ is attached to each commitment x_i, $1 \leq i \leq n$, before applying a pile-scramble shuffle:

$$\underbrace{\boxed{?}\boxed{?}}_{x_1}\underbrace{\boxed{?}\boxed{?}}_{x_2}\cdots\underbrace{\boxed{?}\boxed{?}}_{x_n} \rightarrow \underbrace{\boxed{?}\boxed{?}}_{x_1}\underbrace{\boxed{?}\boxed{?}}_{x_2}\cdots\underbrace{\boxed{?}\boxed{?}}_{x_n}.$$

That is, the resulting sequence of cards after a pile-scramble shuffle is as follows:

$$\underbrace{\boxed{?}\boxed{?}}_{x_1}\underbrace{\boxed{?}\boxed{?}}_{x_2}\cdots\underbrace{\boxed{?}\boxed{?}}_{x_n} \rightarrow \underbrace{\boxed{?}\boxed{?}}_{X_1}\underbrace{\boxed{?}\boxed{?}}_{X_2}\cdots\underbrace{\boxed{?}\boxed{?}}_{X_n},$$

where $(X_1, X_2, \ldots, X_n)$ is generated by permuting $(x_1, x_2, \ldots, x_n)$ with a random permutation π.

If we turn over the commitments to $X_1, X_2, \ldots, X_n$ one by one from left to right, the first revealed commitment to 1 deserves a randomly chosen commitment from the set $\mathsf{True}(x_1, x_2, \ldots, x_n)$ due to the pile-scramble shuffle. Thus, it suffices to output the number card attached to it as the winner. If $X_1 = \cdots = X_n = 0$, then it suffices to output the rightmost number card as a randomly chosen winner from all players. We construct the protocol based on this principle. However, of course, if we simply reveal the commitments to

Table 1. The resulting y_i and token t where $(X_1, X_2, \ldots, X_5) = (0, 1, 0, 1, 1)$.

i	X_i		t		$y_i = X_i \wedge t$		$t := \overline{X_i} \wedge t$	
1	♣	♡	♡	♣	♣	♡	♡	♣
2	♡	♣	♡	♣	♡	♣	♣	♡
3	♣	♡	♣	♡	♣	♡	♣	♡
4	♡	♣	♣	♡	♣	♡	♣	♡
5	♡	♣	♣	♡	♣	♡ (= t)	-	

$X_1, X_2, \ldots, X_n$ one by one, information about the input value of the winner and the number of 0s among (a part of) the inputs would be leaked. For example, let $n = 5$ and $(X_1, X_2, X_3, X_4, X_5) = (0, 0, 1, 0, 1)$. In this case, X_1, X_2, and X_3 are revealed, and hence, all players learn that at least two players' inputs are 0s and the winner's input is 1. Let the inputs be $(0, 0, 0, 0, 0)$ for another example. In this case, all players learn that all the inputs are 0s. To avoid this leakage, we shall perform the above computation while keeping the input values secret.

For this, we introduce a "token" commitment. A token is used to rewrite each input commitment. That is, the winner is determined by making all of the commitments correspond to 0s except for the first revealed commitment to 1. Specifically, we repeatedly perform an AND computation of an input commitment (from left to right) and the token whose initial value is 1, and replace the input commitment with the output of the AND computation (namely, it outputs 1 if and only if both the input and token are 1s). The token should remain 1 until the AND computation first outputs 1, and be 0 after it outputs 1. This computation is accomplished by performing the AND computation of the token and the negation of each input. To summarize, given an i-th input commitment to X_i and the token commitment to t, we perform the following computation and replace the i-th input commitment with a commitment to $y_i = X_i \wedge t$ and the token commitment is updated by $t := \overline{X_i} \wedge t$ $(1 \le i \le n - 1)$:

$$
\underbrace{\boxed{?}\,\boxed{?}}_{X_i}\,\underbrace{\boxed{?}\,\boxed{?}}_{t} \rightarrow \underbrace{\boxed{?}\,\boxed{?}}_{X_i \wedge t}\,\underbrace{\boxed{?}\,\boxed{?}}_{\overline{X_i} \wedge t}, \tag{6}
$$

where the initial value of the token is $t = 1$. The n-th commitment is replaced with the final token.

Let us take an example. Consider the case where $(X_1, X_2, \ldots, X_5) = (0, 1, 0, 1, 1)$. In this case, y_i and t change depending on X_i and t, as shown in Table 1. First, since $X_1 = 0$, we have $y_1 = 0 \wedge 1 = 0$ and $t := \overline{0} \wedge 1 = 1$. Since $X_2 = 1$, $y_2 = 1 \wedge 1 = 1$, we have $t := \overline{1} \wedge 1 = 0$. Since $y_i = X_i \wedge t$ and $t := \overline{X_i} \wedge t$, once the token t becomes 0, all of the remaining AND computations shall output 0s as shown in Table 1.

To perform (6), it suffices to use the six-card AND protocol [21]; thus, we can implement a card-based covert lottery protocol by using the six-card AND protocol $n-1$ times. As mentioned above, we set the final commitment to $y_n = t$. If $X_1, \ldots, X_{n-1}$ are all 0s, we have $t = 1$, and hence, $y_n = 1$. If there is at least 1 among $X_1, \ldots, X_{n-1}$, we have $t = 0$, and hence, $y_n = 0$. Note that, aside from n input commitments, we use four binary cards for the token and the helping cards in the six-card AND protocol.

4.2   Description

The description of our proposed protocol is as follows.

1. Each player secretly creates an input commitment; we now have n input commitments as follows:

2. Place a number card $\boxed{i}$ above each commitment to x_i and make n piles of cards consisting of three cards:

3. Turn over every number card and apply a pile-scramble shuffle to the sequence of piles:

   Let $X_1, X_2, \ldots, X_n \in \{0, 1\}$ be the values of the resulting commitments after the shuffle.

4. Using a pair of free binary cards, make a commitment to $t = 1$ by placing $\boxed{\heartsuit}\boxed{\clubsuit}$ and turning them over.

5. Let $j = 1$. Perform the following computation $n - 1$ times.

   (a) Taking as input the commitment to X_j and the token commitment to t, perform the six-card AND protocol [21] along with the remaining pair of free cards $\boxed{\clubsuit}\boxed{\heartsuit}$ to obtain the following two commitments:

   Place the former commitment to $y_i = X_j \wedge t$ below the number card as the commitment to X_j was there. Let the latter commitment be the next token t. Note that the two face-up cards $\boxed{\clubsuit}\boxed{\heartsuit}$ that were revealed to determine the output can be reused in the next AND computation.

6. Let the commitment to t be a commitment to y_n.
7. Apply a pile-scramble shuffle again to the sequence of n piles, each of which consists of the commitment to y_i and a number card:

Let $Y_1, Y_2, \ldots, Y_n \in \{0, 1\}$ be the values of the resulting commitments after the shuffle.
8. Turn over the commitments to $Y_1, Y_2, \ldots, Y_n$; there should be exactly one commitment to 1. Then, turn over the number card above it. We have the winner represented by the revealed number card.

4.3 Security

We claim that all face-up symbols opened in an execution of the protocol are uniformly randomly and independently distributed from the inputs and output. Face-down cards are opened in Steps 5(a) and 8 only. In Step 5(a), two cards are opened by the six-card AND protocol. From the security of the six-card AND protocol, these symbols are distributed uniformly randomly and independently from any other values. In Step 8, the commitments to $Y_1, Y_2, \ldots, Y_n$ are opened. We note that only a single Y_i is a commitment to 1 and the others are commitments to 0. From the property of the pile-scramble shuffle, the number i is distributed uniformly randomly among $\{1, 2, \ldots, n\}$ and independently from any other values. Therefore, all face-up symbols are uniformly randomly and independently distributed from the inputs and output.

5   Conclusion

In this paper, we formalized a novel problem that determines who makes the first move in a two-player board game such as Chess and Shogi, and designed a card-based protocol to solve this problem. Instead of randomly deciding the first move by a coin tossing, our protocol takes into account players' preferences. Moreover, we generalized the problem into a multi-player case, and designed a "covert lottery protocol" to solve the problem.

We left to reduce the number of cards and the number of shuffles as an open problem. In card-based cryptography, they are considered to be the most important complexity measures. Our two-player protocol requires four cards and one shuffle. Our multi-player protocol requires $3n+4$ cards and $n+1$ shuffles[1]. We note that it is possible to reduce the number of shuffles by applying the technique

---

[1] If we make X_n be two free cards by a random bisection cut before Step 4, the number of cards can be reduced to $3n + 2$ while the number of shuffles becomes $n + 2$. If we apply the AND protocol based on the encode $\clubsuit = 0$ and $\heartsuit = 1$ [17], we can have a $(3n + 1)$-card n-shuffle protocol or a $3n$-card $(n + 1)$-shuffle protocol.

of the card-based garbled circuits [32]. However, in general, it is difficult to reduce *both* the number of cards and the number of shuffles at the same time.

Another interesting problem is to consider a different problem similar to the covert lottery protocol. For example, it is possible to generalize the covert lottery protocol into a protocol with multiple winners although our protocol has a single winner. As another example, since the covert lottery protocol can be viewed as an election with candidacies, it would be worthwhile to consider a protocol for an election that allows for nominations.

Acknowledgements. We thank the anonymous referees, whose comments have helped us to improve the presentation of the paper. We thank the anonymous reviewer at some conference who have inspired us to present the protocol shown in Sect. 3. This work was supported in part by JSPS KAKENHI Grant Numbers JP19J21153 and JP20J01192.

References

1. Abe, Y., Iwamoto, M., Ohta, K.: Efficient private PEZ protocols for symmetric functions. In: Hofheinz, D., Rosen, A. (eds.) TCC 2019. LNCS, vol. 11891, pp. 372–392. Springer, Cham (2019). https://doi.org/10.1007/978-3-030-36030-6_15

2. Boer, B.: More efficient match-making and satisfiability *The five card trick*. In: Quisquater, J.J., Vandewalle, J. (eds.) EUROCRYPT 1989. LNCS, vol. 434, pp. 208–217. Springer, Heidelberg (1990). https://doi.org/10.1007/3-540-46885-4_23

3. Bultel, X., et al.: Physical zero-knowledge proof for Makaro. In: Izumi, T., Kuznetsov, P. (eds.) SSS 2018. LNCS, vol. 11201, pp. 111–125. Springer, Cham (2018). https://doi.org/10.1007/978-3-030-03232-6_8

4. Costiuc, M., Maimuţ, D., Teşeleanu, G.: Physical cryptography. In: Simion, E., Géraud-Stewart, R. (eds.) Innovative Security Solutions for Information Technology and Communications, pp. 156–171. Springer International Publishing, Cham (2020)

5. Dumas, J.G., Lafourcade, P., Miyahara, D., Mizuki, T., Sasaki, T., Sone, H.: Interactive physical zero-knowledge proof for Norinori. In: Du, D.Z., Duan, Z., Tian, C. (eds.) COCOON 2019. LNCS, vol. 11653, pp. 166–177. Springer, Cham (2019). https://doi.org/10.1007/978-3-030-26176-4_14

6. Fagin, R., Naor, M., Winkler, P.: Comparing information without leaking it. Commun. ACM **39**(5), 77–85 (1996). https://doi.org/10.1145/229459.229469

7. Gradwohl, R., Naor, M., Pinkas, B., Rothblum, G.N.: Cryptographic and physical zero-knowledge proof systems for solutions of Sudoku puzzles. Theory Comput. Syst. **44**(2), 245–268 (2009). https://doi.org/10.1007/s00224-008-9119-9

8. Hashimoto, Y., Shinagawa, K., Nuida, K., Inamura, M., Hanaoka, G.: Secure grouping protocol using a deck of cards. In: Shikata, J. (ed.) ICITS 2017. LNCS, vol. 10681, pp. 135–152. Springer, Cham (2017). https://doi.org/10.1007/978-3-319-72089-0_8

9. Ishikawa, R., Chida, E., Mizuki, T.: Efficient card-based protocols for generating a hidden random permutation without fixed points. In: Calude, C.S., Dinneen, M.J. (eds.) UCNC 2015. LNCS, vol. 9252, pp. 215–226. Springer, Cham (2015). https://doi.org/10.1007/978-3-319-21819-9_16

10. Kastner, J., et al.: The minimum number of cards in practical card-based protocols. In: Takagi, T., Peyrin, T. (eds.) ASIACRYPT 2017. LNCS, vol. 10626, pp. 126–155. Springer, Cham (2017). https://doi.org/10.1007/978-3-319-70700-6_5

11. Koch, A., Schrempp, M., Kirsten, M.: Card-based cryptography meets formal verification. In: Galbraith, S.D., Moriai, S. (eds.) ASIACRYPT 2019. LNCS, vol. 11921, pp. 488–517. Springer, Cham (2019). https://doi.org/10.1007/978-3-030-34578-5_18

12. Koch, A., Walzer, S.: Foundations for actively secure card-based cryptography. In: 10th International Conference on Fun with Algorithms (FUN 2020), pp. 1–27. Leibniz International Proceedings in Informatics (LIPIcs), Schloss Dagstuhl-Leibniz-Zentrum fuer Informatik, Dagstuhl, Germany. https://doi.org/10.4230/LIPIcs.FUN.2021.17

13. Lafourcade, P., Miyahara, D., Mizuki, T., Sasaki, T., Sone, H.: A physical ZKP for Slitherlink: how to perform physical topology-preserving computation. In: Heng, S.H., Lopez, J. (eds.) ISPEC 2019. LNCS, vol. 11879, pp. 135–151. Springer, Cham (2019). https://doi.org/10.1007/978-3-030-34339-2_8

14. Miyahara, D., Hayashi, Y., Mizuki, T., Sone, H.: Practical card-based implementations of Yao's millionaire protocol. Theoretical Comput. Sci. **803**, 207–221 (2020). https://doi.org/10.1016/j.tcs.2019.11.005

15. Miyahara, D., et al.: Card-based ZKP protocols for Takuzu and Juosan. In: Farach-Colton, M., Prencipe, G., Uehara, R. (eds.) 10th International Conference on Fun with Algorithms (FUN 2020). Leibniz International Proceedings in Informatics (LIPIcs), vol. 157, pp. 20:1–20:21. Schloss Dagstuhl-Leibniz-Zentrum für Informatik, Dagstuhl, Germany (2020). https://drops.dagstuhl.de/opus/volltexte/2020/12781

16. Miyahara, D., Sasaki, T., Mizuki, T., Sone, H.: Card-based physical zero-knowledge proof for Kakuro. IEICE Trans. Fundam. Electron. Commun. Comput. Sci. **E102A**(9), 1072–1078 (2019). https://doi.org/10.1587/transfun.E102.A.1072

17. Mizuki, T.: Card-based protocols for securely computing the conjunction of multiple variables. Theoretical Comput. Sci. **622**(C), 34–44 (2016). https://doi.org/10.1016/j.tcs.2016.01.039

18. Mizuki, T., Kugimoto, Y., Sone, H.: Secure multiparty computations using the 15 puzzle. In: Dress, A., Xu, Y., Zhu, B. (eds.) COCOA 2007. LNCS, vol. 4616, pp. 255–266. Springer, Heidelberg (2007). https://doi.org/10.1007/978-3-540-73556-4_28

19. Mizuki, T., Shizuya, H.: A formalization of card-based cryptographic protocols via abstract machine. Int. J. Inf. Secur. **13**(1), 15–23 (2014). https://doi.org/10.1007/s10207-013-0219-4

20. Mizuki, T., Shizuya, H.: Computational model of card-based cryptographic protocols and its applications. IEICE Trans. Fundam. Electron. Commun. Comput. Sci. **E100A**(1), 3–11 (2017). https://doi.org/10.1587/transfun.E100.A.3

21. Mizuki, T., Sone, H.: Six-card secure AND and four-card secure XOR. In: Deng, X., Hopcroft, J.E., Xue, J. (eds.) FAW 2009. LNCS, vol. 5598, pp. 358–369. Springer, Heidelberg (2009). https://doi.org/10.1007/978-3-642-02270-8_36

22. Murata, S., Miyahara, D., Mizuki, T., Sone, H.: Public-PEZ cryptography. In: Susilo, W., Deng, R.H., Guo, F., Li, Y., Intan, R. (eds.) Information Security, pp. 59–74. Springer International Publishing, Cham (2020)

23. Nakai, T., Shirouchi, S., Iwamoto, M., Ohta, K.: Four cards are sufficient for a card-based three-input voting protocol utilizing private permutations. In: Shikata, J. (ed.) ICITS 2017. LNCS, vol. 10681, pp. 153–165. Springer, Cham (2017). https://doi.org/10.1007/978-3-319-72089-0_9

24. Nakai, T., Tokushige, Y., Misawa, Y., Iwamoto, M., Ohta, K.: Efficient card-based cryptographic protocols for Millionaires' problem utilizing private permutations. In: Foresti, S., Persiano, G. (eds.) CANS 2016. LNCS, vol. 10052, pp. 500–517. Springer, Cham (2016). https://doi.org/10.1007/978-3-319-48965-0_30

25. Nishida, T., Hayashi, Y., Mizuki, T., Sone, H.: Securely computing three-input functions with eight cards. IEICE Trans. Fundam. Electron. Commun. Comput. Sci. **E98A**(6), 1145–1152 (2015). https://doi.org/10.1587/transfun.E98.A.1145
26. Ono, H., Manabe, Y.: Efficient card-based cryptographic protocols for the millionaires' problem using private input operations. In: 2018 13th Asia Joint Conference on Information Security (AsiaJCIS), pp. 23–28, August 2018. https://doi.org/10.1109/AsiaJCIS.2018.00013
27. Ono, H., Manabe, Y.: Card-based cryptographic protocols with the minimum number of rounds using private operations. In: Pérez-Solà, C., Navarro-Arribas, G., Biryukov, A., Garcia-Alfaro, J. (eds.) DPM/CBT 2019. LNCS, vol. 11737, pp. 156–173. Springer, Cham (2019). https://doi.org/10.1007/978-3-030-31500-9_10
28. Ono, H., Manabe, Y.: Card-based cryptographic logical computations using private operations. New Gener. Comput. **1**, 1–22 (2020). https://doi.org/10.1007/s00354-020-00113-z
29. Robert, L., Miyahara, D., Lafourcade, P., Mizuki, T.: Physical zero-knowledge proof for Suguru puzzle. In: Devismes, S., Mittal, N. (eds.) SSS 2020. LNCS, vol. 12514, pp. 235–247. Springer, Cham (2020). https://doi.org/10.1007/978-3-030-64348-5_19
30. Ruangwises, S., Itoh, T.: Physical zero-knowledge proof for numberlink puzzle and k vertex-disjoint paths problem. New Gener. Comput. **1**, 1–15 (2020). https://doi.org/10.1007/s00354-020-00114-y
31. Sasaki, T., Miyahara, D., Mizuki, T., Sone, H.: Efficient card-based zero-knowledge proof for Sudoku. Theoretical Comput. Sci. **839**, 135–142 (2020). https://doi.org/10.1016/j.tcs.2020.05.036
32. Shinagawa, K., Nuida, K.: A single shuffle is enough for secure card-based computation of any Boolean circuit. Discrete Appl. Math. **289**, 248–261 (2021). https://doi.org/10.1016/j.dam.2020.10.013
33. Takashima, K., et al.: Card-based secure ranking computations. In: Li, Y., Cardei, M., Huang, Y. (eds.) COCOA 2019. LNCS, vol. 11949, pp. 461–472. Springer, Cham (2019). https://doi.org/10.1007/978-3-030-36412-0_37
34. Takashima, K., et al.: Card-based protocols for secure ranking computations. Theoretical Comput. Sci. **845**, 122–135 (2020). https://doi.org/10.1016/j.tcs.2020.09.008
35. Toyoda, K., Miyahara, D., Mizuki, T., Sone, H.: Six-card finite-runtime XOR protocol with only random cut. In: Proceedings of the 7th ACM on ASIA Public-Key Cryptography Workshop, pp. 1–7. APKC 2020. ACM, New York, NY, USA. https://doi.org/10.1145/3384940.3388961
36. Ueda, I., Miyahara, D., Nishimura, A., Hayashi, Y., Mizuki, T., Sone, H.: Secure implementations of a random bisection cut. Int. J. Inf. Secur. **19**(4), 445–452 (2019). https://doi.org/10.1007/s10207-019-00463-w
37. Ueda, I., Nishimura, A., Hayashi, Y., Mizuki, T., Sone, H.: How to implement a random bisection cut. In: Martín-Vide, C., Mizuki, T., Vega-Rodríguez, M.A. (eds.) TPNC 2016. LNCS, vol. 10071, pp. 58–69. Springer, Cham (2016). https://doi.org/10.1007/978-3-319-49001-4_5
38. Watanabe, Y., Kuroki, Y., Suzuki, S., Koga, Y., Iwamoto, M., Ohta, K.: Card-based majority voting protocols with three inputs using three cards. In: 2018 International Symposium on Information Theory and Its Applications (ISITA), pp. 218–222 (2018). https://doi.org/10.23919/ISITA.2018.8664324
39. Yasunaga, K.: Practical card-based protocol for three-input majority. IEICE Trans. Fundam. Electron. Commun. Comput. Sci. **E103A**(11), 1296–1298 (2020). https://doi.org/10.1587/transfun.2020EAL2025

Hardware-Accelerated Cryptography for Software-Defined Networks with P4

Lukas Malina[1]($\boxtimes$)(iD), David Smekal[1](iD), Sara Ricci[1](iD), Jan Hajny[1](iD),
Peter Cíbik[1,2](iD), and Jakub Hrabovsky[2](iD)

[1] Brno University of Technology, Technicka 12, Brno, Czech Republic
{malina,smekald,ricci,hajny}@feec.vutbr.cz
[2] Netcope Technologies a.s., Sochorova 3226/40, Brno, Czech Republic
{cibik,hrabovsky}@netcope.com

Abstract. The paper presents a hardware-accelerated cryptographic solution for Field Programmable Gate Array (FPGA) based network cards that provide throughput up to 200 Gpbs. Our solution employs a Software-Defined Network (SDN) concept based on the high-level Programming Protocol-independent Packet Processors (P4) language that offers flexibility for network-oriented data processing. In order to accelerate cryptographic operations, we implement main cryptographic functions by VHSIC Hardware Description Language (VHDL) directly in FPGA, i.e., a symmetric cipher (AES-GCM-256), a digital signature scheme (EdDSA) and a hash function (SHA-3). Our solution then uses these widely-used cryptographic primitives as basic external P4 functions which can be applied in various customized security use cases. Thus, our solution allows engineers to avoid hardware development (VHDL) and offers rapid prototyping by using the high-level language (P4). Moreover, we test these cryptographic components on the UltraScale+ FPGA card and we present their hardware consumption and performance results.

Keywords: Cryptography · FPGA · Hardware acceleration · Digital signing · High-speed encryption · P4 · Software defined networks

1 Introduction

Nowadays, many Information Communications Technology (ICT) solutions are based on many-to-one communication or centralized architecture where central servers receive the messages from many end-nodes. These servers manage with simultaneous message processing and maintain parallel sessions that usually require mutual authentication (a server and an end-node), key establishment and data confidentiality and integrity. These security requirements can be managed by various security protocols, such as IP Security (IPSec), Transport Layer Security (TLS), Datagram Transport Layer Security (DTLS), Secure Shell (SSH), etc.

This work is supported by Ministry of the Interior of the Czech Republic under grant VI20192022126.

© Springer Nature Switzerland AG 2021
D. Maimut et al. (Eds.): SecITC 2020, LNCS 12596, pp. 271–287, 2021.
https://doi.org/10.1007/978-3-030-69255-1_18

On one hand, these security protocols are mostly realized as software libraries such as OpenSSL, OpenSSH, Strongswan etc. that implement underlying security primitives, and run on most server OS platforms. On the other hand, managing numerous security sessions in parallel and computing heavy cryptographic operations (for digital signing, key exchange) can burden servers' Central Processing Units (CPUs) and slow down services. In order to speed up the services, security functions are more and more offloaded to cryptographic co-processors or other entities such as FPGA network cards. Those dedicated accelerators with the hardware implementation of algorithms could help servers with heavy operations and would allow better managing the queues of end node transactions. Nevertheless, designing, creating and modifying cryptographic hardware implementations in Application-Specific Integrated Circuit (ASIC) or on FPGA cards can be an obstacle, and skilled development exertion are usually required. Current SDN methods can allow engineers to avoid hardware development and offer rapid prototyping or modifications by using higher-level languages in order to speed up creating and testing. For instance, the Netcope P4 framework provides the high-level synthesis of a P4 description into an FPGA firmware bitstream or an IP core[1]. P4[2] as the domain-specific high-level language can be used for a simple definition of a hardware IP core functionality. Thus, there is no need to develop in VHDL, and a firmware or IP core is automatically generated on-demand from functions that are pre-implemented as VHDL templates.

In this paper, we introduce our hardware-accelerated cryptographic solution that leverages the P4 language as an input interface for the flexible setting of FPGA cryptographic external functions (externs) written in VHDL. This work enhances a P4 workflow by adding a cryptographic support into P4-based packet processing and SDN services. Our solution consists of the hardware implementation of widely used cryptographic schemes used for the acceleration of symmetric encryption, hash function computing and digital signature creation and verification. Further, our HW-based cryptographic accelerator is open to be extended by more schemes that can be set into NIC firmware and customized for specific security functions. The paper organization is as follows: In Sect. 2, the state of the art is explored. Section 3 presents preliminaries with underlying cryptographic schemes used as basic initial components in our solution. Section 4 introduces the design of our FPGA-based cryptographic accelerator and describes P4 workload with main benefits. Section 5 then describes our implementation details, measured hardware resources and possible extensions of our solution. The last section concludes this work.

1.1   Contribution

The contribution of the paper is twofold:

- We present our solution that enhances the P4 workflow in order to provide a secure, simple and reconfigurable interface for users who have no experience

---

[1] https://www.xilinx.com/products/intellectual-property/1-pcz517.html.
[2] https://p4.org.

and skills with the VHDL language (Sect. 4). The users of the proposed cryptographic accelerator can easily customize the setting of secure message processing, and add or remove security functions (provided by cryptographic blocks) by using the P4 language and without direct setting the hardware implementation for the FPFA platform. These benefits are mainly discussed in Subsect. 4.3.

- We implement cryptographic primitives such as AES-GCM-256, SHA-3, EdDSA in VHDL and integrate them as hardware-accelerated blocks into our solution as basic initial blocks. The details are presented in Sect. 5. These primitives can be then called as externs in the P4 language, and users or services can simply and fast reconfigure packet processing by calling these functions. Moreover, our solution can be expanded by more VHDL implementations of various cryptographic primitives that are then used for creating the firmware for the FPGA platform, more details in Subsect. 5.4.

2 Related Work

The related work dealing with hardware-accelerated cryptography has focused mainly on particular cryptography schemes, e.g., AES, SHA-3, ECC schemes, and their security and optimization on various FPGA platforms. Recently, Parrilla et al. [17] introduce a hardware-implemented co-processor for elliptic curve cryptography (ECC) over a Zynq device. The co-processor enables the acceleration of secure services using ECC. The solution can be implemented in various FPGA platforms and enables users to create a secure web/database server. Their design requires 9852 LUTs and provides 8930 scalar-point operations per second when operating at 50 MHz. Turan and Verbauwhede [23] consider the Ed25519 algorithm, which is EdDSA using Edwards curve Ed25519, and X25519 schemes implementation on 7-Series Xilinx FPGAs. Moreover, they combine the Ed25519 curve and the X25519 algorithm in a single module, and its implementation requires around 11.1K LUTs, 2.6K registers, and 16 DSP slices. Islam et al. [13] present a FPGA implementation of a high-speed, low-area, side-channel attacks resistant ECC processor over a prime field. They consider the Ed25519 algorithm and propose a novel hardware architectures for point addition and point doubling operations on Ed25519. For a 256-bit key, a single point multiplication runs at a maximum clock frequency of 177.7 MHz and uses only 8873 slices on the Xilinx Virtex-7 FPGA platform. Moreover, several articles, e.g., [14,16,19], focus on speeding up basic elliptic curve operations on Ed25519 and Curve25519 needed for the implementation of ECC. These works provide remarkable results but focus only on the optimization of ECC operations.

Salman et al. [20] present a hardware accelerator for IPSec on Virtex-4 FPGA. Their solution employs hardware-software co-design and partial reconfiguration techniques. The primitives Advanced Encryption Standard (AES), Secure Hash Algorithm (SHA) and modular exponentiation are accelerated on FPGA, and Hashed Message Authentication Code (HMAC) and ciphers modes are calculated in a software part (C libraries). The Encapsulating Security Payload (ESP) and Authentication Header (AH) protocols accelerate secure traffic flow up to 600 Mb/s. Martinasek *et al.* [15] introduce the architecture and implementation of the encryption system utilizing the IPsec protocol on FPGA network cards. Their implementation is based on the AES encryption algorithm and the Galois Counter Mode (GCM) mode of operation to provide both encryption and authentication of transferred data. Their IPSec flow reaches up to 200 Gbps on the NFB-200G2QL network cards based on the Xilinx Virtex UltraScale+. Furthermore, there are only few works dealing with P4 adopting in FPGA that allow designers to not be familiarised with HDL details and only focus on new ideas in the area of network data processing, e.g., [1,24]. For example, Shen *et al.* [22] introduce a programmable and FPGA-accelerated packet processing engine that performs the encapsulation and decapsulation of GPRS Tunneling Protocol (GTP) packets. Recently, Cao *et al.* [9] present a complex framework for converting P4 programs to VHDL and its implementation on FPGA platforms. Yazdinejad *et al.* [25] also present the architecture for a network programmable packet processor using P4 and FPGA that operates at 320 MHz clock speed. Some works already consider P4 and FPGA for security implementation such as [12,21,26]. For example, Scholz *et al.* [21] propose an extension of the P4 Portable Switch Architecture for hash functions and discuss the prototype implementations for 3 different P4 target platforms: CPU, Network Processing Unit (NPU), and FPGA. Further, Hauser *et al.* [12] propose P4-MACsec, a concept to automatically protect links between switches with MACsec in P4-based secure data network. Nevertheless, authors report on unsuccessful efforts to implement P4-MACsec on the NetFPGA SUME platform. Yazdinejad *et al.* [26] introduce a secure blockchain-enabled packet parser for software defined networking. Their blockchain-enabled Packet Parser (BPP) is implemented and tested on ZedBoard Zynq Evaluation and Development Kit (xc7z020clg484-1) Xilinx in FPGA. Nonetheless, these solutions do not provide complex cryptography accelerators based on FPGA and P4.

3   Preliminaries

This section discusses chosen cryptographic primitives that are implemented in VHDL as initial cryptographic components.

- **Symmetric Cipher AES-GCM-256** - the system uses the AES cipher in Galois/Counter Mode (GCM) with 256 bit secret key for high-speed authenticated encryption. Chosen symmetric cipher, keylength and cipher mode are in line with current NIST recommendation. In August 2018, TLS 1.3 (RFC 8446) pruned of all legacy symmetric algorithms. The remaining algorithms use Authenticated Encryption with Associated Data (AEAD) algorithms, such as AEAD_AES_256_GCM. The AES-GCM-256 encryption is also suitable for high-speed implementations in hardware and is recommended in IPsec Encapsulating Security Payload (ESP), see RFC 4106.
- **Hash Function SHA-3** - the system employs the Secure Hash Algorithm 3 (SHA-3) as a hash function. SHA-3 is based on the Keccak algorithm [5,6] that uses a sponge construction [4] and produces 224, 256, 384 and 512-bit

outputs. SHA-3 can be used for computing HMAC authentication tags or as part of authentication protocols. Moreover, SHA-3 is very widespread and many security libraries support it, e.g., OpenSSH, OpenSSL, Botan, etc.

- **Digital Signature EdDSA** - for digital signing in the system, we implement EdDSA (Edwards-curve Digital Signature Algorithm) [3], that is a version of ECDSA employing a twisted Edwards curve bi-rationally equivalent to the Montgomery curve, Curve25519 [2]. In fact, ECDSA involves curves in classical Weierstrass form, while newer ECDSA versions consider curves in twisted Edwards form, namely EdDSA. The main reason of this change is the high performance, smaller keys requirements, and the better resiliency to side-channel attacks of EdDSA with respect to ECDSA. Accordingly, we decide to employ the Ed25519 version of EdDSA that uses SHA-512 (SHA-2) and Curve25519. The nonce is chosen deterministically as the hash of a part of the private key and the message. Thus, the private key is generated only during the setup phase, and then the Ed25519 scheme does not need a random number generator in order to create signatures. Ed25519 is supported by OpenSSH, OpenSSL, wolfSSL or Botan.

Chosen AES-GCM-256, SHA-3 and EdDSA, as initial cryptographic blocks in our accelerator (see Sect. 4), are often compliant with many current security protocols.

4   Design of FPGA-Based Crypto Accelerator

In this section, we present the design of our FPGA-based cryptographic accelerator system. Firstly, we introduce a top-level architecture of the system. Further, we describe the P4 workflow and its main advantages.

4.1   System Architecture

The architecture of the FPGA-based cryptographic accelerator system is depicted in Fig. 1. The system consists of these main blocks:

- **NP4 Cloud** - represents a Firmware as a Service (FaaS) solution which first converts a user-defined P4 source code into VHDL code and after that produces the firmware for FPGA accelerators. This block contains the library of VHDL components, i.e., cryptographic functions described in Sect. 3 and their VHDL codes in Sect. 5, which are deployed to High-speed Network Interface Controller. The details about P4/VHDL compiler and P4 workflow are provided in Subsect. 4.2.
- **High-Speed Network Interface Controller** (NIC) - provides high-speed (200 Gbps) message processing with a FPGA board (the Netcope NFB-200G2QL) where cryptographic primitives run and are wrapped as external P4 objects in two NP4 Atom modules. Each NP4 Atom module processes 100 Gbps data flow. In our solution, we assume two 100 Gbps data flows that are managed by two separated NP4 Atom modules. Further, the FPGA board

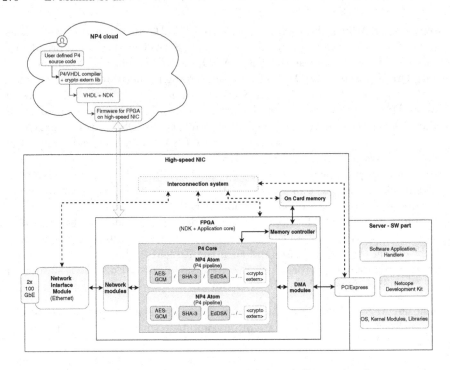

Fig. 1. Top-level Architecture of FPGA-based Crypto Accelerator

contains memory controller for controlling on card memory, Direct Memory Access (DMA) modules that provide fast FIFO-based data transferring between the FPGA board and the host computer, and Network modules that are connected with Gigabit Ethernet network interfaces in order to transfer ingress/egress communication.

– **Server-SW Part** - the software part is used for Network Interface Controller (NIC) configuration and setup, and aggregates generic SW tools (e.g. NP4_atom_tool), handlers and Netcope Development Kit (NDK) that run on Linux OS (CentOS). NDK is the customized product of Netcope Technologies company that enables users to develop applications in VHDL for FPGA targets. NDK provides the set of components for a simple interaction with FPGA parts. Other SW tools enable to set data flow and policy configuration.

4.2   P4 Workflow

The P4[3] is a high-level language designed for Programming Protocol-independent Packet Processors. Three main goals of the P4 language are reconfigurability, protocol independence and target (platform) independence [8].

The P4/VHDL compiler is a tool that compiles a P4 source code to VHDL and maps it on an FPGA platform. This compiler provides an easy way how

---

[3] https://p4.org.

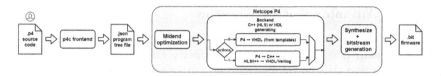

Fig. 2. Compilation process steps

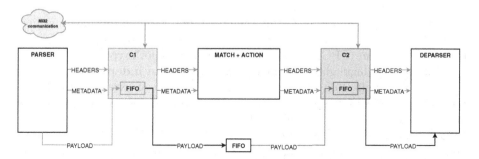

Fig. 3. Extended P4 pipeline for cryptographic external objects usage

to build applications for FPGA accelerators. It is built on the reference p4c[4] compiler with updated midend and proprietary backend for an FPGA platform. The compiler is modular and uses HLS (High Level Synthesis) for generating of actions. To be noted that HLS compiles a C++ description of circuit to VHDL as an intermediate step. The other parts are compiled to VHDL directly.

The compilation process, which describes how the P4/VHDL compiler makes bitstream for FPGA from a P4 source file, is depicted in Fig. 2. A basic pipeline, which processes packets, consists of three main parts. The Parser block parses headers and payload to separate fields used in subsequent stages. The Match and Action block implements all the tables and performs the actions, specified in the source code, on packets' headers or metadata values. The last part is the Deparser block, which joins all modified headers and payload back to a resulting packet. For support of cryptographic external objects, in this case cryptographic VHDL modules, we design an extended P4 pipeline, shown in Fig. 3. The extended P4 pipeline consists of basic P4 pipeline blocks and two additional control blocks C1 and C2 for cryptographic external objects. The C1 control block is designed for usage of external objects that do not need to use modified fields or data from tables stored in the Match and Action block. The second one, the C2 control block, is situated between the Match and Action block and the Deparser block. The C2 control block is designed for external objects that need to use data from the Match and Action block or should be used as the last element after all processing in the Match and Action block has finished.

---

[4] https://github.com/p4lang/p4c.

4.3   Main Advantages of P4 Workflow

We consider the fully automated translation process of a P4 code into the functional bitstream (Fig. 2) as one of the primary benefits of our P4 workflow. Any change a user does in P4 code can be simply applied to the final bitstream by rerunning a translation process without the need for any knowledge of the internal system design changes (Fig. 3). For instance, when a user adds a new external cryptographic object or replaces existing one with another type in the P4 code, the user only has to restart the translation without knowing anything about their implementations (VHDL code in our case) and how they differ for the particular platform (FPGA in our case). The support for cryptographic external objects in P4 highlights its primary goal – **platform independence** – and simplifies the application of cryptography in the form of external objects for processing of network traffic in FPGA at the same time. No need for mastering or even understanding of specialized platform-dependent language, like HDL for FPGA, is another advantage of our P4 workflow. Users only describe a desired behavior of the system including various supported cryptographic operations as a P4 source code, which we assume the users are familiar with. The P4 workflow hides the internal design and implementation of cryptographic operations in an FPGA and only provides the user the final firmware. The P4 workflow and its benefits can be compared to the common well-known software compilers. They also hide the different internals of various processors from the user and only provide the final executable file with the goal to simplify the process of pushing the desired performance into the target platform.

5   Hardware Implementation and Results of Cryptographic Blocks and P4 Core

This section presents our implementation details of chosen initial cryptographic components in VHDL (Subsect. 5.1) and their results of synthesis utilized on the FPGA platform (Subsect. 5.2). In Subsect. 5.3, we present hardware resources required by P4 core, and the chosen example of the customized cryptographic accelerator and possible extensions are described in Subsect. 5.4.

5.1   Hardware Implementation of Cryptographic External Blocks

We implement widely used 3 cryptography schemes, i.e., SHA-3, EdDSA and AES-GCM-256, as atomic 3 VHDL-based modules (externs) for our accelerator. The target FPGA platform of our implementation is a chip from Xilinx, namely Virtex 7 UltraScale+ with the designation xcvu7p-flvb2104-2-i. To be noted that our implementations are wrapped for the P4 pipeline requirements for one 100 Gbps throughput, i.e., 200 MHz as a minimal frequency and 512-bits data bus. Hence, our implementations of cryptographic components in VHDL are not focused on performance or hardware resources efficiency but are focused on the trade-off of both performance, reasonable occupancy of hardware resources, and compatibility with the frequency and data bus requirements.

Hash Function SHA-3

The SHA-3 component consists of 2 subcomponents, namely *Padding Block* which implements the alignment of the input message, and *Hash Block* which is used to compute the hash (the Keccak core function). The Data input (64-bit) is received by the Padding subcomponent that performs an alignment based on the number of valid bytes (input *BYTES_VLD*) in the message block. The alignment is performed only if the received block is the last block of the message (input *LAST_BLOCK*). The output of the Padding subcomponent is aligned data that is passed to the Hash subcomponent. Once the Hash subcomponent receives the data and begins the compute, the Padding subcomponent is reset and additional data can be received for the alignment. The output of the Hash subcomponent is the final 512-bit hash. The data is marked as valid only if the last block of the message was received. After processing the whole message, the subcomponent must be reset, i.e., reset the subcomponent's internal registers. In Appendix A, Fig. 4 depicts the block diagram of the SHA-3 component, and Table 4 presents all used input and output signals.

Digital Signature EdDSA

We implement all main EdDSA phases, i.e., public key generation, signature creation and signature verification, in VHDL and their soundness is verified by using general test vectors for the Ed25519 scheme. The implementation consists of the following subcomponents (blocks): Modular multiplication, Modular division, Addition of points on elliptic curve, Scalar multiplication on elliptic curve, and Hash function SHA-512. The subcomponent for modular multiplication employs the Montgomery algorithm for multiplying two inputs that are firstly converted to Montgomery form. Modular division is implemented by using a hardware algorithm which is based on an extended algorithm for finding the largest common divisor. The addition of points uses extended homogeneous coordinates instead of affine coordinates. Thus, fewer operations are required. Scalar multiplication is implemented by using the Montgomery Ladder algorithm. The hash function SHA-512 are based on the freely available component[5] under the MIT license. The key generation component generates a 32-byte public key from a 32-byte private key. The Signature generation component generates a 64-byte signature from the 32-byte private key, the 32-byte public key and the message at the input. The Signature verification component uses a 32-byte public key, a message, and 64-byte signature at the input, and returns an 1-byte output that determines if the signature is valid or not. Signals of components are summarized in Table 5 in Appendix A.

Symmetric Cipher AES-GCM-256

The implementation of the AES-GCM-256 consists of these components: Expansion, Encryption, Decryption and GCM. The Expansion component expands

---

[5] Component available from: https://github.com/dsaves/SHA-512.

the keys which are passed to the Encryption component as a single signal of 1920 bits. The input signal is the encryption key with the length of 256 bits. The Encryption component contains configurable blocks that perform the operations required for encryption according to the AES-256 standard. The internal blocks of this component perform partial transformation operations, namely, SubBytes, ShiftRows, MixColumns and AddRoundKey. The Decryption component has the same input and output interface as the Encryption component, only performing inverse operations. The GCM component creates the AES-256 block cipher mode. It uses auxiliary components providing computation such as the multiplication of finite fields. Within the structure, the components described above are used to perform encryption and decryption operations. In Appendix A, Table 6 summarizes the input and output signals required in the components.

5.2   Hardware Resources of Cryptographic External Blocks

The hardware resources of the cryptographic modules programmed in VHDL are measured by the synthesis utilized on the Virtex UltraScale+ (XCVU7P).

Hash Function SHA-3

The throughput of one SHA-3 component is approximately 4.51 Gbps. The throughput depends slightly on the length of input messages. The implementation of SHA-3 consumes 3 324 LUTs (Lookup Tables) and 2 715 FFs (Flip-Flops), which are fundamental building blocks inside of an FPGA chip. On one hand, we are able to increase the throughput by using a larger input data width or by performing permutations at higher frequency. Nevertheless, these modifications take a higher number of total hardware resources on FPGA. The results of the synthesis utilized on the Virtex UltraScale+ are summarized in Table 1.

Table 1. Hardware resources on FPGA for SHA-3 component

Component	LUTs	Flip Flops	Frequency [MHz]
SHA-3	3 324	2 715	410
PADDING block	146	584	410
HASH block	3 178	2 120	410

Digital Signature EdDSA

Table 2 shows the results of the synthesis of the subcomponents and main phases employed in the EdDSA scheme. All these results were obtained by synthesis in Vivado 2017.4.1 for Virtex UltraScale+. The first part of Table 2 shows the auxiliary components, i.e., components for calculations needed during the generation and verification of signatures such as modular multiplication, modular division, addition of points on the elliptic curve, scalar multiplication on the elliptic curve and hash function SHA-512. In the second part, three main components for the implementation of the Ed25519 cryptographic scheme are shown, i.e., Public key generation, Signature generation and Signature verification. The comparison of scalar multiplication implementations can be found in Appendix B.

Table 2. Hardware resources on FPGA for EdDSA

Component	LUTs	Flip-Flops	Frequency [MHz]	Time [μs]
Montgomery mult.	1168	783	468,8	–
Modular division	4781	1833	351,1	–
SHA-512	3028	1094	308,5	–
Addition points	7608	3105	330,5	–
Multipl. points	17427	8546	307,7	1075
Public key gen.	25830	12317	307.3	1081
Signature	31024	16706	307.3	2164
Verification	45420	24762	207,2	4502

Symmetric Cipher AES-GCM-256

The results of AES-GCM-256 design from the synthesis utilized on the Virtex UltraScale+ are summarized in Table 3. The maximum operating frequency of the design is 205 MHz. Some sub-components can operate at a higher frequency, but the operating frequency corresponds to the smallest value of all components. The maximum throughput of one AES-GCM-256 core is 26.24 Gbps. The throughput of the cryptography accelerator can be increased by using more AES-GCM-256 cores in parallel.

Table 3. Hardware resources on FPGA for AES-GCM-256 component

Component	LUTs	Flip-Flops	Frequency [MHz]
Expansion	3 123	800	250
Encryption	10 129	898	240
Decryption	15 137	898	222
GCM	8 973	1 238	205
AES-256	28 389	2 596	222
AES-GCM-256	37 362	3 834	205

5.3   Implementation of P4 Core

The resource utilization of P4 Core highly depends on the specific structure of a P4 input file. The increase of the number of P4 tables and their sizes as well as the increase of the complexity and amount of action cryptographic blocks in the P4 code leads to the increase of overall hardware resources consumed in the final design. As an example, we use a simple P4 code with basic bit-wise operations, namely *or*, *xor*, *concat*, *left-shift* and *right-shift*. In this example, the P4 envelope with basic bit-wise operations, and without any cryptographic externs, takes 54k LUTs, 51k FFs, 28 CARRY8, 2.7k F7 Muxes and 192 F8 Muxes.

5.4   Example of Customized Cryptographic Accelerator

Overall hardware resources of the customized cryptographic accelerator directly depends on used security features, e.g., encryption, signing, verification, hash function. For example, if a user chooses and configures the cryptography components such as AES-GCM-256, SHA-3, EdDSA signing in a P4 source code then one simple NP4 Atom (with P4 Core) takes approximately **125k LUTs** and **74k FFs** from maximal 788k LUTs (15.8%), 1576k FFs (4.7%) on the UltraScale+ VU7P board. Thus, the FPGA-NIC device have available hardware resources that can be used for more parallel and comprehensive configurations in P4. Furthermore, the designed FPGA-based cryptographic accelerator can be extended by more cryptographic functions for encryption, key establishment signing and hash functions that have available implementations in VHDL. These VHDL implementations have to be wrapped (for 512 bits data bus and 200 MHz min. frequency) and then stored into the NP4 cloud, i.e., our library of VHDL components. The solution could be extended also by perspective post-quantum cryptographic (PQC) schemes such as CRYSTALS-Dilithium [10] for digital signatures and Kyber [7] or SABER [11] for key establishment. All these PQC schemes are now the third-round finalists of the NIST PQC Standardization Process. In general, PQC schemes can be more memory and computationally expensive than classic asymmetric cryptosystems (RSA, ECDSA). Nevertheless, the hardware acceleration of PQC schemes may improve their performance. There are already several studies dealing with hardware-based PQC implementations. For instance, the implementation of SABER [18] requires 23.6k LUTs and 9.8k FFs with using 250 MHz frequency on the UltraScale+ FPGA platform.

6   Conclusion

In this work, we introduced our design of the hardware-based cryptography accelerator for the programmable network card with the FPGA platform, namely, the Netcope NFB-200G2QL card with the Xilinx Virtex UltraScale+ FPGA chip. Our solution employs the P4 language for flexible setting of the cryptography schemes on the programmable network card. Further, we implemented main cryptography components such as AES-GCM-256 for high speed encryption (up to 26.24 Gbps per component), the SHA-3 hash function (up to 4.51

Gbps per component) and EdDSA signing (up to 462 operations/s per component) and verification (up to 222 operations/s per component). These components can be combined and parallelized in order to increase performance in our P4 based HW accelerator. In our future work, we will extend the system by post-quantum digital signature scheme, optimize components, and test chosen security use cases that combine more cryptography components, e.g., IPSec, DNSSec.

A   Input and Output signals in implemented cryptographic components

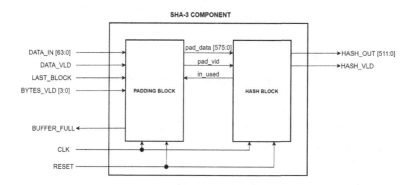

Fig. 4. Block diagram of SHA-3 component with Input/Output signals

Table 4. Input and output signals in SHA-3 component

Signal	Width	Type	Note
DATA_IN	64 b	Input	Input data
DATA_VLD	1 b	Input	Valid input data
LAST_BLOCK	1 b	Input	Last block of msg
BYTES_VLD	4 b	Input	Number of valid byte
BUFFER_FULL	1 b	Output	Full buffer
HASH_OUT	512	Output	Final hash
HASH_VLD	1 b	Output	Valid hash
CLK	1 b	Input	Clock
RESET	1 b	Input	Reset

Table 5. Input and output signals in EdDSA component

Signal	Width	Type	Note
SECRET	256 b	Input	Secret key
PUBLIC	256 b	Input	Public key
MESSAGE_PART	256 b	Input	Part of message
MSG_LEN	64 b	Input	Length of message
SIGNATURE	512 b	Input	Signature to verify
SIGNATURE_GEN	512 b	Output	Gener. signature
SIGNATURE_VLD	1 b	Output	Verification
DONE	1 b	Output	Final hash
ADDRESS	2 b	Output	Message address
CLK	1 b	Input	Clock
RESET	1 b	Input	Reset

Table 6. Input and output signals in AES-GCM-256 component

Signal	Width	Type	Note
KEY	256 b	Input	Input encryption key
KEYS_ALL	1920 b	Output	Block of encryption keys
RX	128 b	Input	Plaintext
KEYS	1920 b	Input	Block of encryption keys
TX	128 b	Output	Ciphertext
HASH_OUT	512 b	Output	Final hash
IV	96 b	Input	Initialization vector
H	128 b	Output	Additional verified data
AUTH_TAG	128 b	Output	Verification mark
OUT_DATA	128 b	Output	Ciphertext in GCM mode
VLD	1 b	Input	Valid data
RDY	1 b	Output	Correct output ciphertext
CLK	1 b	Input	Clock
RESET	1 b	Input	Reset

B   Comparison of Scalar Point Multiplication Implementations on FPGA

Table 7 and Fig. 5 show the comparison of the hardware implementations of scalar point multiplication on EC 25519. The results of implementation created within this work are compared with the hardware implementations in the related works [14,16,19,23]. Regarding to the comparison of hardware sources, the work [14] takes the highest number of resources, i.e., 26 483 look-up tables and 21 107 flip-flops. On the other hand, the work [16] uses the smallest part of the FPGA platform with 3 472 look-up tables and 8 680 flip-flops. Our implementation trades of performance and hardware resources, with 17 427 look-up tables and 8 546 flip-flops.

Table 7. Comparison of scalar point multiplication on EC 25519 implementations

Work	LUTs	Flip-Flops	Frequency [MHz]	Cycles [-]	Time [μs]
Our work	17 427	8 546	307.7	330 754	1 075
[14]	26 483	21 107	115	13 639	118
[19]	12 989	2 705	87	3 858	44
[23]	11 148	2 656	82	–	1 467
[16]	8 680	3 472	137.5	–	628

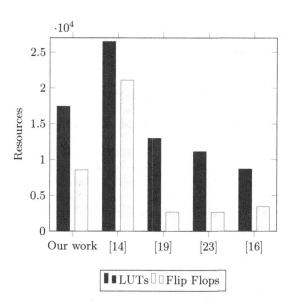

Fig. 5. Comparison of scalar point multiplication on EC 25519 implementations

References

1. Benáček, P.: P4-to-VHDL: How we built the fastest p4 FPGA device in the world. In: 6th Prague Embedded Systems Workshop, p. 43 (2018)
2. Bernstein, D.J.: Curve25519: new Diffie-Hellman speed records. In: Yung, M., Dodis, Y., Kiayias, A., Malkin, T. (eds.) PKC 2006. LNCS, vol. 3958, pp. 207–228. Springer, Heidelberg (2006). https://doi.org/10.1007/11745853_14
3. Bernstein, D.J., Duif, N., Lange, T., Schwabe, P., Yang, B.Y.: High-speed high-security signatures. J. Cryptograph. Eng. 2(2), 77–89 (2012). https://doi.org/10.1007/s13389-012-0027-1
4. Bertoni, G., Daemen, J., Peeters, M., Van Assche, G.: On the Indifferentiability of the sponge construction. In: Smart, N. (ed.) EUROCRYPT 2008. LNCS, vol. 4965, pp. 181–197. Springer, Heidelberg (2008). https://doi.org/10.1007/978-3-540-78967-3_11
5. Bertoni, G., Daemen, J., Peeters, M., Van Assche, G.: The keccak SHA-3 submission. Submission to NIST (Round 3), vol. 6, no. 7, p. 16 (2011)
6. Bertoni, G., Daemen, J., Peeters, M., Van Assche, G.: Keccak. In: Johansson, T., Nguyen, P.Q. (eds.) EUROCRYPT 2013. LNCS, vol. 7881, pp. 313–314. Springer, Heidelberg (2013). https://doi.org/10.1007/978-3-642-38348-9_19
7. Bos, J., et al.: Crystals-kyber: a CCA-secure module-lattice-based KEM. In: 2018 IEEE European Symposium on Security and Privacy (EuroS&P), pp. 353–367. IEEE (2018)
8. Bosshart, P., Daly, D., Gibb, G.: P4: programming protocol- independent packet processors. ACM SIGCOMM Comput. Commun. Rev. 3(44), 87–95 (2014)
9. Cao, Z., Su, H., Yang, Q., Shen, J., Wen, M., Zhang, C.: P4 to FPGA-a fast approach for generating efficient network processors. IEEE Access 8, 23440–23456 (2020)
10. Ducas, L., et al.: Crystals-dilithium: a lattice-based digital signature scheme. IACR Trans. Cryptograph. Hardware Embedded Syst. 2018, 238–268 (2018)
11. D'Anvers, J.-P., Karmakar, A., Sinha Roy, S., Vercauteren, F.: Saber: module-LWR based key exchange, CPA-secure encryption and CCA-secure KEM. In: Joux, A., Nitaj, A., Rachidi, T. (eds.) AFRICACRYPT 2018. LNCS, vol. 10831, pp. 282–305. Springer, Cham (2018). https://doi.org/10.1007/978-3-319-89339-6_16
12. Hauser, F., Schmidt, M., Häberle, M., Menth, M.: P4-MACsec: dynamic topology monitoring and data layer protection with MACsec in p4-based SDN. IEEE Access 8, 58845–58858 (2020)
13. Islam, M.M., Hossain, M.S., Hasan, M.K., Shahjalal, M., Jang, Y.M.: FPGA implementation of high-speed area-efficient processor for elliptic curve point multiplication over prime field. IEEE Access 7, 178811–178826 (2019)
14. Koppermann, P., De Santis, F., Heyszl, J., Sigl, G.: X25519 hardware implementation for low-latency applications. In: 2016 Euromicro Conference on Digital System Design (DSD), pp. 99–106. IEEE (2016)
15. Martinasek, Z., Hajny, J., Smekal, D., Malina, L., Matousek, D., Kekely, M., Mentens, N.: 200 GBPS hardware accelerated encryption system for fpga network cards. In: Proceedings of the 2018 Workshop on Attacks and Solutions in Hardware Security, pp. 11–17 (2018)
16. Mehrabi, M.A., Doche, C.: Low-cost, low-power FPGA implementation of ed25519 and curve25519 point multiplication. Information 10(9), 285 (2019)

17. Parrilla, L., Álvarez-Bermejo, J.A., Castillo, E., López-Ramos, J.A., Morales-Santos, D.P., García, A.: Elliptic curve cryptography hardware accelerator for high-performance secure servers. J. Supercomput. **75**(3), 1107–1122 (2019). https://doi.org/10.1007/s11227-018-2317-6
18. Roy, S.S., Basso, A.: High-speed instruction-set coprocessor for lattice-based key encapsulation mechanism: saber in hardware. IACR Cryptol. ePrint Arch. **2020**, 434 (2020)
19. Salarifard, R., Bayat-Sarmadi, S.: An efficient low-latency point-multiplication over curve25519. IEEE Trans. Circuits Syst. I Regul. Pap. **66**(10), 3854–3862 (2019)
20. Salman, A., Rogawski, M., Kaps, J.P.: Efficient hardware accelerator for IPSec based on partial reconfiguration on Xilinx FPGAs. In: 2011 International Conference on Reconfigurable Computing and FPGAs, pp. 242–248. IEEE (2011)
21. Scholz, D., et al.: Cryptographic hashing in p4 data planes. In: 2019 ACM/IEEE Symposium on Architectures for Networking and Communications Systems (ANCS), pp. 1–6. IEEE (2019)
22. Shen, C.A., Lee, D.Y., Ku, C.A., Lin, M.W., Lu, K.C., Tan, S.Y.: A programmable and FPGA-accelerated GTP offloading engine for mobile edge computing in 5G networks. In: IEEE INFOCOM 2019-IEEE Conference on Computer Communications Workshops (INFOCOM WKSHPS), pp. 1021–1022. IEEE (2019)
23. Turan, F., Verbauwhede, I.: Compact and flexible FPGA implementation of Ed25519 and X25519. ACM Trans. Embedded Comput. Syst. (TECS) **18**(3), 1–21 (2019)
24. Wang, H., et al.: P4fpga: a rapid prototyping framework for p4. In: Proceedings of the Symposium on SDN Research, pp. 122–135 (2017)
25. Yazdinejad, A., Parizi, R.M., Bohlooli, A., Dehghantanha, A., Choo, K.K.R.: A high-performance framework for a network programmable packet processor using p4 and FPGA. J. Netw. Comput. Appl. **156**, 102564 (2020)
26. Yazdinejad, A., Parizi, R.M., Dehghantanha, A., Choo, K.K.R.: P4-to-blockchain: a secure blockchain-enabled packet parser for software defined networking. Comput. Secur. **88**, 101629 (2020)

Security Analysis Using Subjective Attack Trees

Nasser Al-Hadhrami$^{(\boxtimes)}$ ⓘ, Matthew Collinson$^{(\boxtimes)}$ ⓘ, and Nir Oren$^{(\boxtimes)}$ ⓘ

University of Aberdeen, Aberdeen AB24 3UE, UK
{r01nama,matthew.collinson,n.oren}@abdn.ac.uk

Abstract. Subjective attack trees are an extension to traditional attack trees, proposed so to take uncertainty about likelihoods of security events into account during the modelling of security risk scenarios, using subjective opinions. This paper extends the work of subjective attack trees by allowing for the modelling of countermeasures, as well as conducting a comprehensive security and security investment analysis, such as risk measuring and analysis of profitable security investments. Our approach is evaluated against traditional attack trees. The results demonstrate the importance and advantage of taking uncertainty about probabilities into account. In terms of security investment, our approach seems to be more inclined to protect systems in presence of uncertainty (or lack of knowledge) about security events evaluations.

Keywords: Attack trees · Risk analysis · Subjective logic

1 Introduction

In [1], we defined a new model of attack trees (ATs), called a Subjective Attack Tree (SAT), that takes uncertainty about likelihoods of successful attacks (in literature, also referred to as security events) into account. The SAT model aims to address the limitations of traditional probabilistic attack trees [6,14,15], which use precise values for likelihoods of security events. In many situations, it is difficult to elicit accurate probabilities due to lack of knowledge, or insufficient historical data, making the evaluation of risk in existing approaches unreliable. The SAT model allows for *uncertainty* modelling about likelihoods, via *subjective opinions* in the formalism of Subjective Logic [9]. We also discussed how subjective opinions are propagated in the model, via the gates of AND and OR, to compute a subjective opinion on the root node.

The work in [1], however, still lacks several important components for a useful and effective risk and decision analysis. A comprehensive security analysis requires, in addition to likelihoods of attacks, additional metrics such as cost of attack, impact, cost of security investments, etc. Several works have considered the formalism of defense tress, models that add defense mechanisms (i.e., countermeasures) to ATs, e.g. [8,12,16]. These models make use of such metrics to conduct a complete security and risk analysis, and study the efficacy of

D. Maimut et al. (Eds.): SecITC 2020, LNCS 12596, pp. 288–301, 2021.
https://doi.org/10.1007/978-3-030-69255-1_19

proposed countermeasures using economic terms such as Return on Investment (ROI) and Return on Attack (ROA) [2,17]. Any security or security investment analysis makes use, as an essential component, of probabilistic values. Since likelihoods in the SAT model are subjective opinions, it is essential to discuss how security or security investment analysis is conducted, showing at the same time how to handle uncertainties in the model for an effective decision analysis.

In this paper, we extend the SAT model by allowing for the conducting of a comprehensive analysis of security (e.g., risk measuring) and security investment with ROI index to determine which countermeasures are more profitable. This paper thus makes the following contributions. (1) we discuss the adding of countermeasures to the SAT model, and how these countermeasures reduce risk in presence of uncertainty about probabilities. (2) we conduct security and decision analysis, including risk computation, and security investment analysis using ROI index. (3) we conduct an experimental evaluation that compares the security and investment analysis in SATs with the one in traditional ATs.

In Sect. 2, we give an overview of subjective logic, followed by an overview of the SAT model in Sect. 3. In Sect. 4, we discuss the adding of countermeasures to SAT model. In Sect. 5, we discuss security and security investment analysis in SATs. In Sect. 6, we demonstrate the usability of our approach in the context of security analysis using the scenario of DDoS attack. In Sect. 7, we evaluate our approach against traditional ATs. Finally, in Sect. 8, we conclude the paper, discussing prospects for future work.

2 Subjective Logic

Subjective logic [9] is a formalism for reasoning under uncertainty that extends probabilistic logic by allowing also for uncertainty degrees to be expressed about probability values, via subjective opinions. In subjective logic [9], a subjective opinion represents the probability distribution of a random variable complemented by an *uncertainty* degree about the distribution. Let us assume a proposition X such as *the workstation is compromised*. The validity of X is uncertain in general, but we can assume there is a "ground truth" probability p_x that X is *true*, and $p_{\bar{x}}$ (i.e., $1 - p_x$) that X is *false*. This makes X a binary random variable over the domain $\mathbb{X} = \{x, \bar{x}\}$. Little amount of evidence supporting this proposition, or a lack of relevant knowledge, will affect giving the exact probabilities p_x and $p_{\bar{x}}$. As such, the analyst needs to give a subjective opinion about them, expressed in terms of *beliefs* and *uncertainty*.

A subjective opinion on a binary random variable X, called a *binomial opinion*, is a tuple $\omega_X = \langle b_x, d_x, u_x, a_x \rangle$, representing the *belief, disbelief* and *uncertainty* that X is true at a given instance, and a_x is the *prior* probability (also called the base rate) that X is true in the absence of observations. A *prior weight* $W > 0$ is defined indicating the strength of the prior assumption. An opinion's parameters must satisfy: a) $b_x, d_x, u_x, a_x \in [0, 1]$, and b) $b_x + d_x + u_x = 1$. For a given binomial opinion ω_X, the corresponding *projected probability distribution* $\mathbf{P}(x) : x \to [0, 1]$ is determined as $\mathbf{P}(x) = b_x + a_x \cdot u_x$, where $\mathbf{P}(x)$ represents the probability estimation of x which varies from the base rate value, in the case of complete ignorance ($u_x = 1$), to the actual probability in case that $u_x = 0$.

A binomial opinion translates directly into a Beta distribution. The value of a Beta-distributed random variable X is determined from N_{ins} independent observations. Let $n_x, n_{\bar{x}}$ be the total number of observations supporting $X = x$ and $X = \bar{x}$ respectively. Then the Beta parameters $\alpha_X = \langle n_x + W a_x, n_{\bar{x}} + W(1 - a_x) \rangle$, where a_x is the prior assumption, and W is a prior weight indicating the strength of the prior assumption. Unless specified otherwise, we assume $a_x = 0.5$, and $W = 2$, yielding a uniform distribution for the prior assumption.

Given a subjective opinion $\omega_X = \langle b_x, d_x, u_x, a_x \rangle$, we compute the corresponding Beta parameters $\alpha_X = \langle \alpha_x, \alpha_{\bar{x}} \rangle$ as $\alpha_X = \langle \frac{W}{u_x} b_x + W a_x, \frac{W}{u_x} d_x + W(1 - a_x) \rangle$. Conversely, given Beta parameters $\alpha_X = \langle \alpha_x, \alpha_{\bar{x}} \rangle$, a transformation from the Beta distribution to a subjective opinion is given as $\omega_X = \langle \frac{\alpha_x - W a_x}{S_X}, \frac{\alpha_{\bar{x}} - W(1 - a_x)}{S_X}, \frac{W}{S_X}, a_x \rangle$. where S_X is the *Dirichlet strength* of the beta distribution. Equations for computing the Dirichlet strength, mean, and variance directly from a subjective opinion are discussed in [4].

3   An Overview of Subjective Attack Trees

A Subjective Attack Tree (SAT) [1] is an extension to traditional attack trees, proposed so to take uncertainty about likelihoods of security events into account during the modelling of security risk scenarios, via subjective opinions. Fig. 1 shows an example SAT with three possible paths (ways) an attacker can choose to achieve their main goal (MG). These paths begin by the execution of the following security events: (SE_1 and SE_2), SE_3, and (SE_4 and SE_5). Taking the first path with security events SE_1 and SE_2 as an example, the subjective opinions on them, respectively, are denoted by ω_{SE_1} and ω_{SE_2}. The subjective opinion on sub-goal 1 (ω_{SG_1}) is computed from the *conjunction* of ω_{SE_1} and ω_{SE_2}, and the subjective opinion on the main goal (ω_{MG}) is computed from the *disjunction* of ω_{SG_1} and ω_{SG_2}. The subjective opinion on MG represents the *belief* that an attacker can successfully achieve their main goal, the *disbelief* that an attacker can successfully achieve their main goal, and the *uncertainty* degree about the distribution of these belief and disbelief masses.

In SAT model, subjective opinions are propagated through AND gate using the *conjunction* operator of subjective logic [9], and the *disjunction* operator in case of OR gate. Figure 2(b) shows an example computation of a subjective opinion on event Z via OR gate.

4   Adding Countermeasures to SATs

The SAT model does not take into account defense mechanisms that can be implemented by the defending organization and the costs sustained for security investments. We discuss the adding of countermeasures to the SAT model with

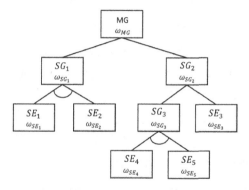

Fig. 1. A Subjective Attack Tree (SAT) model.

Fig. 2. Computing an opinion on event Z via (a) AND gate, and (b) OR gate.

the aim to reduce risk (i.e., likelihood of successful attacks). Countermeasures in our approach can be placed at any node in the tree as per the approach in [16]. Adding countermeasures to ATs models in general is aimed to minimise the likelihood of attacks. In the SAT model, the likelihoods are subjective opinions, so we discuss how these opinions are affected when adding countermeasures.

Each added countermeasure should be associated a value representing the effectiveness of the countermeasures in reducing risk. In most existing approaches, the effectiveness value of a countermeasure is expressed as a percentage, and the likelihood of an attack in presence of the countermeasure is then calculated by multiplying the likelihood value with the given percentage for the countermeasure's effectiveness. However, when there is uncertainty about the likelihood (as in SATs), the calculation would differ. In SATs, adding a countermeasure does not reduce the uncertainty about the likelihood of an event, but the belief mass and base rate. Therefore, the effectiveness value will affect only the belief mass and base rate while maintaining the same uncertainty value. The disbelief mass is calculated by subtracting the total value of the resulting new belief mass and uncertainty from one. Formally, assuming $\omega_{SE} = \langle b_{se}, d_{se}, u_{se}, a_{se} \rangle$ is the subjective opinion about a security event SE, C a potential countermeasure to reduce risk, and CE the countermeasure effectiveness. We compute the opinion about SE with countermeasure C, denoted by $\omega'_{SE} = \langle b'_{se}, d'_{se}, u'_{se}, a'_{se} \rangle$, as follows

1. $b'_{se} = b_{se} \times (1 - CE)$

2. $a'_{se} = a_{se} \times (1 - CE)$
3. $u'_{se} = u_{se}$
4. $d'_{se} = 1 - (b'_{se} + u'_{se})$

Figure 3 shows an example SAT model with two applied countermeasures (ovals), and how they reduce risk according to the above discussion.

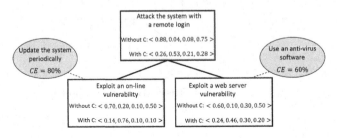

Fig. 3. A SAT model with two countermeasures (ovals), showing how they reduce likelihoods (i.e., opinions) on the leaves, and subsequently on the root node.

5   Security Analysis in SATs

5.1   Risk Computation

In the context of risk analysis, risk is typically computed using the well-known formula $risk = probability \times impact$. In ATs, the computation of risk is often done at the root node (i.e., risk caused by the successful achievement of the attacker's goal). In SATs, we deal with subjective opinions rather than probabilities, and so the risk calculation is different. Risk calculation in SATs depends basically on how the impact value was represented. In literature, most existing approaches represent impact as single values within the interval [0, 1], and very rare is represented as a beta distribution, e.g., [13] for characterizing earthquake damage. In this paper, we demonstrate how risk is computed in case that the impact is a single value and in case is given as a beta distribution.

In contrast to the traditional one, risk calculation in our approach results in a distribution of risk (loss) values in the form of a beta distribution. This is because that there is an uncertainty distribution about the likelihood, expressed in subjective opinions, and these opinions, as discussed in Sect. 2, have one-to-one correspondence to beta distributions. The loss distribution is therefore a beta distribution, provided that the impact value belongs to the interval [0, 1].

Risk Computation with a Single Value of Impact: when the impact is given as a single value within the interval [0, 1], risk is calculated as follows. First, we multiply the projected probability of the subjective opinion (see Eq. 2) with the impact value to obtain the mean of risk, R_μ. Second, we compute the Dirichlet strength of the subjective opinion (see [4]), as this would represent also the Dirichlet strength of risk S_R. Having R_μ and S_R, we can compute the Beta parameters of risk as follows: $\alpha = \langle R_\mu . S_R, (1 - R_\mu) . S_R \rangle$.

Example 1. Suppose the subjective opinion about security event SE is $\omega_{SE} = \langle 0.6, 0.2, 0.2, 0.5 \rangle$, and the impact is 0.4. The mean of risk $R_\mu = 0.7 \times 0.4 = 0.28$, where 0.7 is the projected probability of ω_{SE}. The Dirichlet strength of ω_{SE} is 10, and so $S_R = 10$. Accordingly, $\alpha = \langle 0.28 \times 10, (1 - 0.28) \times 10 \rangle = \langle 2.8, 7.2 \rangle$. The beta distribution of risk in this example is shown in Fig. 4 (a).

Risk Computation with a Beta Distribution Representation of Impact: when the impact is given as a beta distribution, we compute risk as follows:

1. we translate the given subjective opinion into the corresponding beta distribution, and then compute its mean and variance.
2. we compute the mean and variance of the impact from the given beta parameters of the impact distribution.
3. we use the product operator of independent Beta-distributed random variables (see [4]) to compute the mean and variance of risk.
4. we use these mean and variance of risk to compute its beta parameters.

Example 2. Suppose an opinion about event SE is $\omega_{SE} = \langle 0.9, 0.0, 0.1, 0.5 \rangle$. Suppose also the impact I is represented as a beta distribution with shape parameters $\alpha = \langle 18, 4 \rangle$. The risk distribution is then obtained by first computing the mean and variance of both the likelihood (ω_{SE}) and impact distributions. This yields $\mu_{SE} = 0.95$, $\sigma^2_{SE} = 0.00226$, $\mu_I = 0.75$, and $\sigma^2_I = 0.0075$. Using the product operator [4], we obtain the mean and variance of risk R as $\mu_R = 0.7125$ and $\sigma^2_R = 0.0.00805$. Using these values, we obtain beta parameters for risk as $\alpha = \langle 17.41, 7.03 \rangle$. The risk distribution is shown in Fig. 4(b).

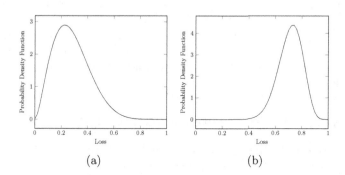

(a)   (b)

Fig. 4. The beta distributions of loss (risk) in (a) Example 1 and (b) Example 2, where "0" indicates no risk and "1" the risk is catastrophic.

Since both representation of impact (the single value and beta distribution representation) yields a beta distribution for risk, for simplicity, in the rest of the paper, we model impact as single values. Our approach of decision analysis takes into account the uncertainty about a likelihood or about risk, so we discuss in the next section, how we deal with uncertainty for risk and decision analysis.

5.2   Dealing with Uncertainty for Decision Analysis

In our approach, metrics such as likelihood and risk are defined as beta distributions (given that subjective opinions, for likelihoods, can be translated into the corresponding beta distributions) rather than single values. For decision analysis, it is important to handle the uncertainty in such metrics, as we will see in the next section. We discuss in this section two possible approaches to reason about risk (or likelihood) in presence of uncertainty. These approaches are (1) reasoning with the most expected value, and (2) reasoning with best and worst-case scenarios via confidence intervals.

Approach 1: Reasoning with the Most Expected Value: In this approach, security managers use the most expected value about a likelihood (or risk) for decision-making. In case of likelihood, the most expected value is the projected probability of the subjective opinion, and it is the mean in case of the risk distribution. This approach yields a single value of risk, and therefore the decision analysis would be similar to the traditional approaches of risk assessment, except that in our approach the uncertainty value is taken into account when computing the most expected value.

Approach 2: Reasoning with Confidence Intervals for Best and Worst-Case Scenarios: In this approach, risk is represented by a range of possible values, determined by lower and upper bounds with a given confidence level, rather than single values, allowing for best- and worst-case scenarios to be considered. In literature, several approaches exist to compute confidence intervals of a beta distribution, e.g., [5,10]. A simple approach is the one discussed in [11], wherein the lower bound of the confidence interval is determined as $1 - BETAINV(1 - \alpha/2, n - k + 1, k)$, and the upper bound as $BETAINV(1 - \alpha/2, k + 1, n - k)$, where α is the level of statistical significance, k the number of events observed, and n the sample size. $BETAINV()$ is the cumulative distribution function of a beta distribution. The lower and upper bounds calculated from these two equations will determine the range of possible values that the risk value is likely to be within.

5.3   Analysing Security Investment: ROI Analysis

Return on investment (ROI) [17] is an economic metric that is widely used to measure the profit obtained by the implementation of a specific countermeasure CM_i (thereby evaluating the efficacy of an investment or comparing the efficacy of a number of different investments). ROI directly measures the amount of return on a particular investment, relative to the investment's cost. According to [17], ROI for a security investment is defined as

$$ROI = \frac{(\text{Risk exposure} \times \%\text{Risk mitigated}) - \text{Investment cost}}{\text{Investment cost}} \tag{1}$$

In AT models, *risk exposure* represents risk at the root node. Since countermeasures do not affect impact value directly (the impact value at the root node is the same apart from whether there were countermeasures applied or not), but rather the likelihood of an event occurrence [16], we may consider risk exposure as the *likelihood* (in SAT, the *subjective opinion*) about the goal (i.e., the top event) when we come to compute ROI. *% Risk mitigated* is the amount of the percentage risk mitigated as a result of applying a specific countermeasure. Unlike traditional probabilistic values, it is difficult to calculate directly such a percentage because the uncertainty value and base rate at the root node might change when applying a countermeasure to the model. Therefore, we have first to resolve uncertainty in the subjective opinions, using one of the approaches discussed in Sect. 5.2, to be able to compute the percentage risk mitigated, and use this percentage in the above ROI formula.

As an example, suppose the subjective opinion at the root node without countermeasure CM_i is $\omega_{goal-without-CM_i} = \langle 0.65, 0.15, 0.20, 0.85 \rangle$ and with the countermeasure is $\omega_{goal-with-CM_i} = \langle 0.42, 0.25, 0.33, 0.72 \rangle$. Suppose also we want to reason about risk using the most likely value, i.e., the projected probability of each subjective opinion. The projected probability of $\omega_{goal-without-CM_i}$ is 0.82, and it is 0.66 for $\omega_{goal-with-CM_i}$. The percentage risk mitigated is then calculated as $1 - \frac{0.66}{0.82} \times 100 = \%19.5$. For abbreviation, we denote such a calculation for risk mitigated by RM.

Investment cost is the cost of the applied countermeasure. Based on the above discussion, we re-define ROI for a countermeasure CM_i as

$$ROI_{CM_i} = \frac{(R_{sys} \times \%RM) - C_{CM_i}}{C_{CM_i}} \tag{2}$$

where R_{sys} is the system risk, i.e., the opinion on the root node ω_{goal}, with an uncertainty treated according to the approaches in Sect. 5.2. In other words, R_{sys} can take any of the following values: the projected probability of ω_{goal}, the lower bound of the desired confidence interval, or its upper bound. A countermeasure CM_i is only profitable if $(R_{sys} \times \%RM) > C_{CM_i}$, and this is satisfied when the risk value is withing the scale of $[0, 100]$ rather than $[0, 1]$ [3]. Therefore, we calculate risk as $R_{sys} \times 100$. If ROI is zero or a negative number, the investment is not profitable. Otherwise, it is financially justified, and so the higher value of ROI the higher desired an investment. Suppose in the given example above, the cost for implementing CM_i is \$20. ROI_{CM_i} is then $(82 \times 0.195) - 20)/20 = -0.2$. Since ROI is negative, the countermeasure is not profitable.

6   An Illustrative Example

To demonstrate the usability of our approach in security analysis, we use the example of DDoS attack discussed in [7] as a case study. To simplify the example, we show only portions of the complete scenario for implementing DDoS attack as depicted in Fig. 5. The effectiveness of each countermeasure is shown in Fig. 5, and their costs of implementation (in \$) are given as follows: $C(CM_1) = 10$, $C(CM_2) = 20$, $C(CM_3) = 15$, and $C(CM_4) = 20$.

Further, the model shows the impact values (below the subjective opinions). The propagation of impact values follows the approach in [15]. In case of OR gate, we choose to propagate the maximum value of impact to consider the worst-case scenario in calculating the impact at the root node. We do so because the analyst has to be prepared for the worst possible consequence (i.e., the attack with maximum impact) and because the attacker's capabilities and preferences cannot be known in advance. In case of AND gate, the impact values are propagated in the model according to formula defined in [8]. However, since our impact scale is $[0, 1]$ and not $[1, 10]$, we redefine the propagation rule of impact values as follows $1 - \prod_{i=1}^{n}(1 - I_{A_i})$, where n is the number of children nodes.

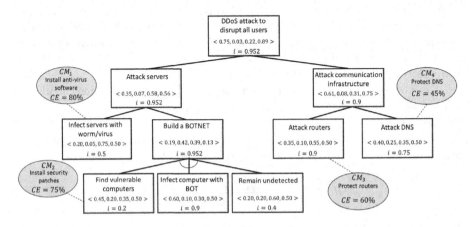

Fig. 5. The SAT model with countermeasures (ovals) for the DDoS attack scenario. The values below the subjective opinions are the impact values.

Table 1. The subjective opinion on the root node, risk mitigated, and ROI for each countermeasure in the DDoS attack scenario.

Applied countermeasure	Subjective opinion on goal	Risk mitigated	ROI
CM_1	$\langle 0.56, 0.13, 0.31, 0.72 \rangle$	18%	0.70
CM_2	$\langle 0.67, 0.09, 0.24, 0.81 \rangle$	09%	−0.57
CM_3	$\langle 0.61, 0.14, 0.25, 0.74 \rangle$	16%	0.01
CM_4	$\langle 0.68, 0.04, 0.28, 0.84 \rangle$	03%	−0.85

The subjective opinion about DDoS attack is $\langle 0.75, 0.03, 0.22, 0.89 \rangle$, and the impact is 0.952. Therefore, the risk is a beta distribution with parameters $\alpha = \langle 8.19, 1 \rangle$. The mean of risk is 0.9, representing the most likely value of risk. The 95% confidence interval of the risk distribution is $[0.833, 0.967]$, representing the lowest and highest possible values. Security managers, unlike in traditional risk assessment approaches, can use these values to reason about risk and make decisions as per their risk attitudes.

We now turn our attention to the analysis of security investment, using ROI index. Applying each countermeasure would result in a reduction in the subjective opinion about the top event, i.e., ω_{goal}. Table 1 shows the subjective opinion about DDoS attack when applying each countermeasure, and the percentage risk mitigated after resolving uncertainty about the subjective opinions using the most likely value approach. Using Eq. 2, we obtain ROI for each countermeasure as shown in Table 1. As appear, two countermeasures, CM_2 and CM_4, since their ROI are negative numbers, should be excluded. The only two countermeasures that are profitable are CM_1 and CM_3, and CM_1 is more profitable than CM_3. However, ROI for CM_3 approaches from zero, and so it does not seem to be significantly financially justified. As a result, the security manager may think of applying CM_1 (install anti-virus software) as a possible security solution against the DDoS attack.

7   Experimental Evaluation

We use the SAT model in Fig. 6 as an example model to conduct an evaluation of our approach against traditional ATs in terms of security and security investment analysis. The model contains two countermeasures CM_1 and CM_2 applied to the security events SE_1 and SE_2, respectively. The subjective opinions about the four security events were established so as to contain relatively high uncertainty values. Propagating these opinions led to also a relatively high uncertainty (0.38) about the likelihood on the root node. The uncertainty values in the opinions lead to several different underlying probability values in contrast to a 0 uncertainty. For example, the probabilities of 0.75, 0.6, and 0.55 might represent possible truth values for the opinion about SE_4 ($\langle 0.40, 0.25, 0.35, 0, 50 \rangle$). In this example, the uncertainty value has affected only the belief mass of the

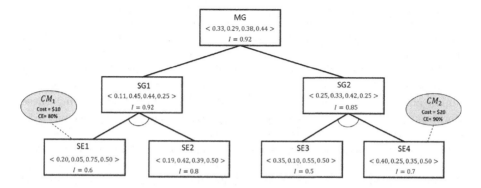

Fig. 6. A SAT model with two countermeasures. The values below the subjective opinions are impact values.

probability distribution of 0.75, affected only the disbelief mass of the probability distribution of 0.6, and affected both the belief and disbelief masses of the probability distributions of 0.55. Based on such a discussion, we generated probability values for the four security events (assuming they represent truth values) as follows: $Prob(SE_1) = 0.3$, $Prob(SE_2) = 0.25$, $Prob(SE_3) = 0.4$, and $Prob(SE_4) = 0.45$. Accordingly, the probability at the root node is 0.24.

First, we began by comparing the risk outcomes from the SAT model of Fig. 6 with the risk obtained from applying traditional risk analysis using the above set of probabilities. In case of the SAT model, the risk obtained is a beta distribution with parameters $\alpha = \langle 4.6, 5.4 \rangle$ and mean 0.46. The 95% confidence interval of the risk distribution is $[0.39, 0.52]$. In case of the AT approach, the risk obtained is the single value 0.24. Suppose the security manager would only protect the system against the attack if the risk is greater than 0.45. It is evident that *in case of the AT approach, the system would not be protected. In case of the SAT model, there are cases in which the security manager would choose to protect the system.* If they rely on the most likely value (the mean of risk), or if the are too pessimistic and wish to consider the worst case scenario (via the upper bound of the confidence interval), they will go for protecting the system, since both values are greater than the defined threshold value. However, the decision would be the same as in the AT approach if they are optimistic and wish to consider the best case scenario (via the lower bound of the confidence interval).

Table 2. The projected probability of each subjective opinion about the attack with and without countermeasures and their 95% confidence interval.

Subjective opinion on attack	Projected probability	95% Confidence interval
$\langle 0.33, 0.09, 0.38, 0.44 \rangle$	0.5	$[0.29, 0.71]$
$\langle 0.27, 0.32, 0.41, 0.26 \rangle$	0.37	$[0.12, 0.61]$
$\langle 0.14, 0.44, 0.42, 0.27 \rangle$	0.25	$[0.03, 0.47]$

Next, we evaluated security investments (with ROI index) using the two approaches. In the SAT model, the subjective opinion about the attack without countermeasures is $\langle 0.33, 0.09, 0.38, 0.44 \rangle$. When applying each of CM_1 and CM_2 to the model, the resulting subjective opinions are $\langle 0.27, 0.32, 0.41, 0.26 \rangle$ and $\langle 0.14, 0.44, 0.42, 0.27 \rangle$, respectively. The projected probability of each subjective opinion and their 95% confidence intervals are given in Table 2. Using these information and cost of each countermeasure, we considered three scenarios to compute ROI for each countermeasure: (1) the most likely scenario (based on the projected probability), (2) the worst-case scenario (based on the lower bound of the confidence interval), and (3) the best-case scenario (based on the upper bound of the confidence interval). We denote the ROI calculated from the first scenario by ROI_μ, and by ROI_{lower} and ROI_{upper} for the other two scenarios, respectively. The ROI values obtained for each countermeasure are all positives (except in one case) as shown in Table 3.

Table 3. ROI values for each countermeasure in case of SAT model (ROI_μ, ROI_{lower}, and ROI_{upper}) and in case of AT approach (ROI_{pro}).

Countermeasure	ROI_μ	ROI_{lower}	ROI_{upper}	ROI_{pro}
CM_1	0.3	0.6	0	−0.49
CM_2	0.25	0.29	0.17	−0.24

In case of AT approach, the ROI obtained for each countermeasure, denoted by ROI_{pro}, is −0.49 for CM_1 and −0.24 for CM_2 (see Table 3). Clearly, none of the countermeasures are profitable, unlike in the SAT model, wherein the two countermeasures are financially justified in the three defined scenarios, except with the worst-case scenario for CM_1, in which ROI returned a 0 value.

Analysing the above results, our experiments clearly demonstrate the importance of taking uncertainty into account when conducting security analysis using models such as ATs, as doing so can lead to completely different security decisions. In terms of risk analysis, the SAT model offers a more flexible approach to decision-making by allowing to consider different scenarios (e.g., the best and worst-case scenarios), and so allowing security managers to take decisions based on, for instance, their risk attitudes, or the organisation' financial capabilities. In terms of security investments analysis (with ROI index), it seems that taking uncertainty into account results in higher ROI values for countermeasures (in contrast to a 0 uncertainty). This means that the chance to apply a countermeasure in the SAT model is higher, which could be also interpreted as follows: *our approach seems to be more inclined to protect systems in case of uncertainty (or lack of knowledge) about security events evaluations.*

8   Conclusions and Future Work

We extended a previous work on subjective attack trees by allowing for the modelling of countermeasures as well as conducting a comprehensive security and security investment analysis with ROI index. We showed how to calculate risk in SATs, and how to handle uncertainty for decision-making. Finally, we evaluated our approach against traditional attack trees, showing that SATs lead to different outcomes in contrast to ATs, and in terms of security investment, they seem to be more inclined to protect systems in presence of uncertainty about security events evaluations.

As future work, we will extend the analysis by allowing for additional metrics to be considered, such as cost of attack, allowing us to study another financial index, namely return on attack (ROA). With both ROA and ROI, we quantify the nature of the competition between the attacker and the defender. We will study how uncertainty might affect such a competition, and how the best countermeasures can be selected under uncertainty about the two indexes.

References

1. Al-Hadharami, N., Collinson, M., Oren, N.: Modelling security risk scenarios using subjective attack trees. In: Proceedings of the 15th International Conference on Risks and Security of Internet and Systems (CRISIS 2020). Springer (2020, to appear)
2. Bistarelli, S., Dall'Aglio, M., Peretti, P.: Strategic games on defense trees. In: Dimitrakos, T., Martinelli, F., Ryan, P.Y.A., Schneider, S. (eds.) FAST 2006. LNCS, vol. 4691, pp. 1–15. Springer, Heidelberg (2007). https://doi.org/10.1007/978-3-540-75227-1_1
3. Bistarelli, S., Fioravanti, F., Peretti, P.: Defense trees for economic evaluation of security investments. In: First International Conference on Availability, Reliability and Security (ARES 2006), p. 8. IEEE (2006)
4. Cerutti, F., Kaplan, L., Kimmig, A., Şensoy, M.: Probabilistic logic programming with beta-distributed random variables. In: Proceedings of AAAI, pp. 7769–7776 (2019)
5. Daly, L.: Simple SAS macros for the calculation of exact binomial and Poisson confidence limits. Comput. Biol. Med. **22**(5), 351–361 (1992)
6. Edge, K., Raines, R., Grimaila, M., Baldwin, R., Bennington, R., Reuter, C.: The use of attack and protection trees to analyze security for an online banking system. In: 2007 40th Annual Hawaii International Conference on System Sciences (HICSS 2007), p. 144b. IEEE (2007)
7. Edge, K.S.: A framework for analyzing and mitigating the vulnerabilities of complex systems via attack and protection trees. Technical report, School of Engineering and Management, Air Force Institute of Technology, Wright-Patterson AFB, OH (2007)
8. Edge, K.S., Dalton, G.C., Raines, R.A., Mills, R.F.: Using attack and protection trees to analyze threats and defenses to homeland security. In: MILCOM 2006–2006 IEEE Military Communications Conference, pp. 1–7. IEEE (2006)
9. Jøsang, A.: Subjective Logic. Springer, Cham (2016). https://doi.org/10.1007/978-3-319-42337-1
10. Julious, S.A.: Two-sided confidence intervals for the single proportion: comparison of seven method by Robert G. Newcombe, Statistics in Medicine 1998; 17: 857–872. Stat. Med. **24**(21), 3383–3384 (2005)
11. Julious, S.A.: Calculation of confidence intervals for a finite population size. Pharm. Stat. **18**(1), 115–122 (2019)
12. Kordy, B., Mauw, S., Radomirović, S., Schweitzer, P.: Foundations of attack–defense trees. In: Degano, P., Etalle, S., Guttman, J. (eds.) FAST 2010. LNCS, vol. 6561, pp. 80–95. Springer, Heidelberg (2011). https://doi.org/10.1007/978-3-642-19751-2_6
13. Lallemant, D., Kiremidjian, A.: A beta distribution model for characterizing earthquake damage state distribution. Earthq. Spectra **31**(3), 1337–1352 (2015)
14. Pieters, W., Davarynejad, M.: Calculating adversarial risk from attack trees: control strength and probabilistic attackers. In: Garcia-Alfaro, J., et al. (eds.) DPM/QASA/SETOP-2014. LNCS, vol. 8872, pp. 201–215. Springer, Cham (2015). https://doi.org/10.1007/978-3-319-17016-9_13
15. Roy, A., Kim, D.S., Trivedi, K.S.: Cyber security analysis using attack countermeasure trees. In: Proceedings of the Sixth Annual Workshop on Cyber Security and Information Intelligence Research, pp. 1–4 (2010)

16. Roy, A., Kim, D.S., Trivedi, K.S.: Attack countermeasure trees (ACT): towards unifying the constructs of attack and defense trees. Secur. Commun. Netw. **5**(8), 929–943 (2012)

17. Sonnenreich, W., Albanese, J., Stout, B., et al.: Return on security investment (ROSI)-a practical quantitative model. J. Res. Pract. Inf. Technol. **38**(1), 45 (2006)

Author Index

Printed in the United States
By Bookmasters